The Ethnomethodological Movement

Approaches to Semiotics
95

Mouton de Gruyter
Berlin · New York

The Ethnomethodological Movement

Sociosemiotic Interpretations

by

Pierce J. Flynn

Mouton de Gruyter
Berlin · New York 1991

Mouton de Gruyter (formerly Mouton, The Hague)
is a Division of Walter de Gruyter & Co., Berlin.

⊗ Printed on acid-free paper which falls within the guidelines of
the ANSI to ensure permanence and durability.

Library of Congress Cataloging in Publication Data

Flynn, Pierce Julius, 1953—
     The ethnomethodological movement : sociosemiotic
interpretations / by Pierce Julius Flynn.
     p.   cm. — (Approaches to semiotics ; 95)
     Includes bibliographical references and index.
     ISBN 0-89925-566-3 (acid-free paper)
     1. Ethnomethodology.   2. Culture—Semiotic models.
3. Semiotics. I. Title. II. Series.
HM24.F59   1990
306′.01—dc20   90-13350
                                             CIP

Deutsche Bibliothek Cataloging in Publication Data

Flynn, Pierce J.:
The ethnomethodological movement : sociosemiotic
interpretations / by Pierce J. Flynn. — Berlin ; New York :
Mouton de Gruyter, 1991
    (Approaches to semiotics ; 95)
    ISBN 3-11-012000-3
NE: GT

Typesetting: Asian Research Service, Hong Kong. — Printing: Gerike GmbH, Berlin. —
Binding: Lüderitz & Bauer, Berlin. — Printed in Germany.

To the strange
half mystic
wonder of reality

Acknowledgments

I would like to thank all those scholars and friends who have been influential in the production of this study and the learning contours that underlie it. Bennetta Jules-Rosette has been a constant inspiration and catalyst in my intellectual growth. Harold Garfinkel, Aaron Cicourel, Hugh Mehan, Howard Schwartz, Reyes Ramos, Susan Wedow, Beryl Bellman, Houston Wood, and Gerald Platt all helped build my experience in ethnomethodology. Joseph Gusfield, Mounira Charrad, Alain J.-J. Cohen, and Theodore Schwartz have provided incisive criticism and help on my analysis of ethnomethodology as a knowledge domain. Emanuel Schegloff, Mel Pollner, Nick Maroules, and Paolo Fabbri provided important oral history and advice. Sam Edward Combs, Susan Lucille Phaneuf, Ken Liberman, Janet Lee Meihls, Peter Hayward, Armando Arias, Jurgen Streeck, Phyllis Baker, Margaret Crowdes, Debbie Emmelman, Chantale Hétu, Alberto Restrepo, Randy Coplin, Harriet Fleisher, Marti Tum Suden, David Lane, Lorna Luker, and Karol Dudziak have all shared the University of California, San Diego's local culture of graduate training and knowledge with me. The University of California, San Diego faculty Fred Davis, Jacqueline Wiseman, Rae Blumberg, Jack Douglas, and Bennett Berger have each given me the benefit of their insights.

Thomas A. Sebeok and Dean and Juliet Flower MacCannell have given me valuable support and insight into semiotics. Laurence Ratier-Coutrot, Gerard Lemain, A. J. Greimas, Michel Maffesoli, Bruno Latour, Benjamin Mattalon, and Georges Lappasade all contributed essential support and guidance on my visits to Paris.

I thank my family and friends for their understanding and support. Drs. Pierce and Helen Flynn, Elsie Brown, Bill, Art, Mary, Bob, Tom, and John, Monica, Jean-Marie, Peter, and Elaine have supported me in every conceivable way. James Combs, Lisa Elizabeth Phaneuf, Peter F. Gach, Lucille, Phil, and Denise Gratia Phaneuf, Lisa Ellen Neely, and Susan J. Bowen have all provided special assistance during this project. The wonderful staffs of the University of California, San Diego Department of Sociology, the Central Library, the Housing Office, the Loan Office, Financial Aid, and the Office of Graduate Studies and Research have played essential roles. The members of the Laboratory for Ethnographic and Audiovisual Studies (LEAVS) have furnished this study with their invaluable discussion, ideas, and suggestions. Susan Lucille Phaneuf and Michael Vierling provided the excellent production and editorial work on this manuscript. I thank all those others that I have been unable to mention here.

La Jolla, May 1990   Pierce J. Flynn

Contents

There is a discipline in it, and a part of the discipline consists of the refusal to have it any other way, regardless of the cost.
Garfinkel (Hill and Crittenden 1968:130)

The feature of this social science is to make of it a members' work.
Garfinkel (Hill and Crittenden 1968:118)

I mean, too, that such practices consist of an endless, ongoing, contingent accomplishment.
Garfinkel (1967a:1)

Introduction

The ethnomethodological movement has been historically perceived by its followers, critics, and observers as revolutionary, misguided, radically innovative, and trivial. It has been accused of being a sect, as well as being called a foundational new discipline with deep consequences for all of the social sciences. In this study I utilize an eclectic sociology of knowledge and a sociosemiotics approach to explore the ethnomethodological movement's historical construction as a rebellious neosociological domain of thought; the poetics of ethnomethodological discourse, language, and texts; the dynamics of its transmission into Europe; and a comparison of the historical development of the ethnomethodological movement with the modern semiotics movement in the United States and Europe. The resulting aisthesis or aesthetic perception attempts to view the ethnomethodological movement's articulative strategies from within.

Ethnomethodology is a sociological movement that began in 1954 around the work of Harold Garfinkel and a small group of cohorts. Ethnomethodology studies the technical details of how participants in social settings use common sense to manage their membership, biographies, language, and knowledge in order to accomplish naturally organized ordinary activities. Ethnomethodology has defined itself as constituting a radically reflexive form of sociological inquiry, which, although it addresses the classical sociological problems of social order delineated by Durkheim and Parsons, is distinct from most all other forms of professional sociology. Several excellent introductions to ethnomethodology's theoretical and methodological system exist (Mehan and Wood 1975a; Schenkein 1978a; Leiter 1980; Handel 1982; Benson and Hughes 1983; Heritage 1984d; Sharrock and Anderson 1986a). The purpose of this study is to investigate the practical context of ethnomethodology's own presence as a professional sociological discipline.

Intellectual movements within the social sciences have received only sparse description and analysis. While the social sciences traditionally have researched and written on knowledge production in religions, ideological groups, everyday life, and other sciences, only little has been written on collective knowledge creation by sociologists them-

selves. My study concentrates on how the ethnomethodological movement has utilized text and talk as both objectifications and significations
of an intellectual culture. In so doing, the ethnomethodologists have
achieved notoriety and knowledge in the fields of modern and postmodern sociological endeavor. This work explores ethnomethodology as a
specialized social science discipline. I attempt to analyze how ethnomethodology has been constructed by several generations of researchers
utilizing practical documentary and semiotic practices to produce its
corpus of knowledge and texts.

The perspective of this work

The interpretation and analysis of an intellectual movement in the
sociohistorical context of the contemporary social sciences requires
methods for examining the "situated hermeneutics" of paradigm construction. The perspective that I take in the present study is an attempt to
address certain neoclassical questions posed in the sociology of knowledge, history of sociology, intellectual history, sociology of intellectuals,
sociology of science, sociology of religion, and sociology of social
movements. This approach then attempts an initial synthesis of these
earlier approaches with new interpretive methods and analytical techniques borrowed from semiotics, interpretive anthropology, studies in the
literary production of ethnography and knowledge, analyses of discourse
systems, the new intellectual history, and ethnomethodology itself. The
resulting synthesis is a new form of the sociology of knowledge and the
sociology of intellectual movements in social science disciplines.

Humanistic understanding can be likened to a conversation with the
past through the medium of its significant texts. La Capra (1983) has
offered this metaphor of conversation as a new goal of intellectual
history, and it is applicable to the study of intellectual movements
in the social sciences. My approach to thought movements in general
and the ethnomethodological movement in particular is to examine the
situated hermeneutics of paradigm construction by utilizing texts and
talk as signs or emblems of locally produced membership within an
intellectual domain. My concentration is on examining how various
individuals have fashioned themselves and their thought into intellectual

collectivities and intellectual communities. My approach is to explore how this has been accomplished via the production, use, and interpretation of significant texts and textual practices situated in a vibrant social context.

My approach is based on the interpretive assumption that all "cultural objectifications" (Mannheim 1952a:33-83; 1982:55ff) are inseparable from the situations of their production and use. I mean by "cultural objectifications" all cultural objects and forms, including membership in intellectual movements, texts, accounts, careers, professional identities, translations, and generations. These cultural formations are produced and established historically through and within the selective interpretive work of persons involved and engaged in any particular domain of knowledge, at any particular time.

Memberships, generations, theoretical lineages, textual interpretations, and intellectual movements "exist" only to the extent that persons engage and produce these cultural forms "contingently," i.e., relative to one's ongoing practical procedural purposes situated in a time and place. The sociology of knowledge of Mannheim, and ethnomethodology's adaption of it (cf. Garfinkel 1967a: 76-103), has long emphasized this relative and contingent character of cultural form. My approach does not appropriate the ethnomethodological movement's cultural objectifications, i.e., texts, membership accounts, perceived generational structures, as authoritative descriptions of the movement. Instead, my work raises the issue of how ethnomethodology's cultural objects are produced and used as emblems, significations, and references of the movement within actual instances of the "local production" of the ethnomethodological movement.

Production and appropriation of intellectual cultural forms and knowledge is carried out by persons who are situated in both private and public domains of discourse and professional and intellectual strategies of organization. Individuals adhere to intellectual movements when it suits their variously constructed interests and plans. When these interests change, so does one's degree of participation in the perceived intellectual movement or body of intellectual organization. This can be "traced" or revealed through an examination of how individuals have used objects such as texts and talk, or written and verbal discourse, relative to a particular domain of knowledge.

My approach in this work is to view the ethnomethodological movement as itself a "reflexive" and "contingent" accomplishment. Thus the ethnomethodological movement as such is seen not in terms of "objectively" existing historical structures of generations and independently existing authoritative lists of membership. Instead, I view the ethno-methodological movement as being situationally constructed each time anyone "references" the movement in practical situations of inquiry, discourse, or professional presentation of self.

The examination of texts in the social sciences for significations of reflexive membership has a starting point in several recent studies of social scientific literary discourse and knowledge production. Gusfield's (1976) work on the literary "rhetoric" of social science has focused new concerted attention on the writing strategies social scientists employ when composing "objective" written reports. Overington (1977a, 1977b, 1977c), O'Neill (1981), and Morrison (1981) represent new approaches to examining specific instances of writing by sociological authors, in prefatory practices, and in introductory sociology texts, respectively. Gilbert (1978) has examined citation and referencing practices in science, a theme I explore in the ethnomethodological movement in Chapter 4. Woolgar (1976) and Knorr and Knorr (1978) have traced the production of science journal articles. McHoul (1982) has worked on ethnomethodology and reading. Mulkay (1985) has experimented with new forms of sociological analysis, drawing on the analysis of discourse and text.

In anthropology a growing number of studies have focused attention on the poetics and politics of ethnographic writing. The "writing culture" movement in anthropology exemplified by the works contained in Clifford and Marcus (1986), Tyler (1985), Webster (1983), and others is bringing a new critical spirit gained from semiotics, discourse analysis, and readings of Foucault, Derrida, and poststructuralist thinkers to bear on anthropological writing and knowledge production. My own work is a current attempt to broaden this critique to sociology through examining the "local" creation of a specific knowledge form and movement: ethnomethodology.

Much of the current interest in the literary production of social science discourse and knowledge forms is a result of and is informed by earlier work in linguistics and literary theory. The so-called "linguistic turn" in the social sciences (cf. Knorr-Cetina and Mulkay 1983:9-11; Lemert 1984; Cicourel 1980; Zito 1984; MacCannell and MacCannell 1982) has effected a focus of attention on the role of written and verbal language play in the interactive constitution of social meaning. Semiotic theorists such as Peirce, Saussure, Hjelmslev, and Greimas have provided new tools for the understanding and analysis of signs and signification systems. Foucault (1972, 1973) has suggested fruitful avenues of histori-cal analyses of discourse formations or "epistemes" (cf. Dreyfus and

Rabinow 1982). The structural linguistics of Bloomfield, the work of Austin (1962), the speech act theory of Searle (1969) and Grice (1975), the generative grammar of Chomsky, and ordinary language philosophy have each encouraged sociologists such as Goffman, conversational analysts, ethnomethodology, and sociolinguistics to pursue new forms of the analysis of spoken and written discourse (cf. Goffman 1981; Gumperz and Hymes 1972; Gumperz 1982; Tannen 1984).

My use of semiotic conceptual and analytical tools is my attempt to construct a new and relevant "sociosemiotics" (cf. MacCannell and MacCannell 1982; Sebeok 1976; Herzfeld 1981; Greimas and Courtés 1982; Jules-Rosette 1982; Gottdiener and Lagopoulas 1986)). Such an approach seeks to locate and analyze local meaning structures and signification systems from the point of view of the producer's use and conceptualization of them. As such it is a synthesis of ethnosemantics, sociology of knowledge, ethnomethodology, and semiotics. New descriptive and analytic technologies are borrowed and adapted from current work in semiotics in an attempt to specify with greater precision the literary procedures of communication at work in the texts.

By concentrating on how "actants" (Greimas and Courtés 1982:5-6) or organizers of systems of discourse and signification construct "contingent" membership and knowledge in intellectual movements through textual procedures, we can begin to better understand the interactive processes of the intellectual and social organization of the sciences. My study of ethnomethodology's construction as a contingent paradigm is an attempt to initiate a more detailed examination of social science knowledge formations and cultural processes. Knowledge production is situated discourse located within changing contexts of immediate relevance.

Ethnomethodology is an organized domain of knowledge production. It takes the form of an intellectual movement when it is perceived as supplying a locus for an alternate or novel program of inquiry for sociology. Social scientists who feel an attraction for ethnomethodology's ideas "attach" themselves to their situationally perceived versions of what ethnomethodology is. This is done via the mechanisms of interpersonal interactions, research practice, intellectual appropriation, and textual referencing. From this activity, the ethnomethodological "movement" is created and formed each time one engages in the work of invoking its being.

Historically, the ethnomethodological movement appears to take on historical contextures relative to each perceiver's situational perception and purposes (cf. White 1973). Various narratives are composed that represent rhetorical versions of the movement's historical facticity, motives, and effects (cf. Ricoeur 1984). For my purposes, the ethnomethodological movement exists as that organized body and formation of discourses that has been and is being assembled by activities of those who wish to be known as "ethnomethodologists" for their various relevant purposes.

For every person and every set of discourses there is a peculiar account of the "history" of the ethnomethodological movement. Occasionally, for the practical purposes at-hand, these narratives correspond and overlap. My version of ethnomethodology's "history" is constructed out of my desire to see a coherent development of thought where, perhaps, there is not such a development. For this reason I have chosen ethnomethodology's texts to stand for, to be signs of, whatever possibly could be such a phenomenon as an "ethnomethodological movement."

In examining the cultural objectifications (texts) that I associate with the ethnomethodological movement, I notice that I am making situated decisions and choices as to what is or is not "ethnomethodology." My method has been to concentrate on how texts are practically referenced and used as "building blocks" of the ethnomethodological paradigm as represented by any particular referencer and builder. Thus, I have looked not so much at the relative theoretical contents of texts. Instead, I have focused on the "work" that writers have done to fashion their discourse so it is commonly "recognized" as "ethnomethodological" by various domains of readers and audiences (cf. Iser 1974; Holub 1984).

My approach has been to "choose" whatever texts have represented themselves as "ethnomethodological" through the variety of textual "knowledge practices" that I index in the following chapters. Generally, these practices are temporally organized literary devices that employ the textual strategies of prolepsis and analepsis. Prolepsis, the evoking of the future in the present, and analepsis, the evoking of the past in the present (cf. Genette 1980:30-84), are manipulated by writers to signify and textually construct a "representation" of intellectual membership, theoretical tradition, and professional "intertextual" location. These practices include the use of "missing whats," "purple-ditto" phases of communication, selective referencing of sources, and "intertextual poetry." Combined together within the situated composition of the printed page, "the ethnomethodological movement" is literally "conjured" up and created for all to see, recognize, and respond to.

The texts that I examine and use in my own interpretive exploration of ethnomethodology are often "co-referenced" between various authors as "standing for" classic and current examples of the ethnomethodological approach, field, or paradigm within sociology. Collective co-referencing strategies compose and construct the "intertextual web" that is the ethnomethodological movement itself.

My investigation of the "situated hermeneutics" of paradigm construction through the production, recognition, and use of textual objects is influenced by the large body of studies in hermeneutics (cf. Palmer 1969; Gadamer 1976; Heidegger 1962; Ricoeur 1985), phenomenology (cf. Husserl 1964, 1970, 1975; Gurvitch 1969; Schutz 1967, 1964; Merleau-Ponty 1962, 1968), and ethnomethodology itself (cf. Garfinkel 1967a; Garfinkel and Sacks 1970; Cicourel 1974b; Lynch 1985a). I concentrate on how the ethnomethodological movement, as an exemplar of new sociological knowledge, is produced and constructed within the "embodied" pursuits of those scholars and researchers who have entertained this particular perspective in sociological discipline. My topic is the creation of representations that are "contingently" formulated, expressed, and manipulated to give a "body" to an intellectual movement in actual occasions of use by professional social scientists.

In order to understand my approach to studying the ethnomethodological movement as an intellectual movement in the modern and postmodern social sciences, it is necessary to survey the existing field of studies of intellectual movements. By doing this, it will be clear that my approach comprises a new form of the sociology of social scientific knowledge. In paying close attention to the "situated micropractices" of the academy (Rabinow 1986:253), I address and continue the neoclassical questions regarding the social genesis of thought posed by the sociology of knowledge beginning with Karl Mannheim (1952a, 1936, 1982, 1986). I accomplish this through a new synthetic form of the sociology of thought that focuses special attention on the "reflexive creation" of the intellectual movement through the variety of "knowledge practices" of those who consider themselves members of the movement.

The history of sociology has traditionally focused attention on sociology's collective production. It has done this primarily through more general descriptions of the historical genesis of social thought in terms of chronological development from St. Simon and Compte to the present. The history of sociology is written primarily by sociologists. As such it presents both a resource and a topic in my study of how sociologists historicize themselves relative to intellectual movements within the discipline. A large number of authors have traced a varied history of sociology from the points of view of the development of the discipline as a whole (Barnes 1948; Gouldner 1971; Maus 1962; Nisbet 1967; Abrams 1968; Therborn 1980; Hinkle 1980; Vidich and Lyman 1985; Tiryakian 1971); the history of individual sociological thinkers (Lukes 1973; Frisby 1984; Wagner 1985; Bendix 1960; Raushenbush 1979; Coser 1984; Loader 1985); and the history of particular sociological schools (Lewis and Smith 1980; Jay 1973; Rock 1979; Faris 1970; Schivendinger and Schivendinger 1974; Parsons 1970).

Intellectual history has provided the important observation that a fact is a pertinent fact only with respect to a frame of reference involving questions that we pose to the past, and it is the ability to pose the "right" questions that distinguishes productive scholarship (Collingwood 1939 in La Capra 1983:31). Heidegger (1962:444-449) has emphasized that the intellectual historian's own questions are themselves situated in a context and a "life world" that cannot be entirely known or made explicit. From this insight, then, I have appropriated a self-reflective or reflexive mode of writing in my study of the ethnomethodological movement, incorporating wherever possible an explication of my own "life world" relative to the domain studied and questions asked. White (1973), La Capra (1983), and Higham and Conkin (1979) have provided me with important directives for pursuing a new form of intellectual history adapted to a sociology of social scientific knowledge practices and text production. Vansina (1965, 1970) has been of great assistance in developing an adapted historical methodology for the study of intellectual oral traditions. Cohen's (1974) study of Herbert Marcuse breaks new ground in the domain of literary theory analysis and intellectual biography.

Numerous studies in intellectual history bear relevance to the study of intellectual movements in the social sciences. H.S. Hughes (1958, 1968, 1975) has written extensively on the development of social thought in Germany and France and on the emigration of German refugee scholars to America during World War II. The latter has a significant importance in the case of the ethnomethodological movement, especially with the arrival in the United States of the German phenomenologists Alfred Schutz and Aaron Gurwitsch. Boyers (1972) has also contributed to an intellectual history of German refugee intellectuals. Studies of European intellectual life in the twentieth century that are relevant to understanding the development of American sociology in general and ethnomethodology in particular include Spiegelberg's (1971) history of the phenomenological movement, Fleming and Bailyn's (1968) history of German intellectual migrations from 1930-1960, Poster's (1975) study of existential Marxism in postwar France, Hirsh's (1981) and

Reader's (1987) intellectual histories of the French "New Left," and Wilkenson's (1981) examination of the intellectual resistance in Europe during World War II. Frances Yates (1964a, b, 1978) has supplied me with important directives for studying intellectual traditions "from within" the traditions' own specialized cognitive "arts." Olafson (1979) has supplied a necessary philosophy of history, historical narrative, and intentional process.

The sociology of intellectuals has successfully advanced the understanding of the role and place of the intellectual in modern societies. Generally these studies have included phenomenological approaches that describe the nature of the self-understanding and perceptions of the individual intellectual in his or her particular ways of thinking or acting (cf. Mannheim 1936; Coser 1965, 1984; Benda 1927; Grana 1964; Berger 1961; Mills 1963; Rieff 1969; Fluer 1976; Touraine 1980) and structural approaches examining the objective, observable position of intellectuals in the social structure (Gramsci 1971; Shils 1961, 1969; Parsons 1969; Gouldner 1979; Collins 1979a, b; Bourdieu and Passeron 1977; Eyeman, Svensson, and Sodergvist 1987). Gella (1976) has presented a useful collection on the theoretical and methodological problems in studies of the intelligensia and intellectuals. Touraine's (1980) and Levy's (1987) studies are particularly important for studying the relationships of intellectuals to social and political movements.

My sociology of social scientific knowledge and intellectual movements takes many of its directives from the classical formulations of the sociology of knowledge. The classical sociology of knowledge has provided the research thematic of examining the existential foundations of knowledge. The development of the sociology of knowledge can be represented as having progressed through three different phases (Stehr and Meja 1984:16; Remmling 1973:3-46; Coser 1975:428-31). The theoretical approaches of Francis Bacon, Auguste Compte, Karl Marx, Friedrich Nietzsche, Vilfredo Pareto, and Sigmund Freud are commonly regarded as the first phase of forerunners of the sociology of knowledge. The second phase can be understood as the process of establishing the sociology of knowledge as an identifiable, distinct specialty in the social science. Max Scheler, Karl Mannheim in Germany, and Emile Durkeheim, Lucien Levy-Bruhl, and Marcel Mauss in France represent the outstanding personages of this phase. The third phase in which much current sociology of knowledge exists can be called the phase of "normalization" (Stehr and Meja, 1984:16) in which much of the more philosophically ambitious goals proposed by

Mannheim have been defined much more narrowly as the sociology of knowledge has become mediated by disciplinary traditions.

It is not surprising that as new translations of unpublished classical texts in the sociology of knowledge have appeared (cf. Mannheim 1982, 1986), and have coincided with a new radical reorientation in how scientific knowledge is being examined sociologically (cf. Knorr-Cetina and Mulkay 1982), a form of a renaissance of the sociology of knowledge is being experienced (cf. Stehr and Meja 1984). A number of writers have examined the "new" sociology of knowledge and its relation to modern knowledge production (cf. Barber1975; Barnes 1977; Bloor 1976; Kulkick 1983). My approach is to form a synthesis between the classical and neoclassical formulations of the sociology of knowledge by exploring the "local" constitution of knowledge in the social sciences. I attempt to present a detailed examination of ethnomethodology as a socio-historically embedded intellectual movement within the sociological discipline. I then detail an aspect of how individuals who have considered themselves "ethnomethodologists" have constructed their paradigm participation and membership through a variety of social and textual "knowledge practices."

I have found a large number of works in the sociology of knowledge relevant to the formation of my approach. Mannheim's work on the "documentary method of interpretation" and the interpretation of Weltanschauung (1952:33-83); historicism (1952:84-133); the problem of generations (1952:276-320); methodology (1936:264-311); and cultural sociology (1982) have been particularly important. Remmling (1975) and Simmons (1978) have provided interpretations of Mannheim's program. Terry Clark's (1973) study of the emergence of the French social sciences and Philippe Besnard's (1983) and Victor Karady's (1983) examination of the Durkheimian group and its social and intellectual context during the founding of French sociology as a new discipline are valuable contributions to the sociology of knowledge in intellectual groups. Besnard's work is particularly important for the way it provides information about the academic careers of all those who collaborated on the *Annee sociologique* journal during Durkheim's lifetime and on the part that each played in constructing the collective enterprise. Lemert (1981, 1986) has examined current fields of French sociology, and Tiryakian (1986) has discussed the challenge presented by present trends toward the development of international sociologies.

Gusfield (1957, 1978) had made relevant studies on the problem of generations in social movements and on the problematics of sociologists' own interests set by the historical events studies. Gusfield (1979, 1981b) has also made a valuable contribution to the examination of the "reflexivity" of social movements' self-construction in public and private domains. Theodore Schwartz (1976) has written on the anthropology of generational structures in time-limited cultures that has relevance to my study of intellectual generations. Ethnomethodologists Wieder and Zimmerman (1974) have examined the generational production of "freaks" culture and knowledge. Jules-Rosette has placed Talcott Parsons's theoretical work relative to concurrent interactions and debates within the phenomenological school (1980b), has surveyed the development of American qualitative sociology (1986e), and has examined the case of Alfred Schutz's international immigration and establishment in American relative to the postwar American sociological context (1987).

All of these works are relevant to the understanding of the development of ethnomethodology as a "new" sociological movement and historical knowledge form.

Recently, the sociology of science has been rejuvenated through a new emphasis on the sociology of scientific knowledge. A large number of studies have recently emerged that utilize a range of approaches to examine the production of scientific knowledge in social context (cf. Knorr-Cetina and Mulkay 1983; Whitley 1984). These approaches include interest theory and the relativist program (Collins 1983; Bloor 1976; Barnes 1977), constructivist/ethnographic studies of scientific work (Knorr-Cetina 1981, 1983; Latour and Woolgar 1979; Traweeks 1982), ethnomethodological studies of scientific practice (Garfinkel, Lynch, and Livingston 1981; Lynch 1985a; Livingston 1983; Morrison 1981; Lynch, Livingston and Garfinkel 1983), scientific discourse analysis (Gilbert and Mulkay 1984; Latour and Fabbri 1977; Woolgar 1976; Bastide 1985; Yearley 1981; Mulkay, Potter, and Yearley 1983; O'Neill 1981; Anderson 1978), a revised Marxian approach to science (Chubin and Restivo 1983), and the use of disciplinary histories (Graham, et al. 1983; Woolgar 1976; Kuhn 1970). These studies bring fresh relevance and directives for examining natural and social scientific knowledge production empirically. My own approach is both informed by and is in dialogue with many of these recent studies.

Whitley (1984:170-171) has characterized the development of ethnomethodology in California as following a pattern of development peculiar to one of his postulated seven major types of scientific fields: the "fragmented adhocracies." Whitley's "types of sciences" organize and control knowledge production and evaluation in different ways, which results in different patterns of intellectual organization. According to Whitley, ethnomethodology's organization as a scientific field displays features of nonstable configurations of specialized tasks and problem areas, and weak coordinating mechanisms that interrelate results and strategies. Where coordination of results does occur, it is highly personal and linked to local control of resources. I analyze various features of this "local control of resources" in Chapter 2.

A sociology of sociology has gradually been emerging. A variety of studies such as Shils (1970, 1972), Friedrich (1970), Mullins (1973), Kuklick (1973), Colfax and Roach (1971), Martindale (1976), and Tiryakian (1971, 1986) have been directing different degrees of attention to sociology as an organized discipline. Turner (1986) has discussed sociology as an academic marketplace. Along with the sociology of knowledge and the history of sociology, these studies contribute differing perspectives on sociology as a paradigm.

Studies on sociological "boundary-keeping" and the foundation of new sociological specialties by S.N. Eisenstadt (1974 a, b, 1977), Gouldner (1970), Loureau (1970), Kuklick (1980), and Gieryn (1983) place attention on the fact that sociology is in a state of crisis and fragmentation due to its traditional self-definitions, boundaries, and delineations. Moreover, as Eisenstadt points out, the "intellectual anti-nomianism" characteristic of the student protests of the 1960s coupled with long trends in the philosophy of the social sciences brought an external and internal demand for sociology to develop "countermodels" such as symbolic interactionism and ethnomethodology (Eisenstadt 1977: 61). Eisenstadt has also remarked on the tendency for sociological "schools" and communities to transform into metaphysical, political, ideological, and analytic paradigms, all of them developing strong "symbolic closure" and esoteric personal or sectarian discourses (1977:62-69). I shall analyze this tendency in the ethnomethodological movement.

A series of studies on the development of sociological subdisciplines by Ben-David (1970), Cole (1975), R. Collins (1979a), Crane (1972), Diner (1975), Gross (1970), Merton (1977), Stehr and Larson (1972), and Hopkins (1984) use a wide variety of methods to analyze sociology's major paradigm characteristics and developmental patterns.

The sociology of religion offers important insights in examining the proposal that many sociological schools display sectarian characteristics such as strong symbolic discourse and esoteric sectarian discourses. Recent developments in the sociology of religion by Robbins, Anthony, and Richardson (1987); Snow (1980); Snow and Machalek (1984);

Beckford (1978, 1985); Jules-Rosette (1978, b, 1987); McGuire (1981, 1983); Hewitt and Stokes (1975); Girton (1975); Hammond (1985); Stark and Bainbridge (1985); and Lofland and Skonovd (1981) have expanded the classical analyses of Durkheim and Weber and the neoclassical analyses of Wilson (1970) and Linton (1943) to focus on the constitution of new religious sects through an examination of the "micropractices" of religious conversion, accounting, and disengagement. Schwartz (1962) has provided an anthropology of a religious movement in the admiralty islands. My study of sectarian features of the ethnomethodological movement selectively utilizes these studies' perspectives on religious organization.

Beckford's (1985:352) analysis of the present state of the sociology of religion comes close to a sociology of knowledge of intellectual movements. He likens the sociology of religion's present position in professional sociology to be similar to that imputed by Alain Touraine to religious groups in postindustrial societies, that is, they are "weakly institutionalized yet strongly integrated" (Touraine 1977:34). The same can be said of the early stages of ethnomethodology's development. Currently, however, the reverse conditions appear to be true: the ethno-methodological movement displays stronger institutionalization in the face of weakening internal integration (see Chapter 3).

Intellectual movements in the social sciences take their place alongside more quotidian movements occurring in mass society. While intellectual movements share a theoretical and ideological content that is certainly more esoteric than many contents found in "everyday life" social movements, nevertheless their structures and processes of organization are comparable.

A sociology of intellectual movements stands embedded within the large body of studies of social movements. Studies by Zald and Ash (1972), Bittner (1963), Gusfield (1981b, 1983), Turner (1969), Ash (1972), Gamson (1975), Obershal (1978), Zald and McCarthy (1978), Lauer (1972), Linton (1943), Tilly (1978), and Piven and Cloward (1979) represent a variety of approaches to the sociological, historical, and interactional appraisal and analysis of social movements. My study of the ethnomethodological movement, while situated in the tradition of movement studies, attempts to introduce a new dimension to the analysis of intellectual movements in sociohistorical context.

Research on the intellectual development of sociology has followed several major thrusts: Shil's (1970) "institutionalization" approach;

Gouldner's (1965, 1970) intellectual history of sociological crisis; Friedrich's (1970) Kuhnian paradigm analysis; Mullin's (1973) communicational structure model; Whitley's (1984) organization and control of knowledge production perspective; and Burt's (1982), Cuppelle and Guterlock's (1986), and Hopkins's (1984) sociometric and structural studies. The first three approaches, while providing important ideas on the centrality of intellectual institutions and traditions, crises resulting from disparities between traditions and new conceptualizations, and paradigm shifts, concentrate on dimensions that tend to overlook the social dynamics of paradigm development.

Mullins and Whitley utilize a more dynamic approach that emphasizes the organization of social interaction within the discipline as central to its development. My approach begins from their models. I focus on a further detailed examination on how a particular intellectual paradigm's communicational structures are reflexively both represented and used to construct that discipline. Thus, I explore how Mullins's (1973:30-31) "transformations of relations" within a theoretical subspecialty or intellectual movement are signified and represented in textual discourse through different generational stages of group development. I examine how a scientific "research front" (Price 1965) or an area defined by bibliographic and literary reference not only "indicate" but form the research organization.

The recent sociometric approach of Cappelle and Guterbeck (1986) has suggested that "formal memberships" in specialty sections within the American Sociological Association offer a unique data base for examining the "connectedness" among sociological subdisciplines. Cappelle and Guterbeck used the ASA's membership records to examine specialty clustering and organizational structure. My approach examines how disciplinary "connectedness" is actually achieved and represented through the varieties of informal and formal "membership" practices and significations. I explore how "membership" in an intellectual movement is a "situated action." Situated actions are produced in particular concrete solutions and are available to the participants for their own recognition, description, and use as basis for further action (cf. Wilson 1986:28). I examine how significations of membership located within textual "object-accounts" (Lynch 1985a:22) reflexively produce the organizational and generational formations of the ethnomethodological movement.

I observe that the ethnomethodological movement displays both similarities and differences to other intellectual movements, especially in sociology. Comparatively, ethnomethodology can be characterized as a "revolutionary" (Mullins 1973:199-300) or "radical" (Bittner 1963) specialty within sociology. By revolutionary I imply the deep rejection or "indifference" (cf. Garfinkel and Sacks1970) to traditional sociological methods and ways of theorizing. Probably the only other movement in sociology that approaches ethnomethodology's revolutionary orientation is radical critical theory (cf. Jay 1973: Mullins 1973:270-293). I characterize ethnomethodology apart from most sociological movements that have built on earlier methods to fashion a new theoretical product. Examples of these "elite" sociological movements (cf. Mullins 1973:300) include standard American sociology, structural functionalism, symbolic interactionism, small group theory, and the new causal theory.

The ethnomethodological movement probably shares general organizational similarities with most intellectual movements in the social sciences. Borrowing again from Mullins (1973:25-26), we can easily see that ethnomethodology displays the following features exhibited by other sociological movements like Chicago sociology, Parsonian structural functionalism, and symbolic interactionism, as well as the international semiotics movement (see Chapter 7). First, these groups exhibit distinct theoretical orientations developed by an intellectual leader, verbalized in a program statement, and supported by intellectual successes. George Herbert Mead, Talcott Parsons, and Herbert Blumer functioned as intellectual leaders for their respective movements. Harold Garfinkel has served as primary intellectual leader for ethnomethodology. Second, there is the appearance of conscious movement development organized and directed by social organizational leaders to secure jobs, acquire students, organize publications, etc. This was achieved by Albion Small for the Chicago School between 1892-1925, by Talcott Parsons and Robert Merton for structural functionalism between 1935-1965, by Herbert Blumer for symbolic interactionism between 1931-1952, and by Thomas A. Sebeok for the semiotics movement. Harold Garfinkel and Aaron Cicourel have served as social organizational leaders for ethnomethodology since 1955, with new social organizational leaders currently active in Boston, Britain, and France (see Chapter 7).

Third, a primary research center or geographical locus arises from where the original ideas are worked out in a close group context and network. The University of Chicago, the Bureau of Applied Research at Columbia University, and the University of California, Berkeley, became these research centers for the Chicago School, structural functionalism, and symbolic interactionism, respectively. The University of

California campuses at Los Angeles and Santa Barbara functioned as the primary early research centers for ethnomethodology.

Fourth, university training centers for graduate students became organized. It is here that new intellectual programs are transmitted and carried out through "generational appropriation." The University of Chicago for the early Chicago School; the University of Chicago, Harvard University, and Columbia University for structural functionalism; the University of California, Berkeley, and the University of Chicago for symbolic interactionism served as student training centers for these movements. Ethnomethodology established the University of California campuses of Los Angeles, Santa Barbara, and San Diego as the primary teaching centers. Boston University is also now a major training center.

Fifth, intellectual movements form bodies of intellectual materials or cultural formations. These include texts, critical materials, ways of communicating, etc. Parsons's (1937) *The Structure of Social Action,* Blumer's (1938) "Social Psychology," Garfinkel's (1967a) *Studies in Ethnomethodology,* and Cicourel's (1964) *Method and Measurement in Sociology* formed both program statements and examples of primary discursive formations within each respective movement.

Ethnomethodology can be distinguished from other sociological schools and movements in terms of its intellectual and social organization. Whitley (1984:159) proposes studying scientific fields as "reputational work organizations." He offers a description of a type of scientific field, the "fragmented adhocracy" that appears to offer a general type under which the ethnomethodological movement could be characterized. A "fragmented adhocracy" presents a combination of high research task "uncertainty" and low degrees of mutual collective dependence that produces a research front that is rather personal, idiosyncratic, and only weakly coordinated across research lines. Participants in the field tend to make relatively diffuse contributions to broad and fluid goals that are highly contingent on local experiences and environmental pressures. Ethnomethodology, much British sociology, management studies, literary studies, and post-1960 American ecology are suggested by Whitley as examples of fragmented adhocracies producing "diffuse, discursive knowledge of common sense objects."

Ethnomethodology stands in contradistinction to those movements or fields that have relatively highly organized mutual dependence and low degrees of research uncertainty such as British social anthropology, Anglo-Saxon economics, biomedical science, and experimental physiology. Because research is weakly coordinated across research sites, yet a social cohesion definitely exists in the ethnomethodological movement, a special technique must be employed to examine the constituent features of its socially contexted knowledge production. For this reason I have chosen to examine the "situated hermeneutics" of ethnomethodology's paradigm production through an explanation of its "textual objects" in an effort to detail how and where the movement's coherence is constructed and sustained.

Outline of the chapters

Chapter One: A generational study

Chapter One examines the generational organization of ethnomethodology's intertextual corpus of knowledge and field of discourse. We observe that ethnomethodology is a case of a specialized social science discipline whose early development displays the properties of an intellectual movement. This chapter utilizes an adaption of various anthropological and sociological representational schemes to represent the working network of the ethnomethodological movement's four generations of researchers. This analysis provides a foundation for the following chapters where we investigate in more detail how ethnomethodology's generations of practitioners assemble their professional knowledge domain. I include an account of my local achievement of membership in ethnomethodology's semantic field as a means of explicating the tacit background from which this study proceeds. I pose questions regarding the organizational form of social science knowledge and how this knowledge is transmitted intergenerationally.

Chapter Two: Ethnomethodology's radical features

Chapter Two examines ethnomethodology's radical features as an intellectual movement and a social science discipline. We see that practical methods by which four generations have organized themselves as an intellectual field and program are embedded in the polemical field of postmodern, post-World War II professional sociology. I examine how ethnomethodology's members have maintained the originality and radical qualities of their approach while managing their professional institutionalization.

Social science disciplines share certain fundamental organizational properties with contemporary radical and religious movements. In this chapter, I explore ethnomethodology's strategies for creating and maintaining itself as a distinctive neosociological field. These organizational strategies will be seen to include various practices observed in radical and religious movements such as the radical questioning of commonsense knowledge, the proleptic production of purity, and practical solutions to organizational tasks like intellectual boundaries and intertextuality. I examine other social science disciplines' dependence on organizational work.

Chapter Three: Garfinkel's intertextual poetry

Chapter Three investigates how ethnomethodology has produced an intertextual corpus of knowledge through the members' utilization of unique genres of speaking and writing. Scientific knowledge in general is interactively produced and embedded in social contexts of research performance and literary convention. We see that ethnomethodology's body of published texts exhibits a poetic structure that is semiotically anchored in its fundamental insights and conceptual themata. I examine how this poetic structure is reproduced and expanded upon by various generations of ethnomethodologists. We observe how poetic expansion is the basis for the creation of neoethnomethodology, or ethnomethodologists' contextual variations and innovations on ethnomethodology's foundational program. This chapter raises issues regarding social scientific practices of semiotic description and communication at the research work site and in written texts.

Chapter Four: The work of referencing

Various approaches have been taken in studying the production of scientific disciplines. These methods include citation analysis (Cole 1975), analysis of scientific communication networks (Mullins 1973), and paradigm revolution (Kuhn 1970). In this chapter I criticize these approaches as being incomplete. I suggest that an investigation of a scientific discipline's referential micropractices in the textual and inter-active domains sheds important light on how disciplinary knowledge and identity is produced and maintained. We observe that the ethnomethodol-ogical movement's disciplinary form and identity has been collectively fashioned by practitioners' usage of analeptic and proleptic practices, or time-ordered indexical signs. These practices are seen to include textual "missing whats," promises of forthcoming publications, refer-ences to membership collectivity lists and unpublished texts, a "purple-ditto" phase of disciplinary textual circulation, references to intellectual sources, and the organizational strategy of invoking the future of the discipline as grounds for present action and representation.

I suggest that the ethnomethodological movement's corpus of texts and social organization be analyzed as temporally ordered practical narratives. We see that an analysis of ethnomethodology's narrative organization and temporal referencing strategies reveals how its mem-bers organize their discursive and interactive field. I pose questions regarding how social science knowledge and discourse are collectively organized, represented, and circulated.

Chapter Five: Local production and documentary verification

This chapter investigates how a discipline's fact production is embedded in practitioners' daily interactions among a local community of research, knowledge, and discourse. I derive a hybridized sociosemiotic style of representation by adopting Garfinkel's (1967a:76-103) analysis of the documentary method of interpretation and applying it reflexively to ethnomethodology's field of discourse and knowledge production. I ex-amine the ordinary interactional assembly and recognition of competent intellectual membership, common working assumptions, research topics, referenced intellectual ancestors and directives, ethnomethodology's "received history," reinterpretations of past research policies, the announcement of disciplinary progress, the location of knowledge in a larger generational context, creations of clarity in situations of "essential vagueness," and common-sense constructs of normative institutionalized features that are used as working schemes of interpretation.

I suggest a semioethnomethodological conceptualization and visual representation of the ethnomethodological movement's interactionally constructed universe of discourse and knowledge. Using a synthesis of the Greimassian semiotic square (Greimas 1976:90-93) and the ethno-methodological conceptualization of the Lebenswelt pair (Livingston 1983; Garfinkel 1985b), I recommend a preliminary representation of the ethnomethodological field of discourse. We observe that this "achieved orderliness" in ethnomethodology's semantic field is a product of the intertwined relations of semanticity and grammaticality. I pose questions concerning the nature of social and natural science fact production and verification.

Chapter Six: Folklore from the field

The sociology of knowledge (Mannheim 1952a:304; 1982:11-18) has suggested that cultural formations such as texts, ideas, and knowledge display signified contents that have a genesis in the collective life experiences of particular historically and culturally located generations of individuals. In this chapter, I utilize a folkloric and semiotic approach to examine the generational location of ethnomethodologists' member-ship accounts and folkloric expansions of the ethnomethodological semantic field. I look at third and fourth generation accounts of members' introduction to and intellectual appropriation of the ethnomethodological movement. I discuss the characteristics of "intellectual conversion" as consisting of a radical change in one's universe of discourse or semantic field.

I discuss the problems of social science disciplines' production of new semiotic vehicles capable of embodying essential disciplinary insights in changing historical, intellectual, and theoretical contexts. Neoethnomethodology, the attempt by later ethnomethodological generations to signify and implement the ethnomethodological move-ment's underlying program in new practical and discursive forms to new disciplinary contexts of reception, is examined as demonstration that the ethnomethodological movement's system of signification is necessarily not fixed nor static. Instead, neoethnomethodology signifies ethnomethodology's potential presence as a contextually pliable program of inquiry.

Chapter Seven: Ethnomethodology around the world in comparative historical perspective

Theoretical paradigms are dependent on common organizational and communicational practices for their professional viability and presence. In the previous chapters we explored how ethnomethodology as a movement and a field of discourse has been composed by member-practioners' generationally embedded organizational, semiotic, intertextual, referential, interactive, and neoethnomethodological practices. In this chapter, I first undertake a sociohistorical investigation of the ethnomethodological movement's historical features in comparison with the international semiotics movement. We observe that the ethnomethodological and semiotics movements are parallel historically, held "first conferences" in 1962, share common intellectual ancestors, have intellectually responded to each others' formulations, and display both similarities and differences in their organizational strategies of disciplinary formation. We see that the semiotics movement has consistently supported ethnomethodology by providing a publication outlet for its texts and that there are clear signs of paradigmatic convergence.

Second, I examine the transmission and reception of ethnomethodology in Paris during 1985-1986. This ethnographic description and analysis is based on my own participation in these events. During 1985 and 1986, while I was studying and conducting research in Paris under a Chateaubriand Fellowship, I was a member of a group of University of California, San Diego "neoethnomethodologists" who facilitated the introduction of the ethnomethodological paradigm into France through a variety of translating, publishing, lecturing, and interfacing work. I look at the structure of the Parisian intellectual scene and context of reception, the economic factors that supported the Franco-American exchange, the intricacies of translating ethnomethodology into French, the historical contours of reception that include the ethnomethodological movement's correspondence to the French tradition of ethnographic surrealism, and a case study of one particular Parisian school, l'analyse institutionelle, and its appropriation of ethnomethodology.

I pose questions about the process of transmission and reception of social science knowledge in new international contexts. I speculate and make suggestions regarding the ethnomethodological movement's current international challenge and discuss the process of indigenous adaption of its theoretical and methodological fields.

Conclusion: Tiresius or knowledge of future events

As well as providing a summary statement of the preceding chapters' lines of argument, the conclusion attempts to supply an answer to the questions posed at the outset of the work: What is the fate and future of the ethnomethodological movement? What does it have to impart to sociological research? How can we learn from the successes and failures of the first four generations of ethnomethodological scholarship and studies? I make recommendations regarding the future of the ethnomethodological movement's knowledge domain, and I suggest articulative strategies relevant to ethnomethodology's future generations. The objective of this investigation is to explore and analyze the ethnomethodological movement's practical creation as an intellectual movement and as a specialized social science discipline. My intention is to convey to the reader a sense of the ethnomethodological movement's unique construction as an analytical style, a vehicle of modern thought, and a postmodern avenue of social investigation and understanding of the social world.

Part I

Chapter One
The Ethnomethodological Movement:
A Generational Exploration

> When I say, therefore, that I am about to propose to you a
> hopeless enterprise, that does not mean I do not think it will
> come off. I mean it is, frankly, insane in the first appearance.
> Garfinkel (Hill and Crittenden 1968:122)

> In the meantime, nothing will sink the boat. I have the money, I
> have the time. I am willing to wait. My friends are sure of me. It is garbage
> now, but tomorrow it will be something else again.
> Garfinkel (Hill and Crittenden 1968:123)

> Our activities are for whoever has the nervous system to withstand it.
> Garfinkel (Hill and Crittenden 1968:130)

This chapter explores ethnomethodology's historical features as an
intellectual movement situated within the field of modern sociological
discourse. To do this I proceed by first examining the ethnomethodological movement's generational structure. After this I present my
own reflexive account of my location in ethnomethodology's fourth
generation of researchers. I proceed by locating my analytical scheme
relative to anthropological analysis of kinship and sociological analysis
of theory group and paradigm formation. We see that the ethnomethodological movement's historical structure is most productively analyzed
through a method that represents ethnomethodology's generational
domains of research. This representation is a composite of ethnomethodologists' accounts and my own working knowledge of ethnomethodology's "received history."

We observe that this analysis of the generational construction of the ethnomethodological movement's field of discourse sheds important light on the question of how social science disciplines and specialties are historically formed. The following chapters examine in more detail how the ethnomethodological movement's generational structure is both productive of and produced by its intertextual corpus of knowledge.

The ethnomethodological movement was begun in 1954 when Harold Garfinkel developed the name "ethnomethodology" to refer to the study of members' methods of using local, common-sense knowledge to construct accountable and intelligible organized cultural contexts (cf. Garfinkel in Hill and Crittenden 1968:8; Garfinkel 1974:15-28). Garfinkel was a student at Harvard with Talcott Parsons in the Department of Social Relations from 1946 to 1952. His work with the German phenomenologists Alfred Schutz and Aron Gurwitsch resulted in a fundamental critique and expansion of Parsons's volunteristic theory of action, which Garfinkel formulated in his 1952 study and subsequent work (see Chapter 2). Heritage (1984b) presents an excellent analysis of Garfinkel's Parsonian and phenomenological theoretical synthesis, which forms the basis of his studies of everyday social life "built solely from the analysis of experience structures" (Garfinkel 1952:1). Garfinkel's pursuit of answers to the problem of social order remains a bedrock for all subsequent ethnomethodological work.

Ethnomethodology became an intellectual movement as Garfinkel was joined by various sociologists and researchers who were formulating similar criticisms and concerns for a reconstruction of sociological methods, theories, and practices. A common ethnomethodological theme became the proper sociological analysis of the social actor's knowledge, taken-for-granted assumptions, and everyday social practices.

As Merleau-Ponty (1962:viii) has said of the phenomenological movement, ethnomethodology became to be "practiced and identified as a manner or style of thinking, that it existed as a movement before arriving at complete awareness of itself as a philosophy."

Ethnomethodology's thematic features

As ethnomethodology has developed, a thematic corpus that is distinctive to its body of studies has arisen. Ethnomethodology's research program and theoretical perspective is set apart from other social science research such as symbolic interactionism and the sociology of everyday life by virtue of its distinctive orientation to social phenomenon. These thematic features can be conceptualized utilizing Mehan, Jules-Rosette, and Platt's (1984) formulation of ethnomethodology's eight distinctive features:

1. Indexical expressions
2. Reflexivity
3. Membership
4. Accountability
5. Local practices and social order
6. Situatedness
7. Unique adequacy of methods and becoming the phenomenon
8. Scenic display

This list of ethnomethodological "themata" (Holton 1978) or distinctive features represents an intertwined and intertextual network of research topics. These features do not constitute a finite corpus. Instead they characterize the work topics of Garfinkel and the different generations of ethnomethodologists. These conceptual themata can be found in various combinations in most ethnomethodological studies. They are research expansions of what I refer to as the ethnomethodological "insight of radical constitution." I develop this notion in Chapter 3.

Indexical expressions

Indexical expressions essentially are communicative products that depend on unstated assumptions and share knowledge for the mutual achievement of sense. Examples are special vocabularies, referential statements, and actions that index a prior socially recognized understanding, like a handshake or a wink. The indexical properties of natural language use are encountered in the reflexivity of members' natural accountability. Members reference constantly their common-sense understanding of social structures of everyday activities. Indexical expressions are essential features of all communication and social action (cf. Bar Hillel 1954).

Reflexivity

Reflexivity is both a phenomenon and a feature characteristic of all social ordering activity. Reflexivity refers to the dynamic self-organizational tendency of social interaction to provide for its own constitution through practices of accountability and scenic display.

The "essential reflexivity of accounts" (Garfinkel 1967e:7) is used by members to create a sense of orderliness for their action as well as constitute the social setting from which they emerge.

Membership

Membership is also a phenomenon and a method for understanding social ordering practices from within social settings. Ethnomethodology places fundamental interest in what a member of a social scene or group has to know and do in order to accomplish recognized membership, performative competence, and identity. Membership stands as the key to the understanding of the other ethnomethodological features. The concept of membership has undergone several changes from the definition of membership as an individual person to member as competent mastery of natural language use and interpretation (cf. Garfinkel and Sacks 1970: 342). This conception bears resemblances to ethnoscience's focus on emic categorization (cf. Tyler 1969).

Accountability

Accountability refers to members' practices of perceiving, describing, and justifying their actions to each other in the local collectivity. Accounting practices in natural science, for example, accomplish both the collective construction and the apparent objectivity of discovered facts and objects. Accountability is thus an essential method by which members reflexively accomplish the creation and management of common-sense understanding of social structures. The activities whereby members produce and manage settings of organized everyday affairs are identical with members' procedures for making those settings accountable (Garfinkel 1967e:1).

Local practices and social order

Local practices are the embodiment of membership and assemble all that is social. Ethnomethodology is the study of people's local practices and methods by which social rationality, knowledge, order, structures, and objects are artfully achieved. Examples of local practices are the local methods by which clinicians manage records and file folders (Garfinkel 1967b:186-207), the methods by which police decide whether a juvenile is breaking the law (Cicourel 1968a), the ways conversants recognize and categorize each other's membership in a group (Sacks 1972c), and the methods that laboratory scientists use to construct a reportable finding and analyzable scientific object (Garfinkel, Lynch, and Livingston 1981).

Situatedness

Situatedness refers to the radically contextual nature of human-sense-making activities. Ethnomethodological studies of social settings seek to discover how structural features are embedded in practical action and common-sense situations of choice. Situated practices are both indexical and reflexively constitutive of the situated members' contexts from which they arise.

The unique adequacy of methods and becoming the phenomenon

The unique adequacy of methods and becoming the phenomenon are methodological devices designed to orient the researcher to the fullest investigation possible of members' ordering procedures "from within" social settings. Unique adequacy of methods refers to the condition that the highest validity is a result of the ethnomethodologists' own achieved competence in the membership domain studied. Becoming the phenomenon is an implementation and expansion of the unique adequacy requirement by the third generation of ethnomethodological researchers (cf. Castaneda 1968; Mehan and Wood 1975a; Jules-Rosette 1975b).

Scenic display

Scenic display refers to members' performative mastery of a social scene's local practices, implicit rules and knowledge, and accountability. Scenic display is the embodied totality of artful membership with which the ethnomethodologist starts and finishes the ethnomethodological investigation. This dimension has been made observable by successive generations' development of research technologies such as incongruity experiments, audiotape transcriptions, and videotape analysis.

Ethnomethodology's topical fields

I group ethnomethodological studies into eight general topical fields: medical settings, legal settings, conversation studies, offices and bureaucratic organizations, educational institutions, religious settings, studies of the arts, and studies of scientific work (see Appendix 5). Examination of the studies in each topical field reveals a local conceptual development that proceeds intergenerationally. In the course of doing research work, the ethnomethodological movement's conceptual themata evolve in ways determined by the phenomenon itself and by the intertextual community of researchers. Conceptual and topical change is embedded in the larger processes of an intellectual movement's management of its own disciplinary character. I examine how conceptual change is intertextually managed in Chapter 4.

Ethnomethodology's ways of working

While ethnomethodology is fundamentally concerned with research methods, it has no official manual of research procedures. Instead, ethnomethodology encourages practitioners to use whatever procedures they can find or invent to make visible the taken-for-granted organizational "work" of everyday life. The ethnomethodological movement has developed local research cultures that emphasize different methodological strategies that are not necessarily exportable to other research sites. For example, some local research groups utilize audiotape and videotape records of activities as their data (cf. Mehan 1979a; Bellman and Jules-Rosette 1977; Lynch, Livingston, and Garfinkel 1982:207; Sacks, Schegloff, and Jefferson 1974; Goodwin 1981; Frankel 1983; Maynard 1986). Methods of transcription and analysis vary between groups. Other studies are directed to the empirical analysis of the embodied activities and competence constitutive of written mathematical proofs (Livingston 1983), laboratory artifacts (Lynch 1985a), and Yaqui sorcery (Castaneda 1968, 1971). Methods are adapted to the specific features of the setting under study in order to reveal its "local" constitution.

New methodological inventions and ethnomethodology's working corpus and "received history" of methods such as conversation analysis, zatocoding, inverted lenses, incongruity experiments, unique adequacy of methods, and displaying the phenomena are discussed in Chapters 2, 4, 5, and 7. I shall discuss in more detail how ethnomethodology's ways of working center on (1) achieving adequate description, (2) describing and analyzing a setting's organizational features, and (3) describing and analyzing the production of cultural objects by members' local practices.

Ethnomethodology's generations

People when asked, "Who's that?" often give identifications which invoke referral to somebody else and set up a relationship between two people...why do they do it that way?

Harvey Sacks (Hill and Crittenden 1968:30)

The ethnomethodological movement may be viewed historically in terms of several networks of "represented" generations. These generations have tried to implement Garfinkel's ethnomethodological program of "the investigation into the rational properties of indexical expressions and other practical actions as contingent ongoing accomplishments of organized, artful practices of everyday life" (1967e:11). This section attempts to delineate ethnomethodology's generational structure through the selective use of members' text-accounts and anthropological representational devices. Ethnomethodology is examined then, as an intellectual movement that shows a self-represented and referenced generational organization. A generational model can provide us with a tool for an initial conceptualizing of the ethnomethodological movement's historical structures as employed by the movement itself.

The question of what marks a generation and where its horizons lie with respect to generational thought, experience, and recognition has been debated by historians and sociologists of knowledge for several decades (cf. Mannheim 1952a:276-323). The boundaries of the collective generation—the "body of living beings constituting a single step in the line of descent from an ancestor"—are not easily fixed; like a single point on a line, the individual generation appears to operate in another dimension and is perceived with difficulty except as a constituent part of the entire pedigree (Nash 1978:1).

The analysis of collective orders and ordering through the use of a generational analytic device is fraught with problematics. I certainly realize the dangers of members in temporal categories of association. Nevertheless, a generational model is undeniably effective in the detailed examination of social organizations and organizing over time (cf. Kriegel 1978: 30). A generation is constituted only when a system of reference has been organized and accepted retrospectively and prospectively as a system of collective identification and order.

Anthropological kinship models

Many anthropological approaches to genealogy and kinship analysis (cf. Hackenberg 1974) share a common and highly disputed problem: to what extent in the specification of genealogical positions of individuals must the anthropologists enter into explanatory schemes of the social universe under study (cf. Plakans 1984:26-33)? As Keesing (1975:119) has summarized, this dispute focuses on the question of whether individuals orient themselves toward each other primarily by reference to the genealogical positions they occupy vis-à-vis each other, or by reference to more inclusive categories that include genealogical positions and make the specification of positions within these larger categories irrelevant. Members of intellectual movements appear to locate themselves by using both of these practical anthropological methodologies. Some ethnomethodologists tend to place themselves or others by reference to the genealogy of their mentors (e.g., Garfinkel, Cicourel, Sacks). Others locate themselves and others with respect to inclusive categories such as ethnomethodological specialties (conversational analysis, science studies, medical studies, etc.), campus localities (University of California, San Diego; University of California, Los Angeles; University of California, Santa Barbara; Boston; Manchester; etc.), or theoretical preference.

Anthropologists have for a long time studied the structure of lineages in village societies and small groups (cf. Hackenberg 1974; Plakans 1984). I utilize this lineage structure to frame my analysis of generations in the ethnomethodological movement. Lineages have an endogenous quality, fragment, and often regroup. I am exploring how these fragmentation and regrouping processes have taken place in the ethnomethodological movement. Following the cognitive anthropologists (Goodenough 1956; Lounsbury 1956; Conklin 1959; Frake 1961; Tyler 1972), I am attempting to formulate an adequate rendering of members of generational and domain categories while at the same time remaining sensitive to the "indexical and situated activities" of members' category creation and usages (Wieder 1970).

The heuristic use of a generational representation

Debate exists among anthropologists as to the best way to formulate the phenomenon of significant links between an entire historical community (cf. Plakans 1986:72). I have chosen a generational domain linkage configuration to reveal the interactive connections between individuals and groups who represent themselves as belonging in the ethnomethodological movement. There appears to exist a network of "genealogical" ties resulting from particular "generational units" (Mannheim 1952a:304), campus locations, represented identities, significant influences, research specialties, and publication networks. My use of the bounded domains is of course a heuristic abstraction useful for the location of specifically represented generational subunits, and it is assumed that represented membership in more than one domain is actually the case. These generational domains represent a composite picture of the ethnomethodological movement's core social groupings. They share a corporate character, a specific identifiable structure, phases of formation, expansion and dissolution, and functions within the larger ethnomethodological community as "members" contingently orient to them selectively.

My use of generation is meant to be heuristically broad and general, referring to historically represented identities and connections between teacher and student groups within the movement. My use of generation is meant to supply a refinement to Mullins's (1973:183-212) communicational stage model of disciplinary development, and draws its source from Mannheim's (1952a:304) analytic use of generation:

> Youth experiencing the same concrete historical problems may be said to be part of the same actual *generation*; while those groups within the same actual generation which work up the material of their common experiences in different specific ways, constitute separate *generation units*.

I have formulated the idea of a generational domain from Mannheim's generation unit. Generation can be analytically used as commonly produced historical units that share experiential contextures and shared objectifications. Mannheim himself saw the potential limitations of generational concept. "Generation" can create an analytical dualism that conceals the more profound interpretations of the member's experiences. Mannheim eventually abandoned the concept of generation because it created a dualism similar to that created by the concept of "class" (cf. Loader 1985:83-84). In my schema, I locate four "generations" of individuals who refer to themselves as doing ethnomethodological studies. This means that somewhere in their work they reference an intellectual identity with ethnomethodological studies. Usually, these individuals are cross-referenced by others referencing a similar identity or "contingent" representation of membership.

1950-1960   first generation Ph.D.'s and fellow travelers
1960-1970   second generation Ph.D.'s and fellow travelers
1970-1980   third generation Ph.D.'s and fellow travelers
1980-1990   fourth generation Ph.D.'s and fellow travelers

Ethnomethodology's generational domains

My decision as to whom to place on the following generational modeling device (Figure 1-1) is founded on sociologists' own representations of themselves as doing "ethnomethodological work." This "representation of identity" is evidenced in print, verbally, and by others who referenced ethnomethodology's members. Often, there have been representations of group membership in ethnomethodology by sociologists who do not consider themselves a part of that working domain of knowledge. Errors have resulted such as the represented membership of Peter Berger and Thomas Luckman (cf. Mullins 1973:199: MacCannell and MacCannell 1982:85; Hopkins 1984). Sociologists who consider themselves "ethnomethodologists" have been quick to correct the public record (cf. Liberman 1983:428).

I have observed that there are common patterns associated with the activity of representing oneself as an ethnomethodologist. Thus, contextual factors like being a Ph.D. student with a "represented member" such as Garfinkel or Aaron Cicourel certainly is relevant to one's creating and sustaining the same professional image. Thus, my chart reveals associational clusters of students in cohort groups producing concerted representation of research and membership that is termed by them "ethnomethodological." Also, there is the existence of "fellow travelers" who, while not producing a doctoral degree with a represented ethnomethodologist, nevertheless align their interests and research with ethnomethodology and signify this textually.

Generally, I have organized individuals into "generational clusters" according to the production dates of their initial cultural objectifications (texts) signifying a represented membership within the movement. In most cases, this has taken the form of a Ph.D. study or an initial published work "in" ethnomethodology. As I explore later in this work, these signifying activities productive of a representation of membership in the movement take a variety of forms and styles that are themselves intimately related to a reflexive construction of a member's "historicity" within the movement and within the larger "popular" culture.

Founding Ancestors   Edmund Husserl   Maurice Merleau-Ponty
                                       Alfred Schutz   Talcott Parsons
                          Aron Gurwitsch

1950 Generation 1

Harold Garfinkel   Erving Goffman

MacAndrew   Churchill   Platt   Cicourel   Bittner   Rose
                                                              Strodtbeck
                                                              Mendlovitz

Bloombaum   Thalmeir   Blum   McHugh

Edgerton   Duster

Jules-Rosette – Lidz   Castaneda   Sacks – Schegloff   Moerman
Walker   Robillard – Bellman   Sudnow – Turner
HARVARD   Girton – Eglin – Schwartz   Speier
                            UCLA   UCB, UCLA

Cavan   Kitsuse

Wilson   Adato

Wieder – Zimmerman
UCLA

Stoddart

1960 Generation 2

Boese – Crowle – Elliot
Hajjar – Jennings – Leiter
Mackay – Mehan – Pollner
Roth – Shumsky – Wood – Handel
Wedow – Ima – Handel
UCSB

Emerson

Narens

Filmer – Silverman – Roche
Atkinson – Drew – Lee – Cuff – Coulter
Heritage – Benson – Hughes – Sharrock
Watson – Wooten
BRITAIN

O'Neill

1970 Generation 3

Twer – Pomerantz – Schenkein
Jefferson – Ryave – Goodwin
Goldberg – Smith – Bellman
UCLA, UCI

Psathas
Coulter
BOSTON

Heap   Lester   Molotch

                      Ramos   Phillips

Figure A

1980 Generation 4

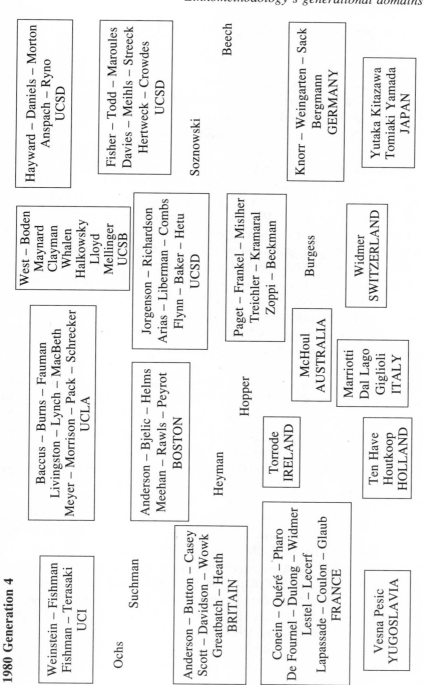

Figure A

The first generation (1950-1960)

I am presenting a "synoptic history" of the ethnomethodological movement's visible generational formations for the practical purpose of giving readers a constructed image of the communicational relationships involved. My basis for assigning individuals to specific generations and domains is as follows. I have located Harold Garfinkel as the first generational progenitor of the ethnomethodological movement. It is he who, in his 1952 study, first began the critical translation of Schutz's phenomenology into a new synthesis with sociological and empirical questions stemming from Parsons's teachings at Harvard. It was Garfinkel who developed the name "ethnomethodology" in 1954 to refer to this approach. It is he who is most often cited by ethnomethodologists as the originator of the first formulations of ethnomethodological ideas. Garfinkel claims that the ethnomethodological movement's ideas and distinctive features were collaboratively developed "in a company of geniuses" (Garfinkel 1985a), a fact that testifies to the inherent limitations of my genealogical configurations. I more fully describe and analyze Garfinkel's central and original contributions in the chapters that follow.

I have placed Aaron Cicourel, Egon Bittner, Milton Bloombaum, Alan Blum, Lindsey Churchill, Troy Duster, Peter McHugh, Gerald Platt, Ed Rose, Fred Thalheimer, and Saul Mendolvitz in coresidence in the ethnomethodological movement's first generation. These individuals stand together as a group identified by their participation and interaction with Garfinkel in the first ethnomethodology seminars and activities at the University of California, Los Angeles, beginning in 1955 and continuing until 1962.

Aaron V. Cicourel is probably the most widely known and influential first-generation ethnomethodologist besides Garfinkel. Cicourel was originally a student of W.S. Robinson at the University of California, Los Angeles in 1955 working on methodology and the problems of how sociologists "make sense" of data. An interest in finding more explicit links between theory and measurement led Cicourel to a two-year collaboration with Harold Garfinkel at the University of California, Los Angeles during 1955 and 1957 (Cicourel 1964:iv). Garfinkel introduced Cicourel to the work of Alfred Schutz, which clarified Cicourel's understanding of the role of theory in method and measurement in sociology. According to Cicourel:

This collaboration (between Cicourel and Garfinkel) proved valuable in understanding how formal sociological theories are tied ambiguously to the subjects' and researchers' common-sense language and thinking.

In 1964, Cicourel produced *Method and Measurement in Sociology*, which analyzed sociology's reliance on common-sense categories. This text formed another controversial pillar for ethnomethodology's developing criticism of traditional sociological methods.

Cicourel left the University of California, Los Angeles in 1955 to do doctoral studies at Cornell. He completed his study in 1957 under Robin Williams at which time he returned to the University of California, Los Angeles. There he and Garfinkel organized an ethnomethodology seminar that included Bittner, Bloombaum, Duster, McHugh, Polk, Platt, and Thalmeir (cf. Mullins 1974:192). He taught at Northwestern in 1959 and at the University of California, Riverside from 1960 to 1965. During 1965-1966 Cicourel taught at Berkeley and facilitated the development of a second generation group of ethnomethodologists, which included Sacks, Schegloff, Moerman, Jefferson, Speier, Sudnow, and Turner. Cicourel chaired Sacks' (1966) dissertation committee, which also included Herbert Blumer and the anthropologist Gerald Berreman.

At Berkeley Cicourel became increasingly interested in linguistics and began to elaborate ethnomethodology's program in relation to anthropological linguistics, such as Hymes, Gumperz, Frake, and Goodenough; to generative grammar and semantics theorists like Chomsky, Greenberg, Katz, and Fodor; and to cognitive psychologists such as Neisser, McNeill, and Norman.

He continued and expanded his dialogue when he went to the University of California, Santa Barbara in 1967 and to the University of California, San Diego in 1972. Cicourel's *Cognitive Sociology* (1973b) provided a summative statement of his ethnomethodological positions centering around the problem of meaning and language (cf. Cicourel 1974b:99-100) and provided a document of his shift from using the term "ethnomethodology" to "cognitive sociology." As a text, *Cognitive Sociology* marks Cicourel's transition of identity as a member of the ethnomethodological movement. Though still known and recognized internationally as an ethnomethodologist, Cicourel began viewing himself during the years 1974 to 1980 as doing a different kind of work, which he preferred to term cognitive sociology or "discourse analysis" (cf. Cicourel 1980). I trace Cicourel's particular shift in his position in the ethnomethodological movement and its display in his texts in Chapter 4.

Karin Knorr-Cetina (Knorr-Cetina and Cicourel 1981:33) presents a good summary of Cicourel's general ethnomethodological emphasis:

> It has perhaps been the major thrust of Cicourel's work to document interactional and organizational accounting procedures and decision-making activities whereby situated events are routinely transformed into summary measures, aggregated distributions, bureaucratic records, and similar macro information.

Cicourel's *The Social Organization of Juvenile Justice* (1968), which was an ethnomethodological study, was reviewed critically by Rock (1968) and Lennon (1973), continuing a pattern of ethnomethodology's cautious reception by the sociological community.

Churchill and Bittner also were graduate students at the University of California, Los Angeles and received their Ph.D.'s in 1961. Both Churchill and Bittner published with Garfinkel. Rose was already in a faculty position at the University of Colorado, Boulder and has remained a "fellow traveler" along ethnomethodology's paths. Rose cofounded the first conferences on ethnomethodology in 1962 with Garfinkel through an Air Force Office of Scientific Research Grant (Garfinkel 1967a:73), participated in the Purdue Symposium on Ethnomethodology (Hill and Crittenden 1968), is listed as doing ethnomethodological studies in Garfinkel's *Preface* (1967a:viii), produced former University of California, San Diego faculty ethnomethodologist Reyes Ramos, and is the originator of "Rose's Gloss" (Garfinkel and Sacks 1970:366).

Also present in the first generation is Gerald Platt, who began as a symbolic interactionist and later worked with Parsons on his study of the American university. Duster, Bloombaum, Thalmeir, and Cavan were early participants but did not become career ethnomethodologists. [Duster's recent work on the micro-macrosociological problem and its reflexive resolution (1981) has been specified as being influential to a recent fourth generational compilation of ethnomethodological studies (cf. Fisher and Todd 1986:xiv).] Blum and McHugh are examples of early participants in the movement who left to develop their ethnomethodologically similar insights in another manner and style and for another professional audience (cf. Blum 1970a, c; Blum and McHugh 1971; McHugh 1968, 1970; McHugh, Raffel, Foss, and Blum 1974).

The second generation (1960-1970)

I have reconstructed the second generation of the ethnomethodological movement to generally include all students and individuals who "reference" themselves with the movement, took ethnomethodological graduate training, completed Ph.D. studies, and published "referenced" ethnomethodological studies during the period 1960 to 1970. This generational segment is a composition of members' accounts and referential activities. It can be conceptualized as a "chapter" of the ethnomethodological movement's story, recognized as such by those who see themselves as its members. For members, this generational "structure of long duration" (Braudel 1972:18) possesses a certain characteristic quality that is bound with the unique mixture of social, intellectual, and political influences existing at the time.

University of California, Berkeley

In 1961 Harvey Sacks, a graduate student of Erving Goffman at the University of California, Berkeley, was making numerous visits to the University of California, Los Angeles to conduct meetings with Harold Garfinkel (Sacks 1963:1). He introduced his Berkeley cohort group, consisting of Emanuel Schegloff, David Sudnow, and Roy Turner to Garfinkel's writings. They began a working group (Sudnow 1971: preface). Sacks participated in the first Conference on Ethnomethodology at the University of California, Los Angeles in 1962 with Garfinkel, Rose, Bittner, and Craig MacAndrew. In 1963 Sacks came to the University of California, Los Angeles as a researcher with Garfinkel, and in 1964 he began lecturing in the University of California, Los Angeles Department of Sociology. In 1963, he began his own research on the ethnomethodological studies of the workings of ordinary and natural conversation activities. His dissertation, inspired by Goffman and Garfinkel, and chaired by Cicourel at Berkeley in 1966, in turn came to stimulate considerable research in that area by his generational cohort group at Berkeley and Los Angeles. Sacks abridged a portion of his dissertation into an article entitled "An Initial Investigation of the Usability of Conversational Data for Doing Sociology" (Sacks 1972c). This article established the ethnomethodological problems of categorization as a central theme in his work and in the work of his cohort network of Jefferson, Moerman, Schegloff (Ph.D. 1967), Speier (Ph.D. 1969), Sudnow (Ph.D. 1967), Turner, and Twer. The current school of conversational analysis has grown out of this early work. Sacks began teaching at the University of California, Irvine in 1967 and published an article with Garfinkel in 1970. Sacks was killed in a car crash in 1975.

Schegloff went to Columbia in 1967 and came to teach at the University of California, Los Angeles in 1971. Sudnow taught at the University of California, Santa Barbara in 1967, at the State University of New York, Stony Brook in 1967, and came to the University of California, Irvine in 1968. He presently lives in New York and teaches jazz piano. Turner taught at the University of British Columbia from 1970 to the present. Speier has taught at the University of British Columbia since 1970.

University of California, Los Angeles

In the early sixties a group of graduate students at the University of California, Los Angeles began working with Garfinkel on dissertation studies. This group included Don Zimmerman (Ph.D. 1966), D. Lawrence Wieder (Ph.D. 1969), and others. Zimmerman wrote his dissertation on the "paper work" involved in record keeping in a public welfare agency. Wieder's dissertation was on the ethnomethodological analysis of the "convict code" used in a Los Angeles halfway house. Both Zimmerman and Wieder lectured at the University of California, Santa Barbara for one year (1967 to 1968) as a way of establishing an ethnomethodological program there that included both Garfinkel's and Cicourel's perspectives. There also existed a group of students and faculty from departments such as anthropology and linguistics who audited Garfinkel's seminars at that time. These "fellow travelers" were deeply influenced by ethnomethodology and carried this influence into their work even though they did not receive doctorates in ethnomethodological studies. This group included Michael Moerman, Carlos Castaneda, Albert Adato, Ken Stoddart, Robert Edgerton, and others.

The third generation (1970-1980)

I refer to ethnomethodology's third generation as those individuals who completed their dissertations "in" ethnomethodology during the period 1970 to 1980. The training of third generation ethnomethodologists has required a complex semiotic practice of transmitting the core ethnomethodological speech, writing, and research genres, developed primarily by the first generation, through the active mediation of the second generation. Although much ethnomethodological training of graduate students has been accomplished by first generation members like Garfinkel and Cicourel, an increasing pattern has been for third and fourth generation students to discover the ethnomethodological paradigm through second generation teaching (see Chapter 6). As we shall examine in more detail in the forthcoming chapters, each generation has created a neoethnomethodology expressive of signified contents specific to their particular spatiotemporal location in the ethnomethodological movement's community of researchers. The ethnomethodological movement's accomplishment of a semiotic unity and a presence as a historical force is achieved through the innovative intertextual and referential practices of its practitioners.

University of California, Los Angeles

A wave of third generation graduate students began their studies at the University of California, Los Angeles in the mid-1960s through the 1970s. Howard Schwartz (Ph.D. 1971), Beryl Bellman (Ph.D. 1970, University of California, Irvine), Lincoln Ryave (Ph.D. 1973), Britt Robillard, Trent Eglin, and Warren Ten Houten conducted doctoral studies with Garfinkel during this period. These students were initiating their studies in ethnomethodology as the earlier members of University of California, Los Angeles's second generation (Sacks, Schegloff, Sudnow, Zimmerman, Wieder, etc.) received their Ph.D.'s and were beginning to teach.

Schwartz went to teach at Harvard in 1970. Thomas Blakeley was one of his first students at Harvard. In 1971, Bellman was teaching in the School of Special Studies at the California Institute of the Arts, and he would later come to teach at the University of California, San Diego.

Students working with Sacks, MacAndrew, and Sudnow at the University of California, Irvine included Gail Jefferson and Jim Schenkein (Ph.D. 1976), Anita Pomerantz (Ph.D. 1975), and Jo Anne Goldberg (Ph.D. 1976). Garfinkel's colloquia at Harvard in 1970 created a Harvard ethnomethodology group that included Bennetta Jules-Rosette, Andrew Walker, and Charles Lidz. Jules-Rosette came to the University of California, Los Angeles to study with Garfinkel in 1970. Reyes Ramos studied with Ed Rose at the University of Colorado, Boulder and finished his dissertation in 1973 while teaching at the University of California, San Diego. Lou Narens and Richard M. Frankel were at the University of California, Los Angeles in 1970. George Psathas, John O'Neill, Harvey Molotch, and Marilyn Lester were professionally established "fellow travelers" who became involved with ethnomethodology during the late 1960s and early 1970s.

University of California, Santa Barbara

In 1967 Aaron Cicourel established an ethnomethodological group at the University of California, Santa Barbara. This group was important for continuing to establish the credibility that the ethnomethodological movement could produce high-quality Ph.D. students and publishable research. Cicourel worked with sociologist Thomas P. Wilson and with Don Zimmerman and D. Lawrence Wieder to implement an ethnomethodological graduate training program that produced over sixteen Ph.D. students between the years 1967 and 1972. This production of successful third generation ethnomethodologists generated continued assurances and legitimation that ethnomethodology was a subdiscipline capable of creating professionals who could teach the new discipline to others.

    This group of students completed doctoral research and dissertations in a variety of areas. Robert Boese (1972) worked on sign language and the acquisition of social structure; Anthony Crowle (1971) analyzed postexperimental interviews using a sociolinguistic analysis; Henry Elliot (1970) studied the similarities and differences between science and common sense; Warren Handel (1972) researched the social process of learning to categorize; Judith Handel (1972) studied perception and constructive process; Ken Jennings (1972) analyzed language acquisition and the development of rational and rationalizable skills; Ken Leiter (1971) studied the structure of teachers' accounts in the classroom; Robert MacKay (1971) completed an ethnography of the classroom and language learning; Hugh Mehan (1971) researched the accomplishment of interactive understanding in educational settings; Mel Pollner (1970) wrote his study on the foundations of mundane reasonings; David Roth (1972) analyzed children's linguistic performances in classroom activity; Marshall Shumsky (1971) made a sociolinguistic analysis of encounter groups' interaction; Susan Wedow (1973) did an ethnomethodological study of astrology and everyday reasoning; and Houston Wood (1968) studied the labelling process on a mental hospital ward. Cicourel was successful in helping many of his dissertation students get published in journals and as coauthors with himself (cf. Cicourel, Jennings, Jennings, Leiter, MacKay, Mehan, and Roth 1974; Cicourel and Boèse 1972a and b; Cicourel and Mehan 1985). Thomas P. Wilson was an already established sociologist at the University of California, Santa Barbara who began doing ethnomethodological work.

Ethnomethodology as a collective movement

As is discussed throughout this work, the inception and development of the ethnomethodological movement has proceeded along a generational and local organization. This organization has been most effective where it has been open and adaptive to local and generational relevances and contexts of reception. This openness has permitted the creation of ethnomethodologies responsive to immediate cultural influences and concerns while remaining faithful to original ethnomethodological programmatic statements. In the late 1960s and early 1970s ethnomethodologists were experiencing the sense of being a collective movement bringing a new and important intellectual truth to the world. In this respect, ethnomethodology bears resemblances to religious, cultural, and political movements existent at that time in America and Western Europe that were expressive of new and radical ideas. Mel Pollner, in an interview with me, commented on this sense of ethnomethodology as a collective movement that was shared by members of the second and third generations at that time:

> PF: How about the idea that ethnomethodology was becoming a revolution, a movement, a sense of a collective endeavor? Did you relate to that?

> MP: Well, I think that Santa Barbara was...one could experience the sense that you were on or within a collective movement. There were students that had ... and faculty that had, a relatively aggressive position vis-à-vis

other aspects of sociology, in the sense you were bringing an important dimension, an important perspective to bear that would just have deep consequences for the rest of the field, and so certainly at Santa Barbara, there was a sense of a close working group of individuals, and so in that sense there was the sense of a movement. To some extent that was also available here at UCLA in the late '60s and early '70s, people like Howie Schwartz, Lou Narens, ...they were here at that time, ...there too...there was that continuation of the sense of being involved in something very important, very serious, consequential, and exciting... and that sense of bringing an important truth to the world. And so there was in that sense a sense of a movement at that time. I don't know to what extent that feeling exists since that time here at UCLA.

University of California, San Diego

In 1970, Joe Gusfield was creating a new sociology department at the University of California, San Diego. Gusfield was given encouragement by University of California, San Diego's trustees to form a unique specialized department that would make a unique contribution to social scientific knowledge. This objective was in line with the young campus's goal for all of its fledgling departments. Gusfield, with his training at the University of Chicago and his years of fieldwork experience in India, Japan, and the United States, envisioned a new kind of sociology department that would encourage scholarship in primarily the qualitatively based forms of ethnographic sociology and social anthropology (Gusfield 1987, personal communication). Gusfield hoped to recruit scholars who were actively examining the philosophical and methodological underpinnings of the sociological discipline and applying their insights to ethnographic research.

Gusfield initially hired Jack D. Douglas, Jerry Skolnick, Bill Wild, and Randall Collins to form the bedrock of the department. Jack Douglas's *The Social Meanings of Suicide* had an ethnomethodological bent that went beyond examining records of suicide to see what the nature of the records actually were. Through Douglas's book, Gusfield was introduced to the work of Harold Garfinkel, which he read and found extremely important because of the emphasis it placed on assumptions and the study of behavior itself, not mere records about behavior.

Gusfield has stated in an interview (1987) his reasons for incorporating ethnomethodology into the nascent department of sociology at the University of California, San Diego:

I began to be concerned with the strands of thought coming from Europe. When I went to Japan (in 1968) I brought with me a copy of *The Savage Mind*, which I had never read, I had never read any of Levi-Strauss. So I was getting more open to what I would call a more idealistic philosophical orientation. When I got back to the states in early 1968, when I had accepted the offer at UCSD and I was faced with what kind of department I would make and who shall I hire, I began to move in the direction of people who had been doing ethnographic work, people who were open, that is not particularly in the quantitative areas because I was determined not to do that because I wanted to train students in fieldwork with more ethnographic orientation.

My interest in ethnomethodology, beyond seeing in it a very effective critique of the heavy quantitative bent, was a capacity to ask kinds of questions about the constituent parts of human behavior that were not being asked in American Sociology, that were somewhat being hinted at in Chomsky and Levi-Strauss in their concern with language to be sure and also that sense about things that were prior to the social structure in the sense that sociologists had talked about, not in the structuralist sense. They led me to see an interpretive scheme or an interpretive paradigm that was inherent in symbolic interactionism that I thought was extremely valuable, it was a new direction. And I wasn't sufficiently aware at the time of nuances and ways of talking about it that I now could do if I wanted to put a different kind of gloss on it and talk about interpretive schemas and the emphasis on interpretive sociology. I saw in it a much more...a set of problems that had been carved out that were not only original but were prior to the kinds of questions sociologists were asking. So the notion that you could talk about the prerequisites for particular kinds of structures or particular sets of interrelationships struck me as extremely important.... In all these senses, ethnomethodology seems to me to be a tremendously important orientation.

Gusfield decided to include an ethnomethodological specialization in the new University of California, San Diego department. Harold Garfinkel was initially offered the position of developing an ethnomethodological program of studies at the University of California, San Diego. Garfinkel declined and it was to Aaron Cicourel that the offer was next made. Cicourel accepted the position that included teaching and research liaisons with the University of California, San Diego Medical School. Cicourel built the ethnomethodological program by bringing Kenneth Jennings, Bennetta Jules-Rosette, and Hugh Mehan. Eventually Reyes Ramos, Beryl Bellman, Susanne Wedow, and Howard Schwartz taught ethnomethodology courses at the University of California, San Diego. Cicourel used his standing in the ethnomethodological tradition, his orientation to empirical research, his administrative skills, and his work in Latin American studies to create a strong ethnomethodological program that immediately began to generate doctoral students.

Great Britain and Europe

At this time (1966-1970) ethnomethodological working groups began in Great Britain as a result of first and second generation ethnomethodologists visiting a variety of English universities. Cicourel and Roy Turner visited Goldsmith's College and contributed to a series of seminars there on the ethnomethodological critique of sociology that later was published as Filmer, Phillipson, Silverman, and Walsh's (1972) *New Directions in Sociological Theory*. Anthony Crowle was hired as a lecturer at Oxford. Garfinkel gave a lecture series at Manchester University as a Simon Visiting Professor in 1973. During this period, J. Maxwell Atkinson, E.C. Cuff, Jeff Coulter, J.R.E. Lee, D. Rod Watson, and Wes Sharrock at the University of Manchester; Paul Drew and John Hughes at the University of Lancaster; Douglas Benson at Plymouth Polytechnic; and John Heritage at the University of Warwick seriously began developing ethnomethodological and conversation studies in Great Britain. Coulter was hired at Boston University and worked with George Psathas to develop an ethnomethodological center there. Filmer visited the University of California, San Diego for a quarter in 1972-1973 and again in 1987 and 1989. Silverman lectured at the University of California, Los Angeles in 1973.

During this period, the ethnomethodological movement began transmitting its ideas to Europe. Aaron Cicourel's "The Acquisition of Social Structure" was first published in Italy in 1968. Cicourel had a series of publications translated into German, including *Method and Measurement* in 1970 (cf. Cicourel 1970a, b; 1973b; 1974b). Garfinkel also was translated into German in 1973 (cf. Garfinkel 1956b; 1959a; 1964a). Harvey Sacks was translated into German in 1971 (cf. Sacks 1967b). Emanuel Schegloff was an invited lecturer in 1975 at the University of Konstanz, West Germany. In 1976, a collection of ethnomethodological papers was published in German as *Ethnomethodologie* (Weingarten, Sacks, Schenkein 1976). Cicourel began developing working relations and exchanges with the University of Konstanz, West Germany.

Cicourel began transmitting ideas to France with the translation of *Cognitive Sociology* in 1973 and an article in *Communications* (cf. Cicourel 1973 Appendix A). Cicourel developed working relations with

Pierre Bourdieu at the Ecole des Hautes Etudes en Sciences Sociales, Paris. Harvey Sacks (cf. Sacks 1973 Appendix A) and Alan Blum and Peter McHugh (1973 Appendix A) were also translated in *Communications*. These networks laid important foundations for the future transmissions of ethnomethodology into France during the 1980s (cf. Chapter 7; Appendix 4).

The fourth generation (1980-1990)

University of California, Los Angeles

In the mid-1970s and 1980's, another generation of new graduate students began to cluster around Garfinkel at the University of California, Los Angeles. This group followed Garfinkel's seminars, attempted to make sense of ethnomethodology's "received history," and began innovatively to master and use Garfinkel's sometimes esoteric speech, writing, and research genres (see Chapter 3) in ways appropriate to their generational intellectual concerns. Melinda Baccus, Stacy Burns, Richard Fauman, Eric Livingston, Michael Lynch, Douglas MacBeth, Louis Meyer, Kenneth Morrison, Christopher Pack, and Friedrich Schrecker began undertaking graduate studies with Garfinkel at that time. Christopher Pack and Ken Liberman were graduate students at the University of California, San Diego who were introduced to ethnomethodology by Cicourel, Mehan, and Jules-Rosette and who participated in this University of California, Los Angeles training. This fourth generation group worked with Garfinkel, Sacks, Schegloff, Sudnow, and others to develop a "neoethnomethodology" that has been termed "ethnomethodological studies of work" (cf. Garfinkel 1986a). This genre of studies investigates the local production of order through an examination of the technical details of organizational phenomena such as natural science, mathematics, jazz piano playing, Kung Fu, lecturing, alchemy, and penguin ethology. As a synthetic fourth generation "neoethnomethodology," the studies of work have innovatively employed and developed a wide variety of new ethnomethodological methods and ways of writing. These seek to analyze locally observable sequences of conduct that make up the details of a discipline's daily work (cf. Lynch, Livingston, and

Garfinkel 1983; Lynch 1985b; Livingston 1983; Baccus 1976; Morrison 1981; Burns 1978a, b, c; Liberman 1980; Pack 1975). This group of students has expanded ethnomethodology's early program to include new uses of the unique adequacy of methods and becoming the phenomena, ethnomethodological "hybridization" with the knowledge system under study, renewed dialogues with semiotics, phenomenology, and relevant critical disciplines, and the development of new semioethnomethodological concepts like the "lebenswelt-pair," laboratory iconization, transitivity, and the sequential analysis of written materials.

University of California, Santa Barbara

At the same time during the mid-1970s and 1980's, Candace West, Douglas Maynard, Deirdre Boden, Steven Clayman, Marilyn Whalen, Jack Whalen, Timothy Halkowsky, Robin Lloyd, Wayne Mellinger and others were developing fourth generation conversational studies with Don Zimmerman, Harvey Molotch, and Thomas P. Wilson, at the University of California, Santa Barbara. This group has developed new expansions of conversation analysis into the areas of power relations between the sexes, plea bargaining, discourse dominance in the Watergate hearings, doctor-patient conversational interaction, in-take processes at public welfare agencies, and other domains.

University of California, San Diego

At the University of California, San Diego, ethnomethodology's fourth generation includes Peter Hayward, Shelly Daniels, Joyce Morton, Renée Anspach, and Ron Ryno who completed dissertations with Cicourel. The ethnomethodologists completing dissertations on medical and educational institutions with Mehan are Sue Fisher, Alexandra Todd, Nicholas Maroules, Phil Davies, Janet Lee Meihls, Alma Hertweck, and Margaret Crowdes. This group has developed a "neoethnomethodology" capable of ethnographically analyzing micro and macro contexts of institutional processes, and has made working bridges with developmental psychology. Graduate students working with Bennetta Jules-Rosette and the Laboratory for Ethnographic and Audiovisual Studies (LEAVS) have included Armando Arias, Phyllis Baker, Sam Combs, Pierce Flynn, Dominique Glaub, Chantale Hetu, Danny Jorgenson, Dominique Lestel,

Ken Liberman, Nick Maroules, Alberto Restrepo and Curtis Richardson .
The LEAVS group has worked with Garfinkel on studies of science and
has been developing a form of neoethnomethodology termed by some
semioethnomethodology. Semioethnomethodology utilizes ethnomethodology, semiotics, life histories, and the sociology of knowledge to
conduct ethnographic explorations of knowledge and belief domains,
textual systems, and new technologies.

Conversation analysis

The development of conversational analysis as a "neoethnomethodology"
has shown the most extensive growth in the second, third, and fourth
generations. With the death of one of its prominent leaders, Harvey
Sacks, in 1975, conversation analysis has artfully faced the challenge of
solidifying and expanding its basic program of the study of the social
organization of talk. Utilizing fundamental ethnomethodological insights
and themata concerning conversation's indexical nature, reflexive temporal order, and interactional work, conversation analysis (cf. Sacks,
Schegloff, and Jefferson 1974; Schenkein 1978a; Psathas 1979; Atkinson
and Heritage 1984) has constructed itself as a neoethnomethodological
discipline that is producing original findings about the formal structure
of situated talk. Conversation analysis has created its own lineage of
researchers and relevant texts. It has been constructing itself as a professionally legitimate analytical subdiscipline through a variety of conceptual referential and organizational strategies (see Chapter 4).

Second, third, and fourth generation ethnomethodologists at all research centers in the United States, Europe, and Canada (see Appendix,
Chapter 7) have utilized conversation analysis as fundamental training
in ethnomethodology whether they specialize in this program or not.
Many include selected analytical conventions of conversation analysis
while textually maintaining a critical theoretical distance (cf. Lynch
1985a; Morrison 1981; Fisher 1979; Maroules 1985). Fourth generation
ethnomethodologists specializing in conversation analysis include David
Weinstein, Arlene Terasake, Pamela Fishman, and Mark Fishman at the
University of California, Irvine; Candace West, Deirdre Boden, Douglas
Maynard at the University of California, Santa Barbara; Jurgen Streeck
at the University of California, San Diego and Free University of Berlin;
and Paula A. Treichler, Richard M. Frankel, Cheris Kramarae, Kathleen
Zoppi, and Howard Beckman. The Interaction Research Group at Boston

University has produced Dusan Bjelic, Albert Jay Meehan, Anne Rawls, David T. Helm, and Timothy W. Anderson. Robert Hopper at the University of Texas-Austin, Richard Heyman at the University of Calgary, Paul Ten Have and Hanneke Houtkoop at the University of Amsterdam, Christian Heath at the University of Surrey, and Brian Torrode at Trinity College, Dublin, all do conversational studies.

Conversation analysis's neoethnomethodological program has possibly had its greatest influence in Great Britain. British third and fourth generation conversation analysts include Graham Button and Nigel Casey at Plymouth Polytechnic, C. Scott at Oxford University, David Greatbatch at University of Warwick, and R.J. Anderson and Maria Wowk at University of Manchester. Bernard Conein, Patrick Pharo, Louis Quéré, and Michel de Fournel constitute a fourth generational cadre of French scholars working with conversation analysis and ethnomethodology.

Ethnomethodology's fourth generation appears to be continuing the intellectual lineage begun in 1952 into new international domains. Included in this generation are the current ethnomethodological students-in-training around the world (see Chapter 7). Despite professional resistance, ethnomethodology's first, second, third, and fourth generations have established themselves in international professional positions and produced students and research networks. In 1990, ethnomethodology increasingly is becoming recognized internationally as a foundational discipline making important contributions to the sociology of science (cf. Knorr-Cetina and Mulkay 1982); the sociology of education, medicine, and law; semiotics (cf. MacCannell and MacCannell 1982); international sociological theory (cf. Alexander, Giesen, Munch, Smelser 1987; Habermas 1981; Pesic 1983; Kitazawa 1984); life historical studies (cf. Denzin 1985); anthropology and linguistic pragmatics. (cf. Levinson 1983) among others (Boden, 1989). New ethnomethodological research groups are forming as ethnomethodologists continue to visit international campuses. Chapter 7 of this work examines a case of ethnomethodology's transmission and influence in France during 1985 and 1986. Yet, the ethnomethodological movement is currently faced with internal contradictions that may threaten its life as an intellectual movement.

Analytical questions

A question posed in this study is what we can learn from the successes and failures of the four generations of ethnomethodological scholarship and studies. What can the sociological discipline learn about its own processes of knowledge production by examining ethnomethodology's development as a subdiscipline? I suggest that ethnomethodology provides a unique case study in the practical production of social scientific knowledge. This knowledge has a historical character that is assembled through members' semiotic practices of reading, writing, speaking, and interacting within the constraints of a larger social, economic, and political field. Ethnomethodological and social scientific knowledge achieves historicized value through the inventive generational appropriation of knowledge structures. Ethnomethodology has historically recognized its own reflexive place in the production of its knowledge (Garfinkel 1967a). Ethnomethodological knowledge has the characteristic of being highly critically aware of its own situated construction as a common-sense formulation dependent on natural language practices (Garfinkel and Sacks 1970; Cicourel 1973b). Understanding social scientific knowledge in particular requires an interpretive process that Lemert (1981:11) in his work on French sociology has called "reading from field to text." The following chapters investigate ethnomethodology's production of its intellectual field, and corpus of texts through attention to its historical and generational horizons.

Ethnomethodology's Received History

Livingston (1983) contributes a fourth generation ethnomethodological "text account" and an analytical mechanism useful for our own analysis of generations in movements. In his dissertation on the foundations of mathematics, Livingston acknowledges Garfinkel as being the pervasive influence on his research:

> This dissertation could not have been written without the assistance, supervision, and support of Harold Garfinkel. His influence has been pervasive *in formulating the problem* of mathematical foundations as a problem in the production of social order and in carrying out the research. (1983:vii).

Later in his study, Livingston develops an idea of a "received history" or a "received topic" of a mathematical theorem (1983:200). He credits Garfinkel with the origination of the notion, saying:

> Again, I am indebted to Harold Garfinkel for making the notions of a "received view," "received history," and "received topic" available as a matter of ethnomethodological interest (1983:118).

Livingston formulates the notion of "received history" to include both a "weak" and "strong" version. The "weak" version specifies that mathematical (or in our case, an ethnomethodological) theorem and its proof are available to the practitioner not only as a useable theorem and proof, but also as a specific theorem and proof that "arises from within" and is responsive to the proper history of their discovery and development (1983: 201). This received historical context includes knowledge of the methods' historical development, their historical importance from the perspective of the discipline, its local applications, etc.

The strong version of the notion of "received history" of a theorem (or theory) refers, in contrast to the preceding, to the "state of the art" (1983: 201) of received ways of actual hands-on proving work. These received "ways of proving" consist of actual in situ members' methods of practically producing the mathematical proof on paper, in front of colleagues, as defense of a position, in an article, analyzing data, etc. According to Livingston, it is by reason of a practitioner's experimental knowledge of and competence with "state of the art" technical methods and stylizations that he or she is able to construct an appropriate and "accountable" history of the theorem in question. Livingston (1983) says:

> It is in the presence of naturally accountable proofs of the theorem that a mathematician is able to find and argue what the *proper history* of that theorem and its proof is.

For the purposes of analyzing ethnomethodology's received history and received topics we can also refer to weak and strong versions of these notions. An ethnomethodological novice or new member-in-training "receives" an integrated program and a history of relevant topical issues, situationally placed by member-mentors in the context of their various research investigations and application, their theoretical and methodological importance, and their potential for importance and innovation. But it is not until the novice and member attempts to perform the ethnomethodological operations that the actual work of ethnomethodology gets done and so achieves a new accountability. The reception of subsequent innovation on received "state of the art" ethnomethodological ways of working, such as achieving adequate description in a "perspicuous setting" (cf. Garfinkel 1985b; Jules-Rosette 1978b, c), analyzing conversation's organizational features in interactive context, formulating an "occasioned corpus" of a setting's features (Zimmerman and Pollner 1970), maintaining critical awareness of the reflexivity of methods and language in situations of research and reporting (cf. Cicourel 1964, 1973b, 1981), or analyzing the production of cultural objects as locally historicized achievements (cf. Garfinkel et al. 1981) provides the grounds of practical performance from which the ethnomethodological practitioner can find and argue what the proper history of the ethnomethodological program is. Emanuel Schegloff (personal communication) told me that it is impossible to comprehend ethnomethodology's history merely through interviews. Instead, one has to "mix sweat" while doing ethnomethodological work and then come to understand its history.

A comparative generational glossary

I have assembled a comparative generational glossary of ethnomethodology to illustrate the generational development of ethnomethodology's distinctive thematic features (see Appendix 1). The glossary presents textual examples of the formulations and use of these features by four generations of ethnomethodologists. It is possible to observe the development of the ethnomethodological style of thinking as well as "neo-ethnomethodological" supplements to that style.

The intertextual dictionary sheds significant light on the generational evolution of ethnomethodology's conceptual distinctive features. The group formulations, definitions, and applications show differences in contextual application, while retaining a core meaning. Ethnomethodology's distinctive thematic features of indexical expressions, reflexivity, membership, becoming the phenomenon and unique adequacy of methods, accountability, local practices of order, situatedness, and scenic display are not static objects. They are considered by members to change in the using of them. Nevertheless, how they change is still a product of ethnomethodological members' practical generational negotiations. The distinctiveness of the ethnomethodological approach is supported by members who produce a practical recognition as to the correct or incorrect expansions and applications of the distinctive features.

A life history account

In the next section I offer my own reflexive account of working in the ethnomethodological movement's knowledge domain. I present this account for the purpose of locating my analysis within the fourth generation members' interpretation of ethnomethodology's intellectual field. Participation in intellectual fields ultimately consists of subjective appropriation as well as objective conceptualization. In presenting this narrative of my introduction to the ethnomethodological movement, I am utilizing a methodological tradition in anthropology, sociology, and ethnomethodology that calls for an explication of the observer's own reflexive presence, competence, and understanding in the domain studied. This tradition has been described as "dialogical anthropology" (Tedlock 1979), "reflexive ethnography" (Jules-Rosette 1978a, b; Rabinow 1977; Rosaldo 1980; Castaneda 1968), "unique adequacy of methods" (Garfinkel 1985b; Livingston 1983), and "becoming the phenomenon" (Mehan and Wood 1975a).

Changes in disciplinary outlook

My working membership in the ethnomethodological movement began with a series of changes in disciplinary outlook during 1976. Having spent the previous two years as an undergraduate studying organic chemistry, genetics, physics, mathematics, and molecular biology at the University of California, San Diego, I was experiencing an inner and outer demand for a more complete field and domain of practical inquiry and academic questioning. Having been immersed in the discipline of natural scientific studies for two solid years following a period of liberal arts exposure at another California college and a year sabbatical, I encountered ethnomethodology while in a state of conscious transition between intellectual and social worlds.

My world was at that time teetering between thought systems. Feeling the movements of what I deemed to be the rudiments of a deep self-inquiry coursing through my nervous system and brain channels, I knew then, in the mid-1970s, that thoughts' worlds were relative – so relative that I had to find out what, in fact, was the appropriate universe of discourse in which to put my money, my mouth, and my mind. My mind sought balance between frames of reference that, on the one hand, were able to supply and furnish an exactitude of microscopic attentions to the actual seen and felt world and, on the other hand, could fluidly move up and down the ladder and scale of the macrocosm itself. This was not easy to do. Given the particular climate of America in 1976, with paradigm revolutions occurring simultaneously with bicentennial celebrations, foolproof world views were a hard commodity to stumble across, conjure up, or latch onto. Encountering ethnomethodology at just about the time I was considering searching elsewhere than the university's classroomed halls was a fortuitous break for a California dreamer like me.

Seeing ethnomethodology's view toward the daily goings-on that people normally spell *r-e-a-l-i-t-y* was a welcome orientation for me. It was an orientation because it provided the first profound lexicon and conceptual net for an undergrowth of thoughts and real insights I had been cultivating for years. Up until my discovery of ethnomethodology as a thought system I had not possessed the adequate concepts, verbiage, and writerly architecture for putting these perceptions, these impressions, into an organized scheme of explication, let alone further organized inquiry.

A first exposure

I remember the first exposure I had to ethnomethodology. It was a consequence of being in a very intense University of California, San Diego biochemistry course during the start of the fall quarter, 1976. I was working at a deli-grocery store in Solana Beach (the type that are so popular in California) and had met some new friends over the course of the previous summer. Of course, none of these situations were causally related to me deciding to enroll late into Professor Reyes Ramos's Sociology of the Mexican-American Family course, but they furnished some of the living context surrounding my particular receptivity. Upon hearing Professor Ramos speak of a new perspective that treated human beings not in terms of reduced cultural stereotypes, such as "Frito Bandito" and lazy men sleeping underneath cacti, nor in terms of brazen numerical imagery as most of the natural and social sciences were likely to do, but instead in terms of a deep examination of the implicit cultural "strategies" that folks actually and artfully used to accomplish their own sense of human dignity in the world, I took another hard look at the placement of my relevance structures.

Biochemistry was becoming daily more distant from my renewed appreciations of the human sociocultural drama. Working in the deli market at the beach had been affecting me in more ways than one. I was beginning to observe and see new joys in the things inanely and intimately human. I was starting to realize that science had more things to look into than just test tubes and particle accelerators. Combined with periods of renewed self-observation and inquiry, I was in an atmosphere highly conducive to paradigm shift.

I returned Monday morning to Professor Ramos's course eager to find out more about the new sociology, especially ethnomethodology and its cultural strategy. After an invigorating lecture on social science's continued trouble with why people insist on behaving unpredictably, at least relative to numerical surveys, and ethnomethodology's alternative studies of how people create and manage intricate social worlds that surveys always seem downright blind to, I was ready to go one step further. At the end of class I asked Professor Ramos if there were any other courses on ethnomethodology immediately available on campus. He told me that Professor Bennetta Jules-Rosette was teaching a course on the sociology of knowledge and that she used an ethnomethodological approach. If I was lucky, I could be added to the class roster despite the fact that it was the third week of classes.

I was pleased to discover that Bennetta Jules-Rosette's course would be meeting that same morning. I arrived to hear Professor Jules-Rosette speaking about Carlos Castaneda's ethnography of the man of knowledge, Don Juan Matus. She was talking confidently about Castaneda's method of "becoming a member" of the world of Mexican sorcery in order to observe its working from the "inside." This method, she said, was an ethnomethodological device for ensuring the validity and profundity of an ethnographer's findings. It was possible, she said to analyze and interpret the taken-for-granted and tacit knowledge that cultural members used routinely to construct meaning in ordinary and nonordinary settings. "Indexical" meanings and stocks of background knowledge were phenomena in their own right, not epiphenomenal to scientific study. She claimed to have used this method in her own study of African independent church movements that practiced firewalking, prophesy, and faith healing. At that point I began noticing that the colorful clothing she was wearing was traditional African garb, right down to the ankle-length dress and embroidered bead cloth. "Hmm," I thought.

I actually was quite taken and impressed with the ease and analytical acumen with which Bennetta Jules-Rosette seemed to move between descriptions of direct experience and analytical models. Her analytic methods served to highlight certain aspects of the direct experience under examination while leaving the whole of it untouched before your eyes and ears. This, she said that day, was what the "veil of objectivity" could never do. Direct membership could become the key to a new form of description and, she said, we were all already tacit members of innumerable social realities that lay waiting for our own reflexive observation, analysis, and interpretation.

I left the class stunned. Rarely had I heard such personally exciting "news" in a college classroom. Something about what I was hearing made such good sense to me that I felt as if I had known about it and deeply understood it all my life. It was just that now it was being finally inquired into in a respectable college context that had all the legitimizing marks of profound intellectual rigor. I felt that I was experiencing that rare form of intellectual discourse when knowledge becomes true understanding.

I deeply desired to inquire further into whatever it was that I was onto here. I added the class, bought all the books, immersed myself in the thoughts, and found myself less and less drawn to my natural science courses. The wonders of biochemistry aside, I was finding my "exact" science classes becoming less and less relevant and actually seriously lacking just the dimension I was discovering in this newfound region called ethnomethodology. By the close of the quarter I had dropped all my science courses and was taking a full load of ethnomethodology and sociology courses. I knew I appeared to be changing horses in midstream to my friends and family, but I was deeply aware that the changes in vision afforded me by these studies were too valuable not to give full attention to. I appeared to be undergoing a form of scholarly "metanoia" or intellectual conversion.

Appropriation of the field

By the close of that first quarter in 1976, I had begun working with a
group of seven students from my courses. We formed a weekly study
group to read and discuss Bennetta Jules-Rosette's class readings, and in
particular several ethnomethodological core texts including Harold
Garfinkel's *Studies in Ethnomethodology* and Hugh Mehan's and Houston Wood's *The Reality of Ethnomethodology*. The study group included
a sociology graduate student studying ethnomethodology, Sam Edward
Combs. Sam had been working with Mehan at Indiana University and
had come to San Diego to study first in the philosophy department and
then in the sociology department. Also in the group was Susan Lucille
Phaneuf in the Teacher Education Program directed by Hugh Mehan. I
found Garfinkel's *Studies in Ethnomethodology* an intriguing book from
the first. This was the kind of book that was difficult to read yet yielded
great secrets and insights to the truly attentive and dedicated reader-
practitioner. I used Mehan and Woods' *Reality of Ethnomethodology* as a
sort of "source guide" through ethnomethodology's corpus of writings. I
was fond of this book's peculiar "vision" of ethnomethodology as being
reflective of a reality system itself.

Graduate studies

My study of ethnomethodology's texts continued as I entered the graduate phase of my studies in ethnomethodology. I was permitted to take
Hugh Mehan's graduate seminar in ethnomethodology during my senior
year as a form of honors seminar. This played a formative and central
role in my patternings of thought. We started with Merleau-Ponty and his
phenomenology of perception. This led to a general awareness that we
are "condemned" to meaning making. We guided our thinking along the
lines and investigations of Edmund Husserl and Alfred Schutz. If phenomenology is to be regarded as the philosophy of subjectivity's actions,
then ethnomethodology can be considered the empirical examination of
subjectivity's actions translated into the social world. The phenomenological "reduction" or epoché became a focus of serious study for me,

eventually leading me to the philosophy department to take seminars on phenomenology from Professor Frederick Olafson.

We covered major ethnomethodological concepts and applications that winter in Hugh Mehan's home. The setting made for a very conducive environment. The nature of rules, the formulation of accounts, management strategies, and indexical expressions were lectured on and discussed. In 1976, the ethnomethodological consciousness was still in a secondary regrouping state, struggling to iron out its naturally agreed upon important emphases, roots, and history. Professionally, the ethnomethodological movement appeared to me to be still reeling from its awareness that it could not seem to accomplish the work necessary to publish its own journal and organize itself as a subdiscipline.

Disciplinary fissures were already becoming apparent to me. In the course of the seminar, much time was spent juxtaposing ethnomethodology's stance with Durkheim, Weber, Parsons's structural functionalism, Goffman's dramaturgy, symbolic interactionism, as well as the sociologies offered by members of the University of California, San Diego department. Goffman was rumored to be possibly paying a visit to the seminar. Mehan's book, *The Reality of Ethnomethodology*, was newly released and was being used as a main text in the seminar. In it, he and Houston Wood make clear that ethnomethodology is a wholly different kind of enterprise than traditional sociology.

Strangely, I began picking up on other more "internal" currents that I comprehended then only very partially. Certain members within ethnomethodology itself were treated by the seminar's more experienced participants with a certain indifference that I surmised was a form of punishment for disloyalty. It was a little like the Quakers' "shunning" practices. When such an ethnomethodologist was discussed, reference was made to work done before and after certain, unknown to me, cataclysmic acts performed by the person. The point of cataclysm marked a strong differentiation in theoretical and conceptual directions. I began growing more sensitive to certain personal histories that figured predominant in ethnomethodology's success or failure in becoming a coherent movement of thought and application.

One thing I noticed was that my own perspective toward criticism of the sociological field was definitely shaped by my ethnomethodological studies. Since I began my perception of sociology's scope and range through the eyes of the ethnomethodological perspective, I developed a critical penchant toward all forms of common sense sociological reasoning, lay or professional. I sensed a peculiar and growing disparity between my perception of the sociological field and those shared by fellow students, colleagues, and professors in the sociology department. The contests of tenure battles over theoretical and methodological preferences and personal conflicts between departmental cohorts began early to be part and parcel of my ethnomethodological background knowledge.

Interestingly enough, I did not initially interpret the fraternal conflicts between the movement's two most visible figures, Harold Garfinkel and Aaron Cicourel, to be as grave as they actually were until later in my career. This was perhaps because my constructed thought system was a product of a number of existential influences and exigencies. My introduction to ethnomethodology's thought labyrinth was primarily mediated by two currents. The first was the ethnomethodology taught by Bennetta Jules-Rosette. The second was the teaching of Hugh Mehan.

Bennetta Jules-Rosette's ethnomethodology was itself a diversely rich product. Her education had begun at Harvard, under Parsons, similar to Garfinkel's own. She had begun her African field experience in liaison with anthropologists and cross-cultural psychologists because of her participation in Parsons's Social Relations Program. Renee Fox had given her her first research training, and Margaret Mead had lent Bennetta her camera for her first film on Bapostolo singing rituals in Lusaka, Zambia, in 1969. Bennetta had gone to the University of California, Los Angeles to do predoctoral work with Garfinkel in 1970. It was there that she was introduced to the burgeoning ethnomethodological network and school of thought. Her subsequent training in ethnomethodological and sociolinguistic modes of research and analysis led to her being invited by Joe Gusfield and Aaron Cicourel to join the faculty of the newly organized sociology department at the University of California, San Diego in 1972. Her apprenticeship in a unique form of cross-cultural, radically ethnographic ethnomethodology has continued through her subsequent tenure at the University of California, San Diego up until the present time.

Hugh Mehan was a student of Tomatsi Shibutani at the University of California, Santa Barbara. Following his involvement and disinvolvement with the war in Vietnam, he returned to the University of California, Santa Barbara to commence his Ph.D. studies in ethnomethodology with Aaron Cicourel's group (cf. Cicourel et al. 1974). Mehan was part of the group of graduate students in 1968-1969 who attempted to make a synthesis between the University of California, Santa Barbara and the University of California, Los Angeles schools of ethnomethodology represented by Cicourel and Garfinkel respectively. Houston Wood, Mel Pollner, Ken Leiter, Don Zimmerman, D. Lawrence Wieder, and Ken

Jennings were also members of this confraternity. After a sojourn in 1970-1971 at Indiana University's department of sociology, Mehan was also invited by Cicourel to join the University of California, San Diego's growing ethnomethodological contingent. At that time the University of California, San Diego's ethnomethodologists included Cicourel, Mehan, Jennings, Jules-Rosette, and Jack D. Douglas. In 1976, Mehan published an article, "Desecting Ethnomethodology" along with Houston Wood, in *The American Sociologist*, defending ethnomethodology against charges of "sectarianism" made by ASA president Lewis Coser. Mehan pressed through the battles for the University of California, San Diego tenure and emerged victorious. His work continues to specialize in ethnomethodological and developmental studies of classroom and institutional interaction. He is now increasingly furnishing liaisons with cognitive science and cross-cultural psychology.

I decided to continue my studies in sociology and ethnomethodology in the graduate school at the University of California, San Diego. At this time I was noting changes in my seriousness toward the life of the mind. I noticed that my former undergraduate styles of work and study habits were metamorphosing into styles based on dedicated endurance. This exhibited itself in my evolving methods of study. I went from working late at night to working early in the morning and throughout the day. I developed new systems of organization of my files and new techniques for recording and accessing my insights. I began the keeping of a personal journal. I accumulated and organized an extensive library related to my queries and investigations. When it was time to go through the application process to graduate school, I felt that I had already begun graduate studies.

I entered the University of California, San Diego's graduate program in sociology in 1978. I felt I was there to continue my ethnomethodological studies. For the past year I had been working with Bennetta Jules-Rosette on ethnomethodological and semiotic studies of new religious movements. She had invited me to be one of several research assistants going with her to Zambia during the previous summer and I had accepted. Hugh Mehan had invited me to join his research team conducting an ethnomethodological investigation of San Diego county public schools. I accepted and began the research along with the formal graduate curriculum offered by the department. The department itself was an original experiment in grouping some of the most interesting qualitative sociologists in the field into an academic institution.

I observed contradictory events during the initial graduate years. I learned that one did not always mention one's affiliation with ethnomethodology's thought circles to faculty who where engaged in personal and public conflicts with ethnomethodology's personnel. It sometimes became a matter of managing two faces in order to survive as a graduate student. Otherwise one could face unpredictable treatment as a not-yet formed but growing intellectual embryo in a small and ambitious sociology department. Garfinkel had already foreseen such problems for ethnomethodologists. He summarizes them in an interview with Bennetta Jules-Rosette in *Sociétés* (1985a, 1:n.5). He claims that both knowledge of and indifference to sociology's methods and theories are required for ethnomethodological work. In the context of these disciplinary obstacles, I continued my sociological and ethnomethodological training at the University of California, San Diego.

In my graduate training, I was unknowingly, though I always had an undelineated sense of it, a sort of generational product or "cultural object." Being one of a handful of students at the University of California, San Diego who were seriously trying to pursue ethnomethodological training in the graduate levels, my background knowledge was both an intellectual and political creation. In studying with Jules-Rosette and Mehan, I was a fourth generation student of two ethnomethodological lineages as it were, Garfinkel's and Cicourel's. What I gradually became aware of, and this awareness took the entirety of my graduate career, was that I as a cultural object was constantly in the process of being "attached to nature" (cf. Kuhn 1970:187-191). This nature appeared sometimes unnatural. It consisted of being seen both as a legitimate graduate product attached to the department of sociology, as well as being seen as a legitimate "ethnomethodologist" and being attached to some part of the ethnomethodological movement's extremely unstable local visage. This role of being a reproduction that is simultaneously an original production characterizes a "themata" (Holton 1978) of ethnomethodological disciplinary practice.

Many questions regarding ethnomethodology's subdisciplinary status continued to concern me. Having such a far-reaching prospectus and program as ethnomethodology had, why was it that so often its influence only barely got off the ground when it came to displaying a gratifying image of internally contented practitioners? Why was it that so many of ethnomethodology's star students and promising researchers either never got a job in a department or else quit the academic profession altogether? Why did attempts to build a strong network of ethnomethodologists around the world, such as semiotics appeared to have done, fail every time it seemed to be most promising? Is this to be seen only in terms of disciplinary resistance from other movements of thought, or is this also a question concerning ethnomethodology's own achieved sense of inner cohesion?

Initial ethnomethodological insights

Working with Jules-Rosette, Mehan, Cicourel, Bellman, and Schwartz opened my eyes to many previously hazy social phenomena. The nature and nonexistence of much explicit rule use in everyday situations began to become particularly clear to me. The relations between the microworld of interactions and the macroworld of structures began to emerge more problematic. Here was a question of whether we could depend on society's structure to hold up independent of our personal activities and whether we thought our activities actually dramatically structured the macroworld. Reasoning in the practical and scientific modes was also a recurring topic of interest. Seeing into the coherent structure of the world's daily thought rituals provided me with a means to analyze my own perceptions of my own thinking styles. I began to appropriate ethnomethodology's various methods of fine-grained study of the social world including a phenomenological background of field methods, audiovisual technologies, and conversation analysis.

My entrance into ethnomethodology's circles was different from what I had expected. Coming to the social sciences in general from the circles of the natural sciences posed no small invitation to changes in my accustomed methods and modes of thinking. The thought technologies I imported from the exact sciences were a form of mental concentration that excelled at intricately analyzing and dismantling objects and forms into their constituent small parts and microrelationships. My mathematical machinery enabled me to image things and processes in terms of calculi of already decided upon integers and factorials. My way of looking was much more the outcome of an encouraged conformity to prescribed canons of agreed upon logic and predefinition than it was to a spirit of proto-inductive inquiry.

My new thinking style, engendered in the milieu of ethnomethodology's and sociology's more radical inquiry, tended to encourage the same sort of concentration on the constituent parts of things, but with an openness to allow for a sense of newness and un-pregiveness in one's formulations and questions. Also, there was a sense of critical inquiry that sought insight into the processes constituent of what most perspectives called parts. Serious association with the social sciences in general was extremely liberating whenever I encountered this predisposition for investigations into dynamic processes instead of merely analyzing already solidified structures. I felt a sense of unexplainable, yet tangible, mystery returning to my formalized perceptions of the world.

The sense of a ready-made, unquestioned explanation of the world that had been building in the natural sciences was giving way to a new form of seeing into the mysterious underbelly of human activity in the world. This underbelly, this Lebenswelt, radically conditioned any explanation proffered by a science, a religion, or a government. Insight into this quality of radical constitution of the most taken-for-granted reality threw me into entirely new valences of thought's orbit. I began to see that there were literally infinite worlds of entities and processes that I and most people in daily life consider absolutely taken-for-granted, that are in essence made up by the functional activities of members embedded deeply in cauldrons of cultural thought structures, practical actions, and tacit beliefs. These "things" include perceptions of reality itself, definitions of the situation, rules for behavior, public problems, transcendental truths, Gods, identities, emotional reactions, stable knowledges, memories, philosophies, institutions, mental images, public media, laws of the land, presidents, and popes.

Entering the cognitive mode of the social sciences I encountered at the University of California, San Diego, I moved my thinking and acting in new directions that permitted me to grasp more clearly the relativity of thought. I saw that the social sciences interested in pursuing inquiries of a newer kind, namely, those synthesizing the streams of multiple disciplines, were up against a fight with those social sciences aligning more closely with traditional sciences of nature.

At this time, I began to notice a temporal shift in my orientation toward the doing of my intellectual life. Throughout the following years of study and work, I went through a period of rapid "discovery" of ethnomethodological, sociological, and philosophical domains of knowledge. I assimilated and practiced, like languages, sociology's and ethnomethodology's codes, background knowledges, and critical questionings. My mind seemed to explode in the finding and noting of new connections and critical relationships between ethnomethodology's and sociology's ideas and those of neighboring domains and disciplines. Phenomenology, structuralism, sociolinguistics, anthropology, developmental psychology, and semiotics "opened up" for me. Ethnomethodological study proved to be a key and platform for evaluating and translating these other domains into a sense meaningful to my intellectual concerns.

I began my formal graduate program study with great intellectual excitement, yet also with some caution. I was aware of various tensions and conflicts existing between the ethnomethodologists and the rest of the department's faculty. There had been a history of these tensions, though the University of California, San Diego department provided a home for the growing ethnomethodological movement. The code word "sociolinguistics" was utilized in the department as an official title for core seminars in ethnomethodological methods in order to make ethnomethodology more acceptable.

My graduate training progressed as I amalgamated ethnomethodological insights with new studies in the sociology of knowledge, religion, culture, and semiotics. I experienced what I interpreted as sociology's range of responses to ethnomethodology within the University of California, San Diego department. Responses ranged from theoretical appreciation to rather antagonistic suspicion.

My graduate "core" (first and second year) seminars were interesting and offered training in classical, neoclassical, and modern sociological theory and methods. An empasis was placed on ethnographic field methods. Ethnomethodology was taught by Jules-Rosette in her "microsociological methods" seminars, by Mehan in his ethomethodology seminars, and by Cicourel in his seminars on cognitive sociology. My research work provided me with intensive training in the use of videotape ethnography, analysis of conversational transcripts, and other ethnomethodological methods. The challenge was for me to articulate my ethnomethodological training with the more "standard" sociological methods I was being taught in the departmental seminars. This was tricky since my ethnomethodological approach was highly critical of many of the methods and theories taught in those core seminars. I was challenged to formulate my ethnomethodological critiques in ways, language, and representational styles that were acceptable to the presiding instructor's paradigmatic leanings.

The foundation of my graduate curricula was necessarily eclectic, as is most graduate students' training. My task was to critically assimilate and contribute to an emerging paradigm that often lacked clear organizational guidelines and standard sociological legitimization. Along with the required seminars, it was necessary for me to broaden my thinking about relevant debates and dialogues between various schools of thought, especially between ethnomethodology and standard American sociology.

As my graduate training drew to a close, I began to become exposed to semiotics primarily through Bennetta Jules-Rosette's advanced seminars on the sociology of knowledge. There, semiotics was critically examined as a potential expansion of ethnomethodology's programs. A series of conferences at the University of California, San Diego, in 1985, 1986, and 1987, and at the University of California, Los Angeles, in 1990, organized by the newly formed Semiotics Research Project and directed by Jules-Rosette and Alain J.-J. Cohen, brought thinkers together on topics relating to semiotics and the social sciences. Participants included Thomas A. Sebeok, A. J. Greimas, Paolo Fabbri, Manar Hammad, Jean Baudrillard, Louis Marin, Johannes Fabian, Manar Hammao, Dean and Juliet MacCannell, Seymour Chatman, and others. Harold Garfinkel participated in 1985 and 1990. These conferences influenced my thinking about new ways of working with meaning and language.

In 1985 I began working informally with Harold Garfinkel on studies of science as a field of practical action. Garfinkel began visiting Jules-Rosette's seminars at the University of California, San Diego that fall. Plans were made for Garfinkel to teach a two-quarter sequence of seminars on ethnomethodology and science studies. Unfortunately, politics, personality conflicts in the department, and budgetary limitations prevented Garfinkel from teaching at the University of California, San Diego that year. Nevertheless, a group of graduate and postdoctoral researchers at San Diego worked closely with Garfinkel at that time.

During 1985, I collaborated with Sam Combs, Susan Phaneuf, and Dominique Lestel, who was a researcher from the École des Hautes Études en Sciences Sociales in Paris, on a project using ethnomethodology and semiotics to study the social construction of penguin ethology at the Hubbs Marine Research Institute at Sea World in San Diego. Harold Garfinkel became an important consultant and dialogant many times during the research. In 1985 and 1986, I lived and worked in Paris as part of a scholars' exchange program with Gerard Lemaine's Group for the Study and Research of Science at the École des Hautes Études en Sciences Sociales. In Paris, I became involved in various movements to translate ethnomethodology onto the French soil at the École, the University of Paris V (Sorbonne), the University of Paris VIII (St. Denis), and at other locations. (I describe these experiences in Chapter 7.)

Since my return to the United States in 1986, my work has roamed widely through the contingencies of finishing a doctoral dissertation, publishing papers, teaching, researching, and garnering an academic position. Semiotics, ethnomethodology, and the sociology of knowledge remain focii in my work. Throughout all of this, the ethnomethodological movement continued to change.

Conclusion

This work represents a form of neoethnomethodological analysis. My continued training in ethnomethodology's program of methods and technologies of research has provided one foundation for what I have written. As is clear in the following chapters, I synthesize the ethnomethodological corpus with semiotics and the sociology of knowledge to critically examine ethnomethodology's construction as an intellectual movement.

In this chapter, we have observed that ethnomethodology is a neosociological field of discourse that displays a generational organization . The following chapters examine how this generational structure is composed and articulated through the ethnomethodological movement's historically available corpus of knowledge, texts, and research genres. I examine how the ethnomethodological movement has organized itself as a theoretical field and discipline through self-referential practical actions and semiotic literary conventions. This analysis allows me to address questions about the historical organization of social science disciplines and the ethnomethodological movement's future contributions to sociological research.

Chapter Two
Ethnomethodology's Radical Features

To begin with our work is not a mysterious enterprise and we are not
peddling remedies. You may not believe it now, but it is not a cult.
Garfinkel (Hill and Crittenden 1968:3)

If my colleagues find anything recognizable for them, fine and dandy. I
think that with most of it, I can be speaking for them, but there is kind of
agreement in the work that we find our own ways for reasons which I hope,
before the end of the day, will be clear enough.
Garfinkel (Hill and Crittenden 1968:143)

I am not making a bid for entry into a club because I do not think I am ever
going to be a member of that club. It is not because I do not want to be a
member but because there are other reasons.
Garfinkel (Hill and Crittenden 1968:171)

This chapter examines how the ethnomethodological movement has produced itself as a historic disciplinary program through a variety of radical
organizational practices. Ethnomethodology's generations of researchers
organized themselves in ways that were specific to their historical and
interactional context as a newly emerging alternative social science.
These members' organizing practices display properties similar to, yet
distinct from, certain practices used by known radical and religious
movements. This similarity poses larger questions as to the relationship
between modern intellectual movements and other forms of radical and
religious organization.

A heuristic vehicle

As a way of access into ethnomethodology's practical organizing work, I shall use an ethnomethodological analysis heuristically derived from Egon Bittner's (1963) analytical study of radicalism and the organization of radical movements. This analytical scheme is at least partly informed by ethnomethodology's radical organizational features that were emerging at the time this article was written. Bittner is a first generation ethnomethodologist. I suggest that we see that ethnomethodology's radical features were supplying at least part of the intellectual context and practical conditions from which Bittner's analysis was constructed. Therefore, I have chosen this analytical framework from which to frame my observations and analysis of ethnomethodology's historicized organizational strategies.

A word of caution is in order. The purpose of this chapter is to show that ethnomethodology has used practical organizational strategies in forming itself as a technical community of studies. These strategies have changed and adapted as the ethnomethodological movement has produced new generations of researchers in local settings. My analysis points to generalized features of ethnomethodology's organized program of studies viewed as a historical whole from my own perspective as a fourth generation student. The objective here is ultimately to point to the fact that ethnomethodology's achieved historicity as an internally organized intellectual program and movement has been situationally constructed by members. Members' organizational, intellectual, and semiotic practices construct all cases of social science intellectual activity and movement. Ethnomethodology's continued creation of itself as a viable intellectual discipline requires new organizational practices that are adapted to today's generations and intellectual and cultural contexts.

Bittner's analysis of radical movements

I see Bittner's (1963:928-940) work on radicalism and the organization of radical movements as both an example of a member's ethnosemiosis or local signification as well as a suitable vehicle for my own analysis. Bittner wrote this article while completing his study with Garfinkel at the

University of California, Los Angeles and while working at the Langley Porter Neuropsychiatric Institute from 1960 to 1963. Since February, 1962, the ethnomethodological movement had begun holding its Conferences on Ethnomethodology at the University of California, Los Angeles and at the University of Colorado. (These conferences had been funded with the aid of a grant from the U.S. Air Force Office of Scientific Research, cf. Garfinkel 1967a:73). Conference members were Bittner, Garfinkel, Craig MacAndrew, Edward Rose, and Harvey Sacks. Bittner had been a research assistant to Garfinkel and had coded the cases for and coauthored the article "Methodological Adequacy in the Quantitative Study of Selection Criteria and Selection Activities in Psychiatric Out Patient Clinics" that appeared in Garfinkel's *Studies in Ethnomethodology* (1967i:208-261). Bittner's dissertation (1961) at the University of California, Los Angeles was on the relationships between collectivity membership, competence, and "common-sense knowledge of social structures" and was entitled "Popular Interests in Psychiatric Remedies: A Study in Social Control." Bittner originally wrote a version of the "Radicalism" paper entitled "Radicalism: A Study in the Sociology of Knowledge" for the Conference on Ethnomethodology and read it at the Pacific Sociological Association annual meetings in 1962. He changed the title to "Radicalism and the Organization of Social Movements" when he submitted the piece to the *American Sociological Review*.

Constitutive properties

Bittner discussed radicalism as a pure Weberian type of social event, with an aim of defining a radical movement's constitutive properties. He makes clear that his description holds equal force for beliefs and actions that find their primary expression in politics, religion, economics, philosophy, or any other major domain of human concern, regardless of their content. I add to this list intellectual movements and the knowledge domain of ethnomethodology.

Bittner purports that radical movements typically share an interpretive frame in which the validity of the entire corpus of common-sense knowledge and its method is radically questioned. I think this characterization certainly fits ethnomethodology as an intellectual movement. Ethnomethodology's fundamental research policy is in fact the heuristic radical questioning of the entire field of common-sense assumptions. This radical questioning of the validity of common-sense methods is extended into a critique of prevailing ways of doing sociology. This critique had formed a bedrock for those doing ethnomethodological studies.

The corollary to the first feature discussed by Bittner is that radical movements typically seek a unified and internally consistent interpretation of the meaning of the world. Adapting Weber's emphasis on prophecy and the personal charisma of the prophet, Bittner points to the central feature of radical movements as being the juxtaposition to a traditionally sanctioned, heterogeneous interpretation of meaning, a rationally consistent new interpretation. We can observe the ethnomethodological movement's adoption of just such a unified outlook as a member's central scheme of interpretation that, as we shall observe, is morally binding, socially sanctioned, and internally consistent. I must agree, though, with Hayward's (1978) critique of Bittner that says that the focus of membership is always much more than some version of "the group."

I observe the generations of ethnomethodological members engaged in a process of adopting what I term the insight of radical constitution. This collective underlying insight, based on the ethnomethodological movement's adaptation of the phenomenological movement's emphases on "intentional constituting acts of consciousness," provides the point from which radical members create a unity of meaning. The radical ethnomethodological member typically tends to think, argue, act, and write on the grounds of this unifying outlook (see Chapter 3). It is historically clear that all attempts to live or work by an internally consistent schema of interpretation are necessarily doomed to fail. As Bittner says, this must be true "for any doctrinally pure outlook, regardless of its superior virtue, empirical adequacy, economic efficiency, or logical coherence" (p.934). Given this fact of tragic failure, Bittner sees only two ways that "radical revisions" of traditionally sanctioned interpretations of meaning can effectively govern conduct in organized collectivity.

The first way has been described already by Weber (1947:367-373) as the process of routinization of charisma. Here, the radical movement abandons the purity of its doctrine through a slow assimilation of casuistic interpretations, the development of dogma, and the submission to bureaucratization. Most "prophetically inspired" radical movements that remain active for a protracted period of time follow this course of development (though, as Bittner points out, the seed of radicalism remains viable in them, for such dogmatic creeds continue to produce radical prophetic apostasies). In my view, the ethnomethodological movement has not yet followed this routinization, due to its relative youth, to the strength of its current "prophetic" leaders, or to the fact that it is unroutinizable by nature.

Radical organizational tasks

The practical alternative to the first line of development is, according to Bittner, to impose upon the believing members conditions that would make "doctrinal impurity" as difficult and unattractive as possible (p.934). It is a fact that contradictory evidence will assail the believing member during everyday experience. Radical movements have organizational tasks of practically eliminating the possibility that its members will assign to any contradictory experience the significance of counterevidence discrediting the professed faith, doctrine, or teaching.

Bittner (p.934) says:

> ...radical action groups must have some way to reduce the horizon of possible encounters and cause the remaining contingencies of potential embarrassment to be seen as either not pertaining or, when "correctly" seen, further boosting the doctrine.

(I point your attention to Bittner's usage of the ethnomethodological movement's own collective "doctrinal" language and usages in the phrases and words "horizons of possible encounters," and "contingencies of possible embarrassment." cf. see Chapter 3.)

If radical movements, including intellectual movements, retain their doctrinal purity and integrity only as long as they manage to discredit all possible counterevidence or counterideology, then "coping with reversals cannot be left to the occasion of their actual occurrence, and life in radical movements must contain norms of conduct and belief that blanket a maximum of future contingencies" (Bittner, p.935). Normative features in the radical movement organize the loyalty of the members in the way that somehow generates the movement's impetus and power from within.

A movement's sustaining of coherence in the face of prevailing contradictory situations and circumstances is the movement's primary organizational task. I observe this as being the case with intellectual movements. The task of eliminating the possibility that derogatory significance will be attached by members to countervailing experiences such as negative book reviews, disciplinary criticism of and/or scoffing at the intellectual enterprise, defeated hiring attempts and tenure battles, and sociological colleagues and students' nonunderstandings of the intellectual approach arises as practical interactive problems for intellectual movements to solve.

The organizational task proposed by Bittner is composed of three mechanisms, borrowed from Parsons's (1960:199-225) theory of systems analysis. I observe these basic mechanisms to be operative, with varying degrees of success, in the ethnomethodological movement and knowledge domain.

1. Participation in the movement must contain some psychologically satisfying payoffs in return for the members' energy and devotion. The sense of radical critique of traditional sociological theory and methods and the collective formulation of a new approach appears to motivate many ethnomethodological members to participate and remain in the movement. In interviews with persons referring to themselves as doing ethnomethodological work, I have found that for some it is the close proximity to the applications of phenomenological ideas that is a relevant and satisfying contexture. Others report that it is ethnomethodology's and conversation analysis' analytic "tools" for examining complex interactive and conversational events that provided them with an analytic instrument unlike anything currently available in the social sciences. Other members have said that they enjoy ethnomethodology's theoretical compatibility with other relevant cultural and social philosophies, theories, and movements, such as feminism, Marxist praxiology, liberational ideology, humanism, and mysticism. These members refer to these contours as psychologically satisfying and important to their continued work in the domain.

2. There must exist a stable solution of internal system problems to minimize the amount of energy required to maintain internal harmony. I have observed that the ethnomethodological movement as a whole has gone through periods of relative success and failure in finding solutions to the problems of maintaining its internal harmony. Ethnomethodology was first officially formed by Garfinkel in 1954 while working with Saul Mendolowitz on a study of jurors' decision making (cf. Hill and Crittenden 1968:5-11). The ethnomethodological movement developed

into a movement through a series of informal seminars held by Garfinkel at the University of California, Los Angeles beginning in 1955 and essentially continuing until the present. These informal seminars, while consisting of a multitude of members, have fundamentally centered around Garfinkel's lectures on the topic of social order in naturally organized settings.

Garfinkel's developing movement required "authorized interpreters" who could cogently explain what Garfinkel was saying "in so many words." As Bittner points out (p.937), "deputized" interpreters constantly run the risk of causing schisms in the movement "through conspiracy and independent empire-building." This situation of real or imagined schisms has plagued ethnomethodology from its inception. As far as I can tell, there has never been a period entirely free of internal disharmony and accusations of Machiavellian political machinations. I observe that many of the ethnomethodological movement's problems in organizing itself in terms of constructing stable graduate training centers, publishing a collective journal, and transmitting its discoveries to a wider audience through the consistent publication of papers and books and through the organizing of a successful program of meetings and conferences have been due to the problematics of achieving an adequate internal harmony.

The ethnomethodological movement's various states of achieved disharmony have very often utilized maximum amounts of members' energy and diverted the energy away from more constructive avenues of movement stabilization and vigor. Often, just when members perceived a change in the wind regarding increased movement solidarity, schisms would reopen afresh. Lest I be guilty of painting too dark a picture of the ethnomethodological movement's working out of effective solutions to the problems of allocation of authority, distribution of inequality, and negotiations between potentially competent claims, I will only say that this feature of the ethnomethodological movement poses the greatest danger to the movement's existence in the upcoming ten years.

3. Relatively rigid boundaries against the system's environment must exist to prevent energy leaks. I have described these particular strategies further in other parts of this work (cf. Chapters 3, 4, and 5). Typically, any movement's boundaries are effected to reduce "energy leaks" resulting from members' contributions to outside causes such as other competing intellectual boundaries, whether in the form of its peculiarized language, topical focus, literary style, or membership categorization

devices, which can produce a monopolization of a member's interests and energy for the intellectual movement.

Organizational solutions

The following features of belief and action are proposed by Bittner as solutions to the organizational tasks of a radical movement. I am using them as a starting point from which to describe the ethnomethodological movement. This inventory is, of course, encumbered with all the risks and incompleteness of ideal-type constructions. I hope that these constructions make it possible to determine the typological locus of ethnomethodology as a historical phenomenon.

1. A sense of charisma must attach to the movement and its creed. Very often a sense of charisma is directly attached to the personage of the prophetic leader by his or her followers. The ethnomethodological movement has found a way of expressing its charisma through "competent exegetes" and definite leaders, while not locating the charisma solely in the leaders' persons. Instead, the ethnomethodological movement's charisma has resided chiefly in its doctrine and intellectual myth, which has been collectively voiced through mythologized actants (persons, texts, and accounts). I develop this idea further in Chapter 3.

What matters in the ethnomethodological movement is that members see the truth of the myth. Seeing the truth of the myth, that is, adequately understanding the phenomenological insight of radical constitution in the ethnomethodological manner and being able to give a member's account of this understanding, is inseparable from experiencing the collective power this myth lends. Believing the truth of the creed and participating in the movement serves professional careers as well as intellectual growth.

For the ethnomethodological member, it does not matter whether the agency of a personal prophetic leader is involved in the intellectual reception process or not. The power of the myth, the ethnomethodological doctrine proper, is enough. For example, many second and third generation ethnomethodologists received their intellectual "conversion" to ethnomethodology directly from the hands of Garfinkel and Cicourel.

These two leaders both served as "strategically salient symbols" as well as competent exegetes of the doctrine. Nevertheless, many second and third generation members continued their careers at a reasonable distance from either of the two leaders. They transmitted the ethnomethodological doctrine and myth to a third generation of graduate students, many times without the direct transmission of Garfinkel and Cicourel. The mythologized actants and doctrine were enough for adequate transmission of knowledge (cf. Chapter 6).

In my experiences as a fourth generation graduate student within the ethnomethodological movement, I observed students at the University of California, San Diego who had never worked to any great degree with either Garfinkel or Cicourel or Sacks. These fourth generation students had received primary instruction from second and third generation ethnomethodologists. Nevertheless, these graduate students displayed a similar zeal and depth of understanding of, as well as commitment to, the ethnomethodological program as their second and third generation instructors.

Conversation analysis has shown a similar feature in its development. The charisma of conversation analysis as an offshoot movement from the ethnomethodological movement proper, resided in its myth and doctrine, as well as in its leaders. Conversation analysis has shown its greatest systematization and growth as an intellectual movement after the death of its primary founder and leader, Harvey Sacks, in 1975. This points to the fact that the ethnomethodological movement's charisma appears to have become inseparably embodied in its intertextual corpus as well as residing in the personas of its leaders.

The ethnomethodological member learns to partake in the charisma of the movement's collective myth. The participation in the movement's charismatic myth includes the acquiring of competent membership in the collective production of a technical and esoteric natural language community. Such a competence is learned in personal contact and work with first, second, and third generation members. This competence is also learned through the arts of textual, technical, and conversational mimesis. This mimesis, or inventive reproduction, requires members' work in the creative production and recognition of the movement's mythologized codes in situated academic contexts of use. (I further describe members' textual mimesis in Chapter 3.)

For intellectual movements, it is the member's vision and assurance of its collective intellectual charisma that produces the member's strong intellectual and emotional involvement in the movement. It is this collective version of charisma that grounds ethnomethodologists' often radical and seemingly self-righteous expressions to outsiders and sociologists. This sense of charisma is a collective production and a cultural object. As a cultural object, the collective sense of charisma demands a continuous reaffirmation of members to keep it alive.

Ethnomethodologists' reaffirmation work and ceremony strengthens their collective sense of charisma. Ceremonial reiteration, validation, and other outward signs include among other things creative mimesis of the ethnomethodological conversational and literary codes and styles, creative intertextual referencing that produces the appearance of the group's unique identity as a movement, members' creations of the movement's "received histories" (Livingston 1983), members' productions of new generations of students, and periodic professional conferences. (I discuss each of these processes later in the text.)

2. The doctrine that inspires the movement should contain information from outside the realm of everyday life. This condition carries an interestingly paradoxical twist when examined in intellectual movements. This feature is most obviously fulfilled in the oracular speech of a religious prophet and the announced mystical origins of teachings. In ethnomethodology's case, the doctrine contains information from outside the realm of sociology's everyday life, only to lead straight back to inside the realm of common-sensical everyday life.

The ethnomethodological movement consistently receives its heuristic directives from sources outside the domain of the everyday American sociologist's training and experience. These sources range from the difficult writings of the phenomenological movement, such as those by Husserl, Heidegger, Schutz, Merleau-Ponty, Gurwitsch, Carr, Spiegelberg and others, to the elliptic descriptions and policies of Harold Garfinkel himself.

A typical seminar by Garfinkel, Cicourel, or by most ethnomethodologists will immerse the student from the outset into a dialogue with philosophers, linguists, historians, mathematicians, classical physicists, psychologists, anthropologists, and the entire corpus of ethnomethodological writings that, frankly, lays outside of standard sociological education. Seminars, especially by Garfinkel, can be an extreme exercise in the interpretation of unknown tongues. The language employed is itself a testing device to impel listeners into a new and different way of conceptualizing social reality.

Garfinkel's seminar conversations can have the effect of creating a movement doctrine that, because of its neophenomenological and inventive ethnomethodological language, appears to contain information from outside the realm of everyday life. This conversational style can "inspire" members to take the plunge into the serious task of interpreting and applying what Garfinkel is saying.

Garfinkel has in the past frequently announced that the ethnomethodological movement has been on the verge of making new discoveries. He said in the Preface to *Studies in Ethnomethodology* that "it is pointless any longer to doubt that an immense hitherto unknown domain of social phenomenon has been uncovered" (Garfinkel 1967a:ix). Pronouncements such as these do organizational work to inspire intellectual members toward an invisible and unknown discovery that is just out of hand, but nevertheless immanent.

Bittner (p.937) reminds us that in prophetic movements the leadership often receives its divine command under the most unusual circumstances. For example, men become prophets on high mountains, in remote deserts, or after they have given up their ordinary life. This seems to hold for leaders of intellectual movements as well. Very often, leaders of radical movements come from life circumstances that differ radically from the life circumstances of those who believe their teachings. Often, radical leaders formulate or discover their doctrines in prisons, in exile, or in fringe environments such as bohemias. The doctrine acquires a "particularistic" aspect because of these circumstances. In other words, members tacitly maintain that the leader "knows better" because of his or her unique experiences. The leader's source of inspiration and his or her daily life must be mythologized in order to reinforce unquestioned respect.

The mythologization by members of Harold Garfinkel as the founder of the ethnomethodological movement has been accomplished through a variety of "particularistic" practices. To begin with, Garfinkel's personal biography has certain features that stand out as unique from the intellectual and life histories of many of the other scholars who have participated in the movement. Garfinkel was a graduate student of Talcott Parsons in Harvard's Department of Social Relations from 1946 to 1952. He lived in the immediate post-World War II intellectual climate on the American east coast, which was haven for quite a number of refugee German intellectuals and phenomenologists including Alfred Schutz, Aron Gurwitsch, and Felix Kaufmann (cf. Spiegelberg 1971:626-634).

Garfinkel's graduate education consisted of a selective immersion into Parsons's program that left him with a drive to search out the experimental mechanisms responsible for the appearance of social order. His 1952 study entitled *The Perception of the Other: A Study in Social Order* stated its aims as being to develop a "generalized social system built solely from the analysis of experience structures" (Garfinkel 1952:1). In his study Garfinkel relied on his increasing familiarization with the newly discovered immigrant phenomenology of Schutz and Gurwitsch to supply a new vocabulary with which to reformulate his deep criticisms of Parsons's theories. Garfinkel corresponded in letters to Schutz about his study and subsequent papers. In a letter to Schutz (Dec. 5, 1949), Garfinkel described his study work in the following manner:

> Sociological in emphasis, the dissertation is organized around two topics: first, a theoretical consideration of the analytically conceived notions under which the experiences of a party to a social relationship remain continuous; and the effect, experimentally tested, of systematically "destroying" the meaning-structures which comprise the alter ego (as a constituent of the natural attitude, while preventing the adoption of alternative cognitive styles) for the ability of the perceiver to continue to transform the behavioral and verbal materials found in the field of expression into meaningful sequences of expressions of conduct. (reprinted in Wagner 1985:239).

Garfinkel told Schutz of his explorations and his interests in Schutz's essay "On Multiple Realities" and *Der sinnhafte Aufbau* (*The Phenomenology of the Social World*) (Wagner 1985:239). Schutz wrote to Garfinkel that he hoped Garfinkel would "be one of the explorers of this undiscovered treasure island" (Wagner 1985:240).

In his dissertation, Garfinkel essentially took issue with three central problems in Parsons's theory of action: (1) the problems of rationality, (2) intersubjectivity, and (3) reflexivity (cf. Heritage 1984d:7-36). The problem of rationality is the question of what kinds of significance to give to actors' own accounts of their reasons for action. Parsons defined rationality as an internalized comparison with scientific procedure, leading to a normative determination. Garfinkel rejected this view that normative rules and reasoning could be determinative of conduct. He insisted that actors' common-sense judgment based on practical considerations is the crux of social action. The problem of intersubjectivity refers to the explanation of how communication is possible in society. Parsons's theory held that intersubjective knowledge and communication is based on prior social agreement about what words mean. Garfinkel rejected this and insisted that intersubjective communication is radically indexical, context specific, and dependent on ceaseless meaning-producing interactive work. The problem of reflexivity is the degree of conceptualizing the actor's orientations, knowledge, and self-consciousness. The Parsonian theory of value and norm internalization and its resulting determinism had to treat this problem as epiphenomenal. Garfinkel insisted that it is the heart of the problem of social organization, intelligibility, and order.

Garfinkel's utilization of the phenomenological movement as one of his most serious sources has had the practical effect of creating a doctrine originating from a relatively esoteric intellectual domain to begin with. Regardless of phenomenology's descriptive and heuristic worth and brilliance, its unknown dimension resulting from its embedded German origins has supplied Garfinkel himself with an aura of being a knowing interpreter and applier of phenomenology's relatively obscure philosophical (Husserl), psychological (Gurwitsch), and sociological (Schutz) insights and discoveries. Garfinkel's personal acquaintances with Gurwitsch and Schutz, both of whom are now deceased, is further cause for members to identify Garfinkel as a particularistic leader.

I see another factor in Garfinkel's embodiment of a particularistic character that is recognized by members of the movement: his foremost position in ethnomethodology's older, founding generation. The ethnomethodological movement's greatest period of growth and expansion, based on numbers of active graduate students and productive post-Ph.D. careers, began with ethnomethodology's second and third generations. The second generation roughly began in 1962. After Egon Bittner's dissertation at the University of California, Los Angeles, it can approximately be said to have extended to 1972 when the second generation themselves began producing students. Garfinkel and Cicourel were granted special leadership status by the younger generations precisely because they existed in an older, more "learned" generation.

Also, I observe that Garfinkel's, and Cicourel's to some extent, career situation was radically unlike the career situations of most later generation enthomethodologists. Garfinkel came to the University of California, Los Angeles's Department of Sociology in 1954, after only two years of post-Ph.D. job searching. He had gone from Harvard to Ohio State to the University of California, Los Angeles. Garfinkel was to stay at the University of California, Los Angeles, a sort of American intellectual "bohemia" (at least for some scholars), for the rest of his career.

While studying with Parsons, Garfinkel visited Gurwitsch and Schutz and began his phenomenological training and influence. He relied heavily on these phenomenological theorists to help him assemble and create relative career stability in a west coast university comparatively unbound by traditional impediments to the new. This supplied Garfinkel with a work space from which to build his radical enterprises. Without the University of California, Los Angeles stable work site, I think it is possible that the ethnomethodological movement would not have grown in the way it has.

Many later generation ethnomethodologists' professional careers have been characterized by an often extreme difficulty in finding stable work in America's sociology departments. Because of the genuine radicalness of the ethnomethodological doctrine, or for other reasons, ethnomethodologists have exhibited a relatively low survival rate in sociology departments. Garfinkel's, and Cicourel's Santa Barbara and San Diego career situations have been given out-of-the-ordinary, particularistic features of special success and stability by the movement's members. Members rely on these leaders' features of success to orient their own hoped-for careers in ethnomethodology and sociology.

I have heard members of the ethnomethodological enterprise remark that both Garfinkel and Cicourel stand as sorts of symbols or icons to the fact that an American intellectual can espouse theoretically radical doctrines such as ethnomethodology and still remain in the university and sociological systems. It is not insignificant that a large percentage of the ethnomethodological movement's second and third generations were in some way sympathetic or aligned with some form of Californian countercultural movement or attitude. The Universities of California, Los Angeles, Berkeley, Santa Barbara, and San Diego supplied Garfinkel and Cicourel with a certain quality of student. This quality was itself a unique sociohistorical product that was determinitive of the movement's ability to develop.

Mythologized schism

Often, the daily existences of leaders of radical movements are mythologized. The leaders' quotidian experience is mythologized by members to form unquestioned respect or create a paradigmatic example of right conduct or right way of life. The leader may surreptitiously withdraw from all but managed appearances. The leader may appoint and deputize an inner circle of trusted interpreters to manage the routine tasks of homiletics and exegesis. These deputized interpreters always present a risk of potential schisms in the movement through conspiracy, ambition, deception, and independent empire building. The hallmark of the true apostles is that they are faithful and trusted believers, not merely independent, competent interpreters (cf. Zanniecke 1940).

Ethnomethodology's leaders have sometimes managed to appear as withdrawn or semi-inaccessible figures. Except for a special few, access to Garfinkel and Cicourel's working relations can develop into a carefully screened affair. An aura of mystery has often shrouded Garfinkel's personal and professional decision-making practices.

Many members report that working with Garfinkel is a little like working with a Tibetan lama or an Indian yogi. De Mille (1980) hypothesized that Carlos Castaneda used Garfinkel as a model for Don Juan. Some have characterized both Garfinkel and Cicourel as mixing temperamental changes of mood and demeanor with outpours of invaluable advice, support, and brilliance.

The ethnomethodological movement itself has had its share of schismatic moments. It can be speculated that the well-publicized personal and intellectual rift between Garfinkel and Cicourel was due in part to differences between the two leaders regarding "independent empire-building." I place the schism between Garfinkel and Cicourel as occurring publicly around 1970 to 1971. Obviously the schism had been developing as a potential event for years during Garfinkel and Cicourel's close collaborations since 1955. Cicourel's books and papers (1964, 1868, 1970, 1973) had all utilized "community" views and effectively served as competent interpretations of Garfinkel's and the movement's ideas.

Disciplinary polemics

Out of the ordinary, particularistic features of radical doctrines provide for the necessity of authoritative interpretation. Also, these features furnish the grounds for systemically discrediting competing sources of information and external tests or validity of the movement's creed. Critics and outsiders simply did not understand the doctrine's complexity and original inner meaning. Often, because of these features, radicals are unwilling to engage outsiders in polemics on equal terms. Radicals can appear to outsiders as rigid in their convictions, unwilling to learn.

The ethnomethodological movement has been accused by members of the sociological profession of being rigidly sectarian, unwilling to communicate to sociology on equal terms and in "comprehensible language," and of attempting to discredit the entire sociological enterprise. The list of sociological accusers is long (cf. Wallace 1968; Coleman 1968; Atwell 1974; Coser 1975; Hill and Crittenden 1968; Gidlow 1972; Maryl 1973; De Milles 1980). While ethnomethodologists insist that they are not gratuitously "obscurantist" and that the uniqueness of their collective formulations and descriptive language is necessary for the proper revisioning of sociology's true phenomena of interest, many critics claim otherwise. Feeling excluded from the ethnomethodologists' collective vision and code, many sociologists have resorted to crying "sect!" when adequate comprehension of ethnomethodological polemic is not forthcoming.

David Gold said to Garfinkel in 1968 at the Purdue Symposium on Ethnomethodology (which was an attempt to unconfuse sociologists concerning ethnomethodology's program) that it was clear to him that Garfinkel used "a hip jargon," was guilty of a "failure of communication," was "attempting to communicate 'outside' the camp," and that even if ethnomethodology was welcomed inside the "camp" by standard American sociology, this certainly did not give ethnomethodology "a license for language" (Gold, in Hill and Crittenden 1968:253). (It is interesting to note Gold's own display of the collective features of "standard" professional sociology as an intellectual movement in his references to communicating "inside" and "outside" the camp.)

3. On all rungs of membership, there must be an intensive concern for the purity of belief. Radical movements typically value purity of belief over clarity of belief. Very often, purity is only *vaguely* defined. Decisions concerning acceptable levels of orthodoxy are left to the leader's discretion. Intellectual searches for clarity of doctrine alone can be interpreted as evidence of bad faith and disloyalty. The maintenance of purity is a difficult organizational task. The ideal is a conceptual faithfulness joined to authoritative interpretation.

Public disclosure of heresy is one of the most powerful devices that a leader has for maintaining the doctrine's purity. Doctrine abstruseness and purges on the level of the collectivity continuously do the work of cleaning the doctrine of foreign elements. The wrong kind of inquiries can be defined as insults. Purity is important, not only for its own sake, but also because it provides a technology of control, which a movement's leaders can use arbitrarily because of the air of mystique that is attached to the ideal of purity of members of the movement.

Like other radical collectivities, the ethnomethodological movement has constructed the ideal of purity of its core policies and doctrines as an organizational practice. It has maintained the ideal of purity as a produced cultural object. This cultural production has been used by members of the movement to solve a large variety of organizational tasks. The purity has been a collective accomplishment, in spite of the fact that the clarity of the doctrine sometimes has shown wide divergences.

The purity of the ethnomethodological movement's doctrine has been creatively mythologized by the members. The doctrine's "pure" features have been a situational accomplishment developed by members for specific situations of use and local requirements of purity. Members' references to a pure ethnomethodological teaching as opposed to a vulgar teaching are situationally motivated by actual occasions of use, such as in the defense of ethnomethodology's findings against competing theories, in making theoretical comparisons of ethnomethodology's doctrines to other theories, in criticizing another member's novel ideas, or in the practical assembling of membership collectivity lists of who is or who is not in fact doing "pure" ethnomethodology.

Purity and prolepsis

Also, members creatively assume that a pure ethnomethodological doctrine exists, or will exist in the future after more work and research has been done. Members' activity employs prolepsis, the act of representing, signifying, or assuming something in the present as if a future state already existed. Prolepsis is a historical time-sense characteristic of the ethnomethodological movement that will be discussed in the next chapters. Ethnomethodologists routinely participate now in the movement's future purity, clarity, and collective development. In spite of the fact that both purity and clarity are vaguely defined, ethnomethodologists act as if this purity and clarity essentially already exist. Present work is directed to "filling-in" the unclarity. There exists a tacit assumption that the movement can in some way presently ground itself in its future discoveries.

Elsewhere in this text (Chapters 3, 4, and 5) I try to show ethnomethodologists' proleptic practices and time-sense in action. Members regularly cite, make reference to, and ground their decision making on a vital present sense of the movement's future. I develop evidence that similar proleptic practices were common in the nineteenth century radical Marxist movements in Europe.

I can find abundant examples of the purity feature in ethnomethodology's history and writings. Garfinkel implicitly refers to the doctrine's pure features when he says in the preface to *Studies in Ethnomethodology* (Garfinkel 1967a:viii):

> Ethnomethodological studies are not directed to formulating or arguing correctives. They are useless when they are done as ironies. Although they are directed to the preparation of manuals on sociological methods, these are in *no way* supplements of "standard" procedure, *but are distinct from them.* They do *not* formulate a remedy for practical actions... Nor are they in search of humanistic arguments, *nor* do they engage in or encourage permissive discussions of theory.

I have personally engaged in, and have observed other ethnomethodologists engage in, measurements of a text's validity by utilizing many of Garfinkel's standards of ethnomethodological "purity" contained in the excerpt above. I have participated in discussions with ethnomethodologists that have been jokingly, but nonetheless effectively, curtailed because we were engaging in "permissive discussions of theory."

Members of intellectual movements also situationally create and call on collectively referenced standards of purity to find solutions to everyday organizational and communicational tasks.

Zimmerman and Wieder's (1970) reply to Norman Denzin concerning ethnomethodology's uniqueness and distinctness from symbolic interactionism effectively displays ethnomethodological members' use of collectively devised features of purity to identify themselves as a legitimate, original, and distinct intellectual movement. Likewise, Zimmerman's (1976) and Mehan and Wood's (1976) replies to Louis Coser's (1975) presidential address to the American Sociological Association exhibit similar features. Anne Rawls's (1985) reply to Gallant and Kleinman's (1983) article "Symbolic Interactionism vs. Ethnomethodology" also formulates a text that produces member-recognizable features of ethnomethodological doctrinal purity for the purposes of clarifying the differences between ethnomethodology and symbolic interactionism, as "a general response to the discipline as a whole" (Rawls 1985:2).

Ethnomethodological heresy

I find the topic of heresy in the ethnomethodological movement a little more difficult to trace. The Garfinkel-Cicourel schism of 1971 has displayed features common to heretical breaches of other radical movements, for example, the competition for authoritative leadership and spokespersonship, the maintaining of boundaries between the two factions, and the refusal of each party to reference or utilize the other's work after the public disclosure of the heresy. Similar practices have been observed in such movements as the Montanist and Quietist heresies (cf. Knox 1961); Amish, Mormon, and Hutterite aposticies and heresies (cf. Kephart 1982; Wilson 1970; Zablocki 1971); in a variety of radical and extremist movements that utilize the public disclosure of heresy as a weapon of social control (cf. Selznick 1952); and the realm of poetry, where the status of the work of art as an object independent of its creator is cause for heretical controversies (cf. Tillyard and Lewis 1939; Schutz 1964:16).

Heresy-avoiding work such as disclaimers, conditional clauses, and statements of intellectual indebtedness can be witnessed in many ethnomethodologists' written acknowledgments of their indebted sources of inspiration. I present here a brief collection of acknowledgments that do literary, semiotic, and organizational work to make sure that what is being said is not interpreted by another member as heresy, unapproved endorsement, or apostasy:

Exhibit 1

I am deeply indebted to Harold Garfinkel for the teachings and advice that inspired and guided my studies. (Lynch 1985a:xiii)
John O'Neill, Harold Garfinkel, and Michael Lynch have, over the past several years, helped in working out key issues with respect to a serious proposal concerning the analyzability of written material. (Morrison 1981:245)

While the joint authors assisted in the exposition, and while that exposition relies on our joint studies and seminars of Harold Garfinkel, it does *not* reflect a common understanding of ethnomethodology... Their collaboration therefore does *not* constitute an *endorsement* of the chapter as an adequate introduction to ethnomethodological studies. (Lynch, Livingston, and Garfinkel 1982:230)

I am only too conscious of the pitfalls and difficulties inherent in this enterprise of making "good sociological sense" of Garfinkel. The strains of oversimplification and even downright revisionism which inhabit any expository work press all the more insistently on those who would expound truly innovative perspectives. The danger of traducing newly minted insights by rendering them in a more traditional conceptual coinage is an ever-present one. (Heritage 1984d:viii)

The work of Harold Garfinkel (1967, 1970, 1972) has influenced these several studies extensively, and the orientations just recited will exhibit our *indebtedness* quite transparently to those *familiar* with his work. (Schenkein 1978b:6, fn.4)

For Aaron (Cicourel), who first served us the sweet poison. (Mehan and Wood 1975a:viii)

I wish to acknowledge my considerable intellectual debt to Professor Harold Garfinkel. Those familiar with his work will *recognize* in the present research the full extent of this *indebtedness*. (Wieder 1974a:5)

Garfinkel's work on the phenomenological structure of ordinary settings of social activity provided and *continues* to provide an enormous intellectual stimulus for our researches. (Sudnow 1972a:v)

We are all *indebted* to Aaron Cicourel, Harold Garfinkel, Harold Pepinsky, and D. Lawrence Wieder for their critical reading of the first draft of this paper...We are alone *responsible* for whatever defects this chapter may possess... Our *debt* to Harold Garfinkel is a special one... More importantly, as will be evident throughout the chapter, his work and counsel furnished us the critical resources from which we have drawn so *heavily*. (Zimmerman and Pollner 1970:80)

My *debts* to him (Professor Harold Garfinkel) are barely noted by the references in the body of the paper. It might be added that he is far from agreeing with all that I have to say. (Sacks 1963:1)

Here our *debts* to the work of Harold Garfinkel surface. Elsewhere, though they cannot be pinpointed they are pervasive. (Schegloff and Sacks 1973:289)

We owe the possibility of ever having seen the importance of the particularization theme to our acquaintance with Harold Garfinkel; cf. his works of 1967 and 1970. (Sacks, Schegloff, and Jefferson 1974:727, fn.40)

My debt to Schutz's work and Garfinkel's exposition of it will be evident in the pages that follow. The present work began after my association with Garfinkel and may depart significantly from his own ideas about the same or similar topics. I have not had the benefit of his criticisms, but have sought to footnote his ideas contained in published and unpublished works within the limits of not being given permission to quote from them directly. (Cicourel 1964:v)

The articles originated from my studies of the writings of Talcott Parsons, Alfred Schutz, and Aaron Gurwitsch, and Edmund Husserl. For twenty years their writings have provided me with inexhaustible *directives* into the world of everyday activities. (Garfinkel 1967i:ix)

The work of Alfred Schutz, cited in footnote 2, is a magnificent exception. Readers who are acquainted with his writings will *recognize* how *heavily* this paper is indebted to him. (Garfinkel 1964: published in Garfinkel 1967f: 36, fn.1)

Indeed, our analysis has so far been *merely* an application of Husserl's masterful investigations into the structure of our experience. According to him, the factual work is always experienced as a world of preconstituted types. (Schutz 1964:168, fn.10) (Italics are mine on all quotations.)

It is interesting to observe that Lynch (1985a), Schenkein (1978a), Wieder (1974a), Zimmerman and Pollner (1970), Sacks (1963), Cicourel (1964), and Garfinkel (1964a) all use the same shared style and structure of formulating these references of intellectual origination as "recognized indebtedness." These creations of a retrospective conceptual lineage in fact establish a quasi-simultaneity of inner time sense between knowledgeable members of the movement. This sharing of the members' inner time-sense, this living through a vivid present in common, constitutes what Schutz has called the "mutual tuning-in relationship" (cf. Schutz 1964:159-178). These members are effectively united with each other by a time dimension shared in common and mediated by the members' arrangements of signs and knowledge elements. (I develop this else where in Chapter 3.)

We see that in the following reference, Lynch, Livingston, and Garfinkel continue these lineage-establishing practices. In a sense, this practice retrospectively produces the future direction of the purity of the movement's doctrine:

We are heavily indebted to Merleau-Ponty's daemonic discussion of the "intertwining" (1968) and Heidegger's masterful exposition of the question of "the Thing" (1967). (Lynch, Livingston, and Garfinkel 1982:231, fn.6)

We can observe in this textual fragment the authors' re-creation and constitution of a lineage of research that was begun in the phenomenological movement. The authors heuristically use the phenomenologists Merleau-Ponty and Heidegger. They create a poetic mimesis of Schutz's lineage reference to Husserl (in preceding reference) using the words "masterful exposition" in synchrony with Schutz's "masterful investigation" (previous page) This literary practice establishes a sense of a socially derived and socially approved knowledge transmission that creates an "authorized linkage" between knowledge sources. This socially derived and socially approved knowledge is signified as group authorized and group authenticated knowledge and therefore more qualified to become a pattern, or "secondary modelling system" (cf. Sebeok 1976:23; Ivanov 1969) for others in the movement than knowledge originating elsewhere.

4. Members have an obligation to carry the burden of their convictions into their personal lives and careers. Radical movements that possess a comprehensive doctrine tend to insist that practicing members apply the doctrine to all parts of their personal lives. Nothing is so private as to merely be a matter of personal choice or preference when matters of the doctrine or ideology are concerned (Bittner, p.937).

The ethnomethodological movement has established various methodological guidelines and requirements for its practitioners that are similarly situationally highly binding and pervasive. The most pervasive methodological strategy and requirement is that all methods be grounded in a reflexive awareness of its contributions to the constitution of the "discovered" data or findings. The reflexivity requirement insists that practitioners exercise no personal methodological or theoretical preferences or whims that are non-reflexive and ungrounded in rigorous ethnomethodological reasoning.

Because of the nearly all-pervasive depth of the radical philosophical critique phenomenology presents, ethnomethodology, in attempting to seriously apply and work out phenomenology's findings, was effectively required to become a radical movement. By adopting phenomenology's discoveries and insights as an adapted "secondary modeling system" (cf. Ivanov 1969), Garfinkel effectively created a subsequent modeling system that demanded of ethnomethodology's members that they practice a similar, often excruciatingly rigorous, reflexive examination of their own practical methodological foundations.

Ethnomethodological practitioners have frequently spoken of this feature of reflexivity as applied to their own researches and theorizing (cf. Garfinkel 1967a; Cicourel 1964; Wilson 1970b; Wieder 1974a; Mehan and Wood 1975a; Mehan 1979a; Jules-Rosette 1975b, 1978b, c; Lynch 1985a). Ethnomethodologists have often noted that this reflexivity of methods requirement leads sometimes to a form of methodological paralysis or immobilization similar to experiences in Zatocoding (cf. Moers 1951, 1956; Garfinkel in Hill and Crittenden 1968: 205ff; Wood 1969a), to new difficulties in formulating a written report in an adequate fashion (cf. Jules-Rosette 1978a, b), and to a new form of description that utilizes the describer's own experience as an explicit device for looking and narrating (Sudnow 1978; Castaneda 1968, 1971; Jules-Rosette 1975b, 1978c; Mehan and Wood 1975a, b; Livingston 1983; Garfinkel 1985b).

"Methodological antinomianism" in the ethnomethodological movement is a paradoxical phenomenon. Practitioners are mandated not to employ sociologically normalized methods nor to engage in common sociological reasoning that does not reflexively examine its own basis in members' common-sense constructions (Garfinkel 1967a; Garfinkel and Sacks 1970; Cicourel 1973b, 1981). Instead, they are to search for and to invent methods that are adequate and sensitive to the unique feature of the phenomena being studied. What those methods consist of is left up to the ethnomethodologist. As Garfinkel (in Hill and Crittenden 1968:252) says:

> Our interests are not in preinvention, and in fact are not directed to strict methodical search. We *use* methodical procedures *insofar* as we can find such methods for making the *features* of practical reasoning *available for inspection.*

The apparent antinomianism or anomicizing of methods in ethnomethodology is actually tied and tethered to a nearly invisible member's principle. This principle, that of creating an "inspectable" exhibit of a natural phenomenon's constitutive features, relies on the ethnomethodological practitioner's competent creations of a coincidence between methods and phenomenon. The transmission of ethnomethodological methods and technical expertise has much more to do with the member's grasping of the underlying principle than acquiring a mere set of sociological research techniques or administering "compliance documents." By compliance documents, the ethnomethodological movement means:

> "data gathering" instruments which require of respondents that they be answerable to a schedule of verbal or written items designed by the researcher, and that such responses will be taken to be representative of real-worldly descriptions, attitudes, beliefs, and semantic structures. Such documents include survey questionnaires, interview schedules, eliciting strategies and bureaucratically administered self report forms of all kinds. (Garfinkel et al. 1981:133, fn.8)

It can be observed here that in fact the ethnomethodological movement trains its members in an alternative sociological semiosis. Practitioners are taught to read social phenomena as signs and to design methods that in effect cause social phenomenon to display their uniquely signified features in a way fundamentally different than the normative sociological paradigm's way of reading and representing social phenomena.

These features of methodological antinomianism are visible in Garfinkel's diversity of studies, settings, and methods in *Studies in Ethnomethodology* (1967a); in his recent work on scientific activity involving historical reconstructions of scientific discoveries and their practical circumstances of work, such as reproducing Gallileo's inclined plane experiment (Garfinkel 1985b) or analyzing the notebooks and audiotapes of the discovery of the optical pulsar (Garfinkel, Lynch, Livingston 1981); in the ethnomethodological movement's use of such bizarre procedures as inverted lenses, zatocoding, prosthetic limbs, auditory illusions, enjambing, occasioned maps, breaching demonstrations, artificial interviews and psychiatric counseling situations, psychedelic drug use, and becoming the phenomena (see Chapters 6 and 7); in Cicourel and Boesès (1972) demonstrations with deaf sign language (Cicourel 1973b); Zimmerman and Pollner's (1970) guidelines for investigating the "everyday world as a phenomena" in terms of an "occasioned corpus;" and many more ethnomethodological techniques and procedures for making the assemblage of the social world apparent and open to a new research and description. The ethnomethodological movement's often disparate and apparently nonconnected use of methods are actually indicative of a heterogeneity of expression of pervasive underlying principles. The seeming "collage" of ethnomethodological approaches and studies has bewildered many outsiders, leading some to state that the ethnomethodological movement has no coherent methods or that it is unable to transmit them to others. For example, Blau (1969: 119-130) has said that ethnomethodology "presents no clear conceptual framework and no specific procedures for research, and its practitioners neither engage in systematic research nor try to construct systematic theories but comment in quite obscure language on some random observations of human behavior they have made."

I observe that, in contrast to this kind of observation, the ethnomethodological movement has in fact established for its members a methodological requirement of extremely rigorous proportions and consequences. The weight of the movement itself insists that members apply these hidden, underlying reflexive strictures in all areas of their research, writing, and professional discourse.

5. Suffering must be made an integral part of the conception of the progress of the movement, and the movement should exploit outside sentiment against it for its own organizational advantage. Bittner's analysis of radicalism (p.938) points out that since disappointments, failures, and reversals are common in the lives of radical movements, suffering must be accorded a central place in the movement's definition of progress. True progress is to be measured by the amount of resistance encountered from those outside the movement. Suffering is a socially

approved state function to minimize its effects on the morale of the members.

The ethnomethodological movement has itself typified suffering in the ranks of the faithful. It has encountered strong resistance from many parts of the sociological discipline that has been reflected in the movement's difficulty and failure in publishing and in having members hired in sociology departments, and in receiving harsh reviews of its work (cf. Wallace 1968; Coleman 1968; Coser 1975; Gouldner 1970). Ethnomethodological members routinely assume that they run major risks of being misunderstood and even persecuted by the more traditional sociological discipline as well as local sociology departments.

Bittner believes that the official portraits of radical leaders should contain elements of martyrdom to collectively signify the conception of suffering. No reversals of fortune or difficulties should be passed over, and all tragedies must be exploited to increase members' devotion. Bittner (p.938) mentions that often in order to increase their own tolerance for suffering and sacrifice, leaders and members of movements find it worthwhile to actually "rehearse" brutality on each other. Of course, members and believers must learn to value pain, humiliation, and degradation in such a way that "indifference" or actual appreciation of it is possible.

Wittingly and unwittingly, the ethnomethodological movement has occasionally displayed features in response to the outside discipline's reactions that can and have been interpreted by practitioner members as having properties of martyrdom.

Ethnomethodology's leaders, most notably the first generation of Garfinkel and Cicourel, as well as "local" second, third and fourth generation scholars, have tended to dramatize their persecution by the sociological establishment for purposes of historical fact as well as for adding cohesion to the movement's protest. This dramatization can be witnessed in their oral lectures concerning their relations with sociology, in their accounts of their battles for academic tenure in which they suffered because of their ethnomethodological ideas, in their cries of disciplinary misunderstanding, and in their written and published texts.

For example, Garfinkel's written statements sometimes have a practical effect of making him appear, whether intentionally or nonintentionally, as a critical and persecuted leader of a demarcated and somewhat separatist sociological faction:

Our work does not stand then in any modifying, elaborating, contributing, detailing, subdividing, explicating, foundation-building relationship to professional sociological reasoning.... (Garfinkel and Sacks 1970:346).

Bittner also says that for "tactical reasons" (p.938) it is efficient to channel the occurring counteraggressive tendencies of the movement toward some outside adversary. It is important for the movement to establish an adversary who can be succinctly pre-judged as evil, wrong, or damned. The usefulness of an adversary's image makes it possible to moralize by counter example. The adversary's misfortunes actually validate and celebrate the movement's own formulated doctrines and epitomize life outside the movement. The fight against the adversary provides a dynamic program for spreading the movement's doctrine and may represent the only version of the doctrine accessible to believers who lack the intellectual capacity to appreciate its loftier aspects.

The ethnomethodological movement has fought with the sociological establishment for years. For its own purposes of survival, ethnomethodology has had to tangle head-on with sociology critics. When it has chosen not to ignore sociology's criticisms and quarrels, ethnomethodology has formulated professional sociology as both an adversary and a phenomenon. As Garfinkel says:

...because professional sociological inquiries are practical through and through, except that quarrels between those doing professional inquiries and ethnomethodology may be of interest as phenomena for ethnomethodological studies, these quarrels need not be taken seriously. (Garfinkel 1967a:viii).

Such "adversary-work" has given members the opportunity to construct a sense of solidarity as an intellectual collective, as well as furnished the grounds for maintaining a level of critical distance from standard sociology.

Conclusion

I have presented a preliminary analysis of the ethnomethodological movement's radical features. Using Bittner's properties of radical movement organization, I have developed a homologous descriptive comparison with ethnomethodology's generalized organizational features as a form of intellectual movement and program. We have seen that some of the ethnomethodological movement's organizational practices bear resemblance to those employed by members of radical and religious movements.

These radical properties included the radical questioning of the established corpus of taken-for-granted sociological knowledge and the creation of a foundationally unified scheme of interpretation. We have observed general organizational tasks like the production of valued cultural objects, the creation of interactive mechanisms to maintain practical internal working relations, and the formation of intellectual and group boundaries that form a sense of a distinctive enterprise. I suggest that these properties and tasks are general to many innovative intellectual movements. They have been observed in American pragmatism, in Parsons's structural functionalist group at Harvard, the Chicago "school" of sociology, and more recent intellectual theory groups and movements such as new causal theorists, cognitive science, semiotics, and French structuralism.

Ethnomethodology is historically distinctive in its solutions to these general organizational tasks. We have seen that the ethnomethodological movement's past intellectual generations have organized themselves as a discipline through creative practical solutions like producing mythologized collective actants in the form of persons, texts, and contexts; formulating heuristic directives, policies, speech and writing genres, career paths, leadership and relationships to other disciplines that in fundamental ways lay outside disciplinary norms and routines; assembling a social time-sense that proleptically assumes and represents a future programmatic clarity and purity in the face of present vagueness, and analeptically or retrospectively devises a form of historical intellectual lineage; inventing a highly unique semiotic system that places vigorous reflexive requirements on practitioners; and exploiting outside disciplinary criticism and resistance to its own organizational advantage.

Ethnomethodology now faces an organizational task of maintaining its radical stance while managing its own institutionalization. Like all modern social science programs, the ethnomethodological movement must manage the professional practicalities of new generations of students, provision of publishing outlets, communication of its discoveries, creation of an innovative intertextuality and establishment of research networks in new local contexts. The chapters that follow examine how the ethnomethodological movement has produced its intertextual discourse (Chapter 3); how its intellectual generations have used textual referencing strategies (Chapter 4), interactive documentary work (Chapter 5), and generational membership accounts (Chapter 6) to compose the ethnomethodological semantic and phenomenal field; and how the movement's generations have managed ethnomethodology's transmission and dissemination around the world (Chapter 7). These chapters all attempt to form the basis of an understanding of the ethnomethodological movement's present and future organizational directions.

Part II

Chapter Three
Garfinkel's Intertextual Poetry

> ...you want to be careful in thinking that since we do not talk in a
> recognizable way, nothing will come of it .
> Garfinkel (Hill and Crittenden 1968:125)

> What they missed was how the damn talk was tied into the thing he was
> doing as a feature of what he was doing. Now maybe you cannot
> understand that, but that is what we insist on.
> Garfinkel (Hill and Crittenden 1968:126)

> Well, I will tell you what: it is my risk. I will wait it out.
> Garfinkel (Hill and Crittenden 1968:124)

This chapter investigates ethnomethodology's production of an intertextual corpus of knowledge embodied in its unique genres of speaking and writing. Knowledge that is cooperatively produced, referenced, and used as a legitimating base for further studies done in a self-referential community is intertextual knowledge (cf. Kristeva 1980:36-63; Tyler 1985). Ethnomethodology's production of its intertextuality provides an important and central social mechanism for its achievement of a disciplinary coherency, cogency, and cohesion. As we shall see, Garfinkel and the others of the first generation composed intricately detailed ways of formulating insights and knowledge through speaking, writing, and other practical communicative technologies. These technologies were appropriated by successive generations of ethnomethodologists, each with an eye and ear sensitive to relevant contextual necessities and the calling of personal style. In the ensuing creations of neoethnomethodological research, writing, and expression, there has remained a detectable presence of Garfinkel's and the first generation's formulations of ethnomethodology. "Formulations" in ethnomethodological terms are communicational practices of "saying-in-so-many-words-what-we-are-doing" through members' mastery of natural language and competent readership and writership. I shall examine the historical production of these intertextual formulations of knowledge in this chapter and in Chapters 4 and 5.

In attempting this investigation of ethnomethodology's production of intertextual knowledge forms, I shall recommend that viewing ethnomethodology's textual and communicational formulations of knowledge as having a poetic structure may shed valuable light on our phenomenon. Findings from the semiotics of poetry (Riffaterre 1978) have been illuminating. The writerly production of texts consisting of complex syntactical, grammatical, and interpretive structures yields an incisive semiotic unity when properly read and comprehended. I am going to suggest that mastery of ethnomethodology's intertexts requires a mastery of specialized procedures of reading, writing, and speaking. Practitioners' competence in ethnomethodology's knowledge domain implies the acquiring of a form of poetic intelligibility. Such competence is not normally developed in modern social science training because of the prevailing style of positivism. I observe that some of the sociological misunderstanding of ethnomethodology has its origins in differences in social science literacy and rhetorical genres.

Ethnomethodology and the semiotics of poetry

Michael Riffaterre's *Semiotics of Poetry* (1978) presents a theory of poetic structure that affords a very useful tool for understanding ethnomethodology's textual unity that underlies its often difficult phraseology. I propose that we examine ethnomethodology's texts as a form of sociological poetry, or as A.F.C. Wallace has called it, "inspired literature."

John Heritage, in his book *Garfinkel and Ethnomethodology* (1984b:1) has said of Garfinkel's writing style that, "These studies are discussed in a difficult prose style in which dense thickets of words seem to resist the reader's best endeavors, only to yield, at the last, forceful and unexpected insights which somehow remain obstinately open-ended and difficult-to-place." Ethnomethodology presents the sociological reader with an awesome task: to solve the mystery of its phraseology by searching for an underlying message or unity to its pronouncements and texts. Riffaterre's semiotics of poetry claims that "the characteristic feature of a poem is its unity" (Heritage 1984d:2). The interpretive reading of a poem is a quest for unity. Jonathan Culler has commented that in Riffaterre's theory the poem's unity is achieved or perceived by the reader's process of making sense of the text, and is achieved "only when the reader abandons the apparent referential or representational meaning of the discourse and grasps the unifying feature or factor that the various signs of the poem express by indirection" (Culler 1981:81). Riffaterre's theory of poetic structure accounts for the unity that underlies poetic and textual "un-grammaticalities" (Riffaterre 1978:4).

Ethnomethodology has been barraged with criticisms of its often times difficult to understand phraseological style. Wallace (1968:125) has said of *Studies of Ethnomethodology* that "At times the text reads like a very bad interlinear translation of an obscure German philosopher. Serious graduate students, let alone reviewers, may waste hours searching for the meaning of such seemingly oracular non-sentences."

James Coleman (1968:130) has also criticized Garfinkel's difficult discourse structure by saying: "Once again, Garfinkel elaborates very greatly points which are so commonplace that they would appear banal if stated in straightforward English. As it is, there is an extraordinary high ratio of reading time to information transfer, so that banality is not directly apparent upon a casual reading."

A poetic model presents a new way of exploring the dynamics of ethnomethodology's aspects as an intertextual intellectual movement. This model goes beyond the general science communicational model of Mullins (1973) and the paradigm model of Kuhn (1967). By inspecting the member's own ethnosemiosis of reading the group's texts, the inner mechanisms whereby readers and writers become part of an intertextual community can be revealed. This member's readership is constructed essentially in the shared perception of poetic or semiotic unity underlying the group's texts and discourse.

Riffaterre (1978:4) says:

The *ungrammaticalities* spotted at the mimetic (simple referential) level are eventually integrated into another system. As the reader perceives what they have in common, as he becomes aware that this common trait forms them into a paradigm, and that this paradigm alters the meaning of the poems, the new function of ungrammaticalities changes their nature, and now they signify as components of a different network of relationships...Everything related to this integration of signs from the mimesis level into the higher level of significance is a manifestation of *semiosis*.

Ethnomethodological ethnosemiosis

"Ethnosemiosis," or members' local practices of signification (cf. MacCannell and MacCannell 1982; Greimas and Courtés 1982:108), entails the process of going from the mimetic level of meaning into the higher level of significance which is only available to the member. This process is carried out by an intellectual movement member in the activity of writing and reading a group intertext.

Surface readings of Garfinkel's work, for instance, routinely produce responses similar to those of Wallace and Coleman. These responses are much like many of those encountered in a first time, representational, "heuristic" reading of a poem by Blake or Rimbaud or a Zen dialogue. The reader solves the mystery of the poem by discovering that each ungrammaticality or bizarrely composed referential structure is in fact a reference to a hypogram. Each work must be discovered as a variant of a kernel of underlying poetic unity that begs to be unified and to be made intelligible by the reader (cf. Culler 1981:87).

A hypogrammatic interpretation gives us a clue to ethnomethodology's appeal to portions of the young generation of the 1960s and 1970s. Philosophic, "new age," poetic, esoteric, mystical, and occult texts from the East and the hermetic West beckoned to the '60s and '70s American youth to read them in such ways as to make them intelligible through the reader's own practices of the poetic unifying of sense. In a similar way, ethnomethodology's semiotic mediums and its message made its call to these generations. Both ethnomethodology's discursive style and what it pointed to as discoverable features of social reality encouraged the student "to go to great lengths to unify it and make it intelligible" (Culler:1981:87). Ethnomethodology persuaded its member readers to reflexively see both the social world and its own discourse as poetic. This poetic structure of everyday life and members' discourse referenced underlying unities and essential features that were waiting to be dis-covered and identified.

Riffaterre's theory of semiotic unity holds that at the higher levels of significance (for us, the member's view), everything in the poem is a variant of an original work or sentence. A word or phrase is poeticized and comes to function as a poetic sign when it refers to (and if a phrase patterns itself upon) a preexistent word group (Riffaterre 1978: 23). Riffaterre calls this preexistent word group, descriptive system, or thematic complex a "hypogram." Ethnomethodology's hypogram is its collection of member produced, and historicized, discursive and textual themata and words that have been constructed by past semiotic and literary practices. For members, "it is in perceiving a sign's reference to this preexisting phrasing or complex that the reader identifies the sign as 'poetic'" (Culler:1981:87).

Ethnomethodology may properly be termed poetic sociological discourse because of the fact that its texts are composed of highly poeticized elements such as words, phrasings, and images that refer to the groups, preexisting corpus or hypograms.

The difference between poetic styles and nonpoetic styles of sociological discourse can be explained by the way a poetic text "carries" meaning (Riffaterre 1978:1). Garfinkel's and subsequent ethnomethodologists' "poetic" sociological texts assume responsibility for their own "figurative integration" (Tyler 1984:335) as self-consciously formulated and mimetic forms of intertextuality. To some extent, all sociological writing is poetic.

Tyler (1984) has said that "postmodern" anthropology and sociology are in a "crisis of discourse" and a "crisis of poetics." Contemporary social science is awakening to the conception that its discourse is a trope—a way of speaking relative to the purpose of a discourse. Ethnomethodology has in many cases accepted this conception and used it to integrate its own "voice" as a movement. James Clifford in his analysis of anthropological discourse and written ethnography has said that "poetry" is not limited to romantic or modernist subjectivism: it can be historical, precise, objective, and determined by social and institutional contexts (Clifford 1985:26). Institutional poetry often employs words excluded from common usage and possesses its own special grammar.

I do not wish to claim that ethnomethodology is "poetic" while other forms of sociological discourse are "nonpoetic." Instead, my aim is to show that ethnomethodology has consistently expressed itself in figurative ways that are unique to itself as a self-formulated intellectual movement. It is the figurative semiotic unity that I refer to as "intertextual poetry."

Consider for a moment this text from Garfinkel's *Studies in Ethnomethodology* (1967e:9):

By this I mean to call attention to "reflexive" practices such as the following: that by his account practices the member makes familiar, commonplace activities of everyday life recognizable *as* familiar, commonplace activities; that on each occasion that an account of common activities is used, that they are recognized for "another first time"; that the member treats the processes and attainments of "imagination" as continuous with the *other* observable feature of the settings in which they occur; and of the proceeding in such a way that the member "in the midst" of witnessed actual settings recognizes that witnessed settings have an *accomplished* sense, and accomplished facticity, an accomplished objectivity, and accomplished familiarity, an accomplished accountability, for the member the organizational hows of these accomplishments are unproblematic, are known vaguely, and are known only in doing which is done skillfully, reliably, uniformly, with some enormous standardization and as an unaccountable manner.

One can observe here that Garfinkel's poetic discourse is composed of reiterated elements, all of which refer to the ethnomethodological movement's hypogram of the insight of radical constitution. This pre-existing thematic corpus is poetically expressed to sociologically highlight the perceived relationship between social accomplishment and accounting practices.

The collective insight of radical constitution

Ethnomethodology can be characterized as having an essential feature exhibited throughout all its texts and discursive productions. This essential feature is the emphasis on social assemblage or the "insight of radical constitution." This feature is communally produced through poetic practices of writing, thinking, and talking. The radically constitutive features of ethnomethodology can be observed by an examination of its communal "cultural objects" in the form of written texts and spoken programmatics. The radical constitutive insight can be observed as the consistently group referenced "hypogram" or underlying descriptive system or thematic complex. The member's work of reading and writing signs (Baccus 1976; Morrison 1981) that references the group's hypogram of radical constitution is a "literary production" (O'Neill 1981) as well as a conversational, comportmental, and mental product. Ethnomethodology produces its "disengaged cultural object" (Garfinkel,

Lynch, Livingston 1981) in the form of a text through local practices of "literary rhetoric" (Gusfield 1976).

Literary referencing of the group's communally assembled insight of radical constitution can be witnessed as appearing in the following selection of textual excerpts:

Exhibit 1

> Among all the described forms of spontaneity that of *working* is the most important one for the *constitution* of the reality of the world of daily life. (Alfred Schutz 1962:212)

> I shall begin by consulting games. From an analysis of their rules, the concept of the *"constitutive order of events"* will be developed. (Garfinkel 1963:190)

> Can the *"constitutive accent"* be found for situations of "serious" life? I propose that the three properties that are definitive of the basic rules of a game are not particular to games but are found as features of the "assumptions" that Alfred Schutz, in his work on the *constitutive phenomenology* of situations of everyday life (1945, 1951), has called the "attitude of daily life." (Garfinkel 1963:209)

> The demonstrably rational properties of indexical expressions and indexical expressions and indexical actions is an *ongoing achievement* of the organized activities of everyday life. Here is the heart of the matter (Garfinkel 1967e:34).

> By use of the term *occasioned* corpus we wish to emphasize that the features of socially organized activities are particular, contingent *accomplishments* of the production and recognition work of parties to the activity. (Zimmerman and Pollner 1970:94)

> Early ethnomethodology arrived at this *constitutive position* through an *adoption* of Schutz's (1962a, 1964, 1966) and Gurwitsch's reading of Husserl. Schutz (e.g., 1962:11) and Gurwitsch (e.g., 1966:xvi) spoke of the everyday world as *constituted* by "mental acts of consciousness." Garfinkel *transformed* these phenomenologists' mental acts into public, scenic, interactional activities, and *ethnomethodology was born....* Social interactional activities *constitute* social facts; the facts do not exist independently of *constituting practices.* (Mehan and Wood 1976)

> In brief, the overriding preoccupation in ethnomethodological studies is with detailed and *observable practices which make up the incarnate production of ordinary social facts....* (Lynch, Livingston, Garfinkel 1983:206) (All italics are mine.)

The insight of radical constitution is the key to reading ethnomethodology. Grasping the profundity and depth of the full phenomenological implications of the insight into the constitutive assemblage of the taken-for-granted world is the requirement for comprehending the ethnomethodological member's reading. It is the "key to significance in the higher system" (Riffaterre 1978:6). By attempting to perceive the nature of the production of the social world as an ethnomethodologist does, it is possible for the reader to overcome difficulties in the written text, "the ungrammaticalities." Readers achieve a new reading of ethnomethodology by contextualizing the texts in terms of their unique sociohistorical ethnosemiosis.

Two ethnomethodological writers themselves have characterized ethnomethodology's "way of reading." This way of reading sees its own task as countering flaws in standard sociology by careful applications of the constitutive insight. Mehan and Wood (1976:14) wrote: "Ethnomethodology says that sociology ignores these structuring activities when they measure the degree of association among variables. One way of reading ethnomethodology is to see it countering this omission: ethnomethodologists study the social structuring activities that assemble social structures."

The achievement of an ethnomethodological poetic reading

It is precisely because so many critics of ethnomethodology have failed to grasp ethnomethodology in its poetic sense or "hermeneutic reading" and have mainly occupied themselves with a "mimetic reading" of only the surface level of apparently obscure representational signs and words, that ethnomethodology has remained so obstinately an obscured member's phenomenon, "a singularly murky domain... deepened by the development of a number of different jargons for its discussion" (Wallace 1968:124).

Blocked in one's mimetic (surface) reading of the ethnomethodological text with its many mimetic difficulties such as the terms "reflexive practices," "another first time," "quiddity," and "accomplished objectivity," the reader must, according to Riffaterre, consider each of these phrasings as a creative transformation of a group cliché or hypogram and a poetic variant of the original ethnomethodological matrix of sense: "The poem results from the transformation of a word or sentence into a text" (Riffaterre 1978:164).

The member's expansion and conversion of the ethnomethodological matrix into a text through reading and writing practices signals the production of a poetic text. This poetic text has two stages of readings. The first reading is the initial, "heuristic," or "mimetic" reading in which readers attempt to comprehend linguistic signs in a primarily referential fashion; readers "assume that the poem is the representation of an action or a statement about objects and situations" (Culler 1981:81). Readers of the poetic text encounter difficulties in this way of reading "ungrammaticalities." These signs give bizarre and contradictory results when interpreted referentially. For example, Garfinkel's statement:

> I use the term "ethnomethodology" to refer to the investigation of the rational properties of indexical expressions and other practical actions as contingent ongoing accomplishments of organized artful practices of everyday life. (Garfinkel 1967e:11)

can be construed by initial heuristic readers as "the creative ambiguity of a prophet exhorting his followers and confounding the heathen" (Wallace 1968:125) or as "esoteric ruminations" (Coser 1975:78) that move "through tedious and belabored stages to solutions that are, here as elsewhere, trivial" (Coleman 1968:129). "Taken on its own," wrote William Maryl (1973:256), "Garfinkel's presentation of the objectives of ethnomethodology is virtually indecipherable."

Poetic difficulties resist a straightforward mimetic reading and lead to, for the reader intent on comprehending the poem's unity, a second, "retroactive" or "hermeneutic" reading. According to Riffaterre, since serious readers know that "the characteristic feature of a poem is its unity" (1978:2), they are required, if they are to properly interpret the text, perceive another level at which that unity can be seen and the text can become a whole. This level of hermeneutic reading is the member's level of reading. By producing a perception of the poetic unity of ethnomethodology's texts and programs, and then sharing this perception with other cohorts who have achieved a similar level of hermeneutic understanding, communication between reading members becomes discursive tradition (cf. Overington 1977).

Poetic signs

Consider another "poetic" text from Garfinkel et al., (1981). The title itself, *"The Work of a Discovering Science Construed with Materials from the Optically Discovered Pulsar,"* bears a certain surrealistic flavor that warns the reader that this is going to be like no ordinary sociological or philosophical text. Garfinkel, Lynch, and Livingston (1981:140-141) write:

> Their tasks can be collected by speaking of them as the exhibitable-analyzability-of-the-optical-pulsar-again. They consist *of* Cocke and Disney's competent practices in that *in* each other's witnessed practices the exhibitable analyzability exists *as* their competent-practices-evidently. This object, their competent-practices-evidently, was achieved *in*, it consisted *of*, and it was extricated *from* the night's work, and *in situ* of the pulsar's Gallilean independence of their practices, the IGP.

Garfinkel et al.'s words and phrases ("the exhibitable-analyzability-of-the-optical-pulsar-again") function here for the member writer and reader as poetic signs that refer to the same underlying hypogram of radical constitution. The ethnomethodologist as competent reader and writer learns to achieve a coherence and a poetic unity for the text. A member's reading and writing depends on the accomplishment and discovery of a higher level of signification or referential structure that is able to perceive, work out, and grasp the sign relationship between Garfinkel's creative transformations ("their competent-practices-evidently") and the underlying poetic unity or hypogram. This poetic unity must be made intelligible by the ethnomethodologist reader as part of his or her own repertoire of competent literary practices. Such a process is fundamental to all intellectual discursive traditions and schools of thought.

Ethnomethodological poetic mimesis

Subsequent ethnomethodological literary work echoes both Garfinkel's poetic signs and the movement's hypogram of radical constitution. A brief survey of texts can illustrate the social character of ethnomethodology's mimetic usage of poetic signs and codes. In this instance one observes the use of "hyphenated" words:

Exhibit 2

In using the linguistic form *"in-order-to,"* I am looking at the *ongoing process of action* which is *still in the making* and appears therefore in the time perspective of the future. (Alfred Schutz 1962a:71)

From the user's point of view, a relationship of undoubted correspondence is the sanctioned relationship between *the-presented-appearance-of-the-intended-object-that-appears-in-this-presented-appearance.* (Garfinkel 1963: 214)

In addition we construct what Schutz calls *"course-of-action types"* (i.e., typical patterns of behavior) which we impute to anonymous others we do not know. (Cicourel 1964:222)

...their utterance had a dual significance: it was not only observable that they said the content of whatever they said; it was an observable event *that-they-said-anything.* (Schwartz 1971:206-207)

Under the auspices in the attitude everyday life, settings, such as that of the previously mentioned family, maintained their perceivedly stable features over time and may be conceived as instances of, say, *families-in-general,* or families-of-this-or-that-type. (Zimmerman and Pollner 1970:97)

...let us here now locate what in the materials the formulation permits us to observe, to see *the culturally-provided-for orderliness of* ... (Sacks 1972c:37)

If this is so, then it seems that on each occasion in conversation on which a formulation of location is used attention is exhibited to the particulars of the occasion. In selecting "right" formulation, attention is *exhibited* to *"where-we-know-we-are,"* to *"who-we-know-we-are,"* to *"what-we-are-doing-at-this-point-in-the-conversation."* (Schegloff 1972:115)

The abandonment of the dualism leads to the singe phenomenon, an *account-of-social-action,* or an *accounting-of-social-action.* "Telling the code" and more critically the work of "telling the code," is in this view a course of accounting which yields an *account-of-resident-behavior....* (Wieder 1974a:224)

A "chromatic path," an array of "intervals of a fourth," or "alternating half steps and minor third steps" or "up a whole step down two whole steps"– to name some instances of class examples in such terms—such *non-chord-specific-so-to-speak-paths* were elaborated. (Sudnow 1978:177)

So we think of their night's work as this: their unavoidable "situated" practices become *progressively-witnessable-and-discourse-able* as *"the-exhibitable-astronomical-analyzability-of-the-pulsar-again."* (Garfinkel, Lynch, Livingston 1981:135)

This study, then, is in that tradition of research (reviewed above) which is directed at analyzing the practices which compose the *moment-to-moment, day-to-day work* of daily life, included those portions of daily life which are carried out in bureaucratic organizations. (Mehan 1986:18) (All italics are mine)

The preceding textual fragments serve as demonstrations of intellectual members' recognized and oriented to practices of poetic mimesis and writing. These mimetic practices follow a received historical structure of hyphenated-word-segments. This structure was "inherited" from Alfred Schutz, who in the first fragment declares that this linguistic form of hyphenated words ("in-order-to") signifies the observation of "the ongoing process of action which is still in the making." Ethnomethodologists, beginning with Garfinkel and continuing to the present, have adopted this convention as a way of literarily and conversationally representing empirical observations resulting from the application of the insight of radical constitution. This literary device has been mimetically reproduced by members as organizationally relevant to recognizable ethnomethodological discourse. Many other examples of the social character of poetic signs are observable in all intellectual movements' texts.

   For example, in the following textual fragments Zimmerman and Pollner (1970) produce ethnomethodological discourse in a mimetic fashion to Garfinkel's:

Not only do *members* —the jurors and the others—take that reflexivity for granted, but they *recognize*, demonstrate, and make *observable for each other* the rational character of their actual, and that means occasional, practices while respecting that reflexivity as an unalterable and *unavoidable* condition of their procedures and findings." (Garfinkel 1967e:8) (Italics are mine.)

We notice that the apparent orderliness and coherency of the scenes of daily life are matters that *members* are continually and *unavoidably* engaged in *recognizing and making recognizable for each other*. (Zimmerman and Pollner 1970:290) (Italics are mine.)

We observe here Zimmerman and Pollner's intertextual references to Garfinkel's phraseology and figurative language in their mimetic use of several word-icons ("members," "recognize," "unavoidably," "recognizable for each other") and in their use of Garfinkel's "reiterative mode" of using several emphatic word-statements to emphasize the details of an idea ("actual, and that means occasional," "unalterable and unavoidable," "orderliness and coherency," and "continually and unavoidably"). This intertextual mimetic work composes what Eco (1978:272) calls a "movement idiolect" or writing style peculiar to a group.

In semiotic terms, what we observe occurring is the writer's use of "anaphorization" procedures (Greimas 1976:23-27). These procedures are writers' creations of partial identity between usages, thereby creating an intertextual linkage. Anaphorization procedures are discursive condensations of previous expansions that produce "co-referencing" (Greimas and Courtés 1982:62-63) between textual signs. According to Greimas and Courtés, "co-referencing is the relation existing between two signs located at two different places referring to the same object." In ethnomethodology's case, both "hyphenizing" devices and "poetic" mimesis of phraseology serve as co-referenced signs between member-writers who use them to signify and specify the ethnomethodological movement's own specific sociological "object": the constituent features of social orders-in-the-making. Garfinkel has continued an intertextual poetic chain from Alfred Schutz, "hyphenizing," which is creatively anaphorized by successive generations of ethnomethodologists as a literary mechanism of intellectual identity.

Garfinkel's poesis

Ethnomethodology's literary productions are preeminently inventions and mimetic creations of Garfinkel's poetic disposition. What makes ethnomethodology unique as a literary genre is its ability to consistently create a description of the everyday world that is poetically replicated and expanded upon throughout its communal body of texts.

Garfinkel's own pseudo-poetic language has set the tone for much subsequent ethnomethodological literary work. His thinking, speaking, and writing styles are in fact a "poesis" (Heidegger 1971) of the everyday. Garfinkel uses a consciously composed poetic language to talk and write about everyday, ordinary phenomenon. The poetic style of expression is apparent to anyone who has heard him speak about ethnomethodology and who reads his work. Poetic "saying" about the ordinary world is consistent with Garfinkel's stated objective in the opening chapter of *Studies in Ethnomethodology* (1967a:1): "...by paying to the most commonplace activities of daily life the attention usually accorded extraordinary events, seek to learn about them as phenomena in their own right." This treating of the ordinary as extraordinary is a characteristic feature of phenomenological inquiry, and amounts to the creating of a descriptive poetry of the object in itself (cf. Heidegger 1962, 1971; Merleau-Ponty 1962, 1968).

Ethnomethodology's members' vocabulary or "jargon" that has so often been misunderstood as only a "morass of words" that "takes so much time to say so little" (cf. Coleman 1968; Wallace 1968; Coser 1975; Goulder 1970; Blau 1969) is in actuality a member's constructed and accomplished poetic attitude and literary idiolect (Eco 1976:270). According to Eco, an idiolect is a personal style producing mannerisms, imitations, and stylistic habits. Disciplinary misunderstanding has resulted, at least partially, perhaps majorly, from the inability of sociological readers, trained in the predominantly positivistic method of scientific reading, to detect and interpret the poetic element in ethnomethodology's texts.

Perhaps due to American scientific training, which does not actively encourage the nurturing and development of literary and interpretive skills, the sociology audience of ethnomethodology has, for the most part, both misread and misunderstood, and thereby rejected, the radically new voice that ethnomethodology has had to offer the social scientific literary and perceptual field. Gusfield (1976:17) notes the absence of literary awareness in much social scientific reading and writing practice. He provides an interpretation of why "doing science," which presupposes an independence from any literary convention, is in fact one of the most rigid and tightly controlled literary rhetorics of them all:

> ...to be scientific is to exercise a definite *form* over the language in use, *to write* in a particular way which shows the audience that the writer is "doing science." The writer must persuade the audience that the results of the

research are *not* literature, are *not* a product of the style of representation. The style of non-style is itself the style of science. There is a literary art involved in scientific presentation.

Recent work has been focused on examining how a discipline's communal literary practices and style produce its textual objects and "written culture" (cf. Gusfield 1976; Morrison 1981; Garfinkel, Lynch, and Livingston 1981; O'Neill 1981; Clifford and Marcus 1986). Ethnographies, scientific reports, sociological theories, and disciplinary programmatic statements can all be analyzed as creative "icons" (Lynch 1979) embedded in "indefinite horizons" of human literary, interpretive, and readerly sense-making work and artful practice located within specific cultural and historical circumstances.

Ethnomethodology may be viewed as a collection of just these forms of historic literary products. Historically it has required a readerly audience capable of interpreting its various levels of signification, message, and poesis.

Sociological misunderstandings

The Purdue Symposium on Ethnomethodology (Hill and Crittenden 1968) serves as a pertinent document for examining in situ the responses of professional nonmembers to Garfinkel's and other ethnomethodologists' (Sacks, Sudnow, Cicourel, Churchill, Rose) communications in a context of verbal discourse. *The Purdue Symposium* is essentially an edited transcript by Hill and Crittenden and contains some extraordinary instances of attempts at dialogue and interpretation between ethnomethodological members and nonmembers during a conference held at Purdue University in 1968. After two days of "intensive" questions, answers, "soliloquies," debates, missing-the-point, and theoretical "name-calling" by both sides of the communicators, the conference members finally "ran out of gas" (p.252). Garfinkel wanted to do it again another time and hoped "he had awakened" (p.252) everyone's interests concerning ethnomethodological studies. But the overwhelming final commentary by the professional sociologists was not so much concerned with substantive issues, but with the language Garfinkel and his cohorts used to explain and express their program.

For example, Dave Gold said to Garfinkel at the end of the symposium (p.254):

> Harold has admitted he is out of gas. Dick (Hill) says he is out of gas and I am too. I have tried very hard. I have really struggled to follow the argument and somehow to get through. I have struggled with some rough things before. I do not think, as presumptuous as this may sound, that I am stupid and that I cannot get this, yet I have had *extreme difficulty* in following it. This last bit for example, in which you where trying to describe the methodology (Zatocoding), I did not really understand what was "news" and what you were communicating.

Dave Gold also expressed to Garfinkel (Hill and Crittenden 1968: 253) that:

> It is clear to me that you use a kind of *hip jargon*, if you will permit me to coin my own words. It is plain to the rest of us (Anderson, Becker, Costner, Crittenden, De Fleur, Hill, McGinnis, Schuessler, Sheldon, and Tittle) that you cannot stop to define your terms all the time, still you are attempting here to communicate *outside the group*. Now I got an impression, correctly or wrongly, that once ethnomethodology has been accepted and you are welcomed within the camp, that this gives you a kind of *license for language*. You do not question each other's language, and at the same time, there is *not* a great concern with communication to outsiders. Now if you do not want to communicate to others, well and good. That's it.

Richard Hill and Kathleen Crittenden (1968:258) comment that:

> Despite the two days of intense involvement, something less than full communication was achieved. The *"language of ethnomethodology"* may well be required by the complexity of the phenomena which ethnomethodologists take as their central concern. Nevertheless, the statements of some participants in the closing moments of the symposium are evidence of the fact that this is a *language* that continues to be *different* for the non-ethnomethodologists. Perhaps for this is one reason for the Tsoris to which Professor Garfinkel referred in his opening remarks.

Melvin De Fleur (Hill and Crittenden 1968:255) declared that:

> I think one of the shortcomings I see in what you are doing is a kind of conceptual poverty. That is, you do not really try very hard to work out a neat conceptual apparatus. For example, you use *things all strung together with a lot of hyphens between*. Every time you come to communicate an idea to us, it takes twenty minutes. There is a large baggage with that *funny set of phrases*. I have no objection to the set of phrases, but if you had a conceptual apparatus, once we learned the *code*, like the term indexical expression, we could

proceed. If you could nail them down like that, so that once we learned the code, we would not have to have all these elaborate illustrations and ramifications of them, I think it would be an awful lot easier to understand your meaning. Start off by defining certain terms very precisely.

And again Gold (p.255) said:

I have come out of this thing with the fact that the methodology is indeed *mysterious*, and Hal started things a couple of days ago by saying there is nothing mysterious. I do get the impression that it is mysterious, and that it is *non-public*. (All italics are mine.)

These conversational excerpts from the Purdue Symposium exhibit the features of a radical kind of paradigm or "semantic space" (Eco 1976: 125) confrontation. The nonethnomethodologists, Hill, Gold, Anderson, and De Fleur, all point to their trouble and difficulty in interpreting and understanding Garfinkel's, Sack's, Sudnow's, and Cicourel's language as representative of a "code" to which they do not have access. De Fleur even tried to specify actual practices of Garfinkel's language-code as "you use things all strung together with a lot of hyphens between" (p.255).

These excerpts show the difficult "work" nonmembers (and novice members) have to engage in in order to make sense of what Garfinkel and ethnomethodology are saying (see Chapter 6). These instances of difficulty or trouble point to the interpretive work members of the movement have learned to do and take for granted in their everyday associations with collectivity members and their intertextual communications. Eco (1976:126) has said that a code as "language" (or performed language) can be viewed as the competence of the speaker and that this practiced competence is the sum of the individual competences that constitute the code as a collective convention. Such a conception of a group's practiced language as constitutive of its collective code has been investigated by Greimas as the sociosemiotic study of "sociolects," which are "sorts of sublanguages...constituted as social taxonomies, underlying social discourse" (Greimas and Courtés 1982:301-302). Ethnomethodologists themselves have focused considerable research on this phenomenon of a collectivity's natural language use in terms of "membership categorization devices" (Sacks 1972c), membership as natural language competence (Garfinkel and Sacks 1970), and detailed analysis of a collectivity's situated conversational practices and interpretive practices (Cicourel and Boèse 1972a, b; Schegloff and Sacks 1973; Schenkein 1978a; Psathas 1978; Atkinson and Heritage 1984).

Ethnomethodology as a semiotic invention

Garfinkel's and ethnomethodology's language and language use can be interestingly examined as an example of an intellectual collectivity's situated creation and employment of a linguistic code that changes transiently and processually as it formulates its ideas in collective context. The ethnomethodological code is a negotiated biplanar rule that establishes new attractions and repulsions between items from different planes (Eco 1976:126). For example, when Garfinkel says:

> I asked Agnes, "What do you figure the facts are?" She answered, "What do I figure the facts are, or what do I think everyone else thinks the facts are?" This remark may serve as a theme in elaborating Agnes's practical circumstances as a texture of relevances. (1967a:175)

Garfinkel is attempting to establish and communicate "new attractions and repulsions" between items in different semiotic planes. Garfinkel asks Agnes, the transsexual informant that he studied, an ethnographic question that is based on a relativistic viewpoint ("What do you think the facts are?"). Garfinkel then combines the ethnographic question with another "plane" of reasoning, taken from Schutz's constitutive phenomenology ("This remark may serve as a theme in elaborating Agnes's practical circumstances as a texture of relevances"). The "code" assembled in this case represents a common pattern in ethnomethodological work: the ethnomethodological code or theme is the expansion of constitutive phenomenology into the ethnographic or empirical domain of social interaction. These different planes had rarely been related before (at least in sociological literature) and therefore Garfinkel's "code" seems "mysterious" or "confusing" to the sociologist. These different semiotic planes textually represent the usually invisible world of a person's tacit or taken-for-granted ways of managing society's expectations of, in this case, normal sexuality. They are an elaboration, using an adapted phenomenological language, of this taken-for-granted activity in a way that makes invisible social features visible. As such, Garfinkel's code, and that of the ethnomethodological movement as a whole to the degree it shares Garfinkel's project, constitutes a semiotic invention.

This invention can be observed in action in basically every ethnomethodological work, most forcefully in Garfinkel's own expressions. The active establishing of new attractions and repulsions between items from different planes constitutes ethnomethodology's "code." The newness of the result or product constitutes its radically inventive feature. This radically inventive feature of the code (cf. Eco 1976:250) explains why for so many nonethnomethodologists and for so many new members, Garfinkel's discourse appears so difficult to interpret and why it appears "to take so much time to say so little" (Wallace 1968:125). In making counted on, but majorly invisible and undiscussed, tacit and practical practices visible and available for a new description, ethnomethodologists have invented a new language form. Uninitiated hearers and readers can have difficulty with the "invented" new language that can be generated to talk about something barely noticeable and visible.

Garfinkel's iconization

Garfinkel's words produce iconizations (Eco 1976:216; Greimas and Courtés 1982:148) that signify for members the invisible form or feature of which the word is a material expression. Garfinkel's words, such as "indexical expressions," "practical actions," "reflexivity," "unremarkable details," "tokens," "routine work," "rational-for-all-practical-purposes," and "contingencies," all produce icons for members that display, as well as stand for, the "noticed but unseen" features of the taken-for-granted world ethnomethodology is trying to describe.

Eco points to the iconic nature of words and ideals as icons for collectivity's members:

> Every object, event, or act has stimulus value for the members of a society only insofar as it is an iconic sign signifying some correspondence form in their culture. (Eco 1976:165)

Thus, in the same way the word house is an icon of the cultural form or complex combination of forms of which it is a material expression, Garfinkel's words or "things all strung together with a lot of hyphens between" (De Fleur op. cit.) are icons of the ethnomethodologically revealed forms of everyday life of which they, as invented descriptors, are part of the material, textual expression and description. These icons are consensually recognizable and usable by members of the ethnomethodological intertextual community.

It is not simply a matter of opting to use a "hip jargon" (Gold op. cit) that makes a member an ethnomethodologist, but rather the ability or competence to first "see" (Garfinkel op. cit.:9) and to make visible the procedures whereby individuals make social organization' happen. Through this trained "seeing" an ethnomethodologist can both recognize this taken for granted practical work in the society at large, and recognize the ethnomethodological icons that other ethnomethodologists compose and share in making those "seen" settings visible to others. This recognition process is combined with writing practices to compose written text.

Because of the underlying complexity of the phenomena that ethnomethodology investigates, the creation of the code used to cogently connect the iconic descriptors mediated between the different represented planes (i.e., the invisible and the visible) is necessarily a difficult and precarious activity requiring immense amounts of work. This code-composing work demands that the iconic vehicles or descriptive vocabulary not attain a reified stasis or become "slogans" that distract the investigator from searching for the "big prize" that ethnomethodology is really after, that of investigating the local practices that compose social order (Garfinkel 1985a). In other words, ethnomethodology tries not to let its descriptors settle an issue prematurely, as much social science does, by merely attaching a label to a phenomenon. Instead, ethnomethodologists work to let new perceptions and discoveries restructure the codes. As Garfinkel (Hill and Crittenden 1968:252) has said: "Our interests are not in preinvention.... We use methodical procedures for making the features of practical reasoning available for inspection."

Poetic language and narrative arrangements

Garfinkel's use of language is an artistic element in ethnomethodology's textual corpus. His language can be understood as a poetic vehicle consciously composed by the author. This poetic vehicle teases the reader into a more than surface "reading" of, first, his words, and then, ultimately, of the reader's own perception of the phenomenal field of radically accomplished social order and "immortal society." Garfinkel's language of expression bears certain resemblances to the poetic language of Heidegger, who influenced Garfinkel repeatedly. Heidegger speaks here on "The Origin of the Work of Art:"

In the work, the happening of truth is the work. This means that the actual work is here already presupposed as the bearer of this happening. At once the problems of *the thingly feature of this work at hand* confronts us again. One thing thus finally becomes clear: however zealously we inquire into the work's self sufficiency, we shall still fail to find this actuality as long as we do not also agree to take the work as something worked, effected. To take it thus lies closest to us, for in the word "work" we hear what is worked. (1971:58).

Garfinkel, writing in his particular style, shows influence by Heidegger:

> Their central recommendation is that the "activities" whereby members produce and manage settings of organized everyday affairs are identical with members' procedures for making those settings "account-able." The "reflexive" or "incarnate" character of accounting practices and accounts makes up the crux of that recommendation. When I speak of accountable, my interests are directed to such matters as the following. I mean observable-and-reportable, i.e. available to members as situated practices of looking and telling. I mean too that such practices consist of and endless, ongoing, contingent accomplishment...." (1967e:1)

Garfinkel, like Heidegger, builds a poetic text through metonymical and synecdochical constructions. Hayden White (1973:34-35) defines metonomy as an expressive trope through which phenomena are implicitly apprehended as bearing relationships to one another in the modality of part-part relationships, on the basis of which one can effect a reduction of one of the parts to the status of an aspect, feature, or function of the other, e.g., "the roar of thunder." He defines synecdoche as a kind of representation suggesting a qualitative relationship among the elements of a totality in an integrative manner, i.e., synecdoche signifies a totality which possesses qualitative features or properties that constitute the essential nature of all parts that make it up, e.g., "He is all heart." In both Garfinkel and Heidegger's writing, they often employ the superimposition of a synecdoche on a metonomy, e.g., "the 'reflexive' or 'incarnate' character of accounting practices" and "situated practices of looking-and-telling" (Garfinkel 1967e:1); and "the thingly features of the work at hand" (Heidegger 1977:178).

These compositions open multiple corridors of meaning that urge a closer reading and a subsequent inventive application by the reader to his or her own everyday experience and perceptions. Heidegger's use of the word "work" stands as representative of the intertwining of effect and object much in the same way that Garfinkel chooses the word to connote the member's making of both methods and meaning.

Garfinkel and Heidegger can be interpreted by us as representing a distinct descriptive genre. Both authors consciously create description through the mechanism of reflexive language performance. By their very words, both consciously create and display the reality they seek to describe and analyze. This literary feature is characteristic of the phenomenological movement (cf. Speigelberg 1971:672). This can be witnessed in the following texts:

> These absurdities are collected as adumbrating aspects of a coherent phenomenon: the irrelevance of the topics, methods, findings, problems of naturally theoretic social studies of scientists' *work* for the *quiddity* of discovering scientists'—in this case Cocke and Disney's—interests in, their knowledge of, and their practices that compose the *in situ* apt and familiar efficacy of the days' *work*, hereafter "quiddity" or "quiddity of discovering *works*." (Garfinkel, Lynch, and Livingston 1981:133) (Italics are mine.)

and

> But what is thus at work, is so *in* the *work*. This means that the actual *work* is here already presupposed as the bearer of this happening. (Heidegger 1977:178)

Characteristic of much of the phenomenological movement's later descriptive literary style, both Heidegger and Garfinkel write in a poetic language that "confronts" the reader "as a test to be stood." (Heidegger 1971:87)

Phenomenological idiolects

Consider a recent textual fragment by Garfinkel (1987:5) that exhibits his unique poetic idiolect:

> For ethnomethodology the objective reality of social facts, in that and just how it is every society's locally, endogenously produced, naturally organized, reflexively accountable, ongoing, *always, only, exactly, and entirely* member's work, with no time out, and with no possibility of evasion, hiding out, passing, postponement, or buy-outs, is *thereby* sociology's fundamental phenomenon. (Italics are mine.)

In this fragment, Garfinkel displays his reiterative style of expression to express his insights. This style is in part traceable to Aron Gurwitsch's phenomenological sociolect used in *Studies in Phenomenology and Psychology* (1966:138):

> To each act there corresponds to a noema—namely, an object *just, exactly and only just*, as the subject is aware of it and has it in view, when he is experiencing the act in question. (Italics are mine.)

Garfinkel met Gurwitsch in the early 1950s and has referenced him in his work (cf. Garfinkel et al. 1981:fn.21). Garfinkel's own written idiolect employs consistent reiteration devices for emphasis of fundamental points.

Ethnomethodology's texts can be seen as following a different operating structure or narrative arrangement than most social scientific texts and literary genres. Following Gusfield's (1976) work on the literary rhetoric of social scientific texts, we can see that ethnomethodology is unique in its written "performance" in that it holds to the principle that significance is not separable from its body of language. Unlike most social science writing that presupposes that scientific observations and conclusions must be presented in a neutral descriptive language that resembles a clear "window pane" of glass (Gusfield, 1976:16), ethnomethodology places itself contrary to the assumption that language is irrelevant to the enterprise of science. As well as being an integral feature in its own literary genre, ethnomethodology has focused much attention on the problematic nature of this assumption toward language in social science research methods (cf. Garfinkel 1959a, 1967a; Cicourel 1964, 1973b, 1981; Sacks 1963; Zimmerman and Pollner 1970).

The "sequential arrangement" (cf. Gusfield 1976; Sacks, Schegloff, Jefferson 1974) of many of ethnomethodology's texts differ from most social scientific written discourse. When examining the body of ethnomethodological texts, one is struck by the fact that many texts make no attempt to formulate the paper's "findings" in a summarized or "abstract" form in standard social science language or mode of presentation. In social science writing, summary presentations "establish the inference that what is significant about the paper can be separated from the larger body of language" (Gusfield 1976). Ethnomethodology's usual refusal to accommodate this translation of its findings into standard sociological language is consistent with its stance that its way of analyzing the world is both reflected in and constituted by its literary style. Though ethnomethodology often follows the standard convention of establishing a "tension" (Gusfield 1976) between older conventional studies and its new perspective (cf. Garfinkel 1964a; Cicourel 1964, 1973b, 1981;

Zimmerman and Pollner 1970; Mehan and Wood 1975a; Sacks, Schegloff, Jefferson 1974; Mehan 1979a; Cicourel and Mehan 1985: Pollner 1978; Lynch 1982a), it nevertheless very often quickly departs from this convention and plunges right in to its technical analyses without overly great regard for the shoulders of its sociological predecessors (cf. Garfinkel 1949, 1967a; Garfinkel and Sacks 1970; Garfinkel, Lynch, and Livingston 1981; Lynch, Livingston, and Garfinkel 1983; Sudnow 1970, 1978; Schenkein, 1978b; Schegloff and Sacks 1973; Livingston 1983). Often, like a short story or a poem, the ethnomethodological paper seems to have so much new to say or so much to say in a new way that realizing "the vision of a rigorous ethnomethodology" (Sudnow 1978:vi) appears to require not reaching too far "beyond the self contained confines of its own product" (Gusfield 1976:19).

The role of the observer's "voice" or posture toward the object is paradoxically resolved in much ethnomethodology by the assumption of the "unique adequacy" of methods (cf. Garfinkel 1985b; Livingston 1983; Lynch 1985a) or "becoming the phenomenon" (cf. Mehan and Wood 1975; Jules-Rosette 1975b, 1979; Castaneda 1968, 1971). By radically embedding the analysis of a social setting in the member's knowledge and performance of that very setting's special skills and contextures of which the ethnomethodologist is a part, much ethnomethodological writing includes the active voice and refrains from the assumption that a researcher's observations are externalized in any way from that setting's features.

Garfinkel's ways of talking

Garfinkel seems to be in a constant search for a way of speaking about social phenomena of order other than the ways usually used to speak about them. He does not wish to "settle the issue" prematurely merely by attaching a sociological label or "slogan" onto the phenomenon, and therefore ending all further discussion (Garfinkel 1985a). Instead, Garfinkel's practice is to compose a way of speaking about phenomena that "recovers" the phenomena for inspection and examination.

For example, Garfinkel (Garfinkel et al. 1981:158) says:

> We have *to find a way of speaking about the Sacksian IT other than* talking about the "apparent pulsar" or "the pulsar as a reading on the screen" or "as an interpretation of the screen." It's difficult to *recover* what this unfinished *IT* could be, this *IT* that could go away and be gone forever.

Here Garfinkel is working to find a way to speak about the optically discovered pulsar as a cultural object that has the properties of what Harvey Sacks, in his unpublished lectures, called "the vague IT," something in a conversation that is produced, recognized, and understood before it has definiteness of sense or reference. The definiteness of sense is achieved and is emergent during the course of the work of the conversation.

Garfinkel's own way of speaking very often itself shows the properties of "an evidently vague IT," in that its sense is achieved through his own inventive (cf. Eco 1976:245) work and through the working out by the reader of what he is saying and pointing to. His speaking displays "iconization" (Greimas and Courtés 1982:147-148). Greimas describes iconization as a set of procedures or semiotic practices that produce "the meaning of effect of 'reality'," which is termed the "referential illusion." The referential illusion, proposed by Roland Barthes (1974a) is what Garfinkel is, in effect, constituting by his iconization or "referentialization" (cf. Greimas and Courtés 1982:259-261; Sacks and Schegloff 1974) procedures that compose his way of speaking. For example, when Garfinkel says:

> It's difficult to recover what this Unfinished IT could be, this IT that could go away and be gone forever,

he is working at constructing a referential illusion that points to, displays, and somehow makes inspectable the vague phenomena he is investigating. This referential illusion grows more clearly defined with each of his interactionally produced and "locally historicized" iconization procedures or ways of speaking that one designed to represent the invisible features of social order.

I have selected a published transcript (Pack 1986:117-119) to display to readers what I mean. This transcript was produced by Christopher Pack using Gail Jefferson's (cf. Schenkein 1978a:xi-xvi; Jefferson 1984a) notational conventions for conversational analysis. The conversation is between Harold Garfinkel and John O'Neill on the subject of "logical properties of occasioned maps." It took place at the Department of

Sociology, University of California, Los Angeles, in February, 1978. The transcript represents a partial rendering of Garfinkel's conversational style that is often mythologized by members.

Exhibit 3

Rules-of-use
Capitals signify a relative increase in volume.

(())	=	editorial comments
()	=	utterance is untranscribable
(0.0)	=	time of silence in seconds
//	=	interruption starts here
*	=	interruption ends here
—	=	stressed utterance
/	=	upward intonation
•	=	downward intonation
–	=	cutoff phrase
.hh	=	in-breath
=	=	this utterance is closely followed by the next

---

232 HG: alright
235 JO: mmhum
238 HG: Okay
241 JO: churley
243 (33.0)
246 HG: .hh .hh .hh ummm ((tape off)) ((tape on))
248 (24.0)
　　　HG: .hh ((laughter far in background)) .hh I don't want to be talk-
　　　　　ing about discovered topics I want to be talking first about
　　　　　talking first of all about (3.0) My whwhat I'm – I want to be
　　　　　talking about the logical properties of
255　　　occasioned maps (1.0)
258 JO: (mmhuh)
　　　HG: the discovered topic consists of the logical
262　　　properties of occasioned maps
265 JO: (mmhuh)
268 HG: right/
271 JO: okay

HG: Finding then what kind of- what kind of thing the logical prop-
    erties of occasioned maps would then find (1.0) uhhmm (3.0)
    in let's say finding what they would then find ummmm that it's
    a – it's a des – that is (6.0) Finding that this is – that this can
    be – that this will be spoken of as a occasioned – as a discov-
    ered topic would thereby ahh (e3.0) would be dired to be – to –
    to pulling together the logical properties of occasioned maps
    and to erh discovered topics as ahmmm as the ahh – as the –
    the big – as the achievement – as

286   the thing that we're looking to lay out alright;
289 JO: mmmhuh
292 HG: .hh ((clearing throat)) ummmm
294 (75.0)

300 JO: (the – it is how the ark for some uh simplest occasion for
    which uh uhmm the talk ge-gets on the way of occasioned – of
    occasioned – the talk of occasioned maps, it gets under way
    HG: Yeah well * I was going to speak about – let me tell you some
    things – that - that - provide provide motives for interest in
    occasioned maps before * we even – so that coming on occa-
    sioned maps we're coming on to something that – it doesn't –
    it's not that we happened – that I happened to be on the street
    one day and asked, / somebody how • do I get to your hou//se*
    and they drew me a map and I could see from what they drew.
311 JO: ummm
314 JO: No
317 JO: right
320 JO: quite=

Conclusion

We have seen that ethnomethodology's generational development as an
intellectual movement and form of discourse in the social sciences has
been produced through practices of semiotic intertextuality. Intellectual
genres of speaking and writing intertwine with the doing of research and
the formulation of findings in all the sciences. We have observed that

ethnomethodology's generational field of discourse is a cultural product of these historically situated conventions. Ethnomethodology has shown a unique poetic character to its conversational and written texts. This poetic structure reveals an underlying hypogram that semiotically organizes its textual constituents. I have called this hypogram the insight of radical constitution.

The poetic nature of ethnomethodology's first generational texts is transformed into intertextual systems by later generations through semiotic practices like mimesis, inventive iconization, anaphorization, and co-referencing strategies. I suggest that these practices are found in some form in all social and natural scientific movements and genres of speaking and writing. The semiotic formulating procedures are constitutive of the most objective science report and description. This indicates that description in the sciences is dependent on practical semiotic strategies for its objectivity. Objectivity and analyzability are anchored in historically constructed fields of discourse.

Chapter Four
Discovering Imaginable Futures: Ethnomethodology's Work of Referencing

It is by reference to the adequate recognizability of detail, including place names, that one is in this sense a member, and those who do not share such recognition are "strangers."
Schegloff (1972:93)

Any work of art, once accomplished, exists as a meaningful entity independent of the personal life of its creator.
Alfred Schutz (1951, "Making Music Together: A Study in Social Relationship," p.169)

What you provide for are the varieties of ways of looking and thinking. That is what the import of "member" is. It has to do with recognition procedures, not with loyalties.
Garfinkel (Hill and Crittenden 1968:121)

This chapter examines how ethnomethodologists assemble their disciplinary field through practices of textual referencing. I suggest that ethnomethodology's historical facticity as a field of discourse is an assemblage of temporal sign-producing work. Scientific disciplines typically produce knowledge that is embedded in the social context of practitioners' everyday communicational skills and representational styles.

I shall investigate one element of the ethnomethodological movement's historical working context: how researchers have textually referenced their membership in ethnomethodology's domain of knowledge and how this referencing work is constitutive of ethnomethodology's social origination as a historical discipline.

Various methods of investigating scientific group formation such as analysis of communicative networks and quantitative citation analysis offer preliminary representations of the general structure of disciplinary organization. I suggest that an examination of a discipline's organizational micropractices in both the textual and interactive domains will offer advances toward understanding how disciplinary knowledge is produced.

Citation analysis of ethnomethodology

Several studies of emerging scientific specialties have been conducted using the methods of citation analysis (cf. Cozzens 1978; Cole 1975; Cole, Cole, and Deitrich 1978, and Garfield, Malin, and Small 1978) use factor analysis of reference citation data in intellectual groups to "map" the "fine structure" of disciplinary clusters. Clusters of citations to central articles are considered a form of science indicator pointing to the problems communities of scientists regard highly important and relevant.

Hopkins (1984:33-53) has analyzed the cocitation patterns of ethnomethodology across a decade. She uses factors analysis to test Mullins's findings concerning the future life of ethnomethodology as a theory group. Data on cocitation patterns from 1972 to 1976 and 1977 to 1981 leads Hopkins to observe that "although ethnomethodology remains a minority group in sociology there is no evidence in the data analyzed here that it is either dying out or becoming increasingly alienated from the mainstream of the discipline (Hopkins 1984:51). Her findings show that between 1977 and 1981 ethnomethodology's cocitations actually increased 24%, compared to a 17% increase of citations in another sociological theory group, the new causal theorists (cf. Mullins 1972: 213-249) consisting of such sociologists as Blalock, Blau, Coleman, and Stinchcombe.

Hopkin's cocitation accounts can be used to examine the numerical contours of the ethnomethodological movement's presence as a collaborative subspecialty recognized within the sociological discipline.

Figure 4-1 is a multidimensional scaling map of the ethnomethodological movement's citation patterns. This mapping device displays the central location of Garfinkel and Cicourel as ethnomethodology's intellectual leaders as well as ethnomethodology's existence as a distinct subspecialty. Hopkins was unable to describe or label the axes in terms of topical areas and concluded that "further examination of the cited literature would be necessary" (1984:51).

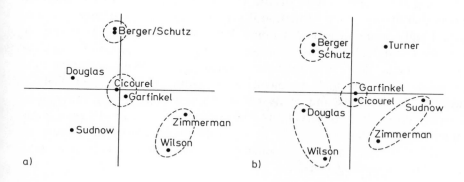

Figure 4-1 Multidimensional scaling map (MDSCAL) of ethnomethodology's primary citation clusters.
Reprinted from Hopkins (1984:50)

Communicational practices and theory group formation

Mullins (1973:19) has described a general communicational model for following the evolution of informal networks of scientists into organized subdisciplines. His model utilizes cocitation patterns, programmatic group texts, formations of organized research and training centers, and prospects for future viability within established scientific disciplines. In his study of ethnomethodology as a theory group he outlines ethnomethodology's stages of growth as a subdiscipline within sociology up to the year 1972. Mullins makes the statement that the future of ethnomethodology as a theory group is dependent on what stage of growth and cohesion as a movement it has achieved by 1982, and whether or not the successful generation of Ph.D. students has been accomplished (Mullins 1973:205).

Mullins alludes to the fact that communicational practices are the key to a theory group's evolution and growth as a movement. Like Kuhn (1970), who utilizes a historical analysis of paradigm shifts as ideas are accepted and rejected when research groups achieve "gestalt shifts" regarding their perceptions of the topics they are analyzing, Mullins shows that theory group formation is a function of group members' intellectual and communicational patterns that develop in stages. I expand on Mullins's and Kuhn's theses of theory group development to include an analysis of the group members' various collectivity practices that assemble the intellectual movement from within the movement itself. I base my perceptions and analyses of ethnomethodology's movement practices on my own observations and experiences as a fourth generation student trained directly in and by the ethnomethodological movement from 1976 to 1987 and on a sociosemiotic methodology that treats text production as signing work.

Referencing practices as production

An analysis of an intellectual movement's referencing practices requires more than an analysis of numerical cocitation patterns. In their work as writers and readers, ethnomethodologists regularly employ the American Sociological Association's (ASA) textual conventions in ways that do more work than merely identifying literary sources. Ethnomethodologists use traditional ways of referencing to signal, to index, and to create their own cohesion as an intellectual movement, enterprise, and program.

Ethnomethodologists' technical work of referencing generally represents the American Sociological Association's normative standards for "successful copy" and the "format of references in a text" (see Figure 4-2). While ethnomethodologists traditionally adhere to the textual form determined by the ASA (except in the case of Garfinkel's (1967a) "nonbook" that violated conventional ASA language uses), most ethnomethodologists interject a nontraditional context.

Social scientific citation practices

Anthropologists, sociologists, and psychologists share a distinctive citation format. Parish (1981:10-20) has outlined several citation practices common to the field. Generally, social scientists document the use of other people's work—the sources of ideas or data used in a paper—by placing citations in the text of the paper or written inquiry. Documentation, for the normal purposes of the sociological discipline, means providing bibliographic references to sources. A citation is a bibliographic reference to a specific source - a book, an article, or other source of information. An in-text citation simply means placing citations in the text of the paper, instead of in the footnotes. In-text citations have become approved methods of citations for the sociological profession. Context footnotes discuss issues and details that are pertinent but not a necessary or direct part of the exposition or argument of the paper.

These disciplinary practices normally do the work of assembling texts in a socially approved way. Manuals for writing such as Parish (1981), Williams (1981), and Strunk and White (1959) refer to sociological members' use of "common knowledge" for deciding when and what to cite.

> You must document, by giving a citation, each and every case where you use someone else's ideas or information, except where it is reasonable to assume that the information or ideas are "common *knowledge*" in the field in which you are writing. (Parish 1981:14)

Discipline-approved writing manuals and guides routinely refer to common-sense features of disciplinary members' knowledge as assumed grounds for making documentary decisions (Garfinkel 1962). What they don't do is make clear how a discipline's "common knowledge" is assembled by these very citation practices and other literary conventions.

Citation and referencing formats and other literary and rhetorical practices are creatively used by disciplinary members in hidden ways. Writing manuals never seem to move past the purely (and merely) normative and technical guidelines into the hidden and artistic domain where references and footnotes poetically speak in double-entendres, and carefully written prosaic language bears connotations only the truly receptive beholder can understand.

Notice to Contributors

The maximum length of an *ASR* paper is typically ten (10) printed pages or thirty (30) typed manuscript pages including space for tables, figures and references. Due to space limitations, we must request contributors to conform to this norm as closely as possible.

To permit anonymity in the review of manuscripts, keep identifying material out of the manuscript. Attach a cover page giving authorship, institutional affiliation and acknowledgments, and provide only the title as identification on the manuscript and abstract.

ASA Multiple Submissions Policy: Submission of a manuscript to a professional journal clearly implies commitment to publish in that journal. The competition for journal space requires a great deal of time and effort on the part of editorial readers whose main compensation for this service is the opportunity to read papers prior to publication and the gratification associated with discharge of professional obligation. For these reasons, *the American Sociological Association regards submission of a manuscript to a professional journal while that paper is under review by another journal as unacceptable.*

SUBMISSION AND PREPARATION OF MANUSCRIPTS

1. Submit three (3) copies and retain the original for your files. Copies may be Xerox, mimeograph or multilith, but not carbons.
2. Enclose a stamped self-addressed postcard for acknowledgment of manuscript receipt. Manuscripts will not be returned unless accompanied by a self-addressed envelope of appropriate size with adequate postage.
3. All copy must be typed, doublespaced (including indented material, footnotes and references) on 8½ by 11 inch white opaque paper. Lines must not exceed six (6) inches. Margins must be a minimum of one inch.
4. Include three (3) copies of an abstract of no more than 150 words.
5. Type each table on a separate page. Insert a location note at the appropriate place in the text, e.g., "Table 2 about here." Send copies, retain originals.
6. Figures must be drawn in India ink on white paper. Send copies, retain originals.
7. Clarify all symbols with notes in the margins of the manuscript. Circle these and all other explanatory notes not intended for printing.
8. Footnotes should not be placed in the body of the text. Type them (doublespaced) and attach them as a separate appendix to the text. Number them consecutively throughout the text. Footnotes are to be kept to a minimum and used only for substantive observations. Source citations are made within the text rather than in footnotes.
9. Acknowledgments, credits and grant numbers are placed on the title page with an asterisk.

REFERENCE FORMAT

A. *In the text:* All source references are to be identified at the appropriate point in the text by the last name of the author, year of publication and pagination where needed. Identify subsequent citations of the same source in the same way as the first, not using *"ibid.," "op.cit.,"* or *"loc. cit."* Examples follow:

1. If author's name is in the text, follow it with year in parentheses. [". . . Duncan (1959) . . ."]
2. If author's name is not in the text, insert, in parentheses, the last name and year, separated by a comma. [". . . (cf. Gouldner, 1963) . . ."]
3. Pagination (without "p." or "pp.") follows year of publication after a colon. [". . . Kuhn (1970:71)."]
4. Give both last names for dual authors; for more than two use "et al." in the text. When two authors have the same last name, use identifying initials in the text. For institutional authorship, supply minimum identification from the beginning of the complete citation. [". . . U.S. Bureau of the Census, 1963:117) . . ."]
5. Separate a series of references with semicolons and enclose them within a single pair of parentheses. [". . . (Burgess, 1968; Marwell et al., 1971; Cohen, 1962) . . ."]

B. *In the appendix:* List all source citations by author, and within author by year of publication, in an appendix titled "References." The reference appendix must be complete and include all references in the text. The use of "et al." is not acceptable in the appendix; list the names of all authors. (See A. 4. for text format.)
If there is more than one reference to the same author and year, distinguish them by the letters, a, b, etc. added to the year. [". . . Levy (1965a:331) . . ."] Give the publisher's name in as brief a form as is fully intelligible. For example, John A. Wiley and Sons should be "Wiley." If the cited material is unpublished, use "forthcoming" with name of journal or publisher; otherwise use "unpublished."
Use no underlining, italics or abbreviations.
Examples follows:

1. *Books:*   Jud, Gerald J., Edgar W. Mills, Jr. and Genevieve Walters Burch
            1970   Ex-Pastors. Philadelphia: Pilgrim Press.
            U.S. Bureau of the Census
            1960   Characteristics of Population. Volume 1. Washington, D.C.: U.S. Government Printing Office.
            Bernard, Claude
            [1865]   An Introduction to the Study of Experimental Medicine. Tr. Henry
            1957   Copley Greene. New York: Dover.

2. *Periodicals:*   Conger, Rand
            Forth-
            coming   "The effects of positive feedback on direction and amount of verbalization in a social setting." Pacific Sociological Review.
            Merton, Robert K.
            1963a   "The ambivalence of scientists." Bulletin of The Johns Hopkins Hospital 112:77–97.
            1963b   "Resistance to the systematic study of multiple discoveries in science." European Journal of Sociology 4:237–82.

3. *Collections:*   Davie, M.
            1938   "The pattern of urban growth." Pp. 133–61 in G. Murdock (ed.), Studies in the Science of Society. New Haven: Yale University Press.

See recent issues for further examples.   **Revised 1975 ASR**

Figure 4-2 American Sociological Association's Guidelines for Journal Contributors.

Transformations of normative practice

Standard, ordinary, and normative literary practices are transformed by intellectual movements' members into new poetic forms that create a tradition that is self-replicating. Semiotic traditions with uniquely specific idiolects (Eco 1976: 270), actants (Greimas 1976: 98), and secondary modeling systems (Ivanov 1969) are assembled through observable and analyzable practices of writing, reading, speaking, acting, and imagining.

The ethnomethodological movement has built itself by assembling its written texts polythetically, that is, by carefully detailed, narratively step-by-step, textual experiences that creatively, artistically, and poetically utilize specific literary practices and formats to produce its unique identity and contribution as an intelligible intellectual collectivity and program. Writing members have done this through hidden, yet nonetheless specifiable, interactive, and temporal devices of semiotic creation and invention.

Referencing as a collective semiotic device

The act of referring to each other in intertextual discourse is a work that members of intellectual movements carry out by means of collectively composed "indexical devices" (cf. Eco 1976:163; Sacks and Schegloff 1974). These indexical devices that accomplish the work of referencing in texts and conversation are situationally constructed mechanisms. These are explicit or implicit practices whereby the writers or speakers make two or more semantic properties or codes coincide to produce an index or a pointing to a feature that connotes a shared underlying pattern of intertextuality and a participation in a larger underlying code.

Other intellectual movements use referencing strategies as well to situationally construct an intertextual paradigm. Natural science groups utilize referencing as persuasion (Gilbert 1977). But ethnomethodology is unique in this use of collective referencing because of the state of the professional sociological context in which it has been done. The reluctance and refusal of the *American Journal of Sociology*, the *Ameri-*

can Sociological Review, and other "standard" sociological journals to publish ethnomethodological articles has provided the incentive for the movement to devise alternative methods of referencing, of private circulation of unpublished work, and of building their enterprise into a semblance of a professional specialty.

For example, ethnomethodological referring work can be seen in Lynch, Livingston, and Garfinkel's (1983:206) statement regarding their program of ethnomethodological studies of natural science:

> The specific studies discussed here address natural science work as incarnate practices of doing laboratory experiments in introductory chemistry (cf. Schrecker 1980), achieving the "followability" of a mathematical proof (Livingston 1978, 1982), reading "state of the art" research materials (Morrison 1980, 1981), producing an orderly series of observatory runs which compose "the interior course of a discovery (Garfinkel et al. 1981), and assembling displays of electron-microscopic photographs. (Lynch 1979, 1982a)

The authors can be observed as following the ethnomethodological code of assembled icons and referencing specific words for the readers. These words are referenced by the practice of inclusion by quotation marks ("followability," "state of the art"). The referenced key words are themselves stylistically created indexical devices that point to elements of the code that were either originated or specially formulated by the ethnomethodologist named in parentheses (e.g., (Livingston)) but that nevertheless display both a retrospective allegiance to original ethnomethodological codes and icons and a license for prospective use by readers. Thus, this form of referential work acts as an "isomorphism" (Greimas and Courtés 1982:163), or the created identity between two or more structures that connect different semantic planes or levels. In this instance, the isomorphism consists of the accomplished coincidence between the past and the future ethnomethodological code.

On another level, the author's referencing work is visible in their conscious construction of an intertextual or dialogical (cf. Todorov 1984) program of studies. This work is accomplished through the practices of textual signaturizing and dating. Thus, the various ethnomethodological studies cited as "(Lynch 1979, 1982a)" are used by the authors as a "document" (Garfinkel 1967a:76-78) of the existence of a larger underlying program of studies of which they are each a part as an intertextual member. In social scientific conventions, this lends an air of respectability to the enterprise and displays that the studies are not disparate and unconnected musings or ruminations, but are in fact parts of a larger, underlying, scientifically legitimate whole.

Also, the choice of ethnomethodological language apparent in this excerpt was chosen by the authors, artistically as well as scientifically, to display the very perceptual competence its codes embody. For example, the ethnomethodological insight of "radical assemblage" or "radical constitution" can be seen emphasized in the word icons:

> doing experiments
> achieving followability
> reading materials
> producing series
> composing discovery
> assembling displays

One can observe the fundamental structure of all ethnomethodological insight and discovery displayed in its sentence structure and wordly locutions: the composition of a cultural object by artful practices of cultural work.

The practices of prolepsis and analepsis

As discussed elsewhere in this work, ethnomethodology can be observed to assemble its identity as a coherent collectivity and an intellectual movement through its practices of prolepsis and analepsis. Prolepsis is the temporal ordering of its future identity through present practices that construct an index to future and forthcoming cultural productions as if those productions were, in fact, existing now. That is, future formulated collective publications are made to stand as present documents of both present and future unity of the movement's programs. For example, in the same article by Lynch, Livingston, and Garfinkel (1983:230), "Temporal Order in Laboratory Work," Lynch et al. say in the first footnote:

> For purposes of this discussion, "ethnomethodological studies of work" will mean work in the natural sciences and will include studies cited in this chapter authored by Burns, Garfinkel, Livingston, Lynch, Morrison, Schrecker, and Wieder. These studies evolved in reference to one another and, of course, in reference to a larger community of ethnomethodological studies in the United States, Canada, and Europe. Studies by these authors have been

published together in *A Manual for the Study of Naturally Organized Ordinary Activities* edited by Harold Garfinkel (1982a, b, c, d). The issues discussed in this chapter are topics with common origins and communal development in these collections.

As well as construing a collectivity membership list for investigators doing ethnomethodological studies of science work, the authors use another indexing device to document the ethnomethodological community's livelihood: the "already published" collections of work with "common origins and communal development."

The author's announcement of availability of such a published collection coincides with the reader's work of reception. The coincidence forms a "signed object" (Garfinkel 1985a) or a "semiotic object" (Greimas and Courtés 1982:216-217) that exists in a manner relative to the writers' and to the readers' treatment of these "ideas as signs" (Eco 1976:165-167). A constructed underlying, coherent, collective ethnomethodological structure with institutionalized features serves then as a scheme for future interpretation for the readers and for the writers (e.g., When I first read this reference I experienced new hope for the future of ethnomethodological studies).

As a matter of fact, only one volume of the collection of ethnomethodological studies referred to here (Garfinkel 1986) has yet to materialize as an incarnate production. Although referenced in a number of other ethnomethodological works since 1982 (cf. Lynch 1982a; Livingston 1983; Heritage 1984d, 1987) ... audiences continue to wait, as well as to project a future, for these volumes that have been announced but not yet published.

In this instance, we can inspect an ethnomethodological practice whereby members of the movement or the program construed, composed, and consulted future institutionalized features of their own collectivity as a present scheme of interpretation and action. These proleptic practices make specific reference to the organized community as a future body of knowledge existing in the present. For all practical purposes, this temporal ordering of the movement's own professionally presented features serves as a warrant or as grounds for managing their present affairs as a professional, publishing group enterprise.

Ethnomethodological prolepsis and praxis

Ethnomethodological prolepsis and historicalization can be witnessed in Garfinkel's preface to *Studies in Ethnomethodology*. Here Garfinkel specifies in a "membership list" those ethnomethodologists who had at that time achieved full member status in the sense of "doing ethnomethodological studies" (a practice he uses in his earlier and later works up to the present, cf. Garfinkel 1967a, 1987; Garfinkel and Sacks 1970; Garfinkel, Lynch, and Livingston 1981). He follows this with a practice of announcing the published, forthcoming, and unpublished ethnomethodological corpus that produces in the writings and reading a sense of the organized intellectual movement. Garfinkel wrote:

> Over the past ten years a group of increasing size has been doing ethnomethodological studies as day to day concerns: Egon Bittner, Aaron V. Cicourel, Lindsey Churchill, Craig MacAndrew, Michael Moerman, Edward Rose, Harvey Sacks, Emanuel Schegloff, David Sudnow, D. Lawerence Wieder, and Don Zimmerman. Harvey Sacks must be mentioned particularly because his extraordinary writings and lectures have served as critical resources.

> Through their studies methods have been made available whose use has established a *domain* of sociological phenomena: the formal properties of common sense activities as a practical organizational accomplishment. An early body of work of considerable size is now either in print or in press. This volume is part of that early corpus. *A later, very large set of materials is currently circulating prior to publication.* Findings and methods are becoming available at an *increasing rate*, and it is pointless any longer to doubt that an *immense hitherto unknown domain* of social phenomena has been uncovered. (Garfinkel 1967a:viii-xi) (Italics are mine.)

This excerpt shows Garfinkel practicing textual organizational methods that produce a sense of intellectual mystique, ("an immense, hitherto unknown domain of social phenomenon"), a delineation of collectivity membership; a sense of burgeoning intellectual movement; ("findings and methods are becoming available at increasing rate"), and a sense of a "very large set of materials" that is circulating unpublished and available to privileged members. These proleptic practices assemble the movement's special textual identity and beckon the reader to engage in a closer reading. By notationally specifying ethnomethodology's corpus of work as representative of a group engaged in a new revolutionary outlook, uncovering an unknown domain, and announcing forthcoming publications that were already available to local members, Garfinkel composed a form of narrative that generated interest in readers looking for alternatives to standard American sociology's reign of method and theory.

Garfinkel (1963, 1964a) utilizes Schutz's "et cetera" assumption or clause to refer to members' assumptions that "as events have occurred in the past, they will occur again in the future" (Garfinkel 1963:212). He points out that the et cetera clause provides members the certainty that present conditions can "be retrospectively reread to find out in light of present practical circumstances what the agreement 'really' consisted of 'in the first place' and 'all along'" (Garfinkel 1967a:47). I observe that the ethnomethodological movement's members have consistently employed the et cetera assumption with their practical professional affairs in their ordinary reliance on the movement's "seen but unnoticed" background expectations. These include ethnomethodology's literary codes, conceptual distinctive features, group oral histories, and collectively accepted way of speaking, reasoning, acting, and writing.

I perceive that a stronger temporal process is also at work in the ethnomethodological movement. This process is prolepsis, the representation or assumption of a future act or development as if it were presently existing or accomplished. Prolepsis is a strong version of Schutz's protention or prospective sense of occurrence (cf. Schutz 1964:172). I see the ethnomethodological movement using this method in the form of textual "missing whats," references to forthcoming movement publications, collectivity membership lists, programmatic tasks, and unfolding consensual vocabulary and other movement promises. This method of movement prolepsis is used by members to create an ordinary sense and certainty that present activities are in fact essentially bound to an intelligible future. Garfinkel calls the et cetera assumption "a method of discovering agreements" (Garfinkel 1967f:74). I call ethnomethodology's use of prolepsis "a method of anticipating the future."

Garfinkel succinctly described et cetera as:

> ...available as one of the mechanisms whereby potential and actual successes and windfalls, on the one hand, and the disappointments, frustrations, and failures, on the other, that persons must inevitably encounter by reasons of seeking to comply with agreements, can be managed while retaining the perceived reasonableness of actual socially organized activities. (Garfinkel 1967f:74-75)

Prolepsis is a movement mechanism whereby the collectivity's intertextual historicized agreement is practically assembled in the first place. The collective assumption of the existence of a recognizable future with presently actualizable and anticipated features is the proleptic process. Garfinkel (1967f:74) has said:

> Adeptness in the deliberate manipulation of *et cetera* considerations for the furtherance of specific advantages is an occupational talent of lawyers and is specifically taught to law school students. One should not suppose, however, that because it is a lawyer's skill, that only lawyers are skilled at it, or that only those who do so deliberately, do so at all. The method is general to the phenomenon of the society as a system of rule governed activities.

I believe that this same social adeptness holds for the proleptic methods as well. The mechanism of prolepsis gives us a glimpse "from within" of what kinds of things make up ethnomethodology's "seen but unnoticed" background of common understandings and how they are related to ethnomethodologists' creation and recognition of stable courses of interpersonal transactions.

The missing whats

Examination of ethnomethodology's textual corpus reveals a finding that a number of referenced texts have never been published. I call these objects "the missing whats." Though unpublished, I have observed that they have encouraged important collective sign-reading work by members. As active reception-producing semiotic objects, the missing whats have served ethnomethodology as promised and presently ontologized "collective actants" (Greimas and Courtés 1982:5-6) or that which is endowed with a common "form of doing" common to all the actors they subsume. These semiotic objects, published or not, effectively have been available to members as historically situated signs standing for the collective intelligibility and cogency of the group enterprise during a specific historical time and space.

As an allusion to the title of Garfinkel's colloquium at the University of California, San Diego in 1971, I have nicknamed the ethnomethodological movement's promised, forthcoming collections of work that have been retrospectively and prospectively referenced, but which have still to publicly appear, as the "missing whats." The list, culled from the movement's oeuvre, is as follows:

1. *Essays in Ethnomethodology* by Harold Garfinkel (referenced in Garfinkel 1963).

2. *Parsons's Primer* by Harold Garfinkel (referenced in Garfinkel 1963; Douglas 1970b; Weingarten, Sacks, and Schenkein 1976; Wieder 1974).

3. *Proceedings of the Conference on Ethnomethodology*, 1962 (referenced in Garfinkel 1964b).

4. *Contributions to Ethnomethodology*, edited by Harold Garfinkel and Harvey Sacks (referenced in Douglas 1970; Schegloff 1967, Garfinkel and Sacks 1970; Zimmerman and Pollner 1970; Wieder 1970; Sudnow 1972; Cicourel 1972; Garfinkel 1972; Schegloff 1972).

5. *Social Aspects of Language*: *The Organization of Sequencing in Conversation* by Harvey Sacks (Engelwood Cliffs; Prentice Hall, forthcoming, 1969) (referenced in Garfinkel and Sacks 1970; Schwartz 1971; Gumperz and Hymes 1972).

6. *The Organization of Conversation* by Harvey Sacks (referenced in Sudnow 1972; Twer 1972; Schegloff 1972).

7. *Aspects of the Sequential Organization of Conversation* by Harvey Sacks (referenced in Schegloff and Sacks 1973; Schenkein 1978a).

8. *The Collected Works of Harvey Sacks*. (New York: Academic Press) (referenced in Schenkein 1978a).

9. *Studies in the Sequential Organization of Conversation* by Harvey Sacks, Emanuel Schegloff, and Gail Jefferson (referenced in Psathas 1979).

10. *Transcripts of Unpublished Lectures*, 1967-1972 by Harvey Sacks (references highly numerous)

11. *A Manual for the Study of Naturally Organized Ordinary Activities* edited by Harold Garfinkel (3 volumes)
    Volume I: *Introduction for Novices*
    Volume II: *Ethnomethodological Studies of Work in the Discovering Sciences*
    Volume III: *Ethnomethodological Studies of Work*
(referenced in Lynch, Livingston, and Garfinkel 1983; Livingston 1983, 1986; Lynch 1985a; Heritage 1984d, 1987; Sharrock and Anderson 1986)

We shall examine in detail the phenomena of two of ethnomethodology's missing whats. The first will be Harold Garfinkel and Harvey Sacks's edited collection of ethnomethodology entitled *Contributions to Ethnomethodology* originally announced in 1970. The second will be Sacks's book on conversation analysis that has been referenced under various titles since 1969. We shall examine how practical collective sign-reading work has been done through the assembling and use of references to these missing whats and how this work builds the larger structures of the ethnomethodological movement.

Contributions to ethnomethodology

Garfinkel and Sacks first mention their forthcoming book in their article "On Formal Structures of Practical Actions" (1970:338-366). In a series of footnotes Garfinkel and Sacks delineate the forthcoming authors and articles for *Contributions to Ethnomethodology*. They announce *Contributions* in the context of declaring that irreconcilable differences exist between "constructive analysis" or professional sociology and ethnomethodology. Garfinkel and Sacks identify an ethnomethodological group of researchers by saying: "Extensive phenomena that constructive analysis has missed entirely are detailed in the ethnomethodological studies of Bittner, Churchill, Cicourel, Garfinkel, MacAndrew, Moerman, Pollner, Rose, Sacks, Schegloff, Sudnow, Wieder, and Zimmerman[6]" (Garfinkel and Sacks 1970). This list is ordered alphabetically rather than generationally.

Footnote six (6) to the previous excerpt contains references to fourteen authors and twenty-seven articles that are deemed by Garfinkel and Sacks to be truly representative of the ethnomethodological paradigm in 1970 (see Appendix 2). Five authors and articles are mentioned as being included in the forthcoming "Harold Garfinkel and Harvey Sacks, ed, *Contributions to Ethnomethodology* (Bloomington: Indiana University Press, in press)" (Garfinkel and Sacks 1970).

Ethnomethodologically, this textual practice can be understood as the movement's group management of its own identity as a "cultural object" (cf. Garfinkel 1967a: 116-185; Garfinkel, Lynch, and Livingston 1981: 137-141, cf., fn. 28). In the same way that Garfinkel's transsexual Agnes "the practical methodologist" produced her own sexuality as a "managed production" that was "accountable for all practical purposes" (Garfinkel 1967a: 180), the ethnomethodological movement produced their own identity as a theoretical paradigm. In a manner analogous to "the work" by which Garfinkel, Lynch, and Livingston's observed astronomers "locally produced" the Optically Discovered Pulsar as an astronomically analyzable "cultural object," the ethnomethodologists produced their own "local historicity" and professionally adequate appearances as a sociological movement through their own "interactionally produced, recognized, and understood" ethnomethodological "competent practices of shop talk and shop work" (Garfinkel, Lynch, and Livingston 1981: 138-139).

These practices consisted of everything interactionally required to present and sustain the occurrence of ethnomethodology as an organized and coherent research program. Of paramount importance in the professional context of American social science was the provision of textual publications for professional members. A condition for an adequate text was that it be rooted in a legitimate intellectual tradition (Gilbert 1977). Since ethnomethodology radically denied the existing professional lineages, and based most of its theory on the little understood German refugee philosophy, phenomenology (cf. Spiegelberg 1971; Hughes 1977; Coser 1985), it was forced by the constraints of the social environment to compose its own "locally produced" lineage and intellectual tradition. This entailed practical methodologies like listing of ethnomethodological "collectivity memberships" in numerous articles, the continuous creation of "forthcoming" collections of movement texts and papers, and the usage of highly indexical technical terminology. All of these practices serve to create and sustain the "recognizability" of ethnomethodology as a historically cogent and coherent research enterprise that functions in a collectivity of competent members. When one closely inspects ethnomethodology's work practices one sees a symbiotic set of historically consistent identity management procedures that accomplish ethnomethodology's identity as an intellectual enterprise and movement.

The members of the ethnomethodological enterprise can be observed coproducing the forthcoming *Contributions* as a developing cultural and semiotic object relevant to their collective interests. Schegloff referenced *Contributions* in his doctoral study (1967:261, 266). In Sudnow's (1972a) ethnomethodological collection entitled *Studies in Social Interaction*, the *Contributions* text was referenced as a forthcoming by Sudnow (1972a: vi, fn. 1), Cicourel (1972:442, fn. 32), and Schegloff (1972:117-118). In another collection of ethnomethodological articles, *Understanding Everyday Life* (Douglas 1970b), *Contributions* was referenced as forthcoming in the general bibliography (1979:343) by Zimmerman and Pollner (1970:93, fn. 36), and by Wieder (1970:128). Cicourel references *Contributions* in Dreitzel (1970b:44). *Contributions to Ethnomethodology* is referenced by Garfinkel (1972:309, fn. 2) as being "in press."

Justifying assertions

This construed cultural object, *Contributions*, has been made recogniz-able to members as providing the possibility of future ethnomethodologi-cal activity. The assembled semiotic object can be seen to serve a variety of practical uses by members. To illustrate with textual example, Garfinkel and Sacks use *Contributions* as a proleptic future object that accomplishes the work of "justifying" a present assertion. In the follow-ing footnote Garfinkel and Sacks (1970:357, fn. 26) use a forthcoming paper to be published in *Contributions* to settle a present issue:

> 26. Because we are required to learn what these practices are by consulting members, we must require of the methods that we use to locate these practices, and of the practices that such methods locate that they satisfy the same constraints. The arguments to *justify the assertion* and to show that the method we use is adequate with respect to these requirements are detailed by Harold Garfinkel, "Practices and Structures of Practical Sociological Reasoning and Methods for their Elucidation," in *Contributions to Ethnomethodology*. (Italics are mine.)

Though *Contributions to Ethnomethodology*, edited by Garfinkel and Sacks, has never been published, it has observably served the intellectual movement as a temporal indexical device.

Sacks's *The Organization of Conversation* as a missing what

A second promised book that has yet to be published is Harvey Sacks's *The Organization of Conversation*. Sacks references his forthcoming manuscript in Garfinkel and Sacks (1970:340, fn. 6). This version of the book was referenced as:

> *Social Aspects of Language: The Organization of Sequencing in Conversation.* Englewood Cliffs: Prentice Hall, Forthcoming 1969

Sacks's book on conversational studies, eagerly awaited as the pro-grammatic statement for the newly developing research domain of conversation analysis, was also referenced as forthcoming under the title

Social Aspects of Language by Schwartz (1971:290) and by Gumperz and Hymes (1972:325, 576).

With the publication of the ethnomethodological anthology (Sudnow 1972a) *Studies in Social Interaction*, we observe a further group formulation of Sacks's influence as a unique source of inspiration for ethnomethodological studies of conversation, and we observe a change in his book's title to *The Organization of Conversation*. Sudnow (1972a:vi) comments on Sacks's significance and his book:

> While graduate students working with Goffman at Berkeley, Sacks, Schegloff, Sudnow, and Turner became influenced by Garfinkel's work, introduced to his writings by Sacks. Sacks began his own research on the workings of the details of conversational activities upon his arrival at UCLA in 1963, and has come to stimulate considerable research in that area. All of those papers in the volume treating conversational structure grow out of Sacks's work. His research on conversation has hither to been available chiefly in the form of unpublished course lectures, which have been mimeographed and circulated each year since 1965. His research on the sequential structure of conversational activities *will appear shortly* in a volume nearing completion."

Sudnow adds footnote 2, which reads: "Harvey Sacks, *The Organization of Conversation*, (Prentice-Hall, in preparation)." Sacks's work on conversants' use of practices involving paired utterances such as question-answers, excuse-pardon, greetings, and conversants' use of a variety of membership categorization and recognition devices was also referenced as a forthcoming text entitled *The Organization of Conversation* by Twer (1972:452, fn. 8) and Schegloff (1972:118, 432).

In 1973, Schegloff and Sacks (1973: 289, 327) referenced Sacks's forthcoming book with the new title *Aspects of the Sequential Organization of Conversation*. They referenced it as part of their procedure of placing their present article in the context of the larger developing program of conversational studies. They said:

> This work is part of a program of work undertaken several years ago to explore the possibility of achieving a naturalistic observational discipline that could deal with the details of social action(s) rigorously, empirically, and formally."

Footnote 1 in the preceding excerpt referenced products of that effort already published or in press, including Sacks's book:

> Products of that effort already published or in press or preparation include: Jefferson (1972), Moerman (1967; 1970), Sacks (1972a, 1972b, in press), Schegloff (1968; 1972, in press) Schenkein (1972).

Sacks died in 1975 in an automobile crash in Laguna Beach, California. Since that time his unpublished lectures from 1967 to 1972 have been organized by Jefferson and used as referential material by a concentrated group of researchers who have access to them (cf. Jefferson 1978; Schenkein 1978a).

The purple-ditto phase

In 1978, Jefferson and Schenkein published a collection of various ethnomethodological articles that worked on conversational studies, *Studies in the Organization of Conversational Interaction* (Schenkein 1978a). In that volume extensive references were made to the unpublished lectures and to the unpublished Sacks manuscript by all of the authors in the volume. Each claimed and referenced membership in the lineage of Sacks's teachings. Competent membership was marked, among other things, by references to the unpublished materials. Schenkein (1978a:249) remarks that the circulation of Sacks's unpublished materials developed into an informal publication system:

> Harvey Sacks routinely taped his lectures and had them transcribed. Initially this was a way to organize his materials, but it subsequently developed into an *informal publication system:* distributing his lectures and other unpublished manuscripts free of charge to anyone who asked for them. A large collection of his transcribed lectures and other manuscripts are available and *will be published shortly.*

Such a local reproduction and circulation phase can be located and observed in many intellectual movements including ethnomethodology. A local reproduction and circulation phase refers to a period of grass-roots production, reproduction, and circulation work by members of the growing intellectual collectivity of unpublished materials usually in terms of available technology and a select circulation network. Since the creation of the printing press, this movement work phase has entailed the use of "technologies of the word" (cf. Ong 1982) to print and reproduce important texts, programmatic statements, and manifestos seen by members as being central to the group's enterprise. This phase can have different lengths of duration depending, probably most importantly, on the availability of materials, publishing outlets, the newness of the approach, and the rate of disciplinary acceptance. Nevertheless, private circulation of new work amongst a core work group is a work practice found in all phases of development. Marx and Engels are known to have produced and privately circulated large amounts of privately published materials to interested cohorts.

I refer to this work phase in the ethnomethodological movement as the "purple-ditto" phase. Early in ethnomethodology's history, in the 1950s and 1960s before the development of the current advanced photocopy technology, assorted ethnomethodological texts and lecture notes were reproduced by "ditto" machines. This process created a characteristic purple print. The reproductions have been referred to by ethnomethodologists as "the purple dittos" and included many of Garfinkel's, Sacks's and others' unpublished papers, notes, and seminar lectures, as well as students' and faculty ethnomethodologists' unpublished works. A common practice was the artful circulation of these texts among members.

The American locus of the ethnomethodological movement has had a relatively long purple-ditto phase of development that has extended up until the mid-1970s. As more anthologies and collections were published (Douglas 1970b; Sudnow 1972a; Turner 1974b), and more publishing outlets were found by members, the purple-ditto phase of the movement began a transition into a new era of visual representation, published availability, and "respectable" textual technologies. Yet, much "hard core" ethnomethodological materials continue to circulate as unpublished working manuscripts, but now they are produced and reproduced on word processors, laser printers, and advanced photocopy machines.

Similar "purple-ditto" work is being conducted now as the ethnomethodological movement spreads into new international contexts. Many current British and French ethnomethodological texts carry references to member-circulated unpublished documents such as transcriptions of Garfinkel's visiting lectures at the University of Manchester (Garfinkel 1973) and at the École des Hautes Études en Sciences Sociales (1984), unpublished lectures by Sacks (1966-1974) and unpublished papers, transcription notations, and lectures by Jefferson (1979b), Pomerantz (1981), and Schegloff (1979c). All these textual objects are evidence of members' work of building a local discipline and intellectual movement.

Referencing unpublished lectures

Schenkein in his volume references Sacks's book as *Aspects of the Sequential Organization of Conversation* and adds a new text, *The Collected Works of Harvey Sacks* (New York: Academic Press. forthcoming). This new text appeared to be Sacks's unpublished lectures.

As already mentioned, Sacks's lectures have been extensively quoted and referenced by "accessed" members in the conversational studies network. For example, Gail Jefferson (1978:220), who was Sacks's associate and "data recovery technician" at the University of California, Los Angeles and the University of California, Irvine (Jefferson 1972: 294), does the work of referencing these unpublished materials in the following way:

> In general, the occurrence of an utterance at a given moment is accountable, and a basic account is that an utterance is produced by reference to the occurrence of a prior, that is, occasioned by it (cf., e.g., Sacks, 1972b, Lecture 4 and Sacks, 1971, April 9).

Jefferson employs an intertextual practice in her explanation of her own referential procedures regarding Harvey Sacks's unpublished lectures. She says that these unpublished materials "are best treated not so much as support for an argument, but as pointers to very interesting talk" (Jefferson 1978:245, fn. 2). As in Garfinkel's case, it can be observed that reference to unpublished materials serve to "justify assertions," "support arguments," and function as "pointers." What makes these practices interesting is that they reference a temporal order that either does not exist yet, exists in the imagined future, or exists now but is unavailable for present use. In each case these practices function to create a form of movement prolepsis, the state of acting in the present temporal field as if something in the future or transcending the present phenomenal field already existed. This procedure of textual prolepsis can be understood as being fundamental and essential to ethnomethodology's collective life as a movement.

In 1979, the following year, another edited collection of conversational studies was published by George Psathas entitled *Everyday Language: Studies in Ethnomethodology* (Psathas 1979). Sacks's book was referenced in another form:

> Harvey Sacks, Emmanuel Schegloff and Gail Jefferson (forthcoming) *Studies in the Sequential Organization of Conversation*, New York: Academic Press.

Members' organizational requests

At present, in 1990, the Sacks materials are still not completely available to wider audiences. Many researchers involved in conversational studies have reported an acute need and hope for the free distribution and publication of Sacks's lectures and book. For example, Benson and Hughes (1983:vii) comment that for British ethnomethodologists this situation has been particularly difficult in attempting to transplant ethnomethodology onto British soil. They remark:

> Although the situation has changed, much of the early ethnomethodological work was only available in mimeograph form and, therefore not widely or easily accessible. To date the most serious gap is the lectures which Harvey Sacks gave through the 1960s until his tragic death in 1975... Here we can only record a general debt to his influence and hope that the lectures soon appear in published form. (1983:vii)

Sharrock and Anderson (1986a:116) make this lament about the situation in 1986 of Sacks's manuscripts and lectures:

> The unpublished lectures of Harvey Sacks were generously provided to inquirers in mimeographed form for many years, but have not yet been published nor, as far as we are aware, is there any immediate prospect of the release of even a selection. These are undoubtedly the main source for getting a proper sense of what Sacks was up to, and only the faintest idea of the quality and range of his thought can be obtained from published papers and the few lectures which have been printed in collections....

Text and transition

Transitions in intellectual membership are also signified through texts. "Defections" have occurred from the ethnomethodological movement as members have chosen new methods and directions for their research. Schismogenesis has occurred over theoretical purity or the practicalities of publishing. Ethnomethodologists have changed the focus of their sociological discourse to include other perspectives, strategies, and empirical fields. Studies of defections and the disengagement process in social movements have been discussed by sociologists such as Zald and

Ash (1966), Bittner (1968), Robbins, Anthony, and Richardson (1978), Snow (1980), and Jules-Rosette (1981a). These studies run the gamut of explanation ranging from public institutional determinations to private, subjective members' interpretations. My approach here is synthesizing "public and private" (Gusfield 1981b) dimensions of change in intellectual movements by looking at how text displays varieties of movement membership.

Aaron Cicourel has placed himself in different positions of membership within the ethnomethodological movement. Following his first collaborations with Garfinkel in 1955, Cicourel has participated in the movement in varying degrees that are signified in his texts. Cicourel's major early work, *Method and Measurement in Sociology* (1964), acknowledges Harold Garfinkel's original expositions and applications of Alfred Schutz's phenomenological philosophy as being an important source of his thought:

> My debt to Schutz's work and Garfinkel's exposition of it will be evident in the pages that follow. The present work began after my association with Garfinkel and may depart significantly from his own ideas about the same or similar topics. (Cicourel, 1964:iv)

Here Cicourel marks the influence of Garfinkel's thinking on his own thought and yet makes clear the potential for his own divergences. Cicourel has consistently produced a multifaceted membership in ethnomethodology as both a leader of the movement and as an independent thinker and researcher. This sometimes has created contradictory signs as to where Cicourel's intellectual "loyalties" lie. This particular tension between a scholar's loyalties to an intellectual movement and to his or her intellectual heterogenity is common and has been discussed by Philippe Besnard (1923:21-22) in the context of the founding of the Durkheimian school of sociology in Paris during the 1890s.

Emblems of identity

Cicourel's paper on the negotiation of status and role in everyday interaction initially written during 1964 to 1965 and subsequently republished three times provides an excellent example of how intellectual products such as texts are used as emblems of identity in intellectual schools and movements. Cicourel's changing identity within the ethnomethodological movement can be traced by following how this particular text has been managed through successive revisions, retitlings, and republications.

The text under consideration here was originally titled "Basic and Normative Rules in the Negotiation of Status and Role" (Cicourel 1970b, 1972) and then revised to "Interpretive Procedures and Normative Rules in the Negotiation of Status and Role" (1973). Cicourel wrote this text in 1964 to 1965 and presented it at an anthropological conference organized by the Institute of International Studies at the University of California, Berkeley (cf. Cicourel 1974f:7). The paper was revised three years later for inclusion in the first ethnomethodological anthology, *Studies in Social Interaction* (Sudnow 1972a). This volume was originally to have been published in 1969, but was delayed until 1972. Cicourel's text was included as an exemplar of the ethnomethodological perspective and school. The editor of the volume, David Sudnow (1972a: vi), described the paper as "an analysis of the traditional concepts of "status" and "role" in interactional inquiries from the standpoint of the ethnomethodological perspective."

Cicourel displayed his anticipation of continued participation in the movement through a footnote (fn.32) citing his forthcoming paper's ("The Acquisition of Social Structure") inclusion in the forthcoming ethnomethodological collection edited by Garfinkel and Sacks, *Contributions to Ethnomethodology*:

> Aaron V. Cicourel, "The Acquisition of Social Structure: Toward a Developmental Sociology of Language and Meaning" in H. Garfinkel and H. Sacks (eds.), *Contributions to Ethnomethodology*, Bloomington: Indiana University Press, forthcoming.

"Basic and Normative Rules" was republished in 1970 in Hans Peter Dreitzel's *Recent Sociology*, No.2 (1970:4-45). Cicourel's text was the article chosen to exemplify "the ethnomethodological paradigm." Dreitzel (1970b:3) characterized Cicourel as an ethnomethodologist saying: "Next to Harold Garfinkel, who invented the term ethnomethodology, Cicourel is the most prominent representative to this school." This version again included the footnote aligning Cicourel's future work with the forthcoming *Contributions* collection. Cicourel's (1968) *The Social Organization of Juvenile Justice* was hailed by Dreitzel (1970:3) as "the broadest empirical study yet produced by an ethnomethodologist." At this time Cicourel was situated squarely within the ethnomethodological program at the University of California, San Diego.

Signs of transition

By 1973 to 1974, Cicourel's texts show signs of his transitioning status within the ethnomethodological movement. Cicourel published *Cognitive Sociology: Language and Meaning in Social Interaction* in 1973 in England and in 1974 in the United States. This book marked a shift from using the term "ethnomethodology" to "cognitive sociology." Cicourel's growing dialogues with linguists, anthropologists, and cognitive psychologists, as well as strained relations with Garfinkel, were leading him to reformulate his work and professional identity. In his Preface (1974b: 7) he articulates himself, even more than ever before, as an eclectic user of ethnomethodological ideas rather than as purveyor of a paradigm:

> For the past eight years my interests have included a deep preoccupation with how language and meaning are constitutive of the way in which everyday social interaction is assembled and represented. I have tried to use the notion of "interpretive procedures" to articulate ideas from writers on phenomenology and ethnomethodology with work on language acquisition and use, memory and attention, or the general idea of information processing.

In *Cognitive Sociology*, Cicourel changes the title of the article most associated with ethnomethodology, the "Basic and Normative Rules," to "Interpretive Procedures and Normative Rules in the Negotiation of Status and Role" (1974:11-41). I think this can be understood as a knowledge practice that is constructive of a new shift in professional identities, especially given Cicourel's continued direction up to the present time. "Cognitive Sociology" and "discourse analysis" have replaced "ethnomethodology" as an intellectual label for his work.

His chapter on "Ethnomethodology" in *Cognitive Sociology* (1974: 99-140) also marks his shift into a new formulation of his identity as an ethnomethodologist. In this paper he refers to himself as an ethnomethodologist addressing new domains: "I have tried to discuss ethnomethodological ideas within the framework of cognition or information processing and information generation" (1974:122).

He thus paints a picture of an ethnomethodologist attempting to open new domains of interdisciplinary application while still referencing a place in the collective program ("our inquiries"):

> In recognizing that we can generate only different glosses of our experiences, the ethnomethodologist tries to understand the pitfalls of viewing indexical expressions as if they could be repaired and thus transformed into context-

free objective statement. *Our inquiries* (italics mine) therefore, cannot ignore the mundanity principle when dealing with substantive outcomes or claims about the structure of syntactic rules, the nature of information processing, the organization of perceptual and linguistic memory, or the elegance of linguistic productions. (1974:123)

Cicourel's signification of transition away from being a central spokesman for the contemporary ethnomethodological movement has continued through his present work. While his work often voices ethnomethodological principles and methods (cf. Cicourel 1980; Cicourel and Mehan 1985), he does not call his position "ethnomethodological," nor does he normally cite Garfinkel's work after 1970. Also, reflexively, Garfinkel and his co-workers have ceased including Cicourel on their published "membership lists" (cf. Lynch, Livingston, and Garfinkel 1983) and decreased their citations of Cicourel in discussions of current ethnomethodological work.

Understanding everyday life

Jack D. Douglas served ethnomethodology as both a purveyor of ethnomethodological ideas and an anthologist while maintaining a personal and critical distance from the movement. Douglas's (1967) *Social Meanings of Suicide* was an early sociological study along ethnomethodological lines that introduced many sociologists to Garfinkel's writings. Douglas was at the University of California, Los Angeles from 1964 to 1967. There he became acquainted with Garfinkel and the ethnomethodologists. Upon coming to the University of California, San Diego in 1968 to start the new sociology department at Joseph Gusfield's invitation, Douglas began editing *Understanding Everyday Life: Toward a Reconstruction of Sociological Knowledge* (1970b). This volume played a major role in the dissemination of ethnomethodology to the sociological world. It contained an introduction by Douglas and ethnomethodological articles by Thomas P. Wilson, Zimmerman and Pollner, Wieder, Cicourel, Roy Turner, Speier, Blum, and McHugh. In his Preface (1975: xi), Douglas conveys his basic alignment with the ethnomethodological positions, yet preserves his own critical distance from the movement:

The essays in this book are critical, theoretical, and empirical. Taken together, I believe they represent the best theory and research being done by those attempting to rebuild sociology. All of these essays share certain fundamental ideas about the scientific inadequacies of the conventional (absolutist) sociologies, and all of them share the fundamental ideas of phenomenological and existential sociology, though to varying degrees. But the reader will find some important differences in basic ideas and in strategies.

Douglas was interested in a reconstruction of the sociological paradigm primarily through studying everyday life situations. For him, the crucial questions were what stance shall we adopt toward everyday life and what methods of analysis shall we use (1970:13). Douglas saw in ethnomethodology at that time a stance and method proceeding from phenomenological and existential philosophical lines, to which he himself was drawn. Ethnomethodology provided a key tool to discovering members' meanings and relating them to situational action.

In his introductory chapter to *Understanding Everyday Life* (1970:32-33), though, Douglas was clear to point out the differences he perceived between "linguistic ethnomethodologists" and "situational ethnomethodologists." By linguistic ethnomethodology, he was referring to Harvey Sacks's, David Sudnow's, and their many co-workers' meticulous analyses of the concrete verbal statements made by individuals. Douglas felt then and still does, that ethnomethodological conversational analysis concentrated too heavily on externally observable data. By contrast, the "situational" ethnomethodologists emphasized and discovered the deep situational meanings of things to members. Garfinkel, Zimmerman, Pollner, Wieder, and Cicourel epitomized this ethnomethodological approach that Douglas deemed "a more creative understanding of everyday life" (1973:33).

Douglas placed himself in critical alignment with the ethnomethodological movement at that time in the sense that he saw his work and ethnomethodological work moving closely in the same direction. He referred to his conception of a new sociology of everyday life as an "enterprise" (1973:34) that included the ethnomethodological strategies. He used a collaborative "we" when speaking of this new enterprise:

> Given the early stage of the work it seems inevitable that *we* shall have great problems in making *our* work objective and shall, consequently, have to make use of our own practically unexplained common-sense understandings of everyday life. (Italics are mine.).

Nevertheless, he allowed himself the license to criticize Garfinkel's approaches as overfocusing on highly routinized settings and over-concentrating on contextual effects, thereby sometimes distorting the realities of everyday life. Douglas argued for the existence of a tension between situational and nonsituational factors (1970a:39-40).

Douglas recognized ethnomethodology's development as a sociological movement in the following footnote to the text of his introduction (1970a:32, fn.39):

> Much of my own understanding of these ideas has necessarily come from numerous personal communications with most of the participants in the (erstwhile) underground movement of *California sociology.*

Douglas's Existential Sociology

Douglas's *Existential Sociology* (1977) marked his move away from his collaboration with the ethnomethodological movement. After a series of methodological and personal differences with the movement (Douglas, personal communication), Douglas differentiated his own work more strongly from ethnomethodology. In *Existential Sociology* (1977:10-11), he describes his work into the "unexpressed forms of human experience" as "moving beyond" ethnomethodology and Husserl's phenomenology in which it was enmeshed. Douglas now described ethnomethodology as having taken an unfortunate linguistic turn that resulted in a loss of depth in the movement:

> Ethnomethodologists came to focus their work on symbolic, common sensi-cally rational, overtly expressed, linguistic accounts. As a result, the enterprise became a narrow one, with little or nothing to say, by self-imposed definition, about the experiences that concern human beings most in their everyday lives. (1977:10)

Douglas builds his *Existential Sociology* on a critique of ethno-methodology's assumptions, methods, and outcomes. No longer is there a common enterprise encompassing the new sociologies of everyday life. Instead Douglas signifies his break with the ethnomethodological movement through textual statements such as this:

Although they started with a critique of positivist methods and absolutist theories of social rules and social order, they (the ethnomethodologists) have ended by reinstituting those methods in a new form of the transcendental ego and the assumption of the rationally accounted for social order. (1977:57)

Thus, we can observe Douglas's intellectual path as taking a trajectory of first being influenced by the ethnomethodological movement through physical and intellectual proximity (University of California, Los Angeles, 1964-1967); then functioning as an allied, though not full, member and purveyor of the movement's ideas through his role as "outside" anthologizer; and finally his breaking away from the movement and establishing a position as a critic of many of ethnomethodology's ideas and strategies.

A narrative analysis of temporal referencing strategies

Ethnomethodology's production of forthcoming texts and "missing whats" is reflexively productive of its own identity as a historicized discipline. "Missing-what" referencing practices are temporal indexical expressions. These indexical expressions accomplish members' group recognition, identification, and spatiotemporal localization through a proleptic and analeptic mechanism. Prolepsis, the evoking of a future state as if it exists in the present, especially characterizes ethnomethodology's semiotic work and historical presence.

I suggest that an intellectual movement's social organization as an intellectual field of discourse *and* its corpus of texts and knowledge be analyzed as temporally indexical narratives. We have seen thus far that ethnomethodology's working social identifiability is intertwined with its local semiotic practices of referencing, intertextuality, and the production of sociolectal communication. I suggest that an examination of how ethnomethodologists order the temporal narrative of their written texts will illuminate properties of how they organize their social presence as a field.

Gerard Genette (1980:35-85) has analyzed writers' ordering of narrative time. He has developed a narratology capable of analyzing writers' temporal ordering of anachronic narratives or narratives that rely on references to both past and future events to sustain the overall temporal framework of the story. He has designated prolepsis as "any narrative maneuver that consists of narrating or evoking in advance an event that will take place later" and analepsis as "an evocation after the fact of an event that took place earlier than the point in the story where we are at any given moment" (1980:40). Both prolepses and analepses are constructed by writers or speakers to illuminate the reader's or hearer's present by creating indexical linkages to either the past or future.

The following ethnomethodological textual excerpt is an anachronic narrative segment that employs both analepsis and prolepsis as time-oriented indexical signs: (excerpt from Lynch, Livingston, and Garfinkel 1982:230).

Textual Excerpt 4-1

01 "While the joint authors assisted in the exposition and while
02 that exposition relies on our joint studies and
03 on the studies and seminars of Harold Garfinkel,
04 it does not reflect a common understanding of
05 ethnomethodology. Instead, the authors urge that
06 the chapter be read as a docent's tour and thereby
07 a bowdlerization done in the interest of
08 not swamping the reader with the technical re-
09 finements that would be required were it the
10 chapter's task to make ethnomethodological studies
11 available to the research practitioner as the
12 constraints of a current situation of inquiry.
13 Their collaboration, therefore, does not con-
14 stitute an endorsement of the chapter as an adequate
15 introduction to ethnomethodological studies. For
16 this, readers are referred to *A Manual for the*
17 *Study of Naturally Organized Ordinary Activities*
18 edited by Harold Garfinkel (forthcoming).

The narrative ordering of this fragment displays a temporally ordered openness of past, present, and future interpretations of ethnomethodological studies. The text first references its origins in "joint studies" and participation in the seminars of Garfinkel. The text writers are fourth generation students working with Garfinkel. The narrative uses analepsis to establish its present state as "not reflecting a common understanding of ethnomethodology" (lines 4 and 5), thereby producing an "open version" of ethnomethodology's field. In Genette's terms, it is a repeating homodiegetic analepsis, or an analepis that is internal to the narrative and retraces its own path (Genette 190:54). This semiotic work creates a paralipsis or a narrative gap by the creation of a conscious omission of some of the constitutent elements needed to complete or close the narrative. This omission or "bowdlerization done in the interest of not swamping the reader"(lines 7 and 8) produces the situation of leaving open the narrative's, and the ethnomethodological movement's, "adequate introduction" (lines 14 and 15) or paradigmatic statement, thereby requiring a retrospective or prospective filling-in. In correspondence with ethnomethodology's observed patterns of using proleptic practices, the narrative gap or paralipsis is partially completed through a proleptic reference to the forthcoming *Manual for the Study of Naturally Organized Ordinary Activities*. The *Manual* as a proleptic object is presently utilized by the ethnomethodologists as an "adequate introduction," thereby allowing the reformed ethnomethodological program and field to remain open to further formations while simultaneously projecting a collaborative professional future. This narrative writing structure corresponds to other evidence that ethnomethodology is presently composed by an open organizational structure encouraging "multiplicities of studies" and generational neoethnomethodologies. Thus, Schegloff's and Sacks's (1973) second generation work on conversational order entitled *"Opening Up Closings"* is an apt description of ethnomethodology's present movement toward establishing a rigorous disciplinary program with organizationally open characteristics, as opposed to earlier organizational practices that tended to narrow and isolate the ethnomethodological movement's field of discourse.

A figure can be constructed that models the temporal order of ethnomethodological referencing practices as well as its social organizing work. Figure 4-3 is an adaptation proposed by Danow (1986:253) of Roland Barthes's "organigram" or a diagram "capable of integrating backtracking and forward leaps" of a text's narrative structure (Barthes 1974b:269).

First, the existence of a referencable ethnomethodological program is exhibited in the previous text through the mentioning of an "adequate" introduction to ethnomethodological studies. The narrative makes a "leap" backwards to a historicized collaborative existence through analepsis, "adequate" functioning as an indexical sign of the movement's contiguity. Next, the future is brought into the present interpretation of

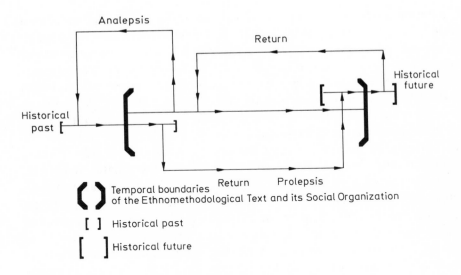

Figure 4-3 Temporal analysis of narrative structure of textual excerpt 4-1

the group's facticity through the introduction of the reference to the forthcoming *Manual.* This "leap forward" is prolepsis, the "evoking in advance of an event that will take place later," and is collectively accomplished through both writers' and readers' participation in indexical sign-making activities. Not only does the future text exist in proleptic time, but the movement's "adequate introduction" is projected there, real enough "for-all-practical-purposes" of the present exposition.

Reference to the past through analepsis is accomplished by an ellipsis or a decided break from the primary plane of collective narrative of the present plot, creating indexical signs to the movement's history. The reader is returned to the present via the future, which is also situated beyond the temporal parameters of the immediate narrative. This "return" rejoins the first narrative by filling-in and making comprehensible what was begun and referenced in the past by referring to what is to occur in the future. The forthcoming *Manual* will make intelligible the past ethnomethodological program of studies for which the present text is not yet an adequate introduction. The past is referred to in order to make comprehensible what is to occur in the future, which is significant to today. Reading the organigram, one can recognize the isotopy between ethnomethodology's temporal strategies and orderings on both the textual and social organizational levels.

Collective prolepsis as a social mode of experiencing time

The ethnomethodological movement employs specialized practices of prolepsis as a social mode of experiencing historical time. Prolepsis itself can be traced as a historical phenomenon occurring in other social movements. For example, Mannheim (1936) has devoted considerable attention to the examination of socially and politically differentiated modes of experiencing historical time (cf. Mannheim 1936:225-6, 244-6, 253-4). In particular, he identifies the practice of prolepsis, or achieving the "virtual existence of the future in the present," as having been a core element in nineteenth century Marxist revolutionary socialist-communism.

The manner or mode in which an intellectual collectivity practically conceives of and experiences historical time displays an important mechanism of its inner organization. Ethnomethodology's movement time-sense bears a very interesting historical resemblance to that employed by the socialist-communist movement of Marx and Engels. In contrast to the nineteenth-century conservative movement in Europe, given voice by the writings of Hegel, and idealizing the past (cf. White 1973), socialist-communist mentality worked to achieve practical everyday experience in which immediacy and presentness of a conceived future became an actual present experience (cf. Mannheim 1936: 229-246).

An excerpt by J. Révai (1920), a communist movement member, is cited by Mannheim (1936:246, fn.44) as a working example of the communists' tendency to manage their affairs through a time-sense that practically actualized the existence of the group's future in the present. The following excerpt by Révai concerns the communists' management of "tactics" or "strategies" (this suggests a comparison to ethnomethodology's interest in the same topics). Révai asserts:

> The present really exists only by virtue of the fact that the past and future exist, the present is the form of the unnecessary past and the unreal future. Tactics are the future appearing as the present . (Das Problem der Taktik 1920:1676).

This idea and its application can be compared by the reader to the ethnomethodological movement's conception of the phenomenological "retrospective-prospective sense of occurrence" (cf. Schutz 1962a) and to its own practical "tactics" in using "the future appearing as the present" (in the aforementioned examples of the proleptic formulation and actualization of membership collectivity listings, forthcoming collections of the movement's articles, programmatic statements, etc.) as a device and a member's method to strategically manage the movement's professional identity.

Prolepsis as a historicized time-sense is a core element in the ethnomethodological movement's achievement of a qualitative differentiation of time and a historical identity. We observe this practice in the ethnomethodological movement's managing of its present professional affairs in terms of future collective realizations. To the degree that the movement tactically relies on a retrospective consultation with its past, it is more proper to speak of an analeptic-proleptic time-sense.

Prolepsis as an ethnomethodological activity transcends mere "waiting" for "prospective" elements to fill-in or clarify present ambiguity (cf. Schutz 1962a:xx). Prolepsis is the imaginative and practical presumption of future projections as virtually existing now, in this present.

Ethnomethodology's practitioners create a multidimensional time-sense in which they imaginatively locate themselves in an identifiable intellectual movement and enterprise. Members produce an imaginative third dimension of time that is practically experienced in the present.

Ethnomethodology's members counterbalance their prolepsis with a retrospective weighing of the past. The past is treated with "indifference" (cf. Garfinkel and Sacks 1970:xx) and is actually used only for heuristic purposes. Heuristic readings of philosophic texts supply only analytic starting points for ethnomethodologists and never conventions (cf. Garfinkel 1967a:ix; Garfinkel and Sacks 1970:345; Garfinkel in Hill and Crittenden 1968:10; Lynch, Livingston, and Garfinkel 1983:231, fn.6).

The revolutionary nature of the ethnomethodological movement has been constructed through a practical union of an indifferent sense of the past and a living presentness of the future. This ordinary union makes it possible to create a historical time-sense of more than one dimension. Instead of an experience of time as a mere traversing from a stable past point to a certain fixed future, the ethnomethodological movement has construed its lived temporality as an active, present, polysemy identifiably retrospective, yet consciously becoming the new.

Conclusion

In this chapter, I have begun to specify how ethnomethodology has developed its disciplinary field through referencing practices. We have observed that intellectual fields of discourse create objects of knowledge and that these knowledge objects are signed with temporally ordered self-references. The references do practical and semiotic labor toward the establishment of a domain of discourse as a historically intelligible program.

We have examined ethnomethodology's unique forms of temporally referenced texts as analeptic-proleptic objects that have been produced by its different generations of researchers. These cultural productions have included "missing whats" or referenced forthcoming published works that have displayed long gaps or ellipses between their announcement and their appearance; references to past works to create ethnomethodological lineages; membership collectivity lists that form representations of the emerging discipline, privately circulated and referenced texts that constitute a "purple-ditto phase" in the group's development; and carefully located and referenced slogans or code words that display membership in an intellectual program as well as accomplish descriptive work.

I have suggested that the textual and social organization of intellectual disciplines can be conceptualized as practical narratives. I have recommended a form of narrative analysis that examines narrative organization through its temporal ordering strategies. I have referred to these temporal strategies as prolepsis and analepsis, and we have observed that they act as temporal indexical signs during members' writing and reading work.

This chapter raises issues regarding the practical production of scientific disciplines. Rabinow (1986:253) has suggested that "the micropractices of the academy might well do with some scrutiny." Ethnomethodology has recommended that the discovering sciences be investigated as sciences of practical action before all else (Garfinkel, Lynch, and Livingston 1981). Knorr-Cetina (1982) has shown that constructivist studies of natural and social science disciplines yield useful findings regarding the manufacture of knowledge. My study has suggested that scientific knowledge and description are socially organized and embedded within group devised ways of speaking, writing, and formulating. These collective signifying processes compose a discipline's distinctive identifying features. The development of these organizational practices over time through successive generations of researchers assembles a discipline's historical coherency, cogency, and creativity. A discipline's public and private representations are a composite of a multiplicity of collectively devised and generationally developed research styles and representational voices.

Ethnomethodology as a distinctive field of discourse serves as a case study of how knowledge is collectively assembled, intellectually circulated, and historically communicated to progressively widening circles of reception. The following chapters will examine in more detail how the ethnomethodological movement's fact production is interactively produced through practitioners' use of documentary procedures (Chapter 5), how ethnomethodology's semantic field is intellectually appropriated and generationally developed in a folklore manner (Chapter 6), and how ethnomethodology's corpus of knowledge has been communicated and established in new international contexts of reception and application (Chapter 7).

Chapter Five
Local Production and Documentary Verification

It is how you accomplish the rational demonstration of your inquiries that is of
interest as a matter of study.
Garfinkel (Hill and Crittenden 1968:194)

You have to have a willingness not only to deal with vague matters, but you
also have to have this willingness to undertake the analysis in the face of an
environment which, by and large, at least tends to be uneasy or maybe worse.
Garfinkel (Hill and Crittenden 1968:136)

We cannot guarantee our students, for example, that from the beginning, in the
department line, that they will know what kind of course of training they can
take. We cannot tell them ... that they are on the right track to a career the end
of which they can see with considerable assurance.
Garfinkel (Hill and Crittenden 1968:136)

Introduction

This chapter examines how intellectual disciplines constitute themselves
in daily interactions between practitioners. Ethnomethodology provides
us with a case of a social science discipline that began as a radical intellectual movement and has attempted to maintain its radical stance in the
face of its institutionalization. We shall observe that the various generations of ethnomethodologists accomplish this maintenance of original
radicality through the daily interactive process of "the documentary
method of interpretation."

I shall investigate how local fact production is embedded in members' production of a recognizable and accountable sense of an intellectual movement's continued presence as a professional discipline. This interactive achievement of a disciplinary field of discourse will be described and conceptualized using a hybridized style of presentation. I have chosen to adapt Garfinkel's (1967a:76-103) analysis of the documentary method of interpretation in professional fact finding to examine the ethnomethodological movement. This adaptation will provide an occasion in which (1) to display some of the intricacies of classic ethnomethodological analysis, (2) to reflexively apply ethnomethodological analysis to its own process of fact production, and (3) to suggest a preliminary "semio-ethnomethodological" conceptualization and visual representation of the process.

Ethnomethodological fact production

Garfinkel's own analysis of lay and professional sociological "fact finding" (1967:76-103) as a situated accomplishment that employs the member's use of the "documentary method of interpretation" can be reflexively folded back and applied to ethnomethodological fact production as well. Garfinkel has never claimed that ethnomethodology is anything but a practical enterprise directed to discovering society's taken-for-granted structures (cf. Garfinkel in Hill and Crittenden 1968: 200-203). Thus, ethnomethodology itself is a topic of interest in its own right.

In his article "Common Sense Knowledge of Social Structures: The Documentary Method of Interpretation in Lay and Professional Fact Finding" (1967:76-103) Garfinkel describes "common culture" as "the socially sanctioned grounds of inference and action that people use in their everyday affairs and that they assume others use in the same way" (p.76). This operational definition of common culture has a recognizable fit with what many ethnomethodologists, in calling themselves ethnomethodologists, actually do as they assemble their semantic and professional field through interpersonal interaction and reasoning.

Garfinkel goes on to say that such "socially sanctioned facts of social life consist of descriptions from the point of view of the collectivity member's interests in the management of his or her practical affairs" (p.78). According to Garfinkel, the discovery of common culture consists of "the discovery from within the society by the social scientist of the existence of common sense knowledge of social structures" (p.78). In investigating ethnomethodology's assemblage of its collective corpus of knowledge, I agree with the perspective of Garfinkel that such a study should be "directed to a description of the work whereby decisions of meaning and fact are managed, and how a body of factual knowledge of social structures is assembled in common-sense situations of choice" (p.73).

Garfinkel continues his analysis of professional sociological inquiry's construction of "fact, hypothesis, conjecture, fancy, and the rest" (p.77) in such a way that certainly leaves open the possibility of this same analysis reflexively turned back upon ethnomethodology itself:

> Nevertheless, a *body of knowledge* of social structures is somehow assembled. Somehow, *decisions* of meaning, facts, method, and causal textures are made. How, in the course of the inquiry during which such decisions must be made, does this occur? (p.78)

Garfinkel specifies "the documentary method of interpretation" of Karl Mannheim as providing "an approximate description" (p.78) of what many sociological researchers, lay, professional, and ethnomethodological actually do. Garfinkel (p.78) quotes Mannheim's own definition of the documentary method as involving the search for "...an identical homologous pattern underlying a vast variety of totally different realizations of meaning" (Mannheim 1952a:57). According to Garfinkel:

> The method consists of treating an actual appearance as "the document of," as "pointing to," as "standing on behalf of" a *presupposed* underlying pattern. Not only is the underlying pattern derived from its individual documentary evidences, but the individual documentary evidences, in their turn, are *interpreted* on the basis of "what is known" about the underlying pattern. *Each is used to elaborate the other.* (p.78)

In Garfinkel's case, the method is observable in the everyday necessity of a member recognizing what a person is talking about, given that he or she does not say exactly what he or she means. It is also observable to be in use when one recognizes common occurrences and objects such as mailmen, friendly gestures, and promises. For Garfinkel, the method is also recognizable in decisions of such sociologically analyzed occurrences of events such as "Goffman's strategies for the management of impressions, Erickson's identity crisis, Riesman's types of conformity, Parsons's value systems, Malinowski's magical practices, Bales's inter-action counts, Merton's types of deviance, Lazarsfeld's latent structure of attitudes, and the U.S. Census occupational categories" (p.78-79).

In our case, the documentary method of interpretation will be observ-able in ethnomethodologists' decisions to view themselves as an identifi-able discipline. We will see how members of the ethnomethodological movement regularly employ the documentary method when they use the identifiable features of themselves as a field to practically manage their professional affairs.

What is ethnomethodological work?

Garfinkel asks:

> How is it done by an investigator that from replies to a questionnaire he finds the respondent's "attitude;" that via interviews with office personnel he reports their "bureaucratically organized activities;" that by consulting crimes known to the police he estimates the parameters of "real crime"? *What is the work* whereby an investigator sets the observed occurrence and the intended occurrence into correspondence of meaning, such that the investigator finds it reasonable to treat witnessed actual appearances as evidences of the event he means to be studying? (p.79)

Garfinkel says that to answer these questions it is necessary "to detail the work of the documentary procedure" (p.79). He designed "a demon-stration" of the documentary method to "exaggerate the features of this method in use and to catch the work of 'fact production' in flight" (p.79).

Garfinkel's demonstration was designed to display the method in the context of a contrived psychotherapeutic conference between an experimenter, disguised as an "advisor", and "subjects" whose personal problems were given random and predetermined "yes" or "no" answers by the advisor in response to their self-formulated questions regarding their present condition and situation. Garfinkel described how the subjects did the work of treating the random answers as documentary evidence or documents of the motivated underlying pattern of the counselor's presumed analysis and legitimacy.

We can examine the ethnomethodological movement's own use of the documentary method as a practice of assembling its collective identity as a movement and as a coherent form of thought through similar "situated reasoning." We can look at the ethnomethodological movement's work of documenting its own "institutionalized features" of itself as a collectivity. This self-documenting work functions as the ethnomethodological movement's scheme of interpretation for future professional decisions.

I now ask, How is it done by an investigator that by researching, reading, and writing he considers himself an ethnomethodologist? What is the work by which the ethnomethodologist sets the observed occurrence (a naturally organized setting) and the intended occurrence (an ethnomethodological descriptive text) into a correspondence of meaning, such that she finds it reasonable to treat witnessed actual appearances as evidences of the phenomena the ethnomethodologist means to be examining and describing?

Interestingly enough, Garfinkel's analysis of the invented counselor-subject exchange provides us with an intriguing point of departure for this analysis of ethnomethodologists' work of documenting themselves into a sociological movement and discipline. Garfinkel follows his transcripts of the interactive exchanges with a list of scenic practices that describe how the demonstration's subjects did the work of treating random answers of "yes" or "no" as documents of a motivated underlying pattern. His list of practices are empirical specifications and generalizations on both Schutz's and Mannheim's observations of the phenomenological structures of everyday reciprocal exchanges (cf. Schutz 1962a, 1964, 1966; Mannheim 1952a, op. cit.).

A heuristic transformation

We can take Garfinkel's list of documenting practices that are scenic to his setting, and transform them so that they fit our scenic setting of ethnomethodologists at work. We can make visible various interpretive, literary, interactive, and reasoning practices that I observe in ethnomethodology's variety of cultural productions in the form of members' discourse, texts, and actions. We can begin to sociosemiotically and ethnomethodologically specify what ethnomethodological members actually do. We shall observe that a core element of this work is a member's search for a common underlying pattern that members recognize and reference as ethnomethodology.

For our heuristic purposes in this analysis, Garfinkel's findings in this study can be summarized according to our specific relevances. Garfinkel's (1967a:89-94) list of advisor -subject documentary practices include

1. Getting through the exchange (or the communicated interaction).
2. Answers were perceived as "answers to questions."
3. There were no preprogrammed questions: the next question was motivated by the retrospective-prospective possibilities of the present situation that were altered by each exchange.
4. Some answers were in search of questions.
5. Work was done to handle incomplete, inappropriate, and contradictory answers.
6. There was a "search" for and a perception of an underlying pattern.
7. Answers were assigned to a scenic source.
8. The vagueness of every present situation of further and future possibilities remained unchanged in light of the clarification furnished by the exchange of questions and answers.
9. In their capacity as members, subjects consulted institutionalized features of the collectivity as a scheme of interpretation.
10. Deciding a warrant for action or a grounds for managing their affairs was identical with assigning the answers a perceivedly "normalized" sense of occurrence.
11. Perceivedly normalized values and sense were not so much assigned as managed.

The key to utilizing these "found" documenting practices for examining the ethnomethodological movement is to make the following transformation onto Garfinkel's original experiment and setting:

1. Transform the counselor into cohorts in the ethnomethodological movement who perform the work of giving legitimation or bestowing membership (e.g., the first generation, generational cohorts, research networks, collective actants, etc.).
2. Transform the subject into new generations of ethnomethodological practitioners searching for reasonable grounds to consider themselves members of ethnomethodology's documentable program of studies.
3. Transform the questions into research, texts, conversation, and actions formulated by the new generations in the context of the ethnomethodological community of work.

4. Transform the answers into cohorts' and members' local accountability, or the collectivity's membership recognition work (i.e., "this is or is not ethnomethodology," or "he or she is or is not doing ethnomethodological work").

In using this scheme for examining ethnomethodology's own interactive work and reasoning of documenting itself as a members' discipline, it is important to remember Garfinkel's (1967a:94) own caveat regarding correlation between the use of the documentary method and membership:

> It is misleading, therefore, to think of the documentary method as a procedure whereby propositions are accorded membership in the scientific corpus. Rather the documentary method developed the advise ("the answer") so as to be *continually "membershipping it."*

An analysis of ethnomethodological documentary practices

In typical situations that I have observed as a fourth generation participant where an ethnomethodological member or a person referencing competence in the field, or member-to-be presents his or her productions of work (in the form of discourse, texts, or actions) to mentors or other members in the movement (at seminars, conferences, meetings etc.) and waits for a response regarding the suitability of the work as far as ethnomethodological practical purposes are concerned, the following documentary work can be typicalized and seen as revealed in the empirically imaginable exchanges. (These generalized interactions represent empirical composites taken from my participation in everyday interaction amongst ethnomethodologists and are used to reveal formal structures of interaction. I expect that readers of this exposition will recognize having been in similar situations of documentary evidence work, whether it be in submitting materials to colleagues, submitting texts to a prospective journal for publication, or presenting one's corpus of work to a tenure or review committee.)

Interactive judgments of a member's work in light of practically established, yet seemingly normative, ethnomethodological standards are used by members as a document of an existing underlying pattern called "ethnomethodology" instituted within the historical context of the ethnomethodological movement. Members presume that criticism and ceremonies that do the work of determining the normal status of their membership "come along with the turf" of their producing text and work in a collective enterprise.

1. Members getting through the details of ethnomethodology's local production.

Members of ethnomethodology's "community" of studies routinely get through interactive processes of formulating discourse, producing texts, and accomplishing actions, all of which are recognizable to other members as "truly ethnomethodological." (Nonmembers also have a way of recognizing the "ethnomethodological" character of the community's products.) The "local production" by members of ethnomethodological cultural and semiotic objects (discourse, texts, actions) is itself a matter of complex interpretive work and documentary assembly. We shall more fully examine this local production in the sections that follow.

An intellectual movement's or a discipline's local production involves, at its core, a documentary method employed by members that treats members' productions as evidence and documents of a commonly assumed, underlying competent membership in a technical, esoteric, and natural language community.

Competent membership and/or the local production of cultural objects can become troublesome if the member fails to produce an adequate object of discourse, text, or action. Usually, especially in the case of novices, members look to the particulars of the local productions, and not to the membership status, as having trouble or failing. But consistent failure to produce an object considered adequate by other members is cause for postponement of the full process of "membershipping" within the movement.

The member may decide that the conditions for local production are not compatible with himself or herself, and decide to effectuate a withdrawal from the collectivity. Practices of disengagement, in which the documentary method is used to document an alien or incompatible collectivity, can be used by members at any time during the course of their membership.

2. Ethnomethodological discourse is routinely perceived by members as motivated by common concerns.

Typically, members hear other members' discourse and read other members' texts as being carefully reasoned "answers" to the collectivity's "questions." In other words, members perceptively assume, and assume that their mentors and colleagues assume it of them, that discussion and textual communications are motivated by a common concern for building a recognizable program of studies. In actualizing this assumption, members have a way of seeing directly into what the mentor and colleague "had in mind." For example, they hear "in a glance" what the other ethnomethodologist is talking about, even though the member is saying it in so many words, i.e., actively using an indexical vocabulary specific to the collectivity. Therefore, the member can know what the other ethnomethodologist means, even though not knowing exactly what the member actually said or how the member said it in so many words.

For example, in the Purdue Symposium on Ethnomethodology (Hill and Crittenden 1968) Garfinkel gives a three-page expansion of Harvey Sacks's one-and-a-quarter-page statement concerning the difference between ethnomethodology and ethnosociology. Garfinkel begins with, "Maybe I can summarize" (1968:14). The idea here is that ethnomethodologist members hear and see a common indexical concern in each other's discursive productions.

3. There are no preprogrammed members' products; the next cultural production is motivated by the retrospective-prospective possibilities of the present situation that are altered by each actual exchange between members.

As Garfinkel (in Hill and Crittenden 1968:252) has said: "Our interests are not in preinvention, and in fact are not directed to strict methodical search." According to ethnomethodological etiquette and protocol, all kinds of methods and textual strategies are usable insofar as they make "the features of practical reasoning available for inspection (Garfinkel, 1968)." Present methods of investigation, discursive and literary strategies, and rhetorics are assumed by all to alter the sense of previous methods, findings, and exchanges between members.

Over the course of exchanges between members of the ethnomethodological movement, a working assumption seems to operate that there is a solution or a discovery or a "big prize" (Garfinkel, personal communication) to be obtained from ethnomethodological studies and research. If the "big prize" or discovery is not immediately and presently obvious, then its identity or "whatness" or "quiddity" (Garfinkel, Lynch, and Livingston 1981) is waiting to be determined by the active search of ethnomethodologists (e.g., "Findings and methods are becoming available at an increasing rate, and it is pointless any longer to doubt that an immense, hitherto unknown domain of social phenomena has been uncovered" (Garfinkel 1967a:ix)). A part of this active search procedure is to continue asking "ethnomethodological" questions and formulating ethnomethodological texts to find out what other members have in mind.

Much effort and work by ethnomethodology's members are devoted to searching for meanings that are intended but are not expressly evident from immediate interpersonal interactions. For instance, upon receiving textual materials from a member, a mentor or colleague typically looks for and reads the text in such a way as to discover the necessary and relevant ethnomethodological iconic signs, indexing devices, and referencing work that stand as documents pointing to the necessary underlying insights that make the text "truly ethnomethodological." If these members' sign productions are not apparently evident and adequately ordered, work on the part of the reading member may or may not be done to "wait" for future and prospective work to fulfill the promise perhaps evidenced there. The reader may actually fill in perceived "tokens" (Garfinkel 1967e:4; Eco 1967:178-180) or indices of future potential on behalf of the writing member in order to preserve the document as standing on behalf of legitimate movement work.

The member delivering the text, on the other hand, actually looks for evidence that the reading member's commentaries point to judgments that can be interpreted as favorable to the continuation and maintenance of the assumed and underlying reciprocally constructed program. If cohorts' support for continuation is not forthcoming, the member either reinterprets the commentary to maintain "membershipping," begins repair work, or stops the work altogether by withdrawal from the perceived program of ethnomethodology or the intellectual field of discourse.

Present exchanges between members motivate the succeeding set of possibilities from among which the next research topic, problem, or article is selected. Future problems to be researched, solved, and written about are products of members' reflections upon previous courses of conversations, commentaries, writings and reviews, and the presupposed underlying general problem. "The ethnomethodological topic" comes to possess features that each actual exchange with fellow members (and nonmembers) documents and extends.

Assembling ethnomethodology's research topics

The underlying ethnomethodological research "problem," in essence, "the how society gets put together; the how it is getting done; the how to do it; the social structures of everyday activities... the how persons, as parties to ordinary arrangements, use the features of the arrangements to make for members the visibly organized characteristics happen" (Garfinkel in Hill and Crittenden 1968:12), is elaborated in its identifiable features as a direct function of the communicational exchange between competent members.

The group sense of their underlying problem to be researched and solved is progressively accommodated to each member's formulation in a text or conversation or action. The members' evaluations and responses motivate the production of fresh new aspects of the collectivity's underlying problem, especially by new generations of students and intellectual practitioners.

In this typicalized (cf. Schutz 1962b:7), but nonetheless empirically based, example of situations in which communicational exchanges are taking place and being made to happen between members of an intellectual community of studies, the underlying pattern of the group's own identity and existence as professional intellectual discipline is elaborated and compounded by members over the series of exchanges. This recognized and documented underlying pattern of group identity is accommodated to each present member's discourse, texts, and actions to maintain the "course of group inquiry," to elaborate what had "really been discovered" previously, and to motivate new possibilities and inquiries as "emerging" features of the movement's underlying, and constitutive, research problems.

4. Phenomenological and ethnomethodological answers in search of questions.

Many ethnomethodological texts by members of the movement provide a practical and contextual "working out" of certain essential insights regarding properties of social order either originally discovered by ethnomethodology or else heuristically borrowed from phenomenological philosophy and other sources as points of departure. Many "classic" texts are valued for the directives they provide as to how ethnomethodologists locate an "occasioned corpus of a setting's features" (Zimmerman and Pollner 1970:94-99) "in and as" the work of assembling a particular social context. A heuristic borrowing from past phenomenological and ethnomethodological discoveries as a way of beginning a new inquiry is referred to as "shedding new light" on the past. The same discovered or "found" principle has been used to provide a basis for examining a number of empirical settings. For example, Garfinkel (1952, 1959a, 1960, 1962, 1963, 1964a) and Cicourel (1964, 1968, 1973b) both "mined" the phenomenological vein of Alfred Schutz's social phenomenology and used Schutz's insights as springboards for ethnomethodological investigations and demonstrations (cf. Garfinkel 1963).

Garfinkel (1967a:37) said regarding his use of Schutz's phenomenology:

> Schutz's fundamental works make it possible to *pursue further* the *tasks* of *clarifying* their nature and operation, of *relating* them to the processes of connected actions, and *assigning* them their place in an empirically imaginable society.

Cicourel (1974f:33) references his use of Schutz as:

> In presenting my discussion I will lean heavily on the writings of Alfred Schutz because I believe he has made more explicit the ingredients of social interaction also discussed by James, Mead, Baldwin, and others.

Instances of this working out of earlier insights by second and third generation ethnomethodological work can be observed first in Beryl Bellman's investigation of Fala Kpelle's practices of secrecy, *Village of Curers and Assassins* (1975). Bellman makes visible his own accepted (and inherited) analytic background expectancies:

> In analyzing the acquired materials I accepted the *guidelines* of the phenomenological and ethnomethodological approaches...I wish to express my gratitude to Professor Harold Garfinkel who has been my mentor for the

past several years, much more whose research and reflections have served as *the basis* for my own work. (p.8)

And again Bellman (1975:16) says:

> In this study we shall deal specifically with secrecy as used by the Fala Kpelle of Sucromu Liberia. To accomplish this we shall *accept* the *programmatic methodological advice* given by Garfinkel, Sacks, Sudnow, Moerman, Cicourel, Schegloff, and other ethnomethodologists to see social facts as "an ongoing accomplishment" of the concerted activities of the daily life, with the ordinary, artful ways that accomplishment is being for members known, used, and taken for granted.

Wieder (1974a:5) acknowledges his foundational orientations that he developed into his study of "the convict code" used by residents at the East Los Angeles Halfway House, as originating in Garfinkel's earlier explorations:

> I wish to *acknowledge* my considerable intellectual debt to Professor Harold Garfinkel. Those familiar with his work will recognize in the present research the full extent of this indebtedness. At UCLA, he served as the chairman of my doctoral committee which served as the basis of this book.

Another third generation student of ethnomethodology, Bennetta Jules-Rosette (1975b:48), states her ethnomethodological point of departure in her investigation and empirical working out of the details of African Apostolic membership through her development of Garfinkel's expansion of Mannheim's "documentary method of interpretation":

> In spite of these problems, I readily made generalizations about Apostolic ritual and *used a documentary method* or pattern-finding approach for describing members' experiences.

She references Garfinkel's use of Mannheim's documentary method in her footnote 16:

> Garfinkel (1959:57-59) provides a more detailed statement of the documentary method of pattern-finding in commonsense and scientific inquiry.

Mehan and Wood (1975b:31) provide us with an example of members' reliance on subsequent reinterpretations of a philosophic base in light of new, personal discoveries:

> Many ethnomethodologists rely on Schutz's concept of reality (e.g., Schutz 1962a, 1964, 1966). I review a portion of this work in Chapter 5. My use of "reality" contrasts with Schutz's view... My view of realities is different. I

do not wish to call one or another reality paramount. It is my contention that every reality is equally real.... My concept of reality, then, has more in common with Wittgenstein (1953) than with Schutz.

This same "search" procedure for studiable topics related to original philosophical insights can be observed in the fourth generation text by Lynch, Livingston, and Garfinkel (1982:231-232, fn.6):

> Our focus upon the irreducible embodiment of the activities exhibiting worldly "reasoning" has a *programmatic origin* in the writings of Merleau-Ponty (1962, 1968) and Heidegger (1962, 1967) ...
>
> It has remained for ethnomethodological studies *to use the incipient topicality* of these expressions to discover and work out the locally produced phenomena of order in and as the ordinary society in identifying features of empirically situated activities. This task has been more than a matter of "applying them to facts" since it has necessitated that the tradition of philosophizing which gave Heidegger and Merleau-Ponty a continued point of departure and return, *be abandoned in a search for* the witnessable varieties of practical actions which animate *topics* of order as non-literary accomplishments.

Reinterpretations of past policies

Over the course of typical interactional exchanges between members of the ethnomethodological movement, a current research finding, idea, or text can provide for reinterpretation of past policies. In the reinterpretation, the past policy becomes reformulated in light of the new discovery. This reformulating activity employs a retrospective revision "in light of new evidence." The previous sense that it had is accommodated to fit new formulations.

An example of this retrospective revising work that involves the ethnomethodological movement's program and collection of research policies can be observed in a recent series of texts that are the result of the collaborative research into natural science activity conducted by Garfinkel, Michael Lynch, and Eric Livingston. An early ethnomethodological "policy" was a research emphasis on members' production of accounts and the reflexive nature of socially situated accounting practices (cf. Garfinkel 1967a; Garfinkel and Sacks 1970; Cicourel 1973b; Wieder 1974a; Zimmerman 1969). Garfinkel (1967e:1) formulated ethnomethodology as the study of the phenomenon that the activities whereby members produce and manage settings of organized everyday affairs are identical with members' procedures for making those settings "accountable", and that the "'reflexive or incarnate' character of accounting practices and accounts makes up the crux of that (the ethnomethodological) recommendation."

Footnoting conceptual progress

In 1981, in their article "The Work of a Discovering Science Construed with Materials from the Optically Discovered Pulsar," Garfinkel, Lynch, and Livingston (1981:131-158) made a powerful comment in a footnote that provided grounds for member practitioners to reevaluate, and ultimately redirect, the working foundations of the ethnomethodological policy toward the study of accounts and accounting practices involved in settings of technical work. In their study of the astronomers John Cocke, Michael Disney, Don Taylor, and Robert McCallister's discovery of the optical pulsar at Steward Observatory on January 16, 1969, Garfinkel, et al., used a tape recording that had recorded the scientists' conversation during the series of observations in which the pulsar was found, to analyze the details of the scientific group's "night's work" (Garfinkel et al. 1981:131-132).

The "night's work" of the astronomers consisted of making the optically discovered pulsar "a radically contingent practical object" (1981:155) that came to assume "natural" properties that could be reproduced and demonstrated to others. Garfinkel et al. (1981:156) say:

> By contrast, the parties in the excerpts below discussed the optically discovered pulsar as something-in-hand, available for further elaboration and analysis, and essentially finished. In these instances, Cocke and Disney speak of IT as an object with analyzable properties which, over the course of subsequent runs, will "fill it out." Instead of being an *"object-not-yet,"* it is now referenced as a perspectival *object* with yet to be "found" and measured properties of luminosity, pulse amplitude, exact frequency, and exact location.

Garfinkel, et al., continue pointing to the phenomenon that it is the practitioners' (and here we could also say the ethnomethodological practitioners') work that *achieves* the local "observability" (1981:139) of the "cultural object," that is the independent Gallilean pulsar. This locally observable and "demonstrable" (1981:139) object is not a physical or a natural object, but a cultural object assembled by the skilled practices of local members who make their object "naturally accountable," that is, "attach it to nature" (1981:142; cf. Kuhn 1970).

Therefore, Garfinkel, Lynch, and Livingston move the earlier programmatic emphasis on the production of accounts to a present emphasis on the "embodied" production of cultural objects that in part depends on natural accountability for its "discovered properties" (1981:141-142). Garfinkel, et al., make this reinterpretation of policy clear in footnote 28 (1981:141, fn.28):

> A first and incorrect understanding takes the Independent Gallilean Pulsar (IGP) to be an account. The IGP can be construed as an achieved account of their night's work, an account that rendered their work in the astronomically adequate terms of the IGP, and is found in the published paper. *But taking the IGP as an account can be irreparably distracting.* It needs to be remembered that Cocke and Disney don't discover an account of the pulsar; they discover an astronomically demonstrable pulsar. *Correctly understood*, the IGP is an object, not a "physical" or "natural" object. In the entirety of its technical astronomical properties, IGP is a cultural object. That object, the IGP, is not an account.

In a later paper Lynch, Livingston, and Garfinkel (1983:220-221) report on their discovery with the astronomers, and in the reporting retrospectively assemble a member's account and reformulation of ethnomethodology's prior policies and "received history" concerning the place of studying accounts. This retrospective assembly or reinterpretation of former methods or research emphases is made "on the basis of results in hand" (1983:221):

> A research policy from early ethnomethodological studies which has been taken up in ethnographic studies of the sciences is that accounts of scientific activities, that is, "inscriptions," factual statements, documentary records, and published reports, become disengaged from the actual course of scientific activity that produced them. The ethnomethodological studies of work discussed here have *gone beyond the earlier emphasis* on the production of accounts of order (or of a sense of social structure) and have *proceeded* to examine the embodied production of *social objects*.

Thus, we observe here an instance of progress in the ethnomethodological field of research built by and composed through member's practices of retrospective reformulation based on new results in hand. These practices of retrospective reformulation are dependent on the members' "situated" and "local" competences with their own forms of practical ethnomethodological research methodology. They constitute the basis of what is referred to by members as ethnomethodology's "received topics" and "received history."

5. Ethnomethodologists' handling of incomplete, inappropriate and contradictory productions.

Where other members' productions (either members' discourse, texts, or deeds) are unsatisfying or incomplete, the members are willing to wait for later productions in order to decide the sense of the previous one. Normally, no text or member's approval or disapproval is so inappropriate or so contradictory that the ethnomethodological "community of cobelievers" (Garfinkel 1967a:96) will not wait for future clarification. If such a practice of waiting for prospective evidence to "fill in" earlier communications and textual exchanges is not maintained successfully by members, the chances are high that a rupture and disengagement between members can occur, and has occurred in the past.

To summarize thus far, we have examined several formal features of typical interactive situations or exchanges between ethnomethodologists where a presentation and interpretation of a group "intertext" (a discourse, written text, or action) is concerned. We have accomplished this through an inventive transformation and reflexive application of Garfinkel's own generalized features found in interactants' usage of the documentary method of interpretation. We are in actuality examining members' use of common sense situations of choice (Garfinkel 1967a: 100) in the production of sociological, and ethnomethodological, findings. These everyday interpretive practices are eternally present, though rarely made explicit, in all situations of popular, scientific, and ethnomethodological knowledge production.

We next turn to the final collection of documentary practices that ethnomethodologists and members of other intellectual movements use to assemble their membership, their literary products, and their domains of knowledge.

6. Ethnomethodologists' "search" for and perception of patterns.

It frequently occurs that when investigators, in whatever domain, perform an action and produce a product they actually find the purpose of the action and product only after a retrospective search and review of his or her already accomplished activities. Insofar as any decision made regarding the status of the action and the product is assigned by the work of this retrospective search and review, the outcome of such situations can be said to occur before the actual "decision." For sociologists, and ethnomethodologists, "such situations occur with dramatic frequency at the time the journal article is being written" (Garfinkel, 1967a:98). Thus, considerations of formal methodology are usually a function of such common-sense situations of choice, decision making, and post-hoc interpretation.

Ethnomethodology is in no way exempt from this everyday, ultimately practical, search for pattern, even after the action is taken and the product is produced. As has already been shown, both ethnomethodology's "received history" as well as its "corpus" of texts, methods, and statused members are fact productions and "cultural objects" that are dependent on members' own common-sense assemblages. Scholars search for coherence and cogency in the face of a swarm of happenings, findings, and consequences.

7. Members' productions are assigned a local source within the larger body of assumed ethnomethodological knowledge.

Members routinely see and hear other cohort's responses to their productions as coming from not only the individual cohort, but also emerging from the larger assumed body of collective knowledge and fact. Thus, any "bit" of members' discourse is actively rendered into a location within the larger corpus of knowledge. This piece of discourse is often elaborated in terms of its perceived scenic location in the collectivity's larger body of fact.

This phenomenon has been described by Polanyi (1966) as the proximal and distal components of tacit knowledge. Members' discourse functions with an oracular character, in this situation, that is dependent on the cohort's active work to scenically locate the oracular utterance within a larger scheme of personal meaning and interpretation. As Polanyi has so succinctly put it, "Thought can live only on grounds which we adopt in the service of a reality to which we submit" (1966:xi).

For example, when some ethnomethodologists hear that I am "constituting an explanendum from members' folk taxonomies," they immediately place this statement both in its context of my immediate performance here, as well as in Garfinkel's larger programmatic statements of ethnomethodological inquiry given in his University of California, Los Angeles lectures in the 1960s and 1970s. Thus a spatial and temporal "fit" is carried out by the knowledgeable member that locates any utterance in the larger body of ethnomethodological tacit knowledge.

8. The "essential vagueness" of every present situation in regards to members' future possibilities.

In the course of a scholar's research and investigations, he or she is likely to find himself or herself addressing a series of technical and practical present situations whose future solutions and outcomes and courses of action are characteristically vague or even unknown. In other words, very often a future, practical course of action relating to research is only sketchily specifiable prior to undertaking the action. That is, for practical methodologists, and ethnomethodologists, the "operational future" is characteristically vague or unknown. The research problem at hand is, in fact, essentially vague and is modified, elaborated, extended, if not created, by the fact and manner of being acted upon.

Very often, it occurs in the actual course of ethnomethodological inquiry that the questions and answers that will have been asked and answered under the various ways of ethnomethodological specification and analysis, given the practical contingencies and exigencies that must be accommodated in doing the work of ethnomethodological inquiry, remain sketchy and open to common-sense decisions even up to the point of composing the results of the inquiry for publication. Very often, the alternative paths to actualize a proposed ethnomethodological prospectus and topical program are characteristically incoherent, unelaborated, and indefinite.

Frequently, it occurs in ethnomethodological investigations that only in the course of actually manipulating a present research situation, and as a function of that actual manipulation, does the nature of the ethno-methodologists' proposed and future state of inquiry become clarified. Thus, the goal of many ethnomethodologists' actually taking action toward a research goal with features he or she does not see clearly in any present moment becomes the practical filling-in of a hunch or a premeditated projection.

In the same way that Garfinkel, et al.'s (1981) observed astronomers, Cocke and Disney, produce a cultural object, the optically discovered pulsar, through a developing sequence of actions beginning with a vague display on an oscilloscopic screen and becoming a "locally embedded phenomena whose 'properties' are come upon in a developing sequence of locally pointed noticings" (1981:149), ethnomethodologists extract and evolve their observations, findings, discoveries, and published reports. Ethnomethodological inquiries, no less than sociological and natural scientific inquiries, are situated inquiries composed of practical actions, practical theorizing, and competent practices that serve to "fill out" the essential vagueness of its own investigations. Ethno-methodology's texts emerge as the temporally developed and achieved demonstration of ethnomethodology's situated inquiries.

The Sacksian IT

Ethnomethodology's inquiries that produce the ethnomethodological text are witnessably vague. Ethnomethodological work and textual objects share the properties of a "Sacksian IT. " A Sacksian IT (cf. Garfinkel et al. 1981:157-158) is a usage developed from Sacks's unpublished lectures and his work on referencing (Sacks 1972a, c; Sacks and Schegloff 1974). The IT refers to the conversational object that is produced and oriented to as understood before its meaning has been clearly defined (cf. Eco 1976: 152-156). Garfinkel et al. (op. cit.), used the notion of the "vague IT" to describe the properties of the astronomers' achieved object (the pulsar).

I am using it here to specify how ethnomethodologists actually produce, recognize, and understand their own researchable and textual objects before these objects have definiteness of sense or reference. This is a proleptic practice of letting an expected goal dwell in the present as grounds for action.

This practice and feature of vague meaning interpretation is observable in conversation analysts' use and dependence upon an assumption that the correspondence between what was actually said in natural conversation and what was recorded, transcribed, and analyzed by them are essentially the same phenomena. Both the writer engaged in conversation analysis and the reader of the written transcript and report must engage in interpretive work that assumes that the "received" transcript, as a cultural product, is from the start in some way understandable and will progressively become actually correspondent with the naturally occurring context from where it was taken. This assumed correspondence is rendered actual in terms of the accepted traditions of conversation analysis methods. These methods and literary devices are themselves dependent on the analysts' and readers' common-sense understandings and labor to transform a priorly vague semiotic product into a clarified and sensible object that is understandably analyzed repeatedly over time.

9. In their capacity as members ethnomethodologists consult institutionalized features of their collectivity as a scheme of interpretation.

Members presuppose known-in-common features of the ethnomethodological collectivity as an intertextual body of common-sense knowledge subscribed to by all "real" members. Members regularly draw upon these presupposed patterns when they assign to other members' discourse, texts, and membership a status as documentary evidence of the distinctive normative features of the ethnomethodological movement and enterprise.

Documentary evidences and the collectivity features of ethnomethodology are referred to constantly between members. Members make specific references to ethnomethodology's own social structures whenever they decide the "ethnomethodological grounds" or warranted character of another's discourse, texts, and membership. These members' references to ethnomethodological social structures, whether by footnotes, conversational allusions, collectivity membership statusing, or referred to grounds for hiring, are treated by members as actually or potentially known in common among all "true" ethnomethodologists.

Ethnomethodological social structures consist of the normative features of the social-intellectual movement seen from within by the members. These normative features are perceived by the member as being in some way definitive of his or her membership in the various ethnomethodological collectivities that are referred to (e.g., conversation analysis, studies of work, cognitive sociology, educational, medical, religious studies, etc.).

Members give very little indication of the explicit collectivity rules for deciding competent membership, prior to the occasions of use of such measurements and standards. Members appear regularly to be disinterested in what the definitive normative social structures are to which their routine interpretations make reference, except when actually engaged in boundary work. The rules for documenting these definitive normative orders seem to come to play only after a set of normative features has been motivated as relevant to an ethnomethodologist's interpretive labor. This member's relevancy is a direct function of the fact that the ethnomethodologists' activities of interpretation and documentation are actually in practice and under way.

Examples of ethnomethodologists' capacity to invoke, consult, and refer to institutionalized features of their collectivity (even when they deny that ethnomethodology is an institutionalized collectivity) as a common-sense scheme of practical interpretation and action are empirically apparent. Members of the movement accomplish this when they depend upon community-developed methods to provide a current situation of inquiry with warranted grounds of demonstration, inference, and action. They accomplish this when they utilize a collectively formulated language to provide a collectively produced reasoned discourse. Members accomplish this when they practically refer to themselves in all matters of professional status, comparison, competition, hiring, publishing, and scientific discovery. Ethnomethodologists accomplish this whenever they do group boundary work of any kind, for they achieve this in "institutionally established terms as matters of competent membership in a technical, esoteric, but nonetheless natural language community" (Garfinkel et al. 1981:141).

10. Members' justification of a discourse, text, or deed's "ethnomethodological" character.

Through the work of constant retrospective-prospective review, ethno-methodologists justify their cultural production's sense and sanctionable status. Members' justifications of discourse, texts, and actions are the grounds for managing their practical and professional affairs. Sanction-able sense and status consists for ethnomethodologists of the compatibil-ity with the collectivity's normative orders of social structures presumed by members to be actually subscribed to and known between one another as competent member ethnomethodologists.

The members' task of deciding the warranted or "ethnomethodologi-cal" character of whatever has been said, written, or done by another is identical to the members' task of assigning values to any discourse, text, or deed. These members' values are (1) its status as a typical instance of an ethnomethodological class of objects and events, (2) its likelihood of occurrence, (3) its comparability with past and future events relevant to the practical purposes of the ethnomethodological movement, (4) the causal conditions of its occurrence, (5) its usefulness or technical efficacy in a set of relationships of local production, (6) its necessity according to the natural and moral order of the ethnomethodological movement.

Ethnomethodological members assign to discourse, texts, and deeds these values while using the normative and institutionalized features of the ethnomethodological movement as a scheme of interpretation. The members' task of deciding whether or not someone else's productions are indeed "truly" ethnomethodological is identical with the task of assigning to these cultural objects their ethnomethodologically perceived normal values and cultural character.

Members' contextual practice of the documentary method of inter-pretation constitutes and manages membership in the ethnomethodologi-cal community.

11. Ethnomethodological members' use of the documentary method constitutes the practice of "membershipping."

Through the work of documenting—i.e., by searching for and determining ethnomethodological patterns, by treating cohort's products and responses as motivated by the intended sense of shared ethnomethodological policies, by waiting for later products to clarify the sense of previous ones, by finding answers to unasked questions—local membership is established, examined, tested, reviewed, maintained, restored, in other words managed.

It must be remembered, therefore, that the documentary method is more than a procedure whereby propositions and products are granted membership in a scientific corpus. Rather, the documentary method of interpretation progressively develops those cultural products to be continually "membershipping" them. The phenomena of membership in the ethnomethodological movement is made real on a day-to-day basis by the documenting work of its members.

Conclusion: a semioethnomethodological representation

I have shown how the ethnomethodological movement's disciplinary field of discourse, identity, and research is composed by varieties of members' interactional activities and reasoning. I have used Garfinkel's analysis of the documentary method of interpretation to show in finer detail how, in typical and idealized situations, members of the ethnomethodological movement as intellectual cohorts create a lived sense of professional identity as ethnomethodologists within a collective movement. As we have seen, this is brought about through contextualized interpersonal interactions that accomplish a group intersubjectivity.

The local production of an intellectual movement on an interactional level proceeds through complex usages of the documentary method by cohorts. Recognition of membership, the formulation of discourse, and the production of texts are carried out by social scientists and ethnomethodologists through a general interpretive process whereby members continuously create interactive verifications of their own and others' local productions and work. This verification, or documentation, is composed in light of interactive, contextual, practically established, yet seemingly normative and constraining local standards created by cohorts. These "locally grammatical" standards are used by members as a "document" of a perceived underlying social pattern that is the local definition of the intellectual movement. These socially accomplished accounts or definitions of the field are then used by members to selectively regulate and control the field and its discursive productions.

I have shown how the ethnomethodological movement has employed such interactive practice and reasoning in its members' recognition of the ethnomethodological character of the enterprise's semiotic products, such as membership and texts, in its motivation by common concerns for building an intellectual program, and in its intersubjective assemblage of legitimate research topics. I have also described the workings of documentary interpretation in the ethnomethodological movement's reinterpretations of past research policies in light of new interests in such a way that it creates the appearance of disciplinary continuity and "progress." I have also shown how ethnomethodologists regularly fill-in incomplete meanings on the assumption of knowing what other ethnomethodologists really mean, how they retrospectively attribute purpose to projects of action and research, and how "essential vagueness" is contextually located within the group's body of knowledge. Finally I have described how members presuppose known-in-common institutional features of the movement when they justify texts, conversations, actions, and membership.

This series of local interpretive processes can be analytically represented by utilizing A. J.Greimas's (1976:79-128) semiotic analysis of the production of legal discourse.

Greimas analyzes the production of juridical discourse as proceeding from two "isotopies" or contrary systematic levels of discourse: a formal legislative discourse consisting of performative and normative enunciations and rules of behavior, and secondly, a referential discourse that is ideological, practical, and related to the present task at hand. These two isotopies depend on each other in a process of mutual interference, and their interaction produces what is called legal discourse. These isotopies are themselves the products of the interactions between a particular semanticity and a particular grammaticality.

Ethnomethodological discourse can be semiotically conceptualized as proceeding from the documentary interaction between members' local semanticity or local meaning production (conversations, texts, actions) and members' grammaticality or local group accountability. Figure 5-1 is a "semiotic square" that displays the series of relationships constitutive of the ethnomethodological discourse domain. This semiotic square should be read in the following manner.

Ethnomethodological discourse is the relation between the movement's local semanticity (S) and grammaticality (G). The semiotic square designates the positions of asemanticity ($\bar{S}$) and agrammaticality ($\bar{G}$). The interaction between the movement's grammaticality (or tacit normative standards) and asemanticity (or nonlocalized ambiguous meaning) is the level of formal ethnomethodological discourse, which exists only as formal rules or standards of discourse. The relation between semanticity (or local meaning) and agrammaticality (or utterances not in conformity with the movements' taken-for-granted rules of discourse) is the level of referential ethnomethodological discourse, which exists as neoethnomethodological discourse anterior to its verification as "ethnomethodological." Ethnomethodological discourse, or discourse that is locally produced and verified by self-referenced members, is the composite relation between these semantic and grammatical interactions.

Ethnomethodological discourse is produced by members through the documentary method of interpretation that is represented by transformation of asemanticity into semanticity ($\bar{S} \rightarrow S$). Verification of ethnomethodological discourse by members is also carried out by the documentary method of interpretation that is the transformation of agrammaticality into grammaticality ($\bar{G} \rightarrow G$).

The analytical representation of the semiotic interactions constitutive of the ethnomethodological movement's discourse domain is itself a "semioethnomethodological" conceptualization. It is my synthesis of the Greimassian semiotic analysis of discourse and the ethnomethodological description of practical action and natural accountability through a description of the workings of a "Lebenswelt pair." A "Lebenswelt pair" is the pair of constitutent segments of a scientific activity containing a first segment consisting of a formal account such as a theorem or proof, and a second segment consisting of the practical interactive work of proving, explaining, or following the first segment (cf. Livingston 1986; Garfinkel 1985b). In my semioethnomethodological analysis, I argue that a social science movement's taken-for-granted normative and local grammaticality is both created and utilized in local situations of semanticity through members' use of a documentary process of interpretation. The remaining chapters describe how the mutually created discourse field of the ethnomethodological movement is folklorically appropriated and accounted for by self-referenced members in different generations (Chapter 6) and how the ethnomethodological universe of discourse is translated and received in international contexts (Chapter 7).

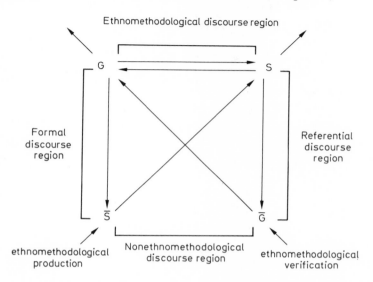

Key:
G = ethnomethodological grammaticality (grammatical accountability)
Ḡ = ethnomethodological agrammaticality
S = ethnomethodological semanticity (practical semantic action)
S̄ = ethnomethodological asemanticity
G + S = ethnomethodological discourse region (constituted by grammaticality and semanticity)
Ḡ + S̄ = nonethnomethodological discourse region (ethnomethodologically agrammatical and asemantic)
G + S̄ = ethnomethodological formal discourse region (ethnomethodological grammatical accounts without practical semantic content)
Ḡ + S = neoethnomethodological referential discourse region (ethnomethodological practical semantic content without traditional ethnomethodological grammaticality)
S̄ → S = ethnomethodological production (transformation of nonethnomethodological practical semantic action into ethnomethodological practical semantic action, implying an identity with the accountable and grammatical form)
Ḡ → G = ethnomethodological verification (transformation of ungrammatical accounts into grammatical accounts, implying identity with the practical semantic actions)

Figure 5-1

Part III

Chapter Six
Folklore from the Field

That is to say, one is already part of a time-ordering apparatus called a social
system. The system's very recognizable features over the course of action is
through and through a time-ordering, time-ordered phenomenon.
Garfinkel (Hill and Crittenden 1968:147)

Let me say it first in an uncomplicated way, then if that is alright I will say it
in a complicated way.
Garfinkel (Hill and Crittenden 1968:176)

Ethnomethodologists do not go into their researches methodologically "empty-
handed," as a corpus of prior studies of work is now usable as a basis for
projecting further studies.
Lynch (1985a:6)

Intellectual movements, as well as popular movements, represent themselves in terms of an oral folkloric tradition. Ethnomethodologists
characterize themselves and their work in ways that form a folklore
of ethnomethodology. Ethnomethodologists engage in folkloric constructions of cultural images of themselves and the ethnomethodological
way of working. These folkloric characterizations or myths become a
part of cultural members' background. They have been called mythoforms (Armstrong 1975:96). The ethnomethodological mythoforms are
celebrated, incarnated, performed, and poeticized whenever members
artfully talk about themselves, think about their community of studies,
and write about their distinctive findings and research styles.
   Ethnomethodology's folklore can be witnessed and shared when one
listens to or reads ethnomethodologists' "verbal art" in the context of
conversations, storytelling, lectures, or written texts (cf. Dundes 1984;

Bauman 1986; Ben-Amos 1972; Dorson 1972; Sebeok 1953). One observes that ethnomethodologists' talk and stories are filled with artful sayings, myths, and proverbs about themselves and their unique ways of looking at and accomplishing the world. I attempt to make visible the ethnomethodological folkloric style by looking at examples of ethnomethodologists as folk narrators.

Garfinkel as folk narrator

Harold Garfinkel can be analyzed as an engaging and masterful raconteur of ethnomethodological folklore. His verbal art consists of a variety of witticisms, proverbs, sayings, figures of speech, and anecdotes expressive of his images of ethnomethodology's local culture. Garfinkel was raised in the Jewish community in Newark, New Jersey. His verbal art is spiced with Yiddish expressions and stylistic play. This verbal style has contributed to ethnomethodology's folk tradition and intertextual poetry (see Chapter 3).

I present several narrative texts that exemplify Garfinkel's verbal creations of proverbial metaphors, aphorisms, heuristic storytelling, illustrative examples, and mythic characterizations of ethnomethodologists. Bauman (1986) has emphasized the necessary interrelationships existing between the act of storytelling or orally performed verbal art (narrated events), the narrative text, and the events recounted in the narrative (narrative events). I shall employ an oral narrative text from the proceedings of the Purdue Symposium on Ethnomethodology that was taped, transcribed and edited by Richard Hill and Kathleen Crittenden (1968). This oral text, although edited, supplies rich examples of Garfinkel's verbal styles in the context of being "in the dock," and explaining ethnomethodology to a symposium of nonethnomethodological sociologists (see Chapters 3 and 7).

Mythic characterizations

Ethnomethodologists, as a local culture and tradition, by and large tend to characterize themselves as "tough characters" and independent "way finders" with "strong nervous systems" and "strong stomachs" for rigorous inquiry and the confutations of the sociological establishment. They see themselves able to persevere in their serious searches and studies despite and in the face of a hostile or indifferent professional environment. The following is Garfinkel's artful verbal characterization (in Hill and Crittenden 1968:136) given at the Purdue Symposium on Ethnomethodology:

> I tell the students, "You want to work with me? You're going to have to find your own way. Part of it I can tell you about and for the rest of it, you're on your own." There are not many students that are willing to undertake that.

> There is a very interesting thing about this score. By and large, we do not get dummies. We just do not have dummies in the enterprise. It is a very odd kind of business, but it is true that we have the bright ones and they are, among other things, rather tough characters. That is to say, it takes a strong nervous system to withstand it. You have to have a willingness not only to deal with vague matters, but you also have to have this willingness to undertake the analysis in the face of an environment which, by and large, at least tends to be uneasy or maybe worse. We cannot guarantee our students, for example, that from the beginning, in the department line, that they will know what kind of course of training they can take. We cannot tell them that they will have been examined repeatedly so as to gain assurance that they are on the right track to a career the end of which they can see with considerable assurance. It happens that our students do well in the end, but it really takes a strong stomach to withstand it. Thus I would say that there is a discipline.

Proverbial metaphors

In the Purdue Symposium, Garfinkel artfully performed the verbal illustration of ethnomethodology's program for an audience of nonmembers with what the audience called "precision and good humor" (p.189). Intermixed with his individual, often complicated, style of speaking,

Garfinkel sauced the conversation with Yiddish folk idioms. These idioms and proverbs grew from his own Jewish folk heritage in Newark. Several examples follow:

> My notion is that we might begin, if you will permit the suggestion, by recitation of what in Yiddish is called *Tsor*is. This means a kind of obstinate, unyielding trouble that does not go away if you use the usual remedies. It is not that it is all that devastating; but on occasion you encounter it, you cannot be indifferent to it. Perhaps you would like to be indifferent, but this is not possible. (p.3)

> Having given all this about what ethnomethodology is, let me tell you the vicissitudes of the term. It has turned into *shibboleth*, and I am going to tell you right now that I cannot be responsible for what persons have come to make of ethnomethodology. (p.10)

> It is being done anyway, so we might as well start with that. Let's not start with, "Here comes the Messiah," or " Here comes the gang." "They finally have rid us of our *Tsoris*." "What kind of nonsense is that?" (p.200)

"That's not the way to Jerusalem"

I have been told by Bennetta Jules-Rosette (1986, personal communication) that in Garfinkel's seminars and lectures in the 1970s, he would use the proverbial expression "That's not the way to Jerusalem." He used this performative device to illustrate various ways that practical sociological reasoning forgot about the indexical nature of their methods and results. This saying resembles various apocryphal expressions found in the Bible, for example, "Jerusalem, Holy City, God scoured you for your handiwork, yet still will take pity on the sons of the upright" (Apocryphal Book of Tobit, 13:1-2).

"Jerusalem" is a motifeme (Dundes 1964) or emic motif category. In both Garfinkel's and Tobit's expressions, Jerusalem seems to function as a motifeme for the "Holy City" or place of truth. Perhaps, for Garfinkel, Jerusalem represents the mythic dwelling place of ethnomethodological studies. A more recent rendering of this mythoform by Garfinkel in the 1980's and 1990's is "This is news from nowhere."

"Ethnomethodology is like a boat without a bottom"

Garfinkel has also used variations of the metaphorical aphorism "ethno-methodology is like a boat without a bottom." He uses this witticism to characterize the ethnomethodological tradition's insistence that it is a foundational enterprise that investigates the taken-for-granted assumptions of all practical reasoning, including its own. Here are several performances from the Purdue Symposium:

> For one thing, if this is a ship that is going down, not everybody has to go down with Garfinkel. That seems clear enough. Although I think that I reminded a previous audience that you need not fear that you are going to sink this boat. It has no bottom. Throw rocks! Do, please, throw rocks! It does not make any difference. (p.143)

> In the meantime, nothing will sink the boat. I have the money. I have the time. I am willing to wait. (p.123)

Garfinkel's heuristic storytelling

Garfinkel, like many ethnomethodologists, tells stories in the context of teaching and talking about ethnomethodology. This is inevitable because ethnomethodologists are continually trying to unite empirical social events with their analytical formulations. Garfinkel is a particularly engaging and masterful oral storyteller. His tellings have a way of drawing the listener in and illuminating the "wondrous details" of everyday practical activities. His verbal artistry is performative ethnomethodology and verbally illustrates what ethnomethodologists are after as phenomena. The following is a telling delivered at the Purdue Symposium:

> I once spent some time in the bowels of Bordentown prison in New Jersey. They had there something called a communication center. Every once in awhile it would clatter and the guard would stand at the machine and there was a guy standing behind him. The guard is standing over here, and every once in awhile the machine goes bang. I really mean that it was banging away. I say to him, "What's going on?" He says, "They are checking in." What is this "checking in"? There were cell blocks connected to this communication

center. Roughly at plus or minus five minutes of the hour every hour, a guard would at each one of these cell blocks go to the end of the block. There would be a call box. If the message arrived plus or minus five minutes of the hour, everything was O.K., which told the guard in the communication center that as far as he is concerned, do nothing. It is not the machine clattering; it is that A has checked in, and nothing is to be done. If a temporarily anticipated message came in more than plus or minus this five minutes of the hour, a big question would arise. It was not that they would know what to do, but instead the telephoning would now begin. "Joe, are you there? Why the hell aren't you calling in?" "I forgot." That kind of thing would start. If they could not raise Joe, then there was more telephoning to the front office which was alerted and which then had to make the decision. Do you alter the whole place in order to see why cell block C did not call in?

I use this as an example of the time of arrival of the message being an integral feature of the message. If you want to ask what is it that the person heard, then apparently you cannot tell without knowing what the orderly system of activities is that they are engaged in at this central place. They invoke this system of activities in order to recognize an organizationally appropriate time of arrival. It is not a clock time just because, after all, plus or minus five is about the hour. It is around noon. *It is an essentially vague notion.* You can ask them, "When ought it to arrive?" This turns out to be a question for which there is no exact numerical procedure whereby that question can be settled. One is stuck with an *irremediably vague* "plus or minus five minutes of the hour." That is for the Bordentown prison. That is at least where I got the big idea about this temporal organization, this temporal ordering of activities as the members do it. They are making it happen in concert for each other in a modelized version. (pp.149-150)

Folklore and scientific knowledge

Contemporary studies of folklore have been increasingly looking to the artfulness of oral literature and cultivating an appreciation of the radical importance of performance as constitutive of "verbal art" (cf. Bauman 1986; Dundes 1975, 1980; Bascom 1977; Ben-Amos 1972; Sherzer 1982; Fine 1984; Hymes 1981; Tedlock 1983; Babcock 1977; Dorson 1972). Many structural studies of folklore have emphasized that understanding of oral narratives must be embedded in syntagmatic and emic contexts of performance (cf. Propp 1968; Sebeok and Ingemann 1956; Dundes 1980;

Greimas 1966, 1971; Maranda and Maranda 1971). Ethnomethodology's folklore and folklife are performed and recognized daily among practitioners in all generations and is constitutive of its knowledge forms. The ethnomethodological movement's example raises questions concerning the constitution of intellectual folk cultures within scientific schools of thought.

Knowledge in the natural and social sciences is culturally organized knowledge. The cultural organization of scientific knowledge includes performative dimensions of local folklore, oral storytelling, and literary artistry that remains to be adequately examined (cf. O'Neill 1981; Gusfield 1976; Mulkay et al. 1985). In the next section, I examine the verbal accounts of two ethnomethodologists who recount their introductions to ethnomethodology's way of knowledge.

I have chosen the interview accounts of Mel Pollner and Nick Maroules to stand as "situationally formulated representations." I have chosen to present their accounts because they best embody the various aspects of ethnomethodology as an intellectual movement that I wish to analyze and because they both most graciously consented to my use of and analysis of their words and recounted experiences in this format.

This chapter explores the issue of whether there are generational differences or similarities in the subjective meaning contextures of ethnomethodology's members. Utilizing folkloric, semiotic, and life historical approaches (cf. Plummer 1983) I examine interview transcripts that create membership accounts of different members. These interviews form situated accounts of particular individuals' constitution of membership in ethnomethodology's field of discourse. I then examine a number of textual excerpts to see if there exists evidence to confirm Mannheim's (1952a:304; 1982:11-18) hypothesis that cultural formations such as texts embody signified contents that have a genesis in the collective life experiences of particular historically and culturally located generations of individuals.

Accounts of intellectual conversion

When we examine folkloric and interview accounts, it is necessary to view the performances as situated constructions. Situationally construed verbal accounts are assembled through retrospection and anticipation, as well as by reference to various organizational modelling systems such as ideologies, "acceptable" versions, generational world views, and beliefs. Research on verbal accounts of religious conversion have shown that as changes occur over time in the organizational rationale and belief structure of a religious group, the structure of members' accounts of conversion show a concomitant change (cf. Beckford 1978). This alerts us to the possibility that interview accounts may be comparable in terms of the member's generation or location in the movement. Such a view, though, forgets that accounts are extremely changeable. They do not describe fixed objective realities. Rather, verbal performances reconstruct past events according to present relevancies and circumstances. Therefore, accounts by differing intellectual generations may all reinterpret the past according to shared present concerns. The particular generational features may be concealed in favor of reference to a commonly imagined present. Nevertheless, an analysis of constructed members' accounts may embody some identifiable generational differences. Our aim will be to investigate this question.

We are going to examine two ethnomethodologists' verbal accounts of intellectual "conversion" into or appropriation of the ethnomethodological field of discourse. Recent studies of religious conversion (cf. Snow and Machalek 1984:172; Lofland and Skonovd 1981) have reconceptualized conversion as a change in one's universe of discourse entailing the displacement of one universe of discourse by another or the placement of a formerly peripheral universe of discourse to the status of a primary authority. Sociological studies of conversion generally place conversion in the context of joining religious movements or sects. For example, Bryon Wilson (1970) outlines distinguishing characteristics of religious movements such as voluntariness, exclusivity, conversion, self-identification, elite status, expulsion, degrees of commitment, and legitimation. Wilson also proposes seven ideal types of sects. McGuire (1981) suggests that conversion into sectarian religious movements is embedded in the social context of special sociocultural dynamics for forming, maintaining, and transforming meaning, identity, and a sense of belonging.

Linton (1943:230) proposed a definition of revivalistic and perpetuitive nativistic movements as sectarian movements arising in the midst of radical cultural change or opposition. Conversion consists here of adopting a new explanation of change. While the ethnomethodological movement has similarities to religious movements, I have adopted the conception of "conversion" as the changing of the universe of discourse in order to emphasize the "secular" character of ethnomethodology's signification system.

Universes of discourse are best conceptualized as semantic universes, or the totality of significations (cf. Eco 1976:75-81; Greimas and Courtés 1982:366). Intellectual appropriation of a new paradigm can be conceptualized in a similar way as the shift of one's semantic universe of discourse from periphery to center. The new universe of discourse serves as the basis of the intellectual's conceptual paradigm and communicative modelling system.

The term appropriation refers to the act of acquiring a new semantic universe as an object of value by subjects' own actions (cf. Greimas and Courtés 1982:15-16). When such a shift occurs in an intellectual's central semantic field, it may be that the corresponding shift in practical intellectual attention bears resemblances to a changed religious consciousness. That is, with the appropriation of a differential semantic universe, one's whole intellectual world-view or perception of the world changes.

What constitutes intellectual appropriation?

I am going to address the issue of what constitutes intellectual appropriation using the ethnomethodological movement as an empirical case. I shall examine what an intellectual appropriation account consists of. I shall then ask whether there are generational differences and similarities in this form of conversion. The following transcripts consist of intellectual transformation accounts from the third and fourth generations of the ethnomethodological movement. I will heuristically use the hypothesis that personal intellectual paradigm transformation implies an appropriation of a new semantic universe of discourse. An analysis of the accounts' composition will illuminate what constitutes these generational versions of intellectual transformation. We can also make some generalizations about the process of intellectual changes of fundamental thought structures.

An interview with Mel Pollner

The following is a transcript of an excerpt of an interview I held with Mel Pollner at the University of California, Los Angeles on November 21, 1986. Pollner is a third generation ethnomethodologist who completed his Ph.D. at the University of California, Santa Barbara in 1971. He has taught at the University of California, Los Angeles since 1968 and has done extensive ethnomethodological research on mundane reasoning, reality disjunctures, traffic court interactions, labeling theory, and self-explicating transactions.

In utilizing this account it is essential to remain critically aware that this account is a construction and a reconstruction of the speaker's experiences, which draw upon available resources at the time of construction to lend them sense. This is not a fixed description of the phenomenon but is a situational construct assembled under the interactive constraints of my own actions as a hearer and questioner as well as the speaker's local performance and accomplishment of a remembered telling.

Exhibit 5
Interview: PF with Mel Pollner
             University of California, Los Angeles, Department of
             Sociology
             November 21, 1986

001   PF: Maybe I could ask you this... could we maybe talk
002   about you ... kind of an informal life history of you
003   and the ethnomethodological movement? Where were you
004   when you first encountered it? What was, as you were
005   telling me before, there were certain people already in
006   the field, there was a certain structure to the field,
007   what drew you to the movement, what was the context,
008   the 1960s. I am interested in that kind of thing.

009   MP: Let me give you a schematic outline and you can tell
010   me what you might want me to elaborate on, if I can ...
011   let me just reflect a moment so I can pull it together ...
012   When I was about to enter graduate school I was a very
013   quantitatively oriented researcher and with very limited
014   kinds of intellectual concerns and initially I was going
015   to go to the University of Wisconsin and I still remem-
016   ber flying out of Madison to get a room with another
017   young man that graduated from what we called at that
018   time CCNY (City College of New York). We were both
019   going to enter sociology at U of W, and we were going out
020   to get a room. He was reading a book on the plane
021   and he said, "You must read this book, there is something
022   very very unusual about it". The book turned out to be
023   *Presentation of Self in Everyday Life*, and I did read
024   the book closely and it was quite fascinating. I thought
025   it was about the naughtiest thing that I had seen in
026   sociology at the time and getting at a level of life
027   that I didn't see anyone having touched on or considered
028   before and I was just very much taken by the power of
029   the work.
030   And one thing led to another and instead of going to U
               of W,
031   I went to the University of Berkeley. I say that because I
032   was so naive at the time I thought Berkeley was a
033   self-contained university. I did not know it was connected
034   to the University of California. I went and I had ...
035   Goffman was at Berkeley at the time. I was living a sort
036   of schizophrenic intellectual existence; on one level I
037   was a statistically oriented researcher, in fact I was
038   an R.A. for Hannan Selvin, who at the time was a known
039   survey researcher emphasizing new multivariate high-
040   powered statistical techniques and, at the same time I
041   had this fascination with Goffman and I was auditing
042   his course, and my wife who was an undergraduate major
043   in sociology was taking a course with Goffman. I would
044   go to his undergraduate courses. So, I was living a sort
045   of schizophrenic intellectual existence. One point
046   Goffman required of undergraduates was a supplementary
047   reading of something in the reserve book room. And my

048	wife Judy went to get it and I went with her, we sat
049	down to read it together. And I really couldn't make
050	sense out of the text for in ... every now and then, this
051	author would report or describe a ... something that
052	looked like an experiment that he had done in public
053	that often involved an infraction of some trivial norm
054	yet it could produce enormous emotional reaction ... and
055	again I didn't fully understand the text, it was written
056	in the most obscure... uh ... of fashion that I had ever
057	encountered and yet, there again, I was intrigued by
058	the power of the examples that were being provided
059	through the manipulation of what seemed to be ... the
060	the most trivial, or the violation of the most trivial
061	aspects or norms of everyday life ... *tremendous* anomic
062	and emotional effects. That man was Garfinkel. And
063	so, the name registered as did the power of what he
064	was doing... I was a research assistant for Hannan
065	Selvin. Our research project ran out of funds so we
066	could no longer do computational work at Berkeley ...
067	however the computer at UCLA was free to those who were
068	supported by NIMH, which our project was an NIMH project.
069	My wife lived in L.A. so we came down, the manifest
070	purpose was to use the computer ... we were living at
071	my wife's parents' house... and I took the opportunity to
072	look up this man Garfinkel and at that time we really
073	hit it off and I began to audit Garfinkel's seminars
074	at the time. I believe ... this was the period 19 ...
075	uh ... 1965, or a period thereabout, I audited Garfinkel's
076	seminars. Garfinkel, in fact, offered me a research
077	assistantship, for, I think it was the summer of
078	1965, it was the summer during which there were the
079	Watts riots, I guess that was '65 ... and he basically paid
080	my way allowing me to do virtually anything I wanted to
081	do and that was my introduction to Garfinkel and my
082	introduction to ethnomethodology.
083	I returned to Berkeley in '66; at that time
084	Aaron Cicourel was teaching there for a year. He knew
085	he was going to be the chair of the department at University of California,

086   Santa Barbara, and fundamentally, the case that he made
087   was if you are interested in ethnomethodology do not
088   expect any support, really intellectual support, at
089   Berkeley, there is none uh ... but do expect it if you
090   come to Santa Barbara. And ... I received my M.A.
091   in 1966 at Berkeley and began in the fall of that year
092   graduate studies at UC Santa Barbara. Now, Henry Elliot
093   and Ted Hajjar came with me from Berkeley. So that in
094   schematic form is my introduction to ethnomethodology.

A narrative analysis

Several things in this transcript tell us it is a conversion or appropriation account referring to a change in the speaker's universe of discourse. The speaker refers to his pre-ethnomethodological biography as a "quantitatively oriented researcher" with "very limited kinds of intellectual concerns" (lines 013 and 014). This retrospective formulation is made in light of his current experiences in the ethnomethodological paradigm. It alerts us to the fact that a process of retrospective interpretation of a past universe of discourse is being undertaken from the working perspective of a new universe of discourse. He refers to his memory of the transition between universes by speaking of his reading of Goffman's *Presentation of Self*, which was "naughty," and getting at an untouched level of life. He recalls being taken by the "power of the work " He refers to an enduing period of "schizophrenic intellectual existence" where he saw himself as suspended between a universe of "multivariate high-powered statistical techniques" and the emerging new semantic universe of Goffman's perceptions of everyday life dramaturgy (line 045). The speaker recounts (lines 047-056) in detail the first encounter with the ethnomethodological semantic universe of discourse. It is in the form of a reserve reading of one of Garfinkel's texts on incongruity experiments (cf. Garfinkel 1964a). The speaker refers to his wife's consensual presence, admits his initial difficulty in reading the author's semiotic style ("I really couldn't make sense out of the text ... it was written in the most obscure ... fashion"). Nevertheless, he was "intrigued by the power" of Garfinkel's reported examples of the manipulation of everyday norms of behavior with the resulting anomic effects. The speaker retrospectively remarks that the encounter with the author made a lasting intellectual impression ("That man was Garfinkel ... the name registered as did the power of what he was doing"). He then produced a description of a sort of intellectual pilgrimage embedded in the context of the financial decline of his former paradigm (line 065). This results in a positive personal interaction with Garfinkel and the beginning of a period of intellectual apprenticeship and work in the new domain of ethnomethodology ("at that time we really hit it off and I began to audit Garfinkel's seminars ... Garfinkel offered me a research assistantship").

It is clear to us that in the preceding narrative Pollner is referring to his process of appropriation of the new semantic field. He begins close interaction with a "collective actant" of the movement (Garfinkel). This period of apprenticeship permits Pollner to assemble the new semantic universe by learning and putting into place ethnomethodology's semiotic system of knowledge procedures, narrative structures, and coreferencing mechanisms. This work accomplishes the "historical anchoring" of his membership in ethnomethodology's domain of figurativized discourse. Historical anchoring (cf. Greimas and Courtés 1982:13-14) is the setting up of a set of intertextual spatiotemporal indices consisting of anthoponyms, toponyms, and chrononyms (see Chapter 3) whose aim is to constitute the similacrum (cf. Baudrillard, 1981:11) of an external referent. This external referent is the new semantic universe. Learning to produce a "referential illusion" (cf. Barthes 1974b:271; Greimas 1976: 30-31) of the semantic universe's "external" historical facticity through intertextual co-referencing and iconization procedures (see Chapter 4) is an essential component of appropriating the new semantic universe at this stage.

A "referential illusion" refers to the discursive representation or "meaning effect of reality" that results from a set of particular discursive procedures. In other words, learning to write and speak "as an ethnomethodologist" consists of implementing shared, taken-for-granted linguistic "mediations" (Vygotsky 1962) such as vocabulary, semantic categories, syntax, pragmatics, and references in a way that constructs an "appearance" of the ethnomethodological domain of knowledge.

As we shall see later, contemporary membership requires competence to invent neoethnomethodological discourse. "Neoethnomethodological" discourse is discourse within the ethnomethodological semantic field but which utilizes new expressive language forms, new methods, and new conceptual linkages.

The account's figurativization

A semiotic analysis of the account itself provides us with further information. Pollner's situated construction of the account references his present location within the ethnomethodological semantic universe. In his preceding account, Pollner uses a set of spatiotemporal indices. These produce the account's historical anchoring (cf. Greimas and Courtés 1982). He inscribes his narrative program within a set of figurative spatiotemporal coordinates. This anchoring actively creates the simulacrum, or the simulated appearance, of the new ethnomethodological semantic universe as an external referent. It also produces the universe's referential illusion as an interactively appropriated semantic field.

Pollner employs three procedures that are constructive of his new discoursivization. These procedures are the use of "anthroponyms," "toponyms," and "chrononyms" to produce the narrative's "figurativization." By figurativization I mean the story's unique way of representing "the real upon the text" (Greimas and Courtés 1982:120) and the historical anchoring of what is said. An "anthroponym" is the designation of actors by proper nouns. A "toponym" is the designation of space by proper nouns. "Chrononyms" are textual designations of specific lengths of time.

Pollner uses anthroponyms ("That man was Garfinkel" and "this man Garfinkel" and "he basically paid my way") to designate Garfinkel as the actant of his intellectual transformation. He uses toponyms ("I was living a sort of schizophrenic intellectual existence" and "a supplementary reading of something in the reserve book room" and "we sat down to read it together" and "my wife lived in Los Angeles, so we came down" and "I took the opportunity to look up this man Garfinkel") to figuratively designate his passing from one semantic space to another. He composes chrononyms ("every now and then" and "it was written in the most obscure … fashion I had ever encountered" and "at that time we really hit it off" and "I began to audit Garfinkel's seminars" and "it was the summer of 1965, it was the summer during which there were the Watts riots") to designate the temporal localization of his changing narrative present. These three figurative procedures semiotically accomplish Pollner's historical anchoring of his narrative account.

These procedures also inform us of Pollner's historical anchoring of his transformed intellectual career. The account is composed from a present localization within ethnomethodology. Its retrospective narrative speaks about Pollner's present topic space, or space of discoursive reference (cf. Greimas and Courtés 1982:181). The narrative consists of figurativizations that articulate Pollner's present topic space. He articulates a sense of present intellectual power ("I was intrigued by the power " and "the name registered as did the power of what he was doing" and "tremendous anomic and emotional effects") (lines 057-064). He anaphorizes, or creates a partial identity between two narrative terms (cf. Greimas and Courtés 1982:13): radical and revolutionary change ("It was the summer during which there were the Watts riots"). He references a present respect for Garfinkel's "actorial modalities" (cf. Greimas and Courtés 1982:193-195) as an intellectual liberator ("and paid my way allowing me to do virtually anything I wanted to do, and that was my introduction to Garfinkel and my introduction to ethnomethodology").

Managing intellectual contingencies

The next part of the transcripted account bears resemblance to an "evaluation and translation" phase represented in many religious accounts of conversion. Here, the new convert begins to practically reorganize his or her world in terms of the new universe of discourse (cf. Jules-Rosette 1975b). Pollner recounts his memories of managing practical contingencies like intellectual support for the new universe of discourse ("do not expect any support, really intellectual support, at Berkeley") (lines 087-089). With his move to the University of California, Santa Barbara for ethnomethodological graduate studies in 1966, Pollner had made his transformation into ethnomethodology.

Comparison: a fourth generation transformation account

The previous analysis of an account by a third generation ethnomethodologist has shown an observable structure. This structure consists of a specific narrative organization and construction. This produced narrative anchors a verbal representation of an intellectual transformation or paradigm change. I have said that this intellectual transformation process consists of an appropriation of a new semantic universe of discourse. I shall now briefly examine a fourth generation (1980-1990) ethnomethodologist's account of his intellectual appropriation of the ethnomethodological movement. We shall examine this account for generational features.

The following life-historical verbal account is from a fourth generation ethnomethodologist, Nicholas Maroules from the University of California, San Diego. He was introduced to ethnomethodology as an undergraduate by a third generation ethnomethodologist, Hugh "Bud" Mehan. Maroules's (1985) dissertation is on the social organization of courtroom sentencing.

Exhibit 6

Interview:	PF with Nick Maroules
	La Jolla, California
	January 17, 1987

001	NM:	It was sometime between 1970 and 1971. At that time I
002		was winding up my sophomore year at Indiana University
003		as a Political Science major. (I was just starting
004		to come over to work with some sociologists. I took a
005		sociology of knowledge course from Larry Hazelrigg and
006		I was deeply impressed by this man ... he was very heavy
007		on Pareto, Weber, and Marx—really a classically
008		trained theorist of some magnitude and depth. I was
009		impressed then, and it wasn't due to the fact that I
010		was young and undeveloped.) At that time I had
011		decided to make sociology my second major and I was
012		oriented to political sociology. At Larry Hazelrigg's
013		insistence I was taking all my studies very seriously,
014		in particular I was taking methodological questions
015		very seriously, taking methodology as a domain of
016		inquiry very seriously. Methodology at Indiana only
017		meant one thing, and that was quantitative, macrosocio-
018		logical designs, technology if you will, quantitative
019		analysis, causal modeling. So I took courses and
020		independent studies in that area... I was really
021		pushing the sociology. I had that summer designed
022		a study of student-voting behavior which required I
023		submit a proposal for an honor's grant of some sort.

024 NM: So I had got all this stuff, money, a computer
025   account, some status, I got an award, and I did this
026   thing under Larry during my junior year. At about
027   this spring—early summer time, Larry suggested that
028   I look into another young sociologist across the hall
029   by the name of Hugh Mehan, and I remember vividly
030   asking Larry, "Well, what does he do?" And he said
031   "He teaches social psychology, and I really think you'd
032   find him interesting."
033   And so shortly thereafter I went over and introduced
034   myself. And I really liked Bud and I planned to take a
035   course from him. We had a long talk that day and it
036   went in the direction of whatever I was capable of
037   recognizing as issues in the philosophy of language.
038   I really enjoyed what he was interested in. Something
039   about this fellow really turned me on. So I then took
040   his course, social psychology, Sociology 232, which
041   met in a large lecture hall and probably had a couple
042   hundred students in it ... It was a large class, there
043   was no question about that. And Bud did some symbolic
044   interactionism; some social construction; Berger and
045   Luckman type stuff; a little Schutzian stuff; he got
046   into Mead of course; Freud; theories of socialization;
047   models of the actor ... But then also went into Goffman;
048   then after Goffman, into *Garfinkel* and I was
049   *absolutely* hooked. There was no question that *this*
050   was the phenomenon worth pursuing. That these were
051   the issues... . It was clear to me at that time ...
052   I know it's difficult to write it this way, we search
053   for metaphors that will allow you to express the
054   relationship between those more traditional phenomenon
055   and these phenomenon ... things like structure and
056   structuring ... uh ... but it always seems to get us,
057   that is people who do this kind of work, into trouble
058   to try to be really serious about things like "this is
059   what's underlying it all" and "this is what's assembling
060   it" in the sense of really the phenomena ... if
061   you go out and *talk* that way people don't take ...they
062   think you are rabid. So you look for these more subtle
063   ways. But to me at that point it was clear to me

064 NM: that this was the stuff. I was *really* turned on ...
065 So I began hanging out more and more with Bud and taking
066 this stuff further and further. After that I got an
067 undergraduate R.A. position for being an honors
068 student and I wanted to work with Bud on this stuff.
069 So from that time on for the next several quarters
070 I either was an R.A. or a T.A. with Bud, and I really
071 learned a lot... .
072 The interesting thing about my introduction substan-
073 tively to ethnomethodology was that Bud was an excellent
074 teacher. These were his first courses, he really
075 had his stuff together. Great lectures! And he
076 *expressed* the phenomenon and the way we would get to
077 it and how it is constituted in ways that you know,
078 one could really understand. But trying to read Gar-
079 finkel was a very painful and difficult experience.
080 And I was always caught up in this thing, that, on
081 the one hand, really digging this stuff and identifying
082 with it and on the other hand, not being sure I really
083 understood what the hell was going on. But you would
084 pick up an ability to string one and two and three
085 lines together, which was almost a kind of passing
086 phenomenon ... what one of my early Garfinkel things,
087 i.e., Agnes, you know, was all about. I was living this
088 thing out. It was really quite interesting.
089 But also Bud of course introduced me to the concept
090 of Aaron Cicourel, as a master sociologist, as *his*
091 guru. And turning me on to the whole ... ethnomethodology
092 at that time was a cultish movement ... I mean this
093 thing was a *force* to be reckoned with. This thing
094 had *momentum*. It was seen as a major threat because
095 it went right for the epistemology and it wasn't
096 fucking around with problems like method and weak
097 theory. This is "turn it inside out!" And it was
098 growing, and people didn't have a sense of what it
099 was going to become and that was fearsome for trad-
100 itionalists. So I identified not only with the subject
101 matter but with the movement, although I was somewhat
102 divorced from it because my only contact was through
103 Bud.

An analysis

We notice immediately that Maroules's account is both similar to and different from Pollner's third generation account. This verbal account similarly follows a narrative structure that identifies it as an intellectual transformation account. The speaker historically anchors his account through figurative devices of anthroponyms ("Bud was an excellent teacher") toponyms ("after Goffman into Garfinkel") and chrononyms ("ethnomethodology at that time"). These devices designate the speaker's transformation into a new semantic universe (ethnomethodology), via a new collective actant (Bud Mehan). He refers to being "hooked" by the "force" of the new position. He cites "passing" practices while acquiring a new competence in utilizing the new universe of discourse (lines 080-088). He identifies himself as part of a collective movement that is perceived as a threat by traditional sociology (lines 94-100).

Maroules states that he "identified not only with the subject matter but with the movement" (lines 100-101). I view this as an indice of his appropriation of perceived membership in the ethnomethodological field. Maroules's dissertation (1985) cites Cicourel as the major influence on the work. His presentational format follows more of the style of Cicourel's rather than Garfinkel's ethnomethodology. His work unmistakably shows the application of ethnomethodological concerns applied in the sociology of law, forming a hybridization of presentation that escapes being labelled "only" ethnomethodological.

The account also exhibits difference. These differences are situated in ethnomethodology's generational structure. Bud Mehan functions as a third generation "collective actant." He interprets that new domain for Maroules. The speaker appropriates the ethnomethodological semantic universe through a third generation actant. This is unlike Pollner, who received his "knowledge transmission" directly from Garfinkel, a first generation actant. Here is a case of a local culture of ethnomethodology developing through an intergenerational transmission process. The speaker learns through a process of "passing" to assemble his local ethnomethodological competence and identity (lines 085-088). He is aware that he is part of the new movement of thought. He is also aware that his knowledge is generationally mediated (lines 101-103). He has to do work to assemble his location in the generational structure of the collective hierarchy.

Generational actants

Intellectuals can undergo a process of conversion when they make fundamental changes in their paradigms or universes of discourse. The previous two verbal accounts have illustrated examples of intellectual transformation into the ethnomethodological movement. An individual's membership is a unique complex of generational contours. The generational features of the "collective actant" can determine the "local version" of the ethnomethodological movement's universe of discourse. The generational collective actant takes the practical form of which texts are read, which research styles are emphasized, which members' works are recognized prioritively. Where a generational collective actant is successively assembled and maintained, a new "school" or local intellectual culture can begin. Multiple generational fields can coexist within a single intertextual semantic universe.

Generational semiotic shiftings within the ethnomethodological semantic field

It is possible to view certain generations of thought movements as expressing differing cultural emphases and folklores and thus developing differing systems of signification within a shared semantic field. The ethnomethodological signitive system serves as a historicized sign-vehicle for differing generational syntheses and voices. Second, third, and fourth generation ethnomethodology is a historically situated set of expansions of collective kernals of meaning.

In my own training as a graduate ethnomethodologist, I found that there was a difference between generations of ethnomethodologists that was visible both in their writings and in their teachings. Second and third generation ethnomethodologists expressed distinctly different sentiments through the ethnomethodological language and theories than did the first generation of ethnomethodologists. Though each generation modeled their discourse along commonly shared ethnomethodological principles, I detected a difference in the underlying experiential contextures that lay behind their words. I found myself confronted with what Mannheim

(1982:87) calls a "transcendence of the conceptual contents" of ethno-methodology's style. The second, third, and fourth generations were employing the first generation's sign system to conceptualize new passions and experiences. They were simultaneously maintaining the core ethnomethodological program. In ways akin to folklore, ethnomethodology's sign system and style were being appropriated and made topically relevant by generations with their own unique contextures of experiences. Ethnomethodology's communal ideas were simultaneously being "expanded and preserved" (cf. Dundes 1964). Several examples can illustrate the generational work of expanding and preserving simultaneously the ethnomethodological movement's folkloric system of signification.

Second, third, and fourth generation emphases

A recurring theme I have observed in much second and third generation work created during the 1960s and 1970s is the attempt to recover the experiencing personal subject as the authoritative source of society and knowledge. This movement of thought was certainly in contraposition to the depersonalizing elements of the military-industrial complex's use of science to host the Vietnam War and positivism's persuasive influence in American culture and academics, what William Blake termed "single vision and Newton's sleep." I find this same emphasis, though in different form, in much fourth generation work as well. The fourth generation's task has been more of a resynthesis of the constitutive subject with the formal structures of its produced objective world. "Decentering" theories such as structuralism and some versions of semiotics seek an emphasis away from phenomenological egos and onto the objective production of signs and structures (cf. Lemert 1979; Eco 1976; Foucault 1973). Ethnomethodology's fourth generation has been attempting syntheses and critiques of these perspectives. They have attempted investigations of human sign and object-producing activities while trying to utilize the phenomenological and hermeneutic subject as a contextual praxeologist (cf. Baccus 1976; Liberman 1985; Combs 1985; Lynch 1985a; Livingston 1986).

Ethnomethodology and liberation

"Early" ethnomethodology provides a radical critique of contemporary social science procedures that attempt to "correct" or repair the man on the street's common-sense knowledge and procedures. This critique was in accord with many of the sentiments of the student youth culture during the 1960s and 1970s who were faced with the results of American science's unsuccessful "correction" of the Vietnamese people's movement of liberation, black American's claims to equality, the fact of ecological imbalance, and the students' own protests against the military-scientific establishment's devaluation of "the man on the street," whether they were chicano farm workers, draft resistors, gay rights activists, women, welfare recipients or the students themselves.

In the Purdue Symposium debate, Garfinkel voiced his critique against sociology's correctives of common-sense knowledge this way:

> For example, the sociologists are forever beginning their descriptive works, "whereas it is commonly held that ..." then comes the *corrective*. The case is otherwise.

> All of this means that the common-sense knowledge of the member is put up against something that we call scientific knowledge, where scientific knowledge is a *competitor* to common-sense knowledge (Garfinkel in Hill and Crittenden 1968:15).

In the 1970s ethnomethodology was taught as a liberation sociology at the University of California, San Diego. Second and third generation ethnomethodologists taught ethnomethodology alongside Paolo Freire's (1968) *Pedagogy of the Oppressed*, and Joseph Chilton Pearce's (1971) *The Crack in the Cosmic Egg* emphasizing that people's practical actions could liberate society and one's mind. In the following excerpt, Mehan and Wood (1975a:238) specifically use and expand Garfinkel's anti-corrective stance as a sign-vehicle that expresses a vision embedded in a distinctive third generation experiential contexture:

> Unlike social science and much earlier ethnomethodology, my ethnomethodology is a *form of life*. It is not a body of theory or of method. I envision ethnomethodology as a collection of practices similar in purpose to the practices artists and craftsmen teach and use. That my understanding is radically unlike contemporary social science seems a virtue to me. In committing itself above all to reporting, social science has shown itself to be a form of life that

denigrates the integrity of non-western, non-male, non-liberal, non-techno-logical realities... My vision of ethnomethodology undermines this practice.

Mehan and Wood signify their own unique place in a third generation formulation and interpretation of ethnomethodology situated in a unique cultural-historical situation. They say "unlike ... much earlier ethnom-ethodology" and "I envision ethnomethodology as ...," thus specifying themselves as a situated generation and form of "neoethnomethodology." They have reinterpreted ethnomethodology's program according to their historically determined life experiences.

Endless reflexivity

The ethnomethodological conception or feature of reflexivity holds a particularly strong charm for the second and third generations (as well as for the fourth generation) in ways that are distinct from the first generation's concerns. The fundamental problem of reflexivity (cf. Garfinkel 1967a) has been interpreted by the second, third, and fourth generations to include dimensions of discovery that the first generation has only alluded to phenomenologically. In concert with the larger cultural contours of the 1960s and 1970s, the younger ethnomethodological generations, as well as many of their students, saw in the problem of reflexivity not only a key to the constitution of society, but a path to the conscious constitution of the self. The realization that "the organized, factual character of any occasion depends reflexively on itself" (Wilson 1970:79) was construed by some to include the "occasion" of the individual and collective psyche and consciousness.

Garfinkel has spoken of an "endless reflexivity" that "illuminates" the features of a setting. The following excerpt illustrates the first generation form from which this message has allowed for a polysemic reading by mystically oriented 60s and 70s students engaged in "New Age" explorations of self:

> One might talk of a kind of endless reflexivity that accounts have in the same way that "talk" folds back on the setting in which it happens to illuminate the features of that setting and thereby illuminate the talk's own features as well (Garfinkel in Hill and Crittenden 1968:208).

Numerous second and third generation works were seriously dedicated to explicating the "reality of reflexivity" (Mehan and Wood 1975a:137-159) in such a way as to highlight and preserve reflexivity as "ultimately an occult phenomenon" (Mehan and Wood 1975a:159; Pollner 1970) and "a theology" (Mehan and Wood 1975a:137). This attention to the inner dimensions of the problem of reflexivity was a theme shared as well by the larger culture of American youth, especially in California (cf. Berger 1981). "New Age" cultural emphases on personal explorations of one's consciousness by means of new religions, psychedelic drugs, rock music, sexual liberations, and returning to nature are all well documented experiental domains shared by a remarkably large portion of the American youth culture in the pre- and post-Vietnam War era of the 1960s and 1970s (cf. Glock and Bellah 1976; Needleman 1970, 1987). Ethnomethodology's graduate students at that time on the campuses of the Universities of California, Los Angeles, Berkeley, Santa Barbara, and San Diego were certainly not untouched by this mind-expanding cultural ground swell. Actually, work done by graduate students in the ethnomethodological movement at that time shows a great preoccupation with applying ethnomethodological insights to areas culturally relevant to California youth culture. The ethnomethodological roots in the phenomenology of perception lent themselves perfectly to the second, third, and fourth generations' new and sometimes visionary quests.

A unique sociocultural climate has embedded each of the ethnomethodological movements' successive generations. Each generation has faced the task of formulating a "neoethnomethodology" that is relevant to current issues, debates, and cultural relevances. Pollner described his perception of cultural ambiance surrounding ethnomethodology's second and third generation at the University of California, Los Angeles in the 1960s.

> ...in the years '68-'69 while I was here I think there was a certain kind of ambiance that was being created by the ... openness and uncertainly of the political environment, and ethnomethodology's ... critical impulses. The ideals of ethnomethodology, the notion of the construction of reality, the notion of taken-for-granted assumptions, these were now being questioned on the political sphere and they seemed to resonate with what ethnomethodology was doing as a general intellectual kind of project. And I think that cultivated a certain diffuse support and congeniality to at least certain dimensions of ethnomethodology ... I think I experienced that in a more direct way than say, in the political climate at an earlier point. (lines 104-121, interview transcript)

Visionary ethnomethodology and the new age

The visionary "new age" lineage of interests in 1960s and 1970s ethno-methodology can be traced by reviewing some of the papers written by young second and third generation members at that time, as well as by examining their later accounts of that period. Garfinkel's and Cicourel's ethnomethodology was used as sign vehicles for aspects of the second and third generation's interests. These transcended or lay somewhat outside of "early" ethnomethodology. The first generation was often aware of the extent and horizons of the second generation's construction and employment of the ethnomethodological sign vehicle in their own culture-specific investigations. Ethnomethodology is a fundamentally radical phenomenological discipline that demands that its practitioners undertake disciplined reflexive examinations of their own social construction of reality.

Some members of the second and third generation found rigorous ethnomethodological inquiry compatible with other types of new age inquiries being undertaken by their generational cohorts through techniques like meditation, mysticism, psychedelic drugs, altered states of consciousness, alternative realities, and new understandings of self and society available at that time. The new forms of social activism and communal sharing characteristic of America's "fourth great awakening" (cf. McGlaughlin 1978), introduced through the agency of young people doing the new mass rock concerts like Woodstock, antiwar demonstrations, civil rights activism, communal living, and the collective nurturing of a growing ecological awareness, provided a climate of reception for the ethnomethodological movement in the universities.

The ethnomethodological system of signification was able to supply referents for complex cultural experiences existing in the 1960s. Mel Pollner has commented in an interview that Carlos Castaneda's presence at Garfinkel's seminars in the late '60s epitomized the unique American context of generational reception reception at the time:

PF: I am interested in how the students at that time resonated with certain historical elements. How about the Castaneda thing? Were you at all involved with that, or did you know anything about this?

MP: ... I knew Castaneda at the time, and I still know him (laughs) ... he was coming to some of Garfinkel's seminars when I was a young faculty member... '68, '69, '70, and it seemed somehow appropriate that, yes, in those political times, yes, there would be a Yaqui shaman or a Yaqui apprentice coming to these seminars and sharing his experiences of being a bird or whatever and it seemed (laughs) in some ways sort of natural and ... it partook of the, at that time, the anything is possible, anything goes climate of events ... that's not saying very much ... but ... It did feed into the overall atmosphere ... his presence. I guess the atmosphere made sense of Castaneda's presence and Castaneda's presence further culted ... cultivated an atmosphere and spirit that was on the edge of things at the time.

Words and ideas are semiotic signs referring to underlying subjective contours of experience. I will now examine some textual excerpts that illustrate the second and third generations' creation and use of specific cultural word-icons: "vision", "perception", and "seeing". These visionary or perceptual words bear a cultural connotation of the transcendence of ordinary, familiar vision that is characteristic of the mystical, ideological and critical dispositions of the fourth great awakening or "new age" culture. Ethnomethodology also offered a transcendency centered on the investigation of the invisible, taken-for-granted assemblage of everyday life structures. I present here a compilation of excerpts from second and third generation writers utilizing compositions of these words that carry distinctive historical-cultural connotations to new age collective streams of experience:

Exhibit 7

The *vision* of ethnomethodology presented in this book is not universally shared by ethnomethodologists. These chapters should be read as a prospectus, not as an authoritative text. (Mehan and Wood 1975a: preface, vii)

My *vision* of ethnomethodology undermines this practice. I do not suggest that social scientists cease studying human phenomenon, only that they begin to use methods that are becoming to the mysterious phenomena ethnomethodology has unearthed (Mehan and Wood 1975a:238)

If my study helps to realize the *vision* of a rigorous ethnomethodology, I would be most pleased. (Sudnow 1978:vi)

I wish to express profound gratitude to ... Professor Harold Garfinkel, who gave me the model and *the spirit* of exhaustive inquiry. (Castaneda 1968, Acknowledgments)

Don Juan stated that in order to arrive at a *"seeing"* one first had to "stop the world." "Stopping the world" was indeed an appropriate rendition of certain states of awareness in which the reality of everyday life is altered because the flow of interpretation, which ordinarily runs uninterruptedly, has been stopped by a set of circumstances alien to that flow. (Castaneda 1973a:xiii)

What I mean is that it was for them a matter of somehow or other in their dealings with each other they managed, if you will permit me to now to use it, to *see*. (Garfinkel in Hill and Crittenden 1968:9)

It was available, somehow or other, for that peculiar way of looking a member has. The peculiar way of searching, of scanning, of sensing, of *seeing* finally, but not only seeing, but *seeing-reporting*. (Garfinkel in Hill and Crittenden 1968:9)

The termination of the apprenticeship meant that I had learned a new description of the world in a convincing and authentic manner and thus had become capable of eliciting *a new perception of the world*, which matched its new description. In other words, I had gained membership. (Castaneda 1973a:xiii)

With our eyes we can *look* at an object, but to the extent that we grasp the inner structure of the object and are able *to see* in a way that transcends merely looking, our perceptions act in concert and it can be said that we gain insight into order. (Ten Houten and Kaplan 1973:60)

Alchemy thus reveals itself as a unique phenomenology which can be encountered in the methods via which it brings its world to *observability*, no less that to accountability, and via which, after its own lights, it presents itself as a rationally defensible enterprise. The methods developed by Harold Garfinkel, it is believed, are singularly suited to provide access to the ways of that accountability in every occasion of their use. (Eglin 1974:155)

In addition to the studies by Garfinkel which we have had occasion to mention, we note his *radical revision* of the problem of common understandings. (Zimmerman and Pollner 1970:101)

There is a striking parallel to this situation in *mystical disciplines*. Instructions are given for aspirants to follow by a teacher. It is understood that the aspirant will not know what these instructions tell him to do, but rather after he is acting and looking in the intended ways ... it will then become clear what. the meaning of the instructions were. (Schwartz 1971:202-203)

These textual excerpts display a semiotic process of generational anaphorization (cf. Greimas 1976:22-23; Greimas and Courtés 1982:13). The iconized words are second and third generation condensed expressions. Anaphorization establishes a relation of partial identity between the established first generation signitive systems and second and third generation cultural relevances. These anaphorization procedures establish and maintain the generational discourse. Garfinkel's excerpts coreference the new uses of the expression, "seeing", used by Castaneda and later generations.

Generational topical relevance

An examination of some of the topics investigated by second and third generation students in the 1960s and early 1970s also shows an underlying cultural world-view or system of experiential themata uniquely relevant to them as a generation. Second and third generation ethnomethodologists began the first ethnomethodological studies of new knowledge systems. For example, in 1973 Warren Ten Houten and Charles Kaplan from the University of California, Los Angeles published *Science and Its Mirror Image*, an investigation of alternative and occult inquiries that are the "mirror image" of naturalistic sciences. Ten Houten and Kaplan found that "appositional inquiries" like the Tarot, the I Ching, sorcery, magic, and psychotropic plant ingestion make use of "synthetic" methods that are the opposite of science's strict cannons of logic: "An emphasis in nonscientific knowledge is that perception of a situation must be compatible with personal knowledge. That is, the personal experience of an inquirer provides a source of authority for knowledge" (Ten Houten and Kaplan 1973:135). Their study displays a concern for exploring the organization of nonscientific knowledge.

Another work that displays a unique generational embeddedness (and was itself extremely influential in forming its own context of reception) was Carlos Castaneda's series of "ethnographic allegories" of his apprenticeships to the brujo, Don Juan Matus. Beginning with the publication of his first book in 1968, *The Teachings of Don Juan: A Yaqui Way of Knowledge*, Castaneda has proceeded to write a series of eight books (1968, 1972, 1973a, 1976, 1977, 1981, 1984, 1987). These describe his essentially ethnomethodological field of studies with the Yaqui shaman that began in 1961 as an anthropology graduate student at the University of California, Los Angeles. Castaneda undertook graduate apprenticeship with Garfinkel and Robert Edgerton in the Department of Sociology. He received a Ph.D. in anthropology from the University of California, Los Angeles in 1973 for his doctoral dissertation entitled *Sorcery: A Description of the World* (1973). *The Teachings of Don Juan* is dedicated to Garfinkel and to Edgerton. Castaneda's descriptions of Don Juan's "separate reality" of sorcery are well known and mirror an understanding of the social world and its investigations that is unmistakably ethnomethodological (cf. Mary Douglas 1975:193-200). Castaneda utilized ethnomethodological concepts like accounts, membership, and the common-sense view of the world to describe the differences between Don Juan's world of sorcery and everyday Western mentalities. Although some critics suspect Castaneda's accounts as being imaginary (cf. De Mille 1976, 1980), nevertheless his influence on certain elements of modern New Age culture and thinking has been immense.

Other ethnomethodologists investigated generationally relevant topics, adapting the ethnomethodological knowledge system as a sign-vehicle through which to carry on these historically relevant explorations. Wood (1969a) used Garfinkel's zatocoding experiments to explore self-consciousness, discovering that "insight too is not 'something' but a temporally unfolding evanescent creation" (Wood 1969a). Eglin's (1973) study of alchemy used Garfinkel's methods to analyze the occult tradition's practices. Schwartz's (1971) study was on mental disorder and the study of subjective experiences and contained comparisons of mysticism and references to Swami Vishnudevananda. Jules-Rosette (1973, 1975b) wrote an account and analysis of her membership in the Apostles of John Maranke, a syncretic African religious movement. Jules-Rosette expanded on the genre of Castaneda, providing first-hand accounts of visionary experiences and "becoming the phenomenon." Bellman (1975) produced a similar ethnomethodological study of the production of Fala Kpelle cosmological categories. Wedow (1973) wrote her dissertation on the ethnomethodology of astrology and astrological practices. Pollner (1970, 1974) analyzed how we routinely construct an intersubjective, objective reality. His ethnomethodological analysis of mundane "primordial theses and the properties of their use" (1974:35) used heuristic comparisons to the "artfulness" of Azande poison oracle's practices and their incompatibility with Western scientific methods of understanding. Zimmerman and Wieder (1977) conducted an ethnomethodological study of countercultural drug users' folklore and knowledge systems. They examined how "freaks" assembled an ethnomethodology of types and situated uses of dope. Silverman's (1975) *Reading Castaneda* utilized Castaneda's accounts of his meetings with the magician Don Juan as a means to analyze sense-making as a socially organized activity. Combs' dissertation (1985) phenomenologically and ethnomethodologically described the world of a tarot reader.

Conclusion: neoethnomethodology

All of these cases illustrate the historical trend of the ethnomethodological movement toward developing generational "neoethnomethodologies." Neoethnomethodology is the attempt to signify ethnomethodology's underlying program in new discursive forms and to new interdisciplinary audiences. Ethnomethodology's goal of rigorously investigating the organizational properties of everyday practical actions from within actual social settings constitutes neoethnomethodology's narrative schema.

Ethnomethodology's second and third generations were beginning to adapt the ethnomethodological semantic universe during the 1960s and 1970s. This adaption process forms the base of the production of neoethnomethodology. The ethnomethodological system of signification is neither fixed nor static. It is elastic enough to accommodate generational developments of figurative discourse and relevant topics. An examination of first, second, third, and fourth generation neoethno-methodology (cf. Garfinkel, Lynch, and Livingston 1981; Schegloff 1986b; Cicourel and Mehan 1985; Jules-Rosette 1986c; Pollner 1986; Atkinson and Drew 1979; Maroules 1985; Combs 1985; Fisher and Todd 1986; West 1986; Maynard 1986; Quéré, Conein, and Pharo 1984) shows that ethnomethodology can be a system capable of sustaining its fundamental analytical program while developing new modes for representing it. This is done through creative forms of intertextual practices, "poetic" license, and folkloric expansion.

Future research is required to trace the generational constitution of social scientific styles of research and writing. As we saw at the start of this chapter, it is often the case that membership in the ethnomethodological movement's domain of knowledge is accompanied by an intellectual transformation experience. This transformation is constituted by an appropriation of a new semantic universe of discourse. It remains to be seen how future generations of ethnomethodologists will organize the transmission and appropriation of ethnomethodological knowledge forms. New forms of ethnomethodology will emerge that are adapted to relevant generation interests, topics, and interdisciplinary links. An organizational task facing the contemporary ethnomethodological movement is the heuristic continuation of the expansion and transmission of its historicized core program. This continuation and expansion proceeds through neoethnomethodological sign vehicles. The historical transmission of a core program through new sign vehicles is a challenge facing all contemporary intellectual movements of thought. New generations of scholars require new presentational styles as well as content. These new styles can embody new paradigmatic discoveries that are made relevant to contemporary problematics, issues, and interests. New sign vehicles and representations will also change the core programs. The ethnomethodological movement is thus continually faced with its own phenomenon of reflexivity and the reflexive construction of social scientific fact.

Chapter Seven
The Ethnomethodological Movement Around the World in a Comparative Historical Perspective

What I am saying is that it is practical through and through in order to get it done. That is the phenomenon. That is the only thing that is of interest.
Garfinkel (Hill and Crittenden 1968:175)

The thing that I feel is that I am being asked to subscribe to recent doctrinaire views, yet I go on doing phenomenological and existential philosophical studies of ordinary activities.
Garfinkel (Hill and Crittenden 1968:114)

You know that what we take for granted is, of course, interesting, but we really ought to get around to it sometime and get a look at it. So what I am proposing is that that damn thing is all I am going to look at. I am not looking at anything else.
Garfinkel (Hill and Crittenden 1968:199)

This chapter examines the ethnomethodological movement in comparative-historical perspective. First, I compare the ethnomethodological movement with the semiotics movement. We observe that the two groups' organizational practices are productive of their essential features as knowledge domains. Second, I explore an instance of ethnomethodology's knowledge transmission into Paris, France, during 1985. I investigate an example of the intellectual and sociocultural context of Paris, ethnographic surrealism, which provides a significant experiential contour for the ethnomethodological movement's reception.

The semiotic and ethnomethodological movements

The semiotics movement and the ethnomethodological movement in the United States are not different in age but are historically *parallel* intellectual movements. Dean MacCannell (a dedicated purveyor of the synthesis and expansion of what he refers to as a "second ethnomethodology" with semiotics) has frequently presented semiotics as chronologically following ethnomethodology on the sociological scene (cf. MacCannell, 1981:74-96, 1986a:165, 1986b). Ethnomethodology and semiotics, in fact, share a synchronous intellectual history. We shall see that it is the two movements' organizational practices that account for their most profound differences.

The ethnomethodological movement has, from the first, utilized and adapted concepts that have been at the heart of the semiotics movement. This borrowing of ideas is an indicator of the two movements' historical proximity of development. Thomas A. Sebeok (1976:5) places the founding of the American semiotics movement in the philosophical writings of Charles Sanders Peirce (1839-1914). Later writers such as Charles Morris (1938) and C.K. Odgen and I.A. Richards (1938) supplied the American audience with further systematizations on the "science of signs." When Alfred Schutz arrived on the American intellectual scene, he found it necessary to enter the debates over the nature of the sign and sign-making activity. Schutz often incorporated discussions of sign systems in his interpretations of phenomenology for the American audience (cf. Schutz 1945a, b, 1951, 1959). In his 1955 "Symbol, Reality, and Society," Schutz (1955:288-292) analyzes Morris's (1946) and Ducasses's (1942) work on sign theory in terms of Husserl's phenomenological model of signs.

Garfinkel has on numerous occasions used or responded to the semiotic movement's ideas. The study of members' use of indexical expressions, which has been central to ethnomethodology's researches, bears a close resemblance to Peirce's definition of the index as one form of sign object. Garfinkel has connected intentional methods of understanding with the ways people speak when they "gloss" a "multitude of sign functions as when we take note of marking, labeling, symbolizing, emblemizing, cryptograms, analogies, anagrams, indicating, miniaturizing, imitating, mocking up, simulating-in-short, in recognizing, and producing the orderly ways of cultural settings" (Garfinkel 1967e:31).

Garfinkel's use of the "token theory of meaning" (Garfinkel 1967b: 202) and the "documentary method of interpretation" (Garfinkel 1967a: 78-79) shares common interest with the semiotics movement concerning the nature of social signifying acts and commonsense referencing systems. Garfinkel and Sacks (1970:343) use I.A. Richard's (1955:17-56) semiotic discussion of "glossing a text" as a "thematic example" of one of the ways readers and speakers use unknown procedures for making texts and conversations comprehensible. In the same article, Garfinkel and Sacks (1970:348, fn. 17) footnote Charles Sanders Peirce as one of many major philosophers who have worked on the nature of indexical expressions. They also include Wittgenstein, Husserl, Russell, Goodman, and Bar-Hillel. Garfinkel has participated in the University of California semiotics conferences in 1985, 1986, and 1990.

Other ethnomethodologists have utilized and attempted to expand upon semiotic ideas. Aaron Cicourel has frequently debated with linguists and semioticians in his work (cf. Cicourel 1973b, 1981) and early on discussed Schutz's theory of signs and communication (1964:212-218). Cicourel has taught at the International Semiotics Summer Institute. Zimmerman (1974) wrote a preface to Wieder's (1974a) book (published by the semiotic movement's publishing arm, *Approaches to Semiotics*) that attempted a theoretical exposition detailing the significance of ethnomethodology "for a semiotic theory that has relevance to the empirical study of human social interaction" (Zimmerman 1974:26). Baccus (1976), Pack (1976), and Liberman (1983) have engaged in theoretical dialogues with semiotics from an ethnomethodological perspective.

Bennetta Jules-Rosette (1977, 1984, 1986a, 1986b) has significantly extended the ethnomethodological synthesis with semiotics. Her early work included explorations of ethnographic film as a sociological research medium that included dialogues with semiotic theory (cf. Jules-Rosette and Bellman 1977). Her later work has dealt directly with synthetic applications of semiotics and ethnomethodology in the context of field work amongst African tourist art producers and the analysis of the tourist art's "messages" (cf. Jules-Rosette (1979b, 1984), the narrative structure of African religious prophecy (Jules-Rosette 1986a). She and A.J.-J. Cohen have organized the Semiotic Lecture Series and Roundtable Conferences held at the University of California, San Diego and Los Angeles during 1985 to 1990 (cf. Cohen 1985) and were pivotal in the organization of the 1986 International Conference on Description in the Social Sciences in Cerisy-La-Salle, France, that provided an opportunity for ethnomethodologists and semioticians to exchange views and ideas. Her recent work has focused on the "sociosemiotics" of Ethiopian jokes (Jules-Rosette 1986c), the contributions of a semiotic perspective to the problems of ethnographic description (Jules-Rosette 1986b), and on the place of semiotic theory in the larger sociological context (Jules-Rosette, 1986d).

The first conferences

The semiotics movement in the United States held its first conferences on semiotics on May 17 to 19, 1962, at Indiana University (Sebeok 1976:21; Sebeok, Hayes, and Bateson 1972). It was sponsored by the U.S. Office of Education (Sebeok, 1976:21). The semiotics movement already had numerous local working groups in Europe, especially in France, Italy, Poland, and the U.S.S.R. The United States conference was organized to discuss the topics of paralinguistics and kinesics but soon widened to include more areas of nonverbal communication, though with a constant reference to language-related issues (Sebeok, 1976:21). It was here that Margaret Mead suggested that this growing field of studies of patterned communication be called "semiotics." "It would be very nice," Miss Mead said,

> ...if we could go away from here with at least a preliminary argument on the use of some phrase that we could apply to this whole field. Kinesics and paralinguistics, after all, are two... We are, I think, conceivably working in a field which in time will include the study of all patterned communication in all modalities, of which linguistics is the most technically advanced. If we had a word for patterned communications in all modalities, it would be useful...many people here, who have looked as if they were on opposite sides of the fence, have used the word "*semiotics*." It seems to me the one word, in some form or other, that has been used by people who are arguing from quite different positions... A lot of people are not going to spend their time on this field unless it is set up for exploration at all levels and in all modalities, but with a great deal from linguists. (Sebeok, Hayes, and Bateson 1972:275).

The first conference on the semiotics movement in the United States provides an interesting contrast to parallel developments that were occurring at the same time in the ethnomethodological movement. Ethnomethodology held its first collective Conference on Ethnomethodology in February, 1962, at the University of California, Los Angeles (Garfinkel 1967a:7.3, fn.12). It was supported by a grant from the Behavioral Sciences Division, U.S. Air Force Office of Scientific Research (Garfinkel 1967a:10). This conference was organized to discuss, among other things, the properties and consequences of the "et cetera clause," an unspoken but understood interpretive device used in common sense understandings and decision-making (Garfinkel 1967a:73-75; Schutz 1962a:3-47). Conference members were Egon Bittner, Harold Garfinkel, Craig MacAndrew, Edward Rose, and Harvey Sacks.

Garfinkel had chosen the name "ethnomethodology" in 1954 to stand for the enterprise he was then beginning to develop. He recounted how he selected the name to the participants at the 1968 Purdue Symposium on Ethnomethodology (Hill and Crittenden 1968:5-8) in the following way:

> Back in 1954 ...when I was writing up these materials I dreamed up the notion underlying the term "ethnomethodology." You want to know where I actually got the term? I was working with the Yale cross-cultural area files. I happened to be looking down the list without the intent of finding such a term. I was looking through their tag lines, if you permit that usage, and I came to a section ethnobotany, ethnophysiology, ethnophysics... Now, how to stick a label on that stuff, for the time being, to help me recall the burden of it? How to get a reminder of it? That is the way "ethnomethodology" was used to begin with. "Ethno" seemed to refer, somehow or other, to the availability to a member of common-sense knowledge of the "whatever." If it were "ethnobotany," then it had to do somehow or other with his knowledge and his grasp of what were for members adequate *methods* for dealing with botanical matter... The member would employ ethnobotany as adequate grounds of inference and action in the conduct of his own affairs in the company of others like him. It was that plain, and the notion of "ethnomethodology" was taken in this sense.

These two pioneering, initial 1962 conferences of the ethnomethodological and semiotics movements were organized in comparable ways. According to Sebeok (1976:22) the first semiotic conference was deliberately organized as a pentad. Its five foci were medicine, specifically communication with words between patient and doctor (Ostuald 1964); psychology, in particular research on extralinguistic phenomena (Mahl and Schalze 1964); pedagogical perspectives in paralinguistic and kinesics (Hayes 1964); cross cultural perspectives (La Barre 1964); and emotive language (Stankiewicz 1964). The published transactions (Sebeok, Hayes, and Bateson 1964) included a summary statement by Margaret Mead calling for "continuing work on the multimodal analysis of communication."

The first conference on ethnomethodology was, according to Garfinkel (1967a:73, fn. 12), organized around discussions of the et cetera clause in the settings of radicalism (Bittner 1963), sociological description (Sacks 1963), Garfinkel's trust experiments (Garfinkel 1963), and his research at the Los Angeles Suicide Prevention Center (Garfinkel 1967a:76-103). Extended discussions and studies were begun at this conference and were continued in published papers by conference participants on the topic of the et cetera clause in the areas of "coding procedures, methods of interrogation, lawyers' work, translation, model construction, historical reconstruction, 'social bookkeeping,' counting, and personality diagnosis" (Garfinkel 1967a:73, fn.12). Conference transcripts have remained unpublished.

The semiotics movement early on made it an aim to establish itself as an interdisciplinary and international endeavor with strong publishing outlets. Unlike the ethnomethodological movement, the semiotics movement by 1966, had held its first full-scale international conference in Poland with representatives from Czechoslovakia, Denmark, France, the German Democratic Republic, Italy, Poland, the U.S.A., and the U.S.S.R. in attendance (Sebeok 1976:24). At this conference, members decided on two "practical" actions: to create an International Association for Semiotics and to establish multiple publication outlets for the movement's work.

By 1969, the International Association for Semiotic Studies had announced three aims; to promote semiotic researches in a scientific spirit to advance international cooperation in this field; and to collaborate with local associations (Sebeok, 1976:24). The Association proposed to achieve these aims by the organization of local, national, and international meetings, and through its sponsorship of an international publication, *Semiotica*. The movement officially began *Semiotica* in 1969 and has subsequently supplemented the journal with three series, *Approaches to Semiotics, Advances in Semiotics, and Studies in Semiotics* to publish book-length contributions, including original monographs, collections, relevant conference proceedings, reprintings, and translations of important works. As we shall see, this practical organizational action by the semiotics movement had very important consequences for the members of the ethnomethodological movement as well.

By 1966, the ethnomethodological movement was majorly developing on the campuses of the University of California, Los Angeles and the University of California, Santa Barbara, though numerous local outposts of interest and application existed such as the University of California,

Berkeley, and the University of Colorado. The ethnomethodological movement was constructing its own form of localized "internationalism" by sending two of Garfinkel's doctoral students, Don H. Zimmerman and D. Lawrence Wieder, to the University of California, Santa Barbara to teach and research with Aaron Cicourel's ethnomethodological group during 1969. This signified an important step in the transmission of knowledge.

Nothing so grandiose or well developed as semiotics' international, interdisciplinary meetings had been assembled by the ethnomethodological movement. While semiotics tended to utilize, and then expand, interdisciplinary networks of already established scholars with a direct interest in semiotic studies, ethnomethodology appeared to be choosing to remain in the relatively local company of sociologists and sociology departments. Though the ethnomethodological movement had been working with a variety of anthropologists and linguists as well, it seemed to be concentrating its organization and development on providing a radical critique and alternative to professional sociology, and on the in-depth training of a new breed of sociology graduate student.

Publishing outlets

By the end of the 1960s, the ethnomethodological movement was not succeeding in putting together a collective journal or an established outlet for publishing members' work. This is an accomplishment the ethnomethodological movement has never been able to realize up to the present moment. Instead, members have had to seek and search out alternative publishers who would print their work. Because of the new and radical nature of their contributions, this has been anything but an easy matter. The *American Sociological Review*, one of the most prestigious publishing arms of the sociological profession, has printed only four ethnomethodological articles: Bittner (1963, 1967b), Blum and McHugh (1971), and Molotch and Boden (1985); *The American Journal of Sociology* published only two ethnomethodological articles: Garfinkel (1956a) and Handel (1979).

Given the situation that few established standard sociological presses would consistently publish ethnomethodology's work and lacking a publishing outlet of its own, the ethnomethodological movement found itself repeatedly turning to *Semiotica* and the related publishing outlets of the semiotics movement. There they found a consistently willing publisher for its new radical studies. From 1972 to the present, the semiotics movement has published over twenty-five ethnomethodological works, including three full-length books. These works include Cicourel (1972), Cicourel and Boèse (1972a), Schenkein (1972, 1974b), Jefferson (1973), Schegloff and Sacks (1973), Moerman and Sacks (1974), Wieder (1974a), Zimmerman (1974), Bellman (1975), Turner (1976), Eglin (1976), Wootton (1981), Heritage and Watson (1980), Jules-Rosette (1979a, 1984, 1986a, 1986c), Liberman (1982), Maynard (1980), Sharrock and Anderson (1986b), Heath (1982), Goodwin (1986), Bjelic (1987), and McHoul (1987).

Ethnomethodology is now just beginning to realize a selective movement publishing outlet in the new series with Routledge and Kegan Paul, London, entitled *Studies in Ethnomethodology*, edited by Harold Garfinkel. So far, four books have come out: Lynch (1985a), Liberman (1985), Livingston (1986), and Garfinkel (1986a). A list of forthcoming publications has been publicly promised. Garfinkel's collection (forthcoming, 3 volumes) was promised in 1983 (cf. Lynch, Livingston, and Garfinkel 1983) with the first volume, *Ethnomethodological Studies of Work*, published in 1986.

Historical milestones

The semiotics movement called the year 1969 a "milestone" year in its history (Sebeok 1976:26). The year 1969 marks the time of the semiotics movement's organization into an interdisciplinary and international association of independent scholars interested in signifying activities, and the concurrent establishment of multiple publishing outlets. These organizational practices have provided for the continuing life of the semiotics movement into the 1980s and beyond. For the ethnomethodological movement, by contrast, 1969 marked its most schismatic year at precisely the point when it most needed to implement practices of organization in order to provide an open and coherent future for itself.

The Symposium on Ethnomethodology was held in 1968 at Purdue University. The symposium was organized by Richard J. Hill and others to provide leaders of the ethnomethodological movement an opportunity to air and confront issues with interested and critical members of the sociological profession (cf. Hill and Crittenden 1968). According to Hill and Crittenden (1968:iii), the driving purpose was to confront questions such as

> Does ethnomethodology constitute a new approach to "doing sociology" or is it an extension of an established tradition? Are ethnomethodologists a group of scholars with a mutual sense of the problematic, or do they constitute a strange movement within sociology? To what degree does ethnomethodology con-stitute a serious methodological critique of traditional sociological practice? Is ethnomethodology a "disaster" or is it something "to get excited about"?

Harold Garfinkel, Aaron V. Cicourel, Harvey Sacks, Edward Rose, David Sudnow, and Lindsey Churchill represented the ethnomethodologists. They squared off with Theodore Anderson, Howard S. Becker, Richard J. Hill, David Gold, Charles Tittle, Melvin L. De Fleur, Herbert Costner, Kathleen Stones Crittenden, Robert McGinness, Eleanor B. Sheldon, and Karl F. Schuessler to discuss the ethnomethodological movement's contributions. While the ethnomethodologists did their best to communicate, the consensus at the end of the two-day symposium was that the ethnomethodologists either could not, or did not, want to communicate their "mysterious" methodology and theories (cf. Hill and Crittenden 1968:252-259).

In the minds of many ethnomethodologists, the series of events in the years immediately following the Purdue Symposium were indicative of the direction the movement was to take throughout the 1970s and the early 1980s. The Purdue Symposium as an event did not stimulate the movement to draw together its ranks in order to generate communicational rallying points. The movement's potential for developing publishing outlets, organized intercampus graduate training centers, and an agenda of conferences with increasingly expanded, open, and interdisciplinary horizons seemed to be blocked by certain mechanisms internal to the movement. Garfinkel and Cicourel's personal cleavage of 1970 to 1971 marked a certain pattern of behaviors among ethnomethodology's members that has proven counterproductive to the serious presentations of the movement's considerable theoretical and methodological contributions.

The ethnomethodological movement has continued to hold local and even international conferences throughout the last twenty years. These conferences have managed to produce important gatherings that have led to subsequent group publications, especially for the ethnomethodological movement's branch of conversation analysis (cf. Psathas 1979; Atkinson and Heritage 1984). Yet, these conferences have yet to accomplish the sort of disciplinary cohesion that is found in the semiotics movement. The conferences included among others, the Conferences on Ethnomethodology that continued to meet after 1962 at the University of California, Los Angeles, the University of California, Santa Barbara, and the University of Colorado; the Boston University International Summer Institutes on Ethnomethodology and Conversation Analysis since 1977; the Didsbury Conversation Analysis Workshop in England in 1973; the Santa Barbara International Conference on Talk and Social Structure in March, 1976, 1986, and the Journée d'Étude sur L'Ethnomethodologie held at the École des Hautes Études en Sciences Sociales, Paris since 1984.

Signs of convergence

The ethnomethodological and semiotic movements today show signs of convergences. The semiotics movement, with its relatively high theoretical syncretism, has begun to look to ethnomethodology as a source of theory and empirical research on the pragmatics of contextual sign communication. The International Summer Semiotics Institute has for the past several years invited ethnomethodologists to deliver lectures. The International Conference on Description in the Social Sciences at Cerisy-La-Salle, France in September, 1986, brought ethnomethodologists and semioticians together on a common problem. MacCannell and MacCannell (1982:84-96) have been calling for a "second ethnomethodology" that is a hybrid form of cultural semiotics rooted in ethnography. Levinson (1983) has claimed that conversational analysis provides a significant contribution to the study of pragmatics in linguistics and semiotics. Fabbri (1985) argues that Greimas and Garfinkel share common sources in phenomenology and share common interests investigating the details of language use and assembled communication in new ways. *Semiotica* continues to publish articles by ethnomethodologists and critical responses to their work.

The future will see the degree to which the ethnomethodological movement and the semiotics movement will cooperate together. I see ethnomethodology as having a need for similar organizational features and solutions as those created by the semiotics movement. Both movements stand in historical isomorphism. Each has developed its own particular strategy for survival as an intellectual field. Continued cooperation and exchange in the conceptual and organizational domains has potential for revolutionary breakthroughs in the study of everyday communication in all modalities.

The ethnomethodological movement in Paris

In November, 1985, Paris was intellectually alive with talk about "l'ethnométhodologie." A special issue of *Sociétés* edited by Bennetta Jules-Rosette had just been published in September entitled "Garfinkel et l'ethnométhodologie" (*Sociétés*, Vol. 1 No. 5, 1985). (See Figure 7-1.) It contains an interview with Garfinkel, the *"Optical Pulsar."* paper (Garfinkel, Lynch, and Livingston 1981), and translations of his and other ethnomethodologists' works. It was believed that Garfinkel was coming to Paris to speak at the Sorbonne and the École des Hautes Études en Sciences Sociales at the end of the month. Special seminars devoted to Garfinkel's recent papers were being held in the Centre d'Études des Mouvements Sociaux at the EHESS and the Sorbonne to prepare for the expected arrival.

I happened to be in Paris that November at the invitation of Professor Gérard Lemaine, director of Groupe d'Études et de Recherches sur la Science, and Professor A.J. Greimas, director of Groupe de Recherches Sémio-linguistique. Both these research groups are affiliated with the École des Hautes Études en Sciences Sociales. I was there as a Châteaubriand fellow sponsored by the French government. I was in Paris to continue comparative work on social studies of science and on semiotics in France and the United States. Researchers from both these Parisian groups had visited the Laboratory for Ethnographic and Audiovisual Studies (LEAVS) (on the University of California, San Diego campus) in 1984 and 1985. I was in Paris with two other LEAVS members as part of an informal exchange between these research groups. I knew and had worked with Harold Garfinkel, and had written several short articles and reviews on ethnomethodology that were translated into French (see Appendix 4), so of course I was extremely interested in

ISSN 0765-3697

SOCIETES

Revue des Sciences Humaines et Sociales

Garfinkel

l'ethnométhodologie

Le champ phénoménal
Sémiotique et ethnométhodologie en Californie
Le syllogisme du sacré
Horowitz

Septembre
1985 - Vol. 1

MASSON
Paris New York Barcelone Milan

N° 5

Figure 7-1 *Sociétés*. Special issue on ethnomethodology, 1985.

following ethnomethodology's Parisian welcome and in personally fostering this exciting new development. The situation in Paris in November of 1985 may prompt the American sociologist to wonder, Why such a big deal about ethnomethodology, and why so late? To find the reasons for this, one must look beneath the surface of Parisian intellectual life. The reasons for Paris's concerted and focused interests in ethnomethodology in 1985 are complex and are intertangled with politics and history.

The promise of Harold Garfinkel's coming to Paris for lectures was raising the intellectual level in some Parisian groups to a near fever pitch. Garfinkel had been in Paris briefly during December, 1984, to speak at a three-day conference on ethnomethodology and description (*Journées d'Étude sur Décrire: Un Impératif?*) held at the École des Hautes Études, sponsored by the Centre d'Étude des Mouvements Sociaux. He had been well received. I learned that it was now hoped that he would give a month-long seminar at the EHESS, as well as invited lectures around Paris.

One year before, in 1984, *Arguments Ethnométhodologiques* had been published by members of the Centre d'Études des Mouvements Sociaux at the École des Hautes Études en Sciences Sociales. (See Figure 7-2.) Articles by Louis Quéré, Bernard Conein, Renaud Dulong, and Patrick Pharo preface first-time translations of portions of Garfinkel's *Studies in Ethnomethodology* (1967), the Purdue Symposium Conference (1968), and Garfinkel and Sacks (1970) "On Formal Structures of Practical Actions." *Arguments Ethnométhodologiques* (Quéré *et al.* 1984) represented a first serious Parisian attempt to critically translate, anthologize, and interpret a major body of ethnomethodological work. Prior to this book, only a few scattered translations of ethnomethodological work had ever appeared in French print (see Appendix 4).

Articles by Cicourel, Sacks, and Schegloff, Blum, Foss, McHugh, and Raffel had been translated for *Communications* (20) in 1973. Cicourel's *Cognitive Sociology* had been translated by 1973 by the Presses Universitaires de France as *La Sociologie Cognitive*. Although Parisian sociologists had made attempts at critically reviewing ethnomethodology (cf. Herpin 1973; Leclerc 1979), *Arguments Ethnométhodologiques* represented, at least for those Parisians that I talked to who were "vraiment" interested in ethnomethodology, the first trustworthy compilation of important translations and analytical reviews.

PROBLÈMES D'ÉPISTÉMOLOGIE
EN SCIENCES SOCIALES

III

Arguments Ethnométhodologiques

Centre d'Etude des Mouvements Sociaux

E.H.E.S.S., C.N.R.S. (L.A. 102)

54, boulevard Raspail
75006 PARIS

Figure 7-2 Arguments Ethnométhodologiques

Various groups of Parisian intellectuals appeared to be very interested in ethnomethodology in November, 1985. It was known that Pierre Bourdieu of the Centre de Sociologie Européen (and editor in chief of *Actes de la Recherches* and Editions Minuit) was very interested in translating and publishing the entirety of *Studies in Ethnomethodology*. I heard it discussed in several Parisian circles that Bourdieu considered ethnomethodology in general, and Garfinkel and Cicourel's work in particular, to be a highly original statement with profound consequences for the social sciences.

The École des Hautes Études en Sciences Sociales group of Louis Quéré, Bernard Conein, Werner Ackerman, Christiane Guiges, and Daniel Vidal next published a two-volume collection of essays on ethnomethodology and its relations to French sociology entitled *Decrire: Un Impératif? Déscription, Explication, Interpretation en Sciences Sociales* in December of 1985. The collection of texts resulted from a conference on ethnomethodology held at EHESS at the Centre d'Étude des Mouvements Sociaux on December 13, 14, 15, 1984. Harold Garfinkel had attended one day of the conference and had given a short talk, which appears as the concluding piece in the collection, entitled, "Sur le Problème des Correctifs" (Ackerman *et al.* 1985b:239-249).

Michel Maffesoli, professor of Sociology at the Sorbonne, editor in chief of *Sociétés* and Librairie des Meridiens, and director of the Centre d'Études sur l'Actuel et le Quotidien and Centre d'Imaginaire, was also supporting Garfinkel's visit. Maffesoli's "formisme" employs an eclectic sociological mix of Simmel, Weber, and, more recently, Alfred Schutz. He studies, and encourages his students to study, the variety of "nouveau" forms of "socialité" found in contemporary everyday life, including orgies, punk rock, bordellos, adventurers, and the strange communities living in Paris's underground catacombs. Maffesoli found Garfinkel's work to be particularly interesting for the detailed study of everyday life, and he invited Garfinkel to speak at the Sorbonne, November 18, 1985.

Associate researchers from the Centre Nationale de Recherche Scientifique (CNRS) who were affiliated with the EHESS, INRP, and the University of Paris, showed interest in ethnomethodology. A number of CNRS researchers had written papers utilizing ethnomethodological concepts and were discussing ethnomethodology's applicability to French social science. These authors include Pierre Achard, Werner Ackerman, Renaud Dulong, Claude Liscia, Jean Marie Maradin, Myriam Pecault,

Patrick Pharo, Michel de Fornel, Louis Quéré, and Daniel Vidal (cf. Ackerman *et al.* 1985).

The semioticians of Paris, notably the Groups de Recherches Sémio-linguistiques, directed by A.J. Greimas, were also excited about Garfinkel's arrival. In the spring of 1985, a number of Parisian semioticians had come to California for the Semiotics Roundtable Conference at the University of California, San Diego. This group included Paolo Fabbri, Louis Marin, and Jean Baudrillard. Garfinkel spoke at this conference on "Details" and was favorably received by the semioticians (cf. Cohen 1985). Garfinkel's visit to Paris was expected to revive the development of a semioethnomethodological movement.

Professor Bruno Latour, a sociologist of science at the École des Mines, had had contact with the ethnomethodological movement since 1976 when he was at the University of California, San Diego teaching and conducting ethnographic research at the Salk Institute (cf. Latour and Woolgar 1979). He had since then published an article by Michael Lynch, one of Garfinkel's students, in an edition of *Culture Technique* (cf. Lynch 1985b). Though not an ethnomethodologist, Latour has used both ethnomethodological and semiotic concepts in his work (cf. Latour 1982; Latour and Fabbri 1977).

The Institute Nationale de Recherche Pedagogique (INRP) had a number of researchers under the direction of M. Derouet who were beginning to work with ethnomethodological ideas in the field of educational research. An informal seminar had been meeting at INRP to discuss Mehan's (1979a) *Learning Lessons* and other ethnomethodologists' works.

The Groups d'Études et de Recherches sur la Sciences (GERS) directed by Gérard Lemaine, with whom I was working, was also interested in Garfinkel. Garfinkel's recent work was on the social phenomenon of scientific discovery. This research group wanted to hear what he had to say. Several of the members of GERS were conducting micro-sociological studies of laboratories and were beginning to employ and cite Garfinkel's work (cf. Lestel 1986).

Perhaps the most curious Parisian group to take an interest in ethnomethodology and in Garfinkel's coming that November was the research cadre called "analyse institutionelle" that was centered at the University of Paris VIII, founded and led by Georges Lapassade and René Lourau. Also called "socianalyse" or "la sociologie d'intervention" (cf. Hess 1981), this school of sociological research seemed to carry a very radical air about it in its insistence that the sociologist must also intervene through a form of militant action into the very institutional structures he or she was attempting to observe. This group believed in the Marxist-Maoist proverb that to know a reality, one must transform it. L'Analyse Institutionelle demanded a "sociologie concréte" rooted in field work and intervention. It was adamantly opposed to mere sociological theorizing or explanation.

Yves Lecerf, an anthropologist from the University of Paris VII (Jussieu) wrote a positive review of *Arguments Ethnométhodologiques* in *Pratiques de Formation* (*Analyses*) (April, 1985), a journal highly influenced by the analyse institutionelle movement. Lecerf claimed that ethnomethodology was coming to Paris to decisively change the face of the social sciences (Lecerf 1984a:165, 171):

> L'année 1984 sera-t-elle, au regard de l'histoire de sciences sociales, celle d'un tournant décisif...Depuis quelques années l'immence d'une irruption en force de l'ethnméthodologie dans les sciences sociales, est une éventualité envisagée par tous les espirits....

In another article in the same edition of *Pratiques*, Lecerf (1984b) called for ethnomethodology to bring a "rapproachement" between a number of Parisian schools of sociology: the school of analyse institutionelle ("la sociologie d'intervention") at the University of Paris VIII; the school of ethnology (descended from Marcel Mauss) at the University of Paris VII; and the Centre d'Étude des Mouvements Sociaux headed by Allain Touraine at the École des Hautes Études en Sciences Sociales. (See Figure 7-3).

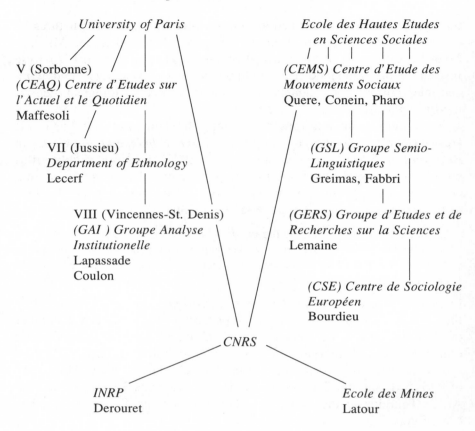

Figure 7-3 The relations of Parisian Schools to Ethnomethodology in November, 1985

The Parisian context of reception

Paris, 1985, provides a case for the observation of how social scientific knowledge is practically transmitted to new cultural contexts of reception via intellectual movements (cf. Jauss 1970; Yates 1978). Intellectual knowledge is communicated by the practical conversational and semiotic practices of culturally situated speakers and hearers. Collective actants are assembled and established by generationally located transmitters and receptors.

On November 18, 1985 a special, ornate lecture hall had been reserved at the Sorbonne for Harold Garfinkel's lecture on ethnomethodology at 5 p.m. The lecture hall was overflowing with people. There was standing room only. My estimation puts the crowd somewhere around two hundred persons. I was able to identify students and faculty from a great variety of Parisian social science groups. One block in particular, whom I did not recognize, seemed unusually noisy and almost tumultuous. This group, I was to find out later that night, was none other than Georges Lapassade with his students.

As it turned out, Harold Garfinkel did not make it to that lecture at the Sorbonne that night. Neither did he make it to Paris at all that Fall of 1985. Instead, one of Garfinkel's students and colleagues, Bennetta Jules-Rosette, came into the lecture hall and gave a talk on ethnomethodology's distinctive features and conceptual aspects. The crowd, at first dismayed at the absence of Garfinkel himself, soon began to listen seriously as Jules-Rosette proceeded to illustrate ethnomethodology's complex program in an excellent and clear French. When her talk was finished, questions began to explode and fly around the hall.

The first questions came from an animated professor, Georges Lapassade, who demanded to know if, contrary to Aaron Cicourel's talk at the EHESS in 1984, the ethnomethodological movement was still alive and if it still claimed a legacy of researching "strange" yet ordinary phenomena from a radical member's perspective, in the line of Garfinkel's and Carlos Castaneda's early works. Lapassade wanted to know if ethnomethodology could be fruitfully used as a method to study such seemingly disparate phenomena as educational institutions and Moroccan trance behavior, and was Cicourel still an ethnomethodologist?

When Bennetta Jules-Rosette said "oui" to these questions, albeit with certain qualifications, then and there began a serious courtship of ethnomethodology's transmitters by Lapassade's group of "institutional analysts." What followed, in terms of frequent invitations to speak, a visiting professorship at the University of Paris VIII for Sam Combs, a student of Jules-Rosette's and a postdoctoral researcher with Garfinkel, publication offers, and numerous opportunities for research collaborations, testified to the perception of a peculiarly strong bond between analyse institutionelle and ethnomethodology. While numerous Parisian groups showed intense interest in ethnomethodology in 1985, that manifested by this group is perhaps the most interesting and curious. We shall examine this "local receptor" of ethnomethodology and the cultural-historical "horizon of expectations" (Jauss 1971) in the next section.

Economic contours of reception

Americans played roles as supporters and brokers for international exchanges of surrealist art in the 1920s and 1930s (cf. Wiser 1983). French support for the ethnomethodological movement displays historical similarities in the economic, cultural, and intellectual conditions necessary for French-American cultural exchange. In 1925, the economic exchange rate was 25 francs to the dollar. This provided an incentive for Americans to visit Paris and, as a result, important cultural liaisons were begun between literary, artistic, and other intellectual domains. In the summer of 1985, the exchange rate of 10 francs to the dollar was also an incentive for American artists and scholars, including myself, to travel to Paris. The French Cultural Ministry's Châteaubriand scholarship program was an open invitation for scholarly exchange. The reception of ethnomethodology in Paris in 1985 was facilitated by the relatively improved economic context. This situation enabled second, third, and fourth generation American ethnomethodologists to travel to Paris and continue the work of translating ethnomethodology into the French intellectual climate.

Translating ethnomethodology

The work of translating texts creates local intellectual cultures. Differences in how ethnomethodological texts were translated into French produced different local lineages of ethnomethodological transmission and reception. A case of this can be observed in the simultaneous translation of Garfinkel's explanation of the origin of the name "ethnomethodology" from the Purdue Symposium on Ethnomethodology (Hill and Crittenden 1968:8-9). This excerpt was translated differently by both Quéré *et al.'s Arguments Ethnométhodologiques* (1985:60-70) and by

Sociétés special issue on ethnomethodology (1985, (5):5-6). Different French translations for key ethnomethodological words such as "accountability" and "unique adequacy" become hotly debated topics of dialogue among competing intellectual factions eager to garner an "approved version" of French ethnomethodology. For example, "accountability" was translated by Jules-Rosette's *Société* teams as "disponibilité"/"disposabilité." *Arguments Ethnométhodologiques* translated in "descriptibilité." Garfinkel "authorized" *Société* versions. Yet, multiple translation styles sprang up as new groups began to adapt ethnomethodology to their intellectual relevances.

Historical contours of receptivity

Paris's present love affair with ethnomethodology bears certain political aims such as proving a possible alternative to the declining Marxist paradigm or a corrective to traditional French social science. As well, the contemporary affinity seems rooted in Paris's perception of correspondence between the ethnomethodological movement and a French approach to ethnography that was developed after the first war, ethnographic surrealism. My growing suspicion that this was indeed the case was heightened when I read James Clifford's "On Ethnographic Surrealism" (Clifford 1981). Clifford put me on the trail of the strong connection between the Parisian tradition of ethnography, started in part by Marcel Mauss and his followers, and the development of surrealist activities in Paris after World War I. The modern ethnographic movement and the surrealist movement developed in very close proximity "in the hothouse milieu of Parisian cultural life" (Clifford 1981:539), sharing members and critical attitudes. This blend of surrealist tendencies with ethnographic methods has survived in Paris and provides much of the inner receptive horizon for ethnomethodology's welcome.

I am going to try to establish how closely related the ethnomethodological and the "ethnographic surrealist" attitudes and practices are. Also, I am going to attempt to show how at least one contemporary Parisian school in particular, l'analyse institutionelle, has been directly influenced by elements of the 1920s and 1930s "surrealist ethnography" movement and how, in the analyse institutionelle movement's present warm welcome of ethnomethodology, it is recognizing a kindred spirit.

Ethnographic surrealism

Ethnographic surrealism refers to a historical disposition toward the empirical world that was founded originally in Paris by members of André Breton's surrealist movement in 1925. Ethnography was wedded to surrealism when in 1929 members of the surrealist movement including Georges Bataille, Robert Desnos, Michel Leiris, Antonin Artaud, Raymond Queneau and others began a journal, *Documents*, that was expressly dedicated to questioning prevailing cultural categories through the use of "ethnographic evidence" taken from both anthropological and amateur researchers (cf. Clifford 1981:548-549). The ethnographic surrealists attributed great influence to Marcel Mauss's lectures on ethnography at the École Pratique de Hautes Études and the Institut d'Ethnologie and formed an informal college, le Collége de Sociologie, designed to support ethnographic studies and direct intervention into social processes. The ethnographic surrealists' aesthetic principle was to begin with reality deep in question and to attempt to juxtapose exotic and strange cultural practices and objects in order to find new human alternatives that could be assembled into new cultural forms.

I characterize ethnographic surrealism and ethnomethodology as sharing several critical orientations toward cultural order: (1) they are both postwar developments, with wartime experiences having a strong formative impact on their collective consciousness; (2) they both poetically and artistically concentrate on the radical assemblage of social reality as a major theme; (3) they both attempt to render the familiar world strange; (4) they both use collage and juxtaposition of found "raw" data as collections of evidence; (5) they both try to supply a new domain of phenomena. Both Garfinkel's ethnomethodological movement and Breton's surrealist movement have arguably developed into far-reaching modern orientations to culture that have exerted influence on modern conceptions of ethnography and empirical sociological research.

The influence of modern warfare on the two movements

The surrealist and ethnomethodological movements were both children of postwar historical contexts and consciousness. They were both products of transitional times when accepted modes of communication were being replaced by something new and more technically modern. For the surrealists, the twilight of World War I imposed on Europe a new cultural style characterized by bursts of "information" such as photographs, newspaper clips, fragments of radio flashes, and the perceptual "shock" of the new modernizing cities (Clifford, 1981:540). I present Walter Benjamin's impressions on the post-World War I apperception that Clifford brought to my attention:

> A generation that had gone to school on a horse-drawn streetcar now stood under an open sky in a countryside in which nothing remained unchanged but the clouds; in a field of force of destructive torrents and explosions was the tiny, fragile human body. (Benjamin 1969:84)

Nadeau (1965:45-58) says that the founding surrealists, Breton, Eluard, Aragon, Peret, and Soupault, "were profoundly affected by the war." Michel Leiris, an early surrealist member, in 1925 at a surrealist banquet in honor of the symbolist poet Saint-Pol-Roux, led a protest against the new French military action in Morocco by opening a window overlooking the boulevard and shouting at the top of his lungs, "Down with France!" He began arguing with a gathering crowd, and a riot ensued on the Boulevard Montparnasse. Leiris, defying the police and mob, was nearly lynched (Nadeau, 1965:114).

In a similar way, the ethnomethodological movement's first generation flowered in the wake of World War II and the Korean War. Its second and third generations were born into the onslaught of the Vietnam War. Harold Garfinkel has said that he learned and developed his distinctive style of teaching and lecturing while serving in the Army as a tank warfare strategy instructor during the Korean War (Garfinkel, personal communication). Hugh Mehan has said that many of his ethnomethodological insights had a source in his experiences as a soldier in Vietnam amongst the traditional mountain people, the Montagnards, who befriended him and attempted to communicate their culture to him in the midst of a cultural genocide (Mehan, personal communication).

The ethnomethodological movement was born on the University of California campuses during the height of the anti-Vietnam War protests. A number of second, third, and fourth generation members participated in the anti-war movements prevalent at that time. All were certainly immersed in the trauma consciousness induced by the Vietnam War that burst through carefully constructed television and media bubbles and shouted for a new resistance and a new revolutionary change. A leaflet entitled "Attention all Military Personnel" distributed by the Berkeley Vietnam Day Committee at the University of California, Berkeley massive "teach in" on May 21 to 22, 1965, attracting over twelve thousand people, gives an idea of dispositions shared at that time by California students:

> The war in Vietnam is not being fought according to the rules. Prisoners are tortured. Our planes drop incendiary bombs on civilian villages. Our soldiers shoot women and children. Your officers will tell you that it is all necessary, that we couldn't win the war any other way. *And they are right.* (reprinted in Jacobs and Landau 1966:256)

In the aftermath of war, reality is no longer a stable, natural, familiar environment but instead has become a shattered, fragmented world that demands new answers to suddenly materialized questions of meaning and sense. As Merleau-Ponty has said (1962:xix), old answers and past poetry will no longer soothe or serve. Humans have now become condemned to meaning simply because they are in this world.

As a direct consequence of modern war time experience, both the surrealist and ethnomethodological movements and dispositions became focused on highlighting and investigating the curious absence of common, binding cultural rules in the society's workings. For the surrealists of 1925, the older generation's rules and traditions had been lies that had led the youth to an early grisly death in a mechanized battlefield (cf. Hughes 1969). For the younger ethnomethodologists, both the hawkish, militaristic government and the Parsonian social science were in league with each other and compromised an establishment. Systematically explainable drives and social norms too quickly became scientifically legitimized stereotypes that were easily manipulated by established powers seeking misguided standards of patriotic duty and justifications for ignoring cries for cultural liberation. For both movements, history had cleansed their perceptions and they now saw reality as it was: a turbulent, changing flux that followed no fixed rules save men and women's localized attributions of sense.

Radical assemblage

The surrealists chose to demonstrate their new found perception into the world's working through means that powerfully displayed the fact of the modern world's often spurious assemblage. "Total art" became a quest for total knowledge and total transformation (Orenstein 1973). Investigations of alternative possible worlds became demonstrations and "ethnographies" of "other" cultural practices, dreams and trance states, simulated states of insanity, and hallucinogenic devices designed to "breach" everyday expectations and taken-for-granted "value hierarchies of the real" (Einstein 1929:95).

The "perceived normality" of values and events are, according to Garfinkel (1963:188), constructions, assemblages, accomplishments, and managements by members and cultural accomplices. The ethnomethodological movement has always been preoccupied with *how* society is put together by consensual artifices and practices, "the locally produced and locally recognized orderliness" of culture (Garfinkel *et al.* 1981:141). The ethnomethodologists, along with the surrealists, have striven to locate tangible instances of society's radical assemblage by citizens' beliefs, practices, and perceptions.

Rendering the routine world strange

Both the surrealists and the ethnomethodological movement utilized idiosyncratic devices and means to "breach" the normal routines of social reality in order to render them strange. The ethnographic surrealists such as Carl Einstein, Marcel Griaule, Andre Schaeffner, and Michel Leiris tended to conduct ethnographies and represent their found evidence in such a way as to "defamiliarize" everyday life and so provoke a new alternative vision. Carl Einstein wrote in *Documents* (1:2 (1929), 95):

> One thing is important: to shake what is called reality by means of non-adapted hallucinations so as to alter the value hierarchies of the real. Hallucinatory forces create a breach in the order of mechanistic processes; they introduced blocks of "a-causality" in this reality which had been absurdly given as such. The uninterrupted fabric of this reality is *torn*, and one inhabits the tension of dualism.

For the ethnographic surrealists, concrete cultural objects, whether foreign or local, were used to play a disruptive, illuminatory role (Clifford 1981:553). African masks, "ready mades" (found objects like Duchamp's bottle rack, discovered at the Parisian flea market, Marché aux Puces), and other objects sauvages were a source of the surrealist's disposition toward forcing a breach of perception and encouraging "making the familiar strange."

Garfinkel has utilized similar "breaching" procedures for rendering the commonplace society "anthropologically strange." In his 1963 paper "A Conception of, and Experiments with, Trust as a Condition of Stable Concerted Actions," he invented a number of "breaches" to make visible the assumptions that make up the attitude of daily life (Garfinkel 1963:217). He led students in "incongruity experiments" such as inventing new rules during a TickTackToe game; engaging friends in conversation and insisting that the person clarify the meaning of commonplace remarks; entering stores or restaurants and treating customers as if they were clerks or a maître'd; spending an hour in their own homes acting toward family members as if they were boarders, i.e., speaking only when spoken to, using only formal address etc.; and having medical school applicants react to a faked medical school intake interview. Garfinkel quoted Schutz's "The Stranger" (1944) and claimed that

> Thus there is a sixth modification. It is possible to induce experimentally the *breach* of these suppositions by deliberately modifying scenic events so as to systematically disappoint these attributions. The attributer's environment should thereby *be made strange to him* and accordingly he should believe himself and act in the presence of others like a stranger. (Garfinkel 1963:237)

Garfinkel's five prior modifications alluded to in the preceding text involved the neonate's or "developing member's" growth into a new world or order, the ceremonial transformation of objects, instrumental transformations of real environments of objects through the use of hallucinogenic drugs such as LSD (Garfinkel discusses the University of California, Los Angeles Alcoholism Clinic's administration of LSD to subjects and the resulting chasms of perception between experimenter and subject (cf. 1963:236); the "discovery of culture" by anthropologists and sociologists; and Schutz's example of the natural "stranger" who finds himself or herself in an alien world.

Garfinkel continued these breaching demonstrations as "aids to a sluggish imagination" in his 1964 paper "Studies of the Routine Grounds of Everyday Activities," which was reprinted in *Studies in Ethnometho-*

dology (1967:35-75). He surrealistically stated that

> For these background expectancies to come into view one must either be a
> stranger to the "life as usual" character of *everyday* scenes, or become
> estranged from them. (Garfinkel (1967a:37)

Garfinkel said (1964a:38) that his "demonstrations" could "provide
reflections through which strangeness of an obstinately familiar world
can be detected." In describing his further experiments with students
acting as boarders or strangers in their own homes, Garfinkel said, in a
way reminiscent of the surrealist Louis Aragon ("Le merveilleux c'est
la contradiction qui apparait dans le réel" = "The marvelous, it is the
contradiction which is apparent in the real'):

> Some information can be obtained if we first ask how a person will look at
> an ordinary and familiar scene and what he will see in it if we require of him
> that he do no more than look at it as something that for him it "obviously"
> and "really" is not. (Garfinkel 1967a:44)

Jean Jamin (1980) has described the ethnographic surrealist group
of 1938, the Collège de Sociologie, in a manner that also accurately
describes the ethnomethodological movement:

> The notions of distantiation, exoticism, representation of the other and differ-
> ences are inflected, reworked, readjusted as a function of criteria no longer
> geographical or cultural but methodological and even epistemological in
> nature: *to make foreign what appears familiar*, to study the rituals and sacred
> sites of contemporary institutions *with the minute attention of an "exotic"
> ethnographer*; and using his methods; to become observers observing those
> others who are ourselves and at the limit, this other who is oneself... The
> irruption of the sociologist in the field of his research, the interest devoted to
> his experience, probably constitutes the most original aspect of the college.
> (translated in Clifford 1981:561)

Surrealist practice attacks the familiar, provoking the eruption of
otherness, the unexpected. Traditional fieldwork, or "constructive
analysis" as Garfinkel puts it, does the reverse, in trying to render the
unfamiliar and different comprehensible through processes of naming,
classifying, explaining, and interpreting. Surrealist fascination with
representations of the "other" (Garfinkel's 1952 Harvard study is entitled
The Perception of the Other) is intended to provoke a defamiliarizing
effect to uncover invisible procedures of the world's assemblage.

Other procedures employed by the ethnomethodological movement bear resemblance to surrealist practices. The use of inverted lenses by Garfinkel and his students to "see again for another first time" the details of doing practical actions (cf. Mehan and Wood 1975:232-233) has a parallel with the surrealists' emphasis on "camera-seeing" (cf. Krauss 1981:31-33). Moholy-Nagy called it the *New vision*: a special form of vision that the camera-eye gives back to the deficient human eye, so now "we may say that we see the world with different eyes" (Moholy-Nagy, 1947:206). Camera-seeing, along with ethnomethodology's use of inverted lenses, blindness, and mechanical arms, hands, and other devices for the handicapped that were designed to make researchers "aware of the way they normally do the world by requiring them to learn to do it otherwise" (Mehan and Wood 1975b:233), acted as a form of "prosthesis," enlarging the capacity of the human body and perception (cf. Krauss 1981:32) and increasing the ways in which the world can be present to vision.

Mehan and Wood's (1975a:237-238) use of "the auditory illusion" to "encourage a direct confrontation with the mutual constitution of persons, objects, and signs" parallels the surrealists' widespread strategy of repetition and "doubling" (cf. Krauss 1981:25-27) especially in their photography. The ethnomethodologists have used audiotapes that repeat a single sound; and over time and shifts in context, one would hear the single sound begin to alter. The surrealists, in a similar manner, would often project double images on their photographs, for "it is doubling that produces the formal rhythm of spacing-two-step that banishes the unitary condition of the moment, that creates within the moment an experience of fission" (Krauss 1981:25). This visual duplication procedure can be witnessed in the photographs by Man Ray, Frederick Sommer, Bill Brandt, Hans Bellmer, and Maurice Tabard. Krauss (1981:25-26) analyzes this surrealist doubling effect by way of comparison with Levi-Strauss's (1970:339-340) description of pure phonetic doubling in the onset of linguistic experience in infancy, saying:

> Repetition is thus the indicator that the "wild sounds" of babbling have been made deliberate, intentional; and that what they intend is meaning. Doubling in this sense is the "signifier of signification."

The ethnomethodological movement's use of zatocoding procedures (cf. Hill and Crittenden 1968:205ff; Mehan and Wood 1975a:230-232) has a certain resemblance to the surrealist movement's "automatic writing" experiments. In zatocoding, the ethnomethodologist first constructs a collection of thoughts, references, and quotes, then begins to construct a catalogue of "descriptors" that will index the collection's contents. New items are added to the collection simultaneously with new indexing descriptors. The resulting examination of "endless reflexivity" (Garfinkel in Hill and Crittenden 1968:208) has produced states such as the following in ethnomethodologists:

> ...the horror of becoming self-conscious of your coding-self... is a feeling that the world does not stand still. That there is no *the* world but a swarm. And the time will be past quitting or saving one's sanity when I begin to feel that that insight too is not "something" but a temporally unfolding and evanescent creation (Wood 1969a:12 quoted in Mehan and Wood 1975:232).

The surrealists relied on the procedure of automatism or "automatic writing" to be less a representation but rather a method for manifestation or recording of the presence of the writer's inner self in the process of sign and meaning production. Like zatocoding also demonstrates, automatic writing and drawing shows that all cursive and visual practice essentially is a production of the artist's manipulation of immediate relevances. Breton writes that "the essential discovery of surrealism is that, without preconceived intention, the pen that flows in order to write and the pencil that runs in order to draw spin an infinitely precious substance" (Breton 1925; translations: S.M. Taylor 1972).

Generational surrealistic supplements

Second, third, and fourth generation ethnomethodologists have improvised on ethnomethodology's knowledge practices. For example, some members supplemented Garfinkel's equipmental breaching experiments in ways relevant to their own immediate concerns. In the 1960s, Garfinkel developed a technique requiring the wearing of inverted lenses. These lenses were prisms that turned the visual field upside down (cf. Mehan and Wood 1975a:232-233). Students were instructed to wear the lenses (a hooded mask-like apparatus) for varying lengths of time ranging from a few minutes to a complete waking day. During this observation period, the person wearing the inverted lenses would be asked to attempt to conduct normal daily tasks such as writing one's name on the board, filling a cup with water, walking down the street, etc. Students would describe their experiences into tape recorders and write them up later in paper form. Experiences range from complete impossibility and paralysis in doing normal, taken-for-granted sight-dependent activities to a gradual revisioning and relearning of normal tasks, "as if for another first time" (Garfinkel 1967a:9; 1985). Students have experienced a sense of the new work required to "embody" (Garfinkel, Lynch, and Livingston 1981:137) a priorly understood social order in such a way that the old social order is still somehow maintained.

It is ethnomethodological folk knowledge that some of the graduate students ingested psychedelics like LSD and marijuana before and while under the influence of Garfinkel's procedures, like the use of the inverted lenses. Their reports later about their experiences with the lenses were typically vivid, colorful and insightful. Garfinkel, and others, interpreted these reports as documenting the success of the procedures. The students had invented a further "supplement" (Derrida 1978) to Garfinkel's procedures. The later generations were expanding Garfinkel's already effective demonstrations to suit their own unique body of historical-cultural experience, biography, and available technologies.

Some ethnomethodologists in the second, third, and fourth generations have reported to me that the controlled use of psychedelic drugs such as marijuana, psilocybin, mescalin, and LSD both complemented and aided their ethnomethodological "looking at the detail of things." It is known and documented (cf. Huxley 1954; Merleau-Ponty 1962:228-229; Castaneda 1968, 1971; Leary 1968; Lilly 1972) that psychedelic and psychoactive substances can cause heightened changes in users' perceptions such that "the doors of perception were cleansed" (Huxley 1954) and reality seen again "as if again another first time." These perceptions were used by some ethnomethodologists to confirm, enrich, and empirically test the detailed look into society's features that they were developing under the rigors of first generation phenomenological methods. A psychedelic drug was a way to create "the break" with the familiar way of looking at things needed to perceive the world's radical assemblage.

Garfinkel used, and still uses, the inverted lens procedure along with others such as "the auditory side-tone-delay effect" (cf. Garfinkel in Hill and Crittenden 1968:161-168; Mehan and Wood 1975a:233), the wearing of masks that leave the student totally blind (cf. Mehan and Wood 1975a:233), the wearing of mechanical and prosthetic arms, hands, legs, and other devices for the handicapped such as spending the day in a wheel chair (cf. Mehan and Wood 1975a; Jules-Rosette, personal communication), using "occasioned maps" to experience the mutual determinations of instructions, signs, persons, and the "objective" world (cf. Mehan and Wood 1975a:230; Psathas 1979:203-228); and "zatocoding" (Garfinkel in Hill and Crittenden 1968:205, 240; Mehan and Wood 1975a:230-232). These procedures provide for the students' seeing anew certain taken-for-granted aspects of the embodied world, as well as for the surrealist aim of making the familiar world strange.

Collections of found data as evidence

The ethnomethodologists attempted the same change or alteration of conventional vision through radical juxtapositions of found empirical evidence. Garfinkel's *Studies in Ethnomethodology* is a collection of essays juxtaposing widely different settings (transsexuals, suicide prevention centers, psychiatric outpatient clinics, breaching experiments, coroners' offices, etc.). Garfinkel's purpose was to "demonstrate" through found evidence the applicability and reality of ethnomethodology's findings. Critics of *Studies* called the book "unreadable," "unrelated excursions into research" (Coleman 1968:126), and a "nonbook...a disconnected collection of papers" (Coleman 1968:126). Serious readings of Garfinkel's *Studies* show that, actually, the book is about a new kind of seeing, a seeing into the radical assemblage of social bodies through unnoticed common-sense activities and practices invisible to conventional sight. The book was composed to deliberately shock the reader into a new sight (cf. Zimmerman 1987).

Both movements have utilized collage, juxtaposition, and collections of "found" evidence as a style of representation. The surrealist's use of collage and ethnographic juxtaposition has been analyzed in the contents of their ethnography (Clifford 1981), their journals (Clifford 1981; Krauss 1981), their photographs (Krauss 1981), their imagery (Matthews 1977), and their artistic "happenings" (Hansen 1965). Collage has the intent to break down conventional "bodies," provoke defamiliarization, and represent phenomena not as continuous wholes but assemblages of symbols and codes (Clifford 1981:552). Surrealist collage was a change in vision.

Other ethnomethodologists continued this tradition of ethnographic juxtaposition with the idea of an "occasioned corpus of a setting's features" (Zimmerman and Pollner 1970). The ethnomethodological movement's widespread use of video and audio technologies contributed to the creation of an ethnomethodological style of "displaying" social features through juxtapositions of audiovisually recorded evidence (cf. Bellman and Jules Rosette 1977; Mehan, Hertweck, Combs, and Flynn 1982). Microinteractions, conversations, and social experiments have been presented in ways that are meant to exhibit concretely what is theoretically being talked about. The shocking sense of the concrete is presented as "raw data" that has been collected and not invented by the ethnomethodologist researcher. The ethnomethodologists and the surrealist ethnographers shared this in common: their reliance on the juxtaposition of raw data in a presentational collage does not attempt to smooth out cultural incongruities in favor of a familiar explanation.

New domains of phenomena

As has become obvious, both movements have attempted to open up entirely new domains of phenomenon. This can easily be attested to in a comparative reading in the two groups' first "manifestos": the preface to Garfinkel's *Studies in Ethnomethodology* and the surrealists' declaration of January 27, 1925. In their manifestos, both movements use a from of definition by negation, claim to be distinct from conventional predecessors, point to new, unmapped domains of study and put forth a list of members. The new domains are similar in both manifestos. The surrealists pronounce that they have nothing to do with literature, that surrealism is a means of total liberation of the mind and all that resembles it, that they intend to investigate the fragility of thought and the shifting foundation of modern society, and that surrealism is a cry of the mind turning back on itself. The ethnomethodologists state that they are distinct from standard sociological procedure, that ethnomethodology has uncovered an immense, hitherto unknown domain of social phenomena, that their study is directed to discovering how modern society consists of members' practical methods, and that the reflexivity of accountability stands as an analyzable feature of reality, as well as establishes its own study.

The context of modern reception in Paris

The ethnomethodological movement's reception in Paris in 1985 was greatly supported by intellectual groups sharing roots in ethnographic surrealism. Michel Maffesoli's Center for Studies of the Ordinary and the Everyday (Centre d'Études sur l'Actual et le Quotidien) at the Sorbonne, and Georges Lapassade and René Lourou's Analyse Institutionnelle movement at the University of Paris VIII, are two good examples. I wish to analyze briefly the case of the Parisian analyse institutionelle movement. My statements are based on my participation in and observation of a number of events in Paris held between members of the analyse institutionelle movement and visiting members of the ethnomethodological movement during 1985-1986. The visiting ethnomethodologists, and I was considered one of them, played a role of *transmitters* of a knowledge domain into a specific historical and cultural *context of reception*. This case allows us to look at an example of how social scientific knowledge is transmitted between diverse cultural groups and intellectual contexts.

Ethnographic surrealism and the analyse institutionelle group

The analyse institutionelle group is a sociological research network that has concentrated its investigations into educational, medical, legal, public welfare, and business institutions. Their program bears a closeness to Cicourel and Mehan's institutional ethnomethodology. They have developed a range of micro-interactive methods that enables the sociologist to go into institutions such as factories or welfare offices and conduct "interventions" that resemble Lewin's T-Groups (cf. Lewin 1948) for resolving social conflicts. The sociologists conduct institutional analysis sessions between large numbers of an institution's members for the purpose of internal problem resolution. I participated in such an "intervention" at a French government plant in May, 1986. Other teams of sociologists conduct sociological investigations of the institutions' internal micro-organizational practices. Members of analyse institutionelle have developed a theory of "transversality" (cf. Hess 1981:201), or contextual institutional determinants, and consider their theory to be in a permanent evolution. Analyse institutionelle has been highly interested in and has supported ethnomethodology as possibly a new theoretical and methodological refinement of their own research program (see Figure 7-4). In interviews and research work, numerous analyse institutionelle researchers have revealed to me what they perceive the two movements' similar orientations to be and what they expect to accomplish by applying ethnomethodology's methods to their research.

My research shows that many of the French sociologists, ethnologists, and psychologists associated with l'analyse institutionelle group such as Lapassade, Lourau, Hess, Coulon, and Lecerf consider themselves part of a French social science research tradition that finds many of its theoretical and methodological directives in the writings of the aforementioned ethnographic surrealist group, le Collège de Sociologie (cf. Hollier 1979). As we have discussed, le Collège, which included Bataille and Leiris, advocated rendering the routine world strange and the direct "intervention" by the sociologist ethnographer into the workings of the society, thereby creating a reflexive and radical sociology. Many of the group's methods resemble those of the early ethnographic surrealists. The leaders of the analyse institutionelle group recognize in the ethnomethodological approach a kindred spirit of radical social investigation that shares certain fundamental similarities to their own approach. These similarities include roots in existential phenomenology, praxeology, and ethnographic surrealism. They also include a strong criticism of prevailing sociological methods. As I have outlined earlier, ethnomethodology's fundamental parallels to the French ethnographic surrealist legacy make ethnomethodology recognizable to certain groups of French thought and practice.

The analyse institutionelle movement was formed by Georges Lapassade and René Lourau around 1966. At first an informal group at Nanterre that included Henri Lefebvre and Jean Baudrillard, among others, it was formally established at the University of Paris VIII, at St. Denis in 1973 (cf. Hess 1981:160-161). This group was dedicated to creating social changes as well as social research by the active "interventions" of the sociologist in the field settings being studied. The institutional analysis group drew on the writings of Marx, Mao, Kurt Lewin, and the ethnographic surrealists for their inspiration (cf. Lapassade 1970, 1971a, b, c; Lourau 1970, 1971; Ardoino 1980; Hess 1975, 1981).

Quel Corps ?

ETHNOMETHODOLOGIE

Identités Sexuelles et Pratiques Corporelles
Échographies de l'Institution Sportive

Figure 7-4 Publication of *l'Analyse Institutionelle* group on ethnomethodology

Several analyse institutionelle writers have emphasized the group's lineage from the Collège de Sociologie. Remi Hess (1981:11-12) introduces his book on institutional analysis, *La Sociologie d'Intervention*, by referring to the movement's common roots in the Collège. Hess quotes Denis Hollier, a historian of the Collège de Sociologie, in his description of both movements as comprising a new form of reflexive sociology that has the potential to "infect" the whole society like a virus:

> Une curieuse opération allait la transformer entre leurs mains: la sociologie ne serait plus une science, mais quelque chose l'ordre d'une maladie, une étrange infection du corps sociale. (Hollier 1979 in Hess 1981)

René Lourau wrote a major study on the Collège de Sociologie entitled *Le gai savior de sociologues* (1977). Lourau's title highlights the presumed connection between the two schools by using the word "gai savior:" "gai" currently is the abbreviation of Groupe d'"Analyse Institutionelle (GAI). In the same edition of *Pratiques de Formation (Analyses)* (9:185:47-57) that contained Yves Lecerf's applause of ethnomethodology, Lourau contributed an article on the use of the field journal method by the surrealist ethnographer Michel Leiris in his work *L'Afrique Fantôme* (1934). Leiris was an original member of Breton's surrealist group, a founder of the Collège de Sociologie, and the secretary-archivist on Marcel Griaule's Mission Dakon-Djibouti expedition to the Dogon tribe in Africa, an expedition that mixed avant-garde art with ethnographic science (cf. Clifford 1981:554-556). Lourau (1985:49) stresses Leiris's preoccupation with the rapports between subjectivity and objectivity in a way similar to Husserlian phenomenology (another parallelism to the ethnomethodological movement). Lourau (1977:57) goes on to say that Leiris's surrealist ethnographic journal presents a model for research, "un nouveau manuel d'ethnographie, de sociologie ou plus généralement de travail intellectuel" (a new manual for ethnography, for sociology, or more generally for intellectual work), and an "instrument of infinite reflection" for analyzing the implications of the researcher in the actual act of fieldwork.

Georges Lapassade, the original founder of institutional analysis, has consistently displayed a surrealist aesthetic in his career. He has been involved in the Parisian literary, artistic, and political avant-garde. Lapassade had been a member of the Arguments group, which was an existentialist-Marxist collective in the 1950s and 1960s (cf. Poster 1975:214); a research assistant and editor of Maurice Merleau-Ponty; a member of Julian Beck's "Living Theatre;" a key organizer of the 1968 student uprising at the Sorbonne; a central figure in the establishment of the revolutionary University of Paris VIII (Vincennes à St. Denis) after the May 1968 demonstrations; and the publisher of numerous books on sociology, psychology, trance, and institutional analysis. He wrote an ethnography on Morocco entitled *Joyeuse Tropiques* as an intellectual comment to Levi-Strauss's *Triste Tropiques*. Lapassade possesses a history of participating in "guerilla theatre," which is fond of interrupting or breaching the routines of daily life by "creating situations" or "happenings." For example, in May 1968, during the student demonstrations in front of the Sorbonne, Lapassade released several hundred white pigeons and balloons. Lapassade claims that his surrealist theatre experience inspired much of his conceptions and applications of "intervention" used by the sociologists in the analyse institutionelle movement (Lapassade 1986). Lapassade's reception and support of ethnomethodology has been vigorous and lively. I have observed Lapassade at nearly every event in Paris that I attended that was directed toward the presentation of ethnomethodology from November 1985 to June 1986. He has said to me that he senses in ethnomethodology a kindred spirit of revolutionary ideas and practices that has as its aim the investigation and uncovering of what is really occurring in society, including the reflexive and active role of the researcher.

The analyse institutionelle group in Paris has recently published a special edition of their journal, *Pratiques de Formation* (Analyses), entitled *Ethnomethodologies* (October, 1986, No.11-12), edited by Lecerf. The format reminds one of an ethnographic surrealist collage in that it juxtaposes numerous short articles on this group's uses of ethnomethodological ideas and theory in numerous settings. The editorial by Ardoino and Lecerf (1986:11) asserts that the publication of Garfinkel's *Studies in Ethnomethodology* in 1967 will be historically as important for its time as the publication of Karl Marx's *Capital* was for its period. Also included in the journal are articles written by Quéré, Conein, and Widmer of the Centre d'Études Movements Sociaux (CEMS) research group at the École des Hautes Études en Sciences Sociales, as well as by Jules-Rosette and by myself. This disparate collection in a way begins to fulfill Lecerf's hope (1984b:60) that ethnomethodology would provide a cause for a rapprochement between different Parisian schools of thought. The diversity of the audiences to the variety of presentations of ethnomethodology and its new applications during 1985 and 1986 bear witness to the local potential that ethnomethodology appears to have in the contemporary French intellectual context.

The analyse institutionelle circle has also published a special edition of *Quel Corps*? (1986) on ethnomethodological research on sexual identity, education, body practices, sports, and trance possession (see Figure 7-4) with articles by Jean-Marie Brohm, Alain Coulon, Georges Lapassade, Remi Hess, Patrick Boumard, and others. Alain Coulon has recently published a book on ethnomethodology entitled *L'Ethno-methodologie* (1987) in the "Que sais-je" series in Paris. Coulon analytically reviews the ethnomethodological movement's major concepts, important research contributions and future relevance for French sociology and institutional analysis. Coulon visited the University of California, Los Angeles to dialogue with Garfinkel and other ethnomethodologists in 1988.

Conclusion: The American and French contexts of the ethnomethodological movement

The American and French "versions" of the ethnomethodological movement possesses some striking similarities and differences. Their similarities lie in the commonly referenced body of ideas that are constituted as the intellectual core of the movement. These "themata" (Holton, 1978), centered around the interpretation and analysis of common taken-for-granted meaning construction, practical activity and reasoning, and indexical expressions, are contextually related by individual scholars to existing and emerging problematics, issues, and fields of study. What is similar to the American and French settings is that these ethnomethodological themata are themselves situationally changed to apply to local intellectual, personal, and political relevances.

Differences in the patterns of the institutionalization of ethnomethodology have arisen in the two countries. Due to, among other things, differences in the scholarly, institutional, political, and cultural traditions in each country, the ethnomethodological movement has taken on distinctly "local" manifestations and patterns of institutionalization, delineation of boundaries, and self-preceptions. This difference in local patterns is in fact common to each institutionalized site of ethno-methodological work, intranationally and internationally. This has been described earlier in this work for the American university system. In

France, institutionalization and boundary definitions are contextually specific to the particular campus formation. For example, the different campuses of the University of Paris each have their own organizational structure, intellectual traditions, and politics situated within the larger Parisian environment. This produces distinctive and unique formulations, translations, and applications of the ethnomethodological "movement" and ideas. In general, Frances's institutionalization of ethnomethodology comes at a time of renewed interest in phenomenology, ethnography, ordinary language, and an emphasis on contextual rather than formalistic theories of meaning.

The link between the intellectual and political aspects of the ethnomethodological movement is found in individuals' situated scholarly and professional work that utilizes discursive representations and recognitions of the "ethnomethodological movement" for their own multifaceted interests, goals, and relevances. This link can be found in texts as the discursive practices that compose the movement itself as a social vehicle.

The current reception of ethnomethodology in Paris is set amidst a specific cultural, intellectual, and economic context. Many elements combine to make ethnomethodology interesting to Parisian social scientists at this particular time. The politics of paradigms are intertwined with artistic sensibilities and tastes. The waning of the structuralist dominance, and a change in Marxism's scholarly appeal has created a unique situation for ethnomethodology to become a possible alternative in French social science. Ethnomethodology currently appeals to numbers of French social scientists because it furnishes an original program of empirical ethnographic research that is attentive to the phenomena of language, meaning, and members' practices in social context. I have shown that an ethnographic tradition does exist in France, one that developed in close proximity to the surrealist movement during the twenties and thirties. The ethnomethodological movement bears certain critical resemblances to this ethnographic surrealist tradition in French social science, a fact which accounts for at least some of the interest being shown to ethnomethodology in Paris today.

This particular example of the transmission of ethnomethodological knowledge into the French culural milieu raises issues regarding ethnomethodology's colletive organizational practices as theoretical paradigm and movement of thought. In the beginning of this chapter I compared the ethnomethodological movement with the semiotics movement in terms of their collective practices as member-organized fields of discourse. We found that by comparison, the ethnomethodological movement showed signs of requiring further development in international organization, consistent collaboration and sharing of ideas through conferences and other means, and provision of publishing outlets for its collective work. If the ethnomethodological movement is to "transplant" itself as an internationally coherent intellectual enterprise, it must provide an organizational structure capable of seriously interacting in the international marketplace of ideas. What is required is an increased openness from all ethnomethodologists to developing an "international competence" (cf. Tiryakian, 1986:155-171) that seeks an active dialogue of ideas and research technologies from the perspective of developing global social sciences as well as increased capacity to train graduate students.

Ethnomethodology is already being received and adapted in numerous campuses around the world (see Appendix A). The challenge of internationalism and the development of indigenous forms of ethnomethodological research adapted to the particular locales' intellectual and cultural context, presents the ethnomethodological movement with its next formidable task. This task can be accomplished through the further development of multiple generational forms ethnomethodology or neo-ethnomethodology. As new stylistic forms of ethnomethodology are composed, commensurate conceptual, and methodological innovations will work themselves out in ways adapted to specialized cultural and topical locales. Adequate graduate training must be offered in order to transmit the movement's contributions in a way productive of sustained academic careers and the future creation of knowledge.

Conclusion
Tiresius or Knowledge of Future Events

Then it becomes whatever you can do with it. What you don't want to
do with it is to announce that there is now an established position
called ethnomethodology.
Harold Garfinkel (1985b)

It's taking any established version that we have of what we are doing and
misreading it. We read it to get from it what today's work requires rather than
remaining respectful of a lineage.
Harold Garfinkel (1985b)

Because there is such a strong result do we lose the effort that has been made
by the company of ethnomethodologists over many years? Of course not,
not at all. Unless you want to abandon your imagination.
Harold Garfinkel (1985b)

This study has argued that the ethnomethodological movement has
constructed itself as a specialized form of social scientific knowledge.
Ethnomethodology's history has been built and structured by its members through a variety of temporal organizational practices. Its historical
form is composed of intellectual generations that have constituted themselves through artful referential and semiotic work. These intellectual
generations have each embodied unique styles of thought, work, and
expression that were functional during specific historical periods and
contexts of socioculturally embedded intellectual discourse. I have
referred to these multiple styles of ethnomethodology as neoethnomethodology, and I have suggested that the present holds continued, yet threat-
ened, possibilities for new ethnomethodological innovations, work, and
interfaces with diverse international contexts, audiences, and disciplines.

I have reviewed the ethnomethodological movement's early history and have observed that it bore organizational similarities to various contemporary radical and religious movements. I have shown that these organizational features functioned as practical devices by which to socially order ethnomethodology's original and unique insights regarding the respecification of society as artful practical action and members' natural accountability. I have described how this early phase made explicit use of tightly ordered intertextual speech and writing genres that functioned to "historically anchor" the ethnomethodological movement's achieved identity as a coherent program of research. Also, I have suggested that in this present stage the ethnomethodological movement seems to be diversifying its neoethnomethodological working, speaking, and writing voices as it moves into new domains of research in the international context. The ethnomethodological movement appears to be developing new iconizations and methods to discover its fundamental phenomena: the identifying details of "lived work" practices constitutive of ordinary society.

If the ethnomethodological movement develops future generations of researchers, it has a chance to reflect on its own "received history" and utilize it as an instructional guide by which to order its own direction as a movement. As I have suggested, the ethnomethodological movement regularly employs proleptic/analeptic practices in the practical composition of its historicity. If it can continue to imagine and fashion its own future as an organizationally open "proleptic object," then ethnomethodology may transcend outmoded and presently useless organizational strategies. By formulating and projecting a working policy of being an intellectual open-door to new local generations of researchers, the ethnomethodological movement may renew its own foundations while simultaneously encouraging the development of new neoethnomethodological voices, methods, and research styles.

I have described how the ethnomethodological movement has constructed itself as a coherent research enterprise, knowledge form, and intellectual movement through the practical establishment of collective actants. These collective actants consist of local ordering devices that have existed as persons, texts, words, and generational semiotic styles. Where a collective actant has been interactively assembled and appropriated, there and then has a local ethnomethodological work site begun to achieve viability. The ethnomethodological movement's actants are changing. New discoveries, methods, texts, and generational leaders are emerging that potentially make possible a more diverse selection of ethnomethodological collective actants capable of being readily used by researchers in different intellectual contexts and fields.

Ethnomethodology can be a foundational discipline making fundamental contributions to both the social and natural sciences. Its technologies for the detailed analysis of interactive social processes can provide an alternative to sociology's other established methods and theories. Established sociological fields such as the sociology of science, knowledge, religion, education, deviance, law and medicine, discourse analysis, sociolinguistics, sociosemiotics, and sociological theory are now implicitly and explicitly utilizing ethnomethodology's methods and concepts. The anthropology of knowledge and religion and the ethnography of speaking are beginning to utilize ethnomethodology. After a twenty-five year period of criticism, misunderstanding, and indifference, other social science disciplines appear to be recognizing ethnomethodology's contributions. Ethnomethodology has a potential of emerging internationally as a foundationally unified model of investigation for the human sciences. Time will tell how the ethnomethodological movement will meet its next organizational challenges.

The local production of the ethnomethodological movement

In describing any movement of thought across intellectual and international domains, a problem arises in finding a link between an intellectual movement and a political one. Throughout this work I have utilized texts to demonstrate how intergenerationally the ethnomethodological movement has embodied and expressed similar world-views, which though not expressly politically formulated, nevertheless carry political consequences. This can be seen exemplified in the case of ethnomethodologists such as Carlos Castaneda, Houston Wood, Kenneth Jennings, and others who chose not to remain in academia because of political and world-view conflicts with the academic system. The ethnomethodological movement, while not being an overtly "political" movement in the United States, has a stronger political character in France.

Eisenstadt (1977:64) has commented that within the contexture of sociology's many "crises" there has arisen a trend of fragmentation and discontinuity in research. This trend has been exaggerated by many in the sociological community to escape the challenges of the crises by "retreating" into philosophical meditations, sectarian research communities, or purely technical aspects of sociological research. He suggests (1977:61) that ethnomethodology may be a form of retreat from crisis and not a new substitute or alternative.

In my view the ethnomethodological movement in America and France has and is functioning simultaneously as an intellectual movement, a world-view, and a political movement of sorts. What ties these aspects together is the contextually defined and implemented strategies of particular members. These strategies use the "ethnomethodological movement" as a symbolic and semiotic vehicle by and through which to accomplish various practical objectives. I suggest that practical motivations are signified in textual representations. Membership in intellectual movements is locally produced on particular occasions for specific purposes, which can include intellectual, professional, political, and metaphysical aims and goals.

A final example of the local production of membership within the ethnomethodological movement through textual signification, purposive referencing work, and local intellectual boundary keeping work can be found exhibited in Deirdre Boden's review article (1986) of Kenneth Liberman's (1985) book *Understanding Interaction in Central Australia: An Ethnomethodological Study of Australian People*. Boden opens her review by saying: "This intriguing book is one of a series of studies in ethnomethodology being brought out by Routledge and Kegan Paul under the general editorship of Harold Garfinkel. As such, it invites enthusiastic examination" (1986:849). Yet Boden concludes her review by saying: "Thus, while Liberman's insights are quite innovative, their ethnomethodological explication is somewhat less than successful" (1986:850).

Between these two statements, Boden, a fourth generation ethnomethodologist and conversation analyst (cf. Boden 1986), both praises Liberman for "going well beyond traditional ethnography" and criticizes Liberman on the grounds that his "ethnomethodological explication" is "unsuccessful," "inappropriate," and "counterproductive." Boden comments that Liberman's book:

> has the makings of another classic study in ethnomethodology, yet I must admit to some reservations both with the book's theoretical stance and the central ethnomethodological aspects of the project. These include an uneasiness with the multiplicity of conceptual frameworks and with the author's approach to analyzing "ordinary discourse." (1986:850).

Boden's ethnomethodological criteria for evaluating Liberman's work are the product of her situated, contingent, local production work. These criteria are contingent expressions situationally "revived" or created by Boden for the practical purposes of writing her review, and justifying her own position relative to her perceived version of "ethnomethodological exposition" for whatever purpose she has. In both Boden's and Liberman's cases, their "ethnomethodological analyses" in reality exist only as contingent expressions within and relative to their own current states of intellectual and professional inquiry. There exists no authoritative text or standard for objectively "testing" or validating ethnomethodological work. Past ethnomethodological "theoretical stance" does not provide a stable ground for future development. What is of interest here are the situated hermeneutics of how past texts are read, interpreted, used, and displayed as signs and emblems of constructed membership in an intellectual movement for a scholar's current professional purposes.

Schutz (1964:159-178) has discussed the "making of music together" as a social relationship involving the shared sense of a pluridimensionality of time between the composer and the beholder. We can examine the making of the ethnomethodological movement's texts in a similar light, by emphasizing the contextual creation of a social sense of inner and outer time between ethnomethodological authors and reader-beholders.

Texts become time-objects communicated through sign composition and sign reading. For our purposes an ethnomethodological text has been defined as a meaningful arrangement of signs in inner and outer time. It is the occurrence of the ethnomethodological movement's inner time, Bergson's durée, which is the very medium within which the movement's textual flow occurs. The flux of signs unrolling in members' inner time is an arrangement meaningful to both the writer and the reader. The text evokes in the stream of consciousness of the ethnomethodologist participating in it a lyrical interplay of recollections, references, protentions, and proleptic anticipations that creatively interrelate the successive literary elements into an intertextual core program and collective enterprise.

The ethnomethodological writer, by the specific means of his or her art, interprets, produces, and arranges the flux of signs in such a way that the consciousness of the beholder is led to refer what he or she actually read to what he or she is led to anticipate will follow immediately in the text and in the projected future. Retrospectively the reader refers to what he or she has just been reading and to what the reader has read ever since he or she began to read ethnomethodology. The reader reads the ongoing flux of signs in a multidimensional medium of inner time.

The specific means of an intellectual movement's literary arts makes use of occurrences in both inner and outer time. Some of these specific practices are essential to any form of textual production in general, while others belong to the particular movement's writing culture itself.

Ethnomethodological literary production has invented and developed its own culture-specific literary practices, which I have described throughout this work. These practices include the creative invention, maintenance, and evolution of ethnomethodology's system of signification and poetic language, its creation of membership categorization devices, its management of methodological adequacy via ability to employ adequately descriptive written forms, its maintenance of itself as an intertextual social movement with disciplinary boundaries to keep, its composition of locally historicized interactive contexts of text production, and its creation of socially derived and approved knowledge forms.

The ethnomethodological movement's inner time sense can be characterized as having a quality of prolepsis, the representation or assumption of a future act or development as if presently existing or accomplished, and analepsis, the representation of a past act as if presently significant. This proleptic/analeptic inner time sense is traceable in its manifestations in the movement's literary, notational and referential systems, its sign production and interpretation practices, and its measurable successes and failures as an intellectual paradigm.

Schutz (1964:278-293) has discussed prolepsis as a mode of experiencing social time. Schutz uses Husserl's conception of projection to describe how it is that our common-sense anticipations of future outcomes actually perceive the outcome as having already occurred. Foresight becomes anticipated hindsight. The future's open horizons are preconceived in the projection of our action as an anticipated state of affairs that we imagine as having already been materialized in the past or in the present. Schutz refers to what William James and George H. Mead have called a "specious present" that contains vitalized elements of the past and the future.

The ethnomethodological movement's referential practices are examples of locally produced, negotiated instances of a social time sense that actively employs a specious or proleptic present. The movement's future projected fulfillment and promise is experienced as a present grounds for action. Past action is interpreted in light of present relevance. Schutz points out with utmost clarity that our retentions, protentions, projections, and anticipations of things to come are essentially "empty reference" to open horizons. They may be fulfilled by the future occurrences or may, as Husserl graphically put it, "explode."

The literary creation of stabilized historicity

In her review, Boden criticizes Liberman's "attempts to breach disciplinary and paradigmatic barriers" as " appearing unconcerned by the considerable differences, for example, between phenomenology, existentialism, and ethnomethodology (*ibid*)." Boden continues:

> Throughout the text, there is an almost relentless attempt to merge these distinct fields at the cost of clear exposition of an intrinsically interesting topic. Author and reader alike are left with precious few pages to examine the more ethnomethodological side of the exposition, which is presented rather sketchily, often by citing unpublished and inaccessible lectures by Garfinkel. There were good reasons for this practice in the past, but the recent explosion of published work in ethnomethodology generally, both in the United States and the United Kingdom, makes this choice both inappropriate and counterproductive.

For some situated reason and reference, it is necessary for Boden literarily to create in this instance the existence of a historically stable "ethnomethodological exposition" that exists independent of Liberman's particular appropriation of the ideas generated by persons who have called themselves "ethnomethodologists" at particular historical times. Boden has made "theoretical ancestry" not only relevant to this analysis of Liberman's text, but as stable grounds for their evaluation and development. Yet, what Boden appears to be doing here is exactly what another ethnomethodologist, Michael Lynch (1985a:20, fn.9) suggests cannot be done to any text viewed from a perspective of situational hermeneutics, that is, treating any texts or initiatives as having an authoritative character independent of the hermeneutical situation (cf. Palmer 1969). Lynch says:

> ...ethnomethodologists provide for "general statements of theory" to be contingent statements rather than organizing principles in an inquiry, where such general statements are produced in the fashion of temporally situated conjectures which locate "resources" on the basis of the current exigencies of the inquiry.

Thus, Boden's statement that Liberman's "rather startling melange of conversation analysis, discourse analysis, and general sociolinguistics" represents a "blurring of distinct fields and their related theoretical underpinnings (that) reduces the strengths of each and thus dilutes the effectiveness of the overall argument," in effect reveals Boden's own "local work" of producing the ethnomethodological position and paradigm. By accentuating Liberman's "blurring of distinct fields" rather than emphasizing his creative appropriation of these domains for the immediate purposes relevant to his ongoing inquiry, Boden has in effect textually created, by a form of analepsis and prolepsis, a historically reified ethnomethodological paradigm whose literarily constructed boundaries exclude Liberman's hermeneutic work. Liberman's treating of ethnomethodological theoretical statements as "temporally situated conjectures" to be appropriated relative to his own course of inquiry is perceived as "ethnomethodologically less than successful" by another ethnomethodologist who has "defined" the enterprise in a particular instance of writing.

Such literary historicizing work seems to be an inevitable tension present in the creation and maintenance of intellectual movements. Conceptual boundaries are drawn whenever one inscribes a written image. This tension has been present within the ethnomethodological movement in the activities of members to define the parameters of the ethnomethodological field (c.f. Mehan, 1990). To transcend this tension, Garfinkel has stated that ethnomethodology is whatever one can make of it:

> Then it becomes whatever you can do with it (ethnomethodology). What you don't want to do with it is to announce that there is now an established position called ethnomethodology... It's taking any established version that we have of what we are doing and misreading it. We read it to get from it what today's work requires rather than remaining respectful of a lineage. (1985a:12-13)

In practice, though, Garfinkel himself has vacillated between allowing for such paradigmatic license and creating more explicit statements as to what is, or who is practicing, ethnomethodology. This can be witnessed in Garfinkel's "membership lists" contained in various articles and books as well as his use of selective intertextual referencing practices.

Liberman's own particular research style can be traced to his unique doctoral studies program at the University of California, San Diego. His Ph.D. was done in the interdisciplinary program in Contemporary

Studies in Language, Society, and Culture in 1981. This program requires that the student be fundamentally trained in one discipline and that he or she undertakes M.A. -level studies in an integrally related discipline or culture area. Liberman's fields of study and respective committee were Studies in Ethnomethodology (Professors Harold Garfinkel and Bennetta Jules-Rosette), Studies in Social Change (Professor Joseph Gusfield), Studies in Ethnolinguistics and Semiotics (Professor Wai-lim Yip, Alain J.J. Cohen, and John Gumperz), and Studies in Phenomenology (Professor Frederik Olafson). Liberman's Ph.D. was received in Sociology and Ethnolinguistics. One can see how Liberman's approach was naturally eclectic while at the same time highly rigorous relative to his topic and inquiry, which was a study of Australian Aboriginal peoples' everyday strategies and struggles over land control rights.

The textual production of intellectual boundaries

One can observe Liberman's own contingent production of ethnomethodological knowledge, parameters, and membership for his practical purposes at-hand in one of his own text-accounts. In the following example Liberman is reviewing Dean and Juliet Flower MacCannell's book *The Time of the Sign: A Semiotic Interpretation of Modern Culture* (1982) for the *American Anthropologist* (1983:428-429). In what appears to be a pattern for newly minted Ph.D.'s in sociology who desire to construct career visibility in particular fields (myself included (cf. Flynn 1985, 1987)), Liberman produces local textual definitions and boundaries between intellectual fields. He creates a literary definition of ethnomethodology relative to semiotics via the medium of his book review. These local definitions or demarcations are constructed to serve his own practical purposes at that particular time, i.e., composing a "book review" in the context of creating an academic career that is sympathetic yet critical of certain versions of semiotics from the perspective of Garfinkelian ethnomethodology. In the review, he works to identify his version of ethnomethodology with Garfinkel's exposition of it, with whom he studied at the University of California, Los Angeles.

Liberman (1983:428) writes:

They (the MacCannells) claim that ethnomethodology suffers from a built-in limitation stemming from its intellectual dependence upon a version of phenomenology based on the Husserlian epoché, which requires that the world be held frozen in brackets, a disconnection of conscious experience from the world. But they provide no illustrations of *whose* ethnomethodology they are considering. (Italics are mine.)

With this emphasis on "whose ethnomethodology," it appears that Liberman is making visible for readers the state of ethnomethodology's various expositions, generational styles, and personages. He locally produces his contingent alignment with Garfinkel's exposition of ethnomethodology through the following writing practices as he comments on the MacCannells' view that semiotics is the "second ethnomethodology:"

> Despite their criticism of ethnomethodology, they see it and semiotics as allies in the search for the ultimate structures of meaning and argue for a rapprochement between them. I believe the two schools are even closer than the MacCannells have learned to appreciate, that in fact the "first" ethnomethodology is the MacCannell's "second" in that ethnomethodology, *particularly Garfinkel's exposition of it*, has had a long-standing opposition to "the disembodied subjectivity" of both the constitutional phenomenologists and constructionist social theorists. (Liberman 1983:429) (Italics are mine.)

By accentuating "Garfinel's exposition," Liberman seems to be differentiating between other ethnomethodologists who have worked close to semiotics, for example, Aaron Cicourel or Bennetta Jules-Rosette. Thus, Liberman chooses to create textually a reflexive affiliation with a perceived Garfinkelian line of ethnomethodology for his relevant purposes.

Liberman, as Boden did in his case, constructs an ethnomethodological standard by which to measure the MacCannells' understanding: "If the MacCannells have read ethnomethodology as being a perpetuation of the subjective viewpoint based on the Husserlian epoché, then they have misunderstood ethnomethodology" (Liberman 1983:429).

This constructed standard consists of Liberman's own understanding of ethnomethodology situated in and made relevant to his purposes in writing the review, establishing himself however indirectly in an ethnomethodological theoretical ancestry, and in playing a part in establishing a new sociological paradigm that includes semiotics and ethnomethodology as collaborative perspectives. His case, as well as Boden's, reveals a fact known but often forgotten: sociological writing is essentially embedded in practical intellectual politics, career establishment, and boundary keeping as well as theoretical exposition. All of us as writers display this phenomenon whenever we engage in writing, no matter how seemingly value-free or objective.

Textuality and authority

What texts say can no longer be treated as final authority or grounds for how they are made relevant for an ongoing particular inquiry. Instead, any inquiry is "equiprimordial" as a "theory" of the text. This hermeneutic observation appears to apply equally to membership in intellectual movements as well as to the historicity and context of the intellectual movement itself. Membership in intellectual movements is a contextual expression created by particular persons on particular occasions for   particular purposes. Membership is assembled and signified by localized procedures of reviving relevant theoretical ancestors, referencing an intertextual collectivity, and appropriating the intellectual movement's resources relative to one's inquires. It also is assembled by conscious, theoretical boundary creation and the historicization of texts as authoritative and stable grounds for paradigm development. Intellectuals and scholars employ varying degrees of situational reasoning in their proleptic-analeptic creation of an intellectual identity and a paradigmatic stance.

Knowledge of future events

In this study I have attempted to elucidate the assumptions, styles, and skilled performances underlying the establishment of the ethnomethodological movement. What can be said about ethnomethodology's knowledge system in relation to the larger traditions of Western social science? What makes ethnomethodology worth examining, and what does it tell us about the present state of social scientific inquiry?

As I have attempted to show, the ethnomethodological movement as a collective scientific enterprise has expanded various ideas in phenomenological philosophy, Parsonian and interpretive sociology, and ordinary language philosophy. Four generations of ethnomethodologists have developed distinctive methods of discovering and analyzing social actors' taken-for-granted assumptions and practical interactive constructions in empirical settings of use. These methods and analyses have been embedded in the ethnomethodological movement's distinctive representational genres, folkloric mythoforms, and organizational practices.

Polanyi (1962:150,274) has articulated that the natural and social sciences commonly engage in scientific controversy based on reasonable and unreasonable doubt. Scientific proofs and findings are often ignored and rejected largely on the general ground that members of the larger community are reluctant to believe what these findings try to prove or that the scientific community condemns the very nature of its argumentation (Jules- Rosette 1987). The ethnomethodological movement inhabits such scientific controversy. As I have shown, many of its critics dismiss it as an eccentric body of "hip jargon," refuse to engage in conceptual point-by-point debates, and accuse it of triviality. Others, including many ethnomethodologists, claim it is not sociology and question ethnomethodology's place in the social scientific field. Some claim the ethnomethodological movement is an esoteric sect. Will its critics eventually persuade and convince the larger sociological domain that there is a "reasonable doubt" about ethnomethodology's findings and contributions? What form will this take? In spite of its present development and recognition, will ethnomethodology eventually be discarded by the social sciences as unusable knowledge or perhaps an irrelevant discipline?

I think the ethnomethodological movement's most critical future problematic lies internal to itself as a movement. Rather than locating future success or failure solely in external disciplinary conditions and responses, I find ethnomethodology's prospects lie within its own organizational adaptations to individually and collectively perceived external and internal conditions.

Mullins has "prophesied" (1973:205) that if the University of California, San Diego, the University of British Columbia, and York began producing students, ethnomethodology's transitions to a specialty status in the social sciences will have been completed. If they did not, it was likely that ethnomethodology would not survive beyond 1983. It would gradually disappear, and its insights parceled out to new groups of sociologists.

What is my prediction for the ethnomethodological movement? From my own position as an analyst it is difficult to predict what will become of the ethnomethodological movement in the coming years. The movement has grown through a foundational period from 1950 to 1960, a revolutionary period from 1960 to 1975, and a normalization period from 1975 to present. Despite mounting international acceptability of ethnomethodological analyses in certain sociological subfields such as the sociology of science, education, medicine, and law, as well as the apparent maturing of conversation analysis as a legitimate subdiscipline, the future of the ethnomethodological movement appears to me to be ambiguous.

The uncertainty of the ethnomethodological movement's future results from various internal contradictions that threaten it with extinction. First, the ethnomethodological movement possesses a "pseudo-aristocratic" or privileged character in its critiques of other sociological movements and theories. Historically, this has prevented creative dialogue between other sociological schools. "Bridge-building" has been discouraged in favor of retaining the purity or uniqueness of the approaches of ethno-methodology and conversation analysis. In-group sanctions have been applied and marginalization has been the reward to members who have intellectually and politically strayed too far from the movement's inner circle, regardless of lip-service to a doctrine of laissez-faire development of the paradigm.

Second, the ethnomethodological movement is in danger of losing its creative originality. With the academic retirement of Harold Garfinkel in 1988 and the retirement of other first generation ethnomethodologists soon following, the movement is inwardly in need of a way of generating a new life if it is to survive. Because of the dependency of the ethno-methodological movement on Garfinkel's original voice, methods, and "intertextual poetry," new radical methods must be found that are capable of stirring up the sociological imagination of new graduate students. So far, these have not been found. Many of the leading ethnomethodologists including Garfinkel, Cicourel, and Schegloff now have relatively few graduate students completing Ph.D.'s. Attention to graduate student training in a way that fosters fresh experiences and reformulations of ethnomethodological insights needs to be carried out before it is too late.

Third, as the ethnomethodological movement passed into a normaliza-tion period within academic sociology, and passed out of its creative, revolutionary period, certain essential features of the "ethnomethodologi-cal experience" may have been lost. After 1970, as the movement appeared unable or unwilling to create and sustain organized research and graduate teaching centers, publication outlets, consistent open conferences, academic positions, and a "synthetic ecumenising" with other international schools of thought, the creative and original forward momentum of the movement seemed to slow down. This slowing was witnessed in the absence of new generations of graduate students who had complete training that included first-hand exposure to different teaching approaches in ethnomethodology, e.g., from Garfinkel, Cicourel, Sacks, Schegloff, Sudnow, Zimmerman, etc., as well as the lack of production of a unified ethnomethodological front in the international interdisciplinary debate.

With the death of Harvey Sacks in 1975, the conversation analysis wing of the movement was left with an accumulation of materials in the form of unpublished lectures and notes. These materials tended to invite applications and intellectual interpretations of Sacks's work, a practice that presents a danger of supplanting the teaching and engendering of an original perspective with mere textual exegesis and guardianship. Garfinkel's retirement, too, will presumably generate a similar interval of conflict over bequeathed textual materials since adequately radical methods for training graduate students have not been sufficiently devised. Whether the ethnomethodological movement will survive Garfinkel's retirement is an open question.

Fourth, the emergence of accusations of ethnomethodological "positivism" aimed mainly at the conversation analysis school (cf. Douglas 1977:56-57) as a result of their minute applications of much of Sacks's and Schegloff's work on conversational transcripts, has split the ethnomethodological movement into two methodological approaches. The two tendencies of "linguistic ethnomethodology," or conversation analysis, and "constitutive ethnomethodology" or Garfinkel's school of phenomenological and existential ethnomethodology, have been covertly, if not openly, at odds with each other at least since 1975 up to the present. This division threatens to deepen, especially after Garfinkel retires and as the conversation analysis school becomes stronger organizationally. Because of the degree of training required to master the philosophical and hermeneutic subtleties of Garfinkel's approach, special effort will be necessary if Garfinkel is to leave behind an adequate scaffolding for the future generations interested in his approach.

Mannheim (1982:239) has asserted that one of the most essential questions posed by the sociology of knowledge is at what stage does an intellectual movement find it necessary to reflect on its own construction? Does this, asks Mannheim, signal immanent dissolution or perfection? I think an answer to this query has been suggested by Jean Baudrillard (1981:11) in his concept of the simulacrum or simulation. The simulacrum, or produced appearance of reality, is the cultural sign that has taken on a life of its own in ways that are distinct from the reality it signifies or represents. For example, television and the media are not mere representations of the external world, but reference themselves as a hyper-real reality that has acquired a predominance and primordiality. Intellectual movements and disciplines reach a stage at which they produce a simulacrum of the approach they embody, organize, and promulgate.

The ethnomethodological movement, like many other social and intellectual movements, has reached such a simulated phase. Garfinkel (Hill and Crittenden 1968:10) alluded to this in 1968 when he said that the name "ethnomethodology" had acquired a life of its own.

Historical studies of the ethnomethodological movement, including this present study, have begun to emerge from within the movement itself (cf. Mehan and Wood 1975a; Leiter 1980; Handel 1982; Benson and Hughes 1983; Heritage 1984d, 1987; Sharrock and Anderson 1986a). These works attempt to produce a passable simulation of what the ethnomethodological movement actually is in historical and theoretical terms. Many of these texts, as well as the most frequently referenced texts of the movement (e.g., Garfinkel 1967a; Cicourel 1964; Sacks, Schegloff, and Jefferson 1974, etc.) presently stand as legitimate simulations of the movement. In fact, they attain an intertextual life of their own that in some sense transcends the actual lived contexts of their production within the movement. There is a danger that the movement can become hypnotized by its own textual and political simulations of itself. This can lead to a state of affairs where the movement effectively ignores its own practical construction on the level of interpersonal relations, graduate training, cultivation of creative originality, and encouragement of interdisciplinary communication. These conditions could result in the extinction of the movement over time.

My suggestion to the ethnomethodological movement is that those who actively consider themselves intellectual members creatively apply the movement's significant discoveries about the intersubjective world to their own field of discourse and action. Reflexive attention to an intellectual movement's Lebenswelt and social production of shared knowledge is essential to its continued life. Paramount is the creative, open training of graduate students, the organization of publishing and career possibilities, free international and interdisciplinary dialogues and conferences, and the flexible creation of its intellectual boundaries and simulations.

I foresee the possibility that the ethnomethodological movement could be utilized by the social sciences in spite of present controversy and uncertainty. Ethnomethodology may be increasingly drawn upon by the hermeneutic and interpretive schools of sociology and anthropology in their pursuit of members' meaning and motivations; by poststructural linguistics and semiotics in their search of new ways of analyzing the syntagmatic, pragmatic dimensions of language use; by phenomenological, existential, critical, and constructivist sociological approaches as these approaches attempt to clarify the social actor's praxis in the everyday world; and ultimately by ethnomethodology's harshest critic, standard American sociology, who may apply ethnomethodology's insights regarding practical reasoning to its research, survey, and quantitative analysis designs.

The fruitful utilization by the social sciences of ethnomethodology's findings will begin with an adequate understanding of the ethnomethodological movement's sociohistorically constructed voices, myths, and forms of knowledge. My objective in this present work has been to provide more of a basis for that understanding. Perhaps someday the social sciences will understand why the ethnomethodological movement has for so long remained at an initial stage, as a problem to be solved, a hope to be realized, and a discipline waiting to be born.

Appendix 1
A Generational Textual Glossary of Ethnomethodology

Ethnomethodology

First generation

Garfinkel (1967:11):

> I used the term *ethnomethodology* to refer to the investigation of the rational properties of indexical expressions and other practical actions as the contingent ongoing accomplishment of organized artful practices of everyday life.

Cicourel (1974:51):

> By *ethnomethodology* I mean the study of *interpretive procedures* and surface rules in everyday social practices and scientific activities.

Bittner (1965:239-55):

> Insofar as the procedure and considerations actors invoke in related terms of rational common-sense constructions to things in the world exhibit some stable properties, they may be called a method. It is, of course, not proper to assume that this method is identical with, or even similar to, the method of scientific inquiry. Garfinkel proposed that in order to differentiate the study of this method from the study of the methods of scientific inquiry it be called *ethnomethodology* .

Second generation

Zimmerman and Wieder (1970:295):

> Whatever the gains or losses of this "radical departure" might subsequently prove to be, proper understanding of what *ethnomethodologists* are trying to do cannot be achieved without explicit recognition of the fundamental break with the sociological tradition discussed above.

Third generation

Mehan and Wood (1975:3):

> For me, *ethnomethodology* is not a body of findings, nor a method, nor a theory, nor a world view. I view it as a form of life (cf. Wittgenstein 1953). It is a way of working which creates findings, methods, theories; it enables its practitioners to enter other realities (e.g., Castaneda 1968, 1971, 1972), there to experience the assembly of world views.

Pollner (1974:27):

> *Ethnomethodological inquiry* is guided by the heuristic "Treat social facts as accomplishments" (Garfinkel 1967). Where others might see "things," "givens," or "facts of life," the ethnomethodologist sees (or attempts to see) *process*; the process through which the perceivably stable features of socially organized environments are continually created and sustained.

Fourth generation

Lynch, Livingston, Garfinkel (1982:206, 208):

> In brief, the overriding preoccupation in *ethnomethodological studies* is with the detailed and observable practices which make up the incarnate production of ordinary social facts, for example, order of service in a queue, sequential order in conversation, and the order of skillfully embodied improvised conduct.... ethnomethodology is, therefore, a *foundational* discipline.

Rawls (1985:138):

> *Ethnomethodology* has articulated a new epistemological position which avoids many of the pitfalls of pragmatism and phenomenology, while nevertheless treading on some of what would appear to be "their" territory.

Lynch (1985:6):

> It is difficult to characterize the corpus of *ethnomethodological studies* of work under a uniform definition of a "field," of a "method," or of a "unified theory." In fact, these studies are distinguished by their irreverence to such terms of characterization.

Indexical expressions

First generation

Garfinkel (1967:4):

> Wherever studies of practical action and practical reasoning are concerned, these consist of the following: (1) the unsatisfied programmatic distinction between substitutability of objective (context free) for *indexical expressions*; (2) the "uninteresting" essential reflexivity of accounts of practical actions; and (3) the analyzability of actions-in-context as a practical accomplishment.

Garfinkel (1967:34):

> The demonstrably rational properties of *indexical expressions* and *indexical actions* is an ongoing achievement of the organized activities of everyday life.

Second generation

Schegloff (1972:87):

> These terms are prototypical members of a class logicians have called "*indexical expressions*," terms whose referent varies with the context of its use.

Wieder (1970:108):

> It has been a recurrent finding of ethnomethodology that, because everyday language use is characterized by the use of *indexical* or occasioned *expressions*, everyday language is used in such a way that is inappropriate to conceptualize its use in terms of rulelike semantics.

Third generation

Leiter (1980:107):

> *Indexicality* refers to the contextual nature of objects and events.

Fourth generation

Baccus (1976:5):

> That "reasonableness" relies on the *indexicality* of the account as an essentially vague referencing device which allows the imagined availability of properties and features of the phenomenon.

Reflexivity

First generation

Garfinkel (1967:7):

> Thereby, the first problematic phenomenon is recommended to consist of the *reflexivity* of the practices and attainments of the sciences in and of the organized activities of everyday life, which is an essential *reflexivity*.

Second generation

Wieder (1974:166):

> Instead, this talk was at the same time part of life in the halfway house, and it was a part that was itself included within the scope of things over which the code had jurisdiction. It is in this sense that talk involving the code was *reflexive* within the setting of its occurrence.

Third generation

Mehan and Wood (1975:13):

> Similarly, the word "indentation" not only takes its meaning from the context in which it appears, it *reflexivily* creates that very context.

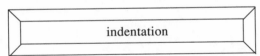

indentation

Wilson (1970:79):

> ...the fundamental problem of *reflexivity* (Garfinkel 1967: 7-9). On the one hand, the objectivity and reality of what is happening on any given occasion depends on the *members* seeing the present occasion as located within a stable, *objective social order*. On the other hand, the members' sense that the features of the social order are objective and real is an *accomplishment* of the members on that same occasion.

Fourth generation

Lynch (1985:22, fn.28):

> In speaking of object-accounts as *"reflexive achievements"* I allude to the way in which in a particular setting, an account does the work of "description" for the practical purposes of the parties in that setting.

Fisher and Todd (1986:xiv):

> We are suggesting, instead, a contextual hermeneutic mode of analysis in which causality resides in a dynamic, *reflexive* process.

Membership

First generation

Garfinkel (1967:1):

> Their central recommendation is that the activities whereby *members* produce and manage settings of organized everyday affairs are identical with *members'* procedures for making those settings "accountable.

Garfinkel and Sacks: (1970:342)

> The notion of member is at the heart of the matter. We do not use the term to refer to a person. It refers instead to the mastery of natural language.

Second generation

Sacks (1966:76):

> From the *member's* standpoint it is the case that for any population N, on some occasion of categorizing its members, the task can be complete if each *member* of the population has had a single category applied to him.

Castaneda (1972:ix):

> For Don Juan, then, the reality of our day-to-day consists of an endless flow of perceptual interpretations which we, the individuals who share a specific *membership*, have learned to make in common.

Third generation

Schenkein (1978:5):

> In sum, our independent studies of turn taking, identity negotiations, compliment responses, story clusters, the recommencement of a meeting, action sequence negotiations, conversational environments for equivocality, amplitude shifts, story beginnings and endings, and dirty jokes are all committed to building nonintuitive descriptions of the organization of conversational interaction as the technical accomplishment of *member* conversationalists.

Fourth generation

Lynch (1985:4):

> Except when presentations of lab work were given in the explanatory format of a "tour," shop talk was produced for recipients who were already familiar with the technical details of the ongoing work.

Maynard (1986:5):

> The presumption here, contrariwise, is that a social organization worthy of intense scrutiny is deeply rooted in *members'* ongoing production of those interactional products that get labeled as plea bargaining, character assessment, deciding facts, and so forth.

Accountability

First generation

Garfinkel (1967:vii):

Ethnomethodological studies analyze everyday activities as members' methods of making those same activities visibly-rational-and-reportable-for-all-practical-purposes, i.e., *"accountable,"* as organizations of commonplace everyday activities.

Garfinkel (1967:1):

When I speak of *accountability* my interests are directed to such matters as the following. I mean observable and reportable, i.e., available to members as situated practices of looking-and-telling.

Second generation

Zimmerman and Wieder (1970:294):

It is this decision to bring such *accounting practices* under investigation as phenomena in their own right without presupposing the independence of the domain made observable via their use that constitutes the radical character of the ethnomethodological enterprise.

Third generation

Benson and Hughes (1983:120):

The *accounts* of the organization's workings are, like formulations, reflexively tied to the setting in which they are produced and of which they are a part.

Leiter: (1980:162)

Accounts, in turn, are any intentional communication between two or more people that covertly or through practical analysis reveal features of a setting and serve the pragmatic interests of the participants.

Fourth generation

Baccus (1976:9):

> In the same way that sign-reading is a natural *account* to the production of an unseen, as a reflexively constituted object, sign-reading can be taken as an *account* of one means whereby the visibility criterion can be met by constituting social objects as worldly phenomena which are *accountably* visible.

Local practices

First generation

Garfinkel (1967:8):

> With respect to the problematic character of *practical actions* and to the *practical adequacy* of their inquiries, members take for granted that a member must at the outset "know" the settings in which he is to operate if his practices are to serve as measures to bring particular, located features of these settings to recognizable account.

Garfinkel (1967:1):

> I mean, too, that such practices consist of an endless, ongoing, contingent accomplishment....

Second generation

Zimmerman: (1970:225)

> ...the problematic topic of sociological inquiry is the member-of-society's "socially organized common *practices*" for detecting, describing, warranting, and accounting for the sensible features of everyday activities. Any socially organized setting, precisely in the way it organizes itself, provides an occasion for the study of these *practices*. The description of the phenomena subsumed under the rubrics of social organization, informal organization, and the like is then a description of these practices. Hence, the present study is not a sociology of organizations per se, but an inquiry into the practices members employ in sustaining the "sense" that their own and others' conduct is orderly and understandable, and reasonable—given the circumstances.

Third generation

Schwartz (1971:250):

> So-called *"member's methods"* of making common sense settings observable which consisted of their methods of talking rationally about those settings were therefore a prime research topic of ethnomethodology.

Fourth generation

Livingston (1983:195):

> Furthermore, and in consequence, in that discovery consists of the just-this endogenous organization of *work practices*, that discovery is irremediably and exclusively available in and as a local enterprise.

Situatedness

First generation

Garfinkel (1967:10):

> The phenomenon consists, too, of the analyzability of *actions-in-context* given that not only does no concept of context-in-general exist, but every use of *"context"* without exception is itself essentially indexical.

Cicourel (1973:124):

> The elaboration of *circumstances and particulars of an occasion* can be subjected to an indefinite re-elaboration of the "same" or "new" circumstances and particulars.

Second generation

Zimmerman and Pollner (1970:103):

> The distinctive features of the alternative perspective, which we offer here, reside in the proposal that the object structures of social activities are situated,

practical accomplishments of the work through and by which the appearance-of-objective structures is displayed and detected.

Third generation

Bellman (1975:16):

Following this recommendation, secrecy is here to be understood as a managed accomplishment *in those settings* where it is itself a mundane feature.

Fourth generation

Lynch (1985:158):

Although such an analysis is deficient as a way to characterize the competence which were productive of the talk, it is of some value to point to how the sensibility of the talk was *local to its productive situations*.

Unique adequacy of methods and becoming the phenomenon

First generation

Garfinkel (1967:vii-viii):

Their study is directed to the task of learning how members' actual, ordinary activities consist of methods to make practical actions, practical circumstances, common sense knowledge of social structures, and practical sociological reasoning analyzable; and of discovering the formal properties of commonplace, practical commonsense actions *"from within"* actual settings, as ongoing accomplishments of these settings.

Second generation

Castaneda (1968:7):

> I carried out the *apprenticeship* first in Arizona and then in Sonora, because Don Juan moved to Mexico during the course of my *training* .

Third generation

Mehan and Wood (1975:227):

> If the purpose of the research is to know the reality of the phenomenon, then the researcher must begin by first *becoming the phenomenon.*

Fourth generation

Lynch (1985:6):

> Garfinkel's maxim of the "unique adequacy" of methods locates a concern in these studies to operate from within the competence systems they describe.

Scenic display

First generation

Garfinkel (1967:1):

> ...that the practices are *done* by parties to those settings whose skill with, knowledge of, and entitlement to the detailed work of that *accomplishment-* whose-competence-they obstinately depend on, recognize use, and take for granted. . .

Garfinkel (1967:29):

> Then the recognized sense of what a person said consists only and entirely in recognizing the *method* of his speaking, of seeing *how he spoke.*

Second generation

Schegloff (1972:117):

> For it is through such resources that the production of a world of particular specific scenes through a set of general formal practices is *accomplished and exhibited.*

Third generation

Bellman (1975:17):

> The decision to speak is for him a reflexive feature of the settings in which he finds himself, for on those occasions he is called upon to say something (if only to *demonstrate* that he is a member in those situations). He must have available techniques to make the decision of what to speak.

Fourth generation

Lynch (1985:11):

> What are considered here to be meaningful exhibits of "the data" are such *instances* of the data under an argument, the data under reading, or the data as documents of an announcement or claim, as can be *witnessed in actual occasions* of lab work.

Appendix 2
Referencing

Collectivity membership list and references to the "missing what," *Contributions to Ethnomethodology*, edited by Harold Garfinkel and Harvey Sacks. The following textual excerpt is found in Garfinkel and Sacks (1970:340-341, fn. 6).

Egon Bittner, "Police Discretion in Emergency Apprehension of Mentally Ill Persons," *Social Problems*, 14 (Winter, 1967), 278-292; "The Police on Skid-row: A study of Peace Keeping, " *American Sociological Review*, 32 (October, 1967), 699-715. Lindsey Churchill, "Types of Formalization in Small-group Research," review article, *Sociometry*, vol. 26 (September, 1963); "The Economic Theory of Choice as a Method of Theorizing," paper delivered at the American Sociological Association meetings, August, 31, 1964; "Notes on Everyday Quantitative Practices," in Harold Garfinkel and Harvey Sacks, eds., *Contributions to Ethnomethodology* (Bloomington: Indiana University Press, in press). Aaron Cicourel, Method and Measurement in Sociology (Glencoe: Free Press, 1964); The Social Organization of Juvenile Justice (New York: Wiley, 1968). Harold Garfinkel, *Studies in Ethnomethodology* (Engelwood Cliffs: Prentice-Hall, 1967). Craig MacAndrew, "The Role of 'Knowledge at Hand' in the Practical Management of Institutional Idiots," in Garfinkel and Sacks, *Contributions*; with Robert Edgerton; *Time Out: A Social Theory of Drunken Comportment* (Chicago: Aldine, 1969). Michael Moerman, "Ethnic Identification in a Complex Civilization: Who Are the Lue?" *American Anthropologist*, 65 (1965), 1215-1230; "Kinship and Commerce in The Thai-Lue Village," Ethnology, 5 (1966), 360-364; "Reply to Naroll," *American Anthropologist*, 69, (1967), 512-513; "Being Lue: Uses and Abuses of Ethnic Identification," *American Ethnological Society, Proceedings of the 1967 Spring Meeting* (Seattle: University of Washington Press, 1968), 153-169. Zimmerman and Pollner, "The Everyday World." Edward Rose, "Small Languages," in Garfinkel and Sacks, *Contributions to Ethnomethodology; A Looking Glass Conversation in the Rare Languages of Sez and Pique*, Program on Cognitive Processes Report No.102 (Boulder: Institute of Behavioral

Science, University of Colorado, 1967); *Small Languages: The Making of Sez*, Bureau of Sociological Research, Report No. 16, Part 1 (Boulder: Institute of Behavioral Science, University of Colorado, 1966). Harvey Sacks, *Social Aspects of Language: The Organization of Sequencing in Conversation* (Englewood Cliffs: Prentice-Hall, 1967); "Normal Crimes: Sociological Features of a Penal Code in a Public Defender's Office," *Social Problems*, 12 (Winter, 1965), 255-276. D. Lawrence Wieder, "Theories of Signs in Structural Semantics," in Garfinkel and Sacks, *Contributions*. Don H. Zimmerman, "Bureaucratic Fact Finding in a Public Assistance Agency," in Stanton Wheeler, ed., *The Dossier in American Society* (in press); "The Practicalities of Rule Use," in Garfinkel and Sacks, *Contributions*; "Paper Work and People Work: A Study of a Public Assistance Agency," Ph.D. dissertation, Department of Sociology, University of California, Los Angeles, 1966.

Appendix 3
Ethnomethodology Around the World

Countries and campuses where ethnomethodology is being taught or practiced:

Canada

University of Calgary
University of British Columbia
La Trobe University
University of Waterloo

England

University of Lancaster
University of Manchester
Oxford University
Plymouth Polytechnic
Manchester Polytechnic
University of London,
    Goldsmith College
University of Warwick
University of York
University of Surrey

France

École des Hautes Études en
    Sciences Sociales (EHESS)
University of Paris V (Sorbonne)
University of Paris VII (Jussieu)

University of Paris VIII
    (Vincenne at St. Denis)
Centre Nationale de Recherche
    Scientifique (CNRS)
Centre Nationale de Recherche
    Pédagogique (CNRP)

Germany

University of Bielefeld
Free University of Berlin
University of Regensburg
University of Hanover

Ireland

University of Dublin, Trinity
    College

Italy

University of Rome
University of Palermo

Japan

Waseda University

The Netherlands

University of Amsterdam

Spain

University of Madrid

Switzerland

University of Fribourg
University of Geneva

Turkey

University of Istanbul

USA

University of California
   Berkeley
   Irvine
   Los Angeles
   Santa Barbara
   San Diego
San Diego State University
Boston University
Brandeis University

City University of New York
Oklahoma State University
Washington University, St. Louis
Washington State University
Wesleyan University
University of Wisconsin
Harvard Medical School
University of Massachusetts
   Amherst
University of Southern Carolina
Queens College
Southern Methodist University
Columbia University
University of Michigan
Adelphi
Marquette
New Mexico Highlands
New School of Social Research
Southern Illinois-Edwardsville
Syracuse University
University of Texas
   El Paso
   Austin
University of Oregon
(Source: American Sociological Association Guide to Sociology Departments, 1986-1987)

Yugoslavia

University of Belgrade

Zambia

University of Zambia

Appendix 4
Ethnomethodology Translated in French

Blum, Alan F. et Daniel Foss, Peter McHugh, Stanley Raffel
  1973   "La rebuffade", dans *Communications*, 20(1973), pp.225-245.
Cicourel, Aaron
  1973   *La Sociologie Cognitive*. Presses Universitaires de France.
  1973   "Sémantique générative et structure de l'interaction sociale"
         dans *Communications*, 20(1973), pp.204-224.
Flynn, Pierce J.
  1985   Book Review. *From a Sociology of Symbols to a Sociology of
         Signs* by Ino Rossi; *The Hermeneutic by Imagination* by Josef
         Bleicher; *The Perspective of Ethnomethodology* by Douglas
         Benson and John Hughes. In *Sociétés: Revue de Sciences
         Humaine et Sociales*, Vol. 1, No. 5, (September):24-25.
  1986a "Les Générations Successives d'Ethnométhodologues aux
         U.S.A." In *Pratiques de Formations* (Analyses), 11-12
         (October):97-102.
  1986b Book Review. *Garfinkel and Ethnomethodology* by John
         Heritage; *The Ethnomethodologists* by Wes Sharrock and
         Bob Anderson. Translated by Dominique Glaub. In *Sociétés:
         Revue de Sciences Humaine et Sociales*. Vol. 2, No. 4 (May-
         June): 36-37.
Flynn, Pierce J. and Sam E. Combs
  1985   Book Review. *An Ethnomethodological Investigation of the
         Foundations of Mathematics* by Eric Livingston; *Art and
         Artifact in Laboratory Science* by Michael Lynch. In *Sociétés:
         Revue de Sciences Humaine et Sociales*, Vol. 1 No. 5:24.
Garfinkel, Harold
  1984a dans *Arguments ethnométhodologiques*, 1984, Louis Quéré
         (ed.) et al. pp.6-10. "Le domaine d'objet de l'ethnométhodol-
         ogie." Extrait de la 'Preface' aux *Studies in Ethnomethodol-
         ogy*, 1967.
  1984b dans *Arguments ethnométhodologiques*, 1984, pp.31-37. "Les
         structures formelles des actions pratiques." Extrait de l'article

"On Formal Structures of Practical Action." By Garfinkel and Sacks, 1970, pp. 338-342.

1984c dans *Arguments ethnométhodologiques*, 1984, pp.54-99 "Qu'est-ce que l'ethnométhodologie?" Ce texte constitue le chapitre 1, des *Studies in Ethnomethodology*, 1967.

1984d dans *Arguments ethnométhodologiques*, 1984, pp. 60-70 "Sur les origins du mot 'Ethnométhodologie'."Extrait du *Proceedings of the Purdue Symposium on Ethnomethodology*, 1968.

1985a dans *Sociétés: Revue des sciences humaines et sociales*, Vol. 1, No. 5, septembre 1985. pp. 5-7 "L'origine du terme 'L'ethnométhodologie'." Extrait du *Proceedings of the Purdue Symposium on Ethnomethodology*, 1968, pp. 5-11.

1985b dans *Sociétés: Revue des sciences humaines et sociales*, Vol. 1, No. 5, septembre 1985. pp. 35-39 "Interview avec Harold Garfinkel: La contribution de l'ethnométhodologie à la recherche sociologique." par Bennetta Jules-Rosette.

1985c dans *Décrire: Une imperatif? Description, explication, interpretation en sciences sociales*. Edited par Ackerman, Conein, Gruigurs, Quéré, Vidal. Ecole des Hautes Etudes Etudes en Sciences Sociales, Paris, 1985, pp. 239-249. "Sur le problème des correctifs." Ce texte est la transcription décrire intervention orale de Harold Garfinkel à Paris.

1986 "Du bon usage de la degradation." In *Sociétés: Revue de Sciences Humaine et Sociales*, No. 11:24-27.

Heritage, John
  1984 *Garfinkel and Ethnomethodology*. London: Polity Press. Extrait (pp.1-5) "Ethnométhodologie: Un défi à la sociolgie 'Conventionnelle'." dans *Sociétés: Revue des sciences humaines et sociales*, Vol. 1, No. 5, septembre 1985, pp.7-9.

Jules-Rosette, Bennetta
  1987 "L'Ethnométhodologie en Perspective." In *Sociétés: Revue de Sciences Humaine et Sociales*, No. 14, Juin: 5-7.

Lynch, Michael
  1985 "La retine exteriorisé: Selection et mathematisation des documents visuelles." dans *Culture Technique*, No. 14, "Les vues de l'esprit", Paris. D.U.F.

Mehan, Hugh
  "Constructivisme sociale dans psychologie et sociologie." dans *Sociologie et Sociétés*, Vol. 14(2):77-96.

Sacks, Harvey
    1973   "Tout le monde doit mentir." dans *Communications*, 20,(1973),
            pp.182-203.
    1984   "Perspectives de recherche." Extrait des "lectures" donneés
            par Harvey Sacks entre 1964 et 1972 dans *Arguments
            ethnométhodologiques*, 1984, pp.138-144.
Schegloff, Emanuel
    1987   "Entre 'Micro-' et 'Macro-': Contexts et l'autre Connections."
            Translated by Dominique Glaub. In *Sociétés: Revue de Sci-
            ences Humaine et Sociales*, No. 14, Juin:17-22.
Signorini, Jacqueline
    1985   *De Garfinkel à la communaute electronique geocub: Essai de
            méthodologie (et recherche de fondements)*. Memoire de
            D.E.A. d'Ethnologie, dirigé par Y. Lecerf, Université de Paris
            VII-Jussieu, Department d'Ethnologie. *Chapitre Trois*: traduc-
            tion de chaptire "3" de Harold Garfinkel *Studies in Ethnom-
            ethodology*, 1967.

Appendix 5
Ethnomethodology's Topical Fields

Selected ethnomethodological studies can be grouped by research topic in the following ways:

Medical settings

Anderson, W. T. 1981a, b
Bittner 1961
Blum 1970b
Cicourel 1985
Coulter 1975, 1979
Emerson, J. 1970a
Emerson, R. & Pollner, 1976, 1981
Fisher 1981, 1982, 1983, 1986
Fisher and Todd 1983, 1986
Frankel 1983
Garfinkel 1956a, 1967
Jules-Rosette 1981a, b
MacAndrew 1969
Robillard and Pack 1980
Robillard et al. 1983
Sacks 1966
Schegloff 1963, 1967
Schwartz 1971
Sharrock 1979
Shumsky 1972
Silverman 1981
Smith, D. 1978
Sudnow 1967
Todd 1982, 1983, 1984
Turner 1972a
Watson 1986
West 1983, 1984
Wood 1968

Legal settings

Atkinson 1981
Atkinson and Drew 1979
Bittner 1967, 1975
Burns 1981, 1986
Cicourel 1968
Emerson, R. 1969
Garfinkel 1949, 1967g
Liberman 1982, 1985
Maroules 1985
Maynard 1983, 1985, 1986
Meehan 1983
Pollner 1974, 1987
Ramos 1973
Sacks 1972d
Sudnow 1965
Wieder 1974
Zimmerman 1984
Zimmerman and Wieder 1977

Conversation studies

Atkinson 1971-84
Atkinson and Drew 1979
Atkinson and Heritage 1984
Atkinson, Cuff, Lee 1973, 1978
Bellman 1975
Boden 1981-89
Button and Casey 1982, 1984
Button, Drew, and Heritage 1986
Cicourel 1973, 1980
Coulter 1979a, b
Fisher and Todd1986
Garfinkel 1967, 1972
Garfinkel, Lynch, Livingston
    1981
Garfinkel and Sacks 1970
Goldberg 1975, 1976, 1978
Goodwin 1979, 1981
Heritage and Watson 1979, 1980
Heyman 1986
Jefferson 1972-86
Jefferson, Sacks, Schegloff 1973
Jefferson and Schenkein 1977,
    1978
Jules-Rosette 1976b, 1980a
Lynch 1985a
Mehan 1971-90
Moerman 1972, 1973, 1977,
    1988
Moerman and Sacks 1974
Pack 1986
Pollner 1987
Pomerantz 1975-84
Pomerantz and Atkinson 1984
Psathas 1979
Ryave 1973, 1978
Ryave and Schenkein 1974
Sacks 1963-84

Sacks and Schegloff 1974
Sacks, Schegloff and Jefferson 1974
Schegloff 1967-88
Schegloff, Jefferson, Sacks 1977
Schegloff and Sacks 1973
Schenkein 1971-86
Sharrock 1974
Sharrock and Turner 1978
Sudnow 1972a, b
Terasaki 1975, 1976b
West 1975-84
Zimmerman and West 1975, 1980

Offices and bureaucratic organizations

Baccus 1981, 1986
Baker 1989
Bittner 1965
Burns 1978b
Garfinkel 1967b
Jules-Rosette 1986
Jules-Rosette and Flynn 1988
Wieder 1974
Wowk 1980
Zimmerman 1966, 1969

Educational institutions/ settings

Boèse 1972
Burns 1978c, 1981
Cicourel and Boèse 1972a
Cicourel and Kitsuse 1963
Cicourel and Mehan 1985
Cicourel et al. 1974
Davies 1978

Educational institutions/ settings (cont'd)

Garfinkel and Burns in press
Hertweck 1986
Jennings 1972
Leiter 1971, 1974
MacKay 1973
McDermott 1976
McDermott et al. 1978
McHoul, A.W. 1978b
Mehan 1971-88
Mehan, Meihls, Hertweck, 1985
Mehan, Hertweck, Combs,
    Flynn 1981
Morrison 1976, 1981
Roth 1974

Religious and mystical settings

Bellman 1975, 1977
Bittner 1963
Castaneda 1968, 1972, 1973
Combs 1985
Eglin 1973
Flynn 1977
Girton 1986
Hayward 1978
Jules-Rosette 1973, 1975, 1976,
    1978, 1979a, 1980a, 1986a
Ryno 1985
TenHouten and Kaplan 1973
Wedow 1973, 1980
Zimmerman and Wieder 1977

Ethnomethodological studies of the arts

Bellman and Jules-Rosette, 1977
Fauman 1980
Flynn 1987a
Garfinkel 1967
Girton 1986
Jules-Rosette 1981a, 1984
Livingston in press
Morrison 1981
Pack 1986
Sudnow 1978, 1980, 1983

Scientific work sites

Burns 1978b
Combs, Lestel, Flynn, Phaneuf
    1985
Garfinkel 1967, 1987, 1990
Garfinkel, Lynch, Livingston 1981
Livingston and Garfinkel 1983
Livingston 1983-89
Lynch 1974-90
Lynch, Livingston, Garfinkel 1983
Morrison 1979, 1981
Robillard 1980, 1986
Robillard and Pack 1980
Robillard, White, Maretzki 1981
Schrecker in press
Wieder 1980

Bibliography

Abrams, P.
   1980   *The Origins and Growth of British Sociology.* Chicago: University of
          Chicago Press.
Ackerman, Werner G., Bernard Conein, Christine Guiges, Louis Quéré, Daniel
          Vidal (eds.)
   1985   *Décrire: Un impératif? Description, explication, interpretation en
          sciences sociales.* a. Tome I. b. Tome II. Paris: Ecole des Hautes
          Etudes en Sciences Sociales.
Adato, Albert
   1976   "Alltägliche Ereignisse – ungewöhnlich erfahren: in Weingarten,
          Sacks, and Schenkein, (eds.). pp. 179-202.
   1980   "Occasionality as a Constituent Feature of the Known-in-Common-
          Character of Topics. *Human Studies* 3:47-64.
Anderson, Digby
   1978   "Some Organizational Features in the Local Production of a Plausible
          Text." *Philosophy of the Social Sciences*, vol. 8, no.1, pp. 113-135.
Anderson, R. J.
   1981   *A Sociological Analysis of Some Procedures for Discerning Member-
          ship.* Unpublished Ph.D. dissertation, University of Manchester.
Anderson, R. J., W.W. Sharrock, and J.A.Hughes,
   1987   "The Division of Labour", paper presented at the conference on
          "Action Analysis and Conversation Analysis", *Maison des Sciences
          de L'Homme*, Paris, September 26-30.
Anderson, W. T.
   1981a *Behavior in Painful Places: Aspects of the Dentist-Patient Encounter.*
          Unpublished Ph.D. dissertation, Boston University, MA.
   1981b "Dentistry as an Activity System: Sequential Properties of the
          Dentist-Patient Encounter." In Anderson, Helm, Meehan and Rawls
          (eds.), *New Directions in Ethnomethodology and Conversational
          Analysis.* New York: Irvington Press.
Anderson, W. T., and D. T.Helm
   1979   "The Physician Patient Encounter: A Process of Reality Negotiation."
          In E. Gartley Jaco (ed.), *Patients, Physicians and Illness* (3rd ed.).
          New York: Free Press.
Aragon, Louis
   1925   "Idees." In *La revolution surrealiste.* Vol. 1 (April, 1925):30.

310   *Bibliography*

Ardoino, J. and Yves Lecerf
1986   "L'ethnométhodologie et l'alternative des sciences sociales." In
Pratiques de Formation (Analyses), (11-12):11-20.

Armstrong, Robert Plant
1975   *Wellspring: On the Myth and Source of Culture.* Berkeley: University
of California Press.

Ash, R.
1972   *Social Movements in America.* Chicago: Markham Publishing Co.

Atkinson, J. M.
1971   "Societal Reactions to Deviance: The Role of Coroners' Definitions."
In S. Cohen (ed.), *Images of Deviance.* Harmondsworth: Penguin
Press, pp. 165-191.
1976   "Order in Court: Some Preliminary Issues and Analyses." Paper
presented at the I.S.A. Conference, Balatonszeplak, Hungary.
1978   *Discovering Suicide: Studies in the Social Organization of Sudden
Death.* London: Macmillan.
1979   "Sequencing and Shared Attentiveness to Court Proceedings." In
George Psathas (ed.), *Everyday Language: Studies in Ethnomethodology.* New York: Irvington, pp. 257-286.
1981   "Ethnomethodological Approaches to Sociolegal Studies." In A.
Podgorecki and C.J. Whelan (eds.), *Sociological Approaches to
Law.* London: Croom Helm, pp. 201-223.
1982   "Understanding Formality: Notes on the Categorization and Production of 'formal' Interaction." In *British Journal of Sociology,* 33:
86-117.
1984a   *Our Masters Voices: Studies in the Language and Body Language of
Politics.* London: Methuen.
1984b   "Public Speaking and Audience Responses: Some Techniques for
Inviting Applause." In J. Maxwell Atkinson and J. Heritage (eds.),
Structures of Social Action: Studies in Conversation Analysis.
Cambridge: Cambridge University Press, pp. 370-409.

Atkinson, J. M. and P. Drew
1979   *Order in the Court: The Organization of Verbal Interaction in
Judicial Settings.* London: Macmillan.

Atkinson, J. M. and C. C. Heath
1976   "Problems in Analyzing Video-taped and Other Observational Data."
Paper presented at the Annual Conference of the British Sociological
Association, Manchester.

Atkinson, J. M. and J. C. Heritage (eds.)
1984   *Structure of Social Action: Studies in Conversation Analysis.*
Cambridge: Cambridge University Press.

Atkinson, J. M., E. C. Cuff, and J. R. E. Lee
  1973   "'Right...er': Prolegomena to the Analysis of 'meeting talk' with Special Reference to the Problem of 'beginnings'." (Didsbury Conversational Analysis Workshop, August, Working Paper No.1) Unpublished manuscript.
  1978   "The Recommencement of a Meeting as a Member's Accomplishment." In *Studies in the Organization of Conversational Interaction.* Jim Schenkein (ed.). New York: Academic Press, pp. 133-154.
Attewell, P.
  1974   "Ethnomethodology since Garfinkel." In *Theory and Society.* 1: 179-210.
Austin, J. L.
  1962   *How to do things with words.* Ithaca, New York: Cornell University Press.
Baccus, Melinda
  1976   "Sociological Indication and the Visibility Criterion of Real World
  (1986) Social Theorizing." Department of Sociology, University of California, Los Angeles. In Garfinkel (ed.) *Ethnomethodological Studies of Work,* vol. III. London: Routledge and Kegan Paul (1986).
  1981   "Multipiece Truck Wheel Accidents and Their Regulations." Unpublished paper, Department of Sociology, University of California, Los Angeles.
Baker, Phyllis
  1989   *Corporate Culture and the Automated Office.* Unpublished Ph.D. dissertation, University of California, San Diego.
Bakhtin, M. M.
  1981   *The Dialogic Imagination: Four Essays by M.M. Bakhtin.* Michael Holquest (ed.), translated by C. Emerson and M. Holquest. Austin: University of Texas.
Barber, B.
  1975   "Toward a New View of the Sociology of Knowledge." In L. Coser, (ed.), *The Idea of Social Structure.* New York: Harcourt, Brace, Jovanovich, pp. 102-16.
Barnes, B.
  1977   *Interests and the Growth of Knowledge.* London: Routledge and Kegan Paul.
Barnes, H. E. (ed.)
  1948   *An Introduction to the History of Sociology.* Chicago: University of Chicago Press.
Barthes, Roland
  1974a   S/Z. Translated by Richard Miller. New York: Hill and Wang.
  1974b   "An Introduction to the Structural Analysis of Narrative." In *New Literary History,* 6(2):237-272.

Bastide, Francoise
    1979   "La foie lave: Approche semiotique d'un texte de sciences expéri-
            mentales." *Documents de Recherches GRSL*, 7.
Baudrillard, Jean
    1981   *Simulacres et Simulation*. Paris: Galilee.
Bauman, Richard
    1986   *Story, Performance, and Event: Contextual Studies of Oral Narrative*.
            Cambridge: Cambridge University Press.
Bauman, Zygmunt
    1973   "On the Philosophical Status of Ethnomethodology." In *The Socio-
            logical Review*, 21, S:5-23.
Becker, Howard
    1986   *Writing for Social Scientists*. Chicago: University of Chicago Press.
Beckford, James
    1978   "Accounting for Conversion." In *British Journal of Sociology*, 29(2):
            249-262.
    1985   "The Insulation and Isolation of the Sociology of Religion." *Socio-
            logical Analysis* 46, 4:347-354.
Bjelic, Dusan
    1987   "On Hanging Up in Telephone Conversation," *Semiotica*, (67)-3-4:
            195-210.
Bellman, Beryl
    1975   *Village of Curers and Assassins: On the Production of Fala Kpelle
            Cosmological Categories*. The Hague: Mouton.
    1977   "Ethnohermeneutics: On the Interpretation of Intended Meaning
            Among the Kpelle of Liberia." In *Language and Thought*,
            McCormick (ed.), Mouton.
Bellman, Beryl and Bennetta Jules-Rosette
    1977   *A Paradigm for Looking: Cross-Cultural Research with Video Media*.
            New Jersey: Ablex Publishing Corp.
Benda, Julien
    1927   *The Treason of the Intellectuals*. (translated by R.Aldington) New
            York: William Morrow.
Benjamin, Walter
    1969   *Illuminations*. New York: Schochen Books.
Benson, Douglas
    1974   "Critical Note. A Revolution in Sociology?" In *Sociology*, S:125-129.
Benson, Douglas and John A. Hughes
    1983   *The Perspective of Ethnomethodology*. New York: Longman.
Berger, Bennett M.
    1961   "Sociology and the Intellectuals: An Analysis of a Stereotype." In
            Lipset, S. M. and N. Smelser (eds.), *Sociology: The Progress of a
            Decade*. New Jersey: Prentice Hall, pp. 37-46.

Berger, Peter and Thomas Luckmann
  1966   The *Social Construction of Reality: A Treatise in the Sociology of
          Knowledge*. New York: Anchor Books.
Bergmann, Jörg R.
  1987   *Klatsch: Zur Sozialform der Dikreten Indiskretion*. Berlin and New
          York: Walter de Gruyter.
Besnard, Phillipe (ed.)
  1983   *The Sociological Domain: The Durkheimians and the Founding
          of French Sociology*. Cambridge: Cambridge University Press.
Betsworth, Roger G.
  1980   *The Radical Movements of the 1960s*. New Jersey: The Scarecrow
          Press Inc. and The American Theological Library Association.
Bittner, Egon
  1961   *Popular Interest in Psychiatric Remedies. A Study in Social
          Control*. Unpublished Ph.D. dissertation, University of California,
          Los Angeles.
  1963   "Radicalism and the Organization of Social Movements." In
          American Sociological Review, 28(S):928-940.
  1965   "The Concept of Organization." In *Social Research*, 32(S):239-255
          and in R. Turner (ed.), *Ethnomethodology*. Harmondsworth, 1974, S:
          69-81.
  1967a   "Police Discretion in Emergency Apprehension of Mentally Ill
          Persons." In *Social Problems*, 14(S):278-292.
  1967b   "The Police on Skid Row. A Study of Peace Keeping." In *American
          Sociological Review*, 32(S):699-715.
  1973   "Objectivity and Realism in Sociology." In George Psathas (ed.),
          Phenomenological Sociology. New York: John Wiley and Sons.
  1975   *The Functions of the Police in Modern Society*. New York: J.
          Aronson.
Bloor, D.
  1976   *Knowledge and Social Imagery*. London: Routledge and Kegan Paul.
Blum, Alan F.
  1970a   "The Corpus of Knowledge as a Normative Order. Intellectual
          Critiques of the Social Order and the Common-sense Features of
          Bodies of Knowledge." In J. C. McKinney and E. A. Tiryakian (eds.),
          Theoretical Sociology. New York: pp. (S):319-336.
  1970b   "The Sociology of Mental Illness." In J. D. Douglas (ed.), *Deviance
          and Respectability*. New York: (S):31-60.
  1970c   "Theorizing." In J. D. Douglas (ed.), *Understanding Everyday Life:
          Toward the Reconstruction of Sociological Knowledge*. Chicago:
          Aldine Publishing Co.

1972   "Sociology, Wrongdoing, and Aphasia. An attempt to Think Greek About the Problem of Theory and Practice." In R. A. Scott and J. D. Douglas (ed.), *Theoretical Perspectives on Deviance*. New York: (S):342-362.

1973   "Reading Marx." In *Sociological Inquiry*. 43(S):23-34.

1974a   *Theorizing*. London: Heinemann.

1974b   "Positive Thinking." In *Theory and Society*, I(S):245-269.

Blum, Alan F. and Peter McHugh

1971   "The Social Ascription of Motives." In *American Sociological Review*. 36(S):98-109.

Boden, Deirdre

1981   *Talk International*. Unpublished masters thesis, University of California, Santa Barbara.

1984a   "Talking with Doctors: Conversation Analysis in Action." (Washington University, St. Louis) Review of *Routine Complications: Troubles with Talk Between Doctors and Patients*, by Candice West. Bloomington: Indiana University Press. In Contemporary Sociology, September, 1986:715-718.

1984b   *The Business of Talk: Organizations in Action*. Cambridge: Polity Press.

1986   Review of *Understanding Interaction in Central Australia: An Ethnomethodological Study of Australian Aboriginal People*. By Kenneth Liberman. In *Contemporary Sociology*, November, Vol. 15(6):849-850.

1989   "Ethnomethodology International." *Contemporary Sociology* 18(6): 958-962.

Boden, Deirdre and S. Bielby

1986   "The Way It Was." *Language and Communication*, Vol. 6, #1/2.

Boden, Deirdre and H. Molotch

1985   "Talking Social Structure: Discourse, Dominance and the Watergate Hearings." In *American Sociological Review*, 50(3).

Boden, Deirdre and Don H. Zimmerman (ed.)

In press *Talk and Social Structure*. Cambridge: Polity Press.

Boèse, Robert

1972   *Natural Sign Language and the Acquisition of Social Structure*. Unpublished Ph.D. dissertation, University of California, Santa Barbara.

Bottomore, T. and Nisbet (eds.)

1978   *A History of Sociological Analysis*. London: Heineman.

Bourdieu, Pierre and J. C. Passeron

1977   *Reproduction in Education, Society, and Culture*. London/Beverly Hills: Sage Publications.

Boyers, Robert (ed.)
    1969   *The Legacy of the German Refugee Intellectuals.* New York: Schocken.

Braudel, Fernand
    1972   "History and the Social Sciences." In P. Burke (ed.), *Economy and Society in Early Modern Europe.* New York: Harper & Row.

Breton, André
    1925   "Le Surrealisme et le Painture." In *La Révolution Surrealiste*, vol. 1, (July, 1925):26-30.
    1972   *Surrealisme and Painting.* Translated by Simon Watson Taylor. New York: Harper and Row.

Brock, Werner
    1949   "An Account of Being and Time." Preface to Martin Heidegger's *Existence and Being*, 1949. New York: Henry Regnery Co.

Brohm, Jean-Marie (ed.)
    1986   *Quel Corps? Ethnomethodologie*, special issue No. 32/33, Dec. (1986).

Bruner, Jerome
    1986   *Actual Minds, Possible Worlds.* Massachusetts: Harvard University Press.

Burgess, M. M.
    1983   *Informed Consent in Routine Contexts.* Unpublished Ph.D. disserta-
    (1986) tion. University of Tennessee, Knoxville.

Burns, Stacy
    1978a   "A Comparison of Geertzian and Ethnomethodological Methods for
    (1986) the Analysis of the Production of Member-Relevant Objects." In Garfinkel (ed), (1986).
    1978b   "A Comparison of March-Olson and Ethnomethodology on the 'Circumstantial' Analysis of Decision-Making Work." In Garfinkel (ed.), (1986).
    1978c   "The Lived-Orderliness of Lecturing." Unpublished paper, Department of Sociology, University of California, Los Angeles.
    1981   "Becoming a Lawyer at Yale Law School." Unpublished paper, Yale Law School, New Haven.
    1986   *An Ethnomethodological Case Study of Law Pedagogy in Civil Procedure,* unpublished monograph, University of California, Los Angeles.

Button, G. and N. Casey
    1982   "Topic Nomination and Topic Pursuit." Mimeo, Plymouth Polytechnic.
    1984   "Generating Topic: The Use of Topic Initial Elicitors." In Atkinson and Heritage (eds.), Cambridge University Press, pp. 167-190.

Button, Graham, Paul Drew, and John Heritage (ed.)
   1986   "Interaction and Language Use." Special Issue, *Human Studies*,
           May (1986).
Casey, N.
   1981   *The Social Organization of Topic in Natural Conversation: Begin-
           ning a Topic.* Unpublished Ph.D. dissertation, Plymouth Polytechnic.
Castaneda, Carlos
   1968   *The Teachings of Don Juan: A Yaqui Way of Knowledge.* Berkeley:
           University of Berkeley Press.
   1972   *A Separate Reality: Further Conversations With Don Juan.* New
           York: Simon and Schuster.
   1973a   *A Journey to Ixtlan: The Lessons of Don Juan.* New York: Simon
           and Schuster.
   1973b   *Sorcery: A Description of the World.* Ph.D. dissertation, Department
           of Anthropology, University of California, Los Angeles.
   1976   *Tales of Power.* New York: Simon and Schuster.
   1977   *The Second Ring of Power.* New York: Simon and Schuster.
   1981   *The Eagle's Gift.* New York: Simon and Schuster.
   1984   *The Fire From Within.* New York: Simon and Schuster.
   1987   *The Power of Silence.* New York: Simon and Schuster.
Chua, Beng-Hua
   1974   "On the Commitments of Ethnomethodology." In *Sociological
           Behavior.* 4(S):71-87.
Chubin, D. E. and S. Restivo
   1983   "The 'Mooting' of Science Studies: Research Programs and Science
           Policy." In Knorr-Cetina and Mulkay (eds.), *Science Observed*,
           pp. 53-84.
Churchill, Lindsey
   1963   "Types of Formalization in Small-group Processes." Review article
           in *Sociometry*, 26(S):373-390.
   1964   "The Economic Theory of Choice as a Method of Theorizing."
           Kongreb-Papier, American Sociological Association.
   1966   "On Everyday Quantification Practices." Kongreb-Papier, American
           Sociological Association, Chicago.
   1971a   "Ethnomethodology and Measurement." In *Social Forces*, 50(S):
           182-191.
   1971b   "Some Limitations of Current Quantitative Methods in Sociology."
           Kongress-Papier, American Sociological Association, Denver,
           Colorado.
   1976   "The Grammar of Questioning." Unpublished manuscript.
   1978   *Questioning Strategies in Sociolinguistics.* Rowley, Massachusetts:
           Newbury House.

Cicourel, Aaron V.
1964   *Method and Measurement in Sociology.* New York: Free Press.
        [Translation: *Methode und Messung in der Soziologie.* Frankfurt: 1970.]
1965   "Family, Status, Social Class, and the Administration of Juvenile Justice." In *Estudios Sociologicas,* Buenos Aires.
1967a   "Fertility, Family Planning, and the Social Organization of Family Life. Some Methodological Issues." In *Journal of Social Issues,* 23(S):57-81.
1967b   "Kinship, Marriage and Divorce in Comparative Family Law." In *Law and Society Review,* I(S):103-129.
1968a   *The Social Organization of Juvenile Justice.* New York: Free Press.
1968b   "Police Records and Official Records." In Roy Turner (ed.), *Ethnomethodology.* Baltimore: Penguin Press. pp. 85-95.
1969   "Language as a Variable in Social Research." In *Sociological Focus,* 3(S):43-52.
1970a   "The Acquisition of Social Structure: Toward a Developmental Sociology of Language and Meaning." In J.D. Douglas (ed.), *Understanding Everyday Life.* Chicago: Aldine Publishing Co. pp. 136-168.
        [Reprinted in: A. V. Cicourel, *Cognitive Sociology.* New York: The Free Press, 1974:42-73.]
        [Translation: "Die Aneignung der sozialen Struktur." In *Sprache in der sozialen Interaktion,* München, 1975:13-68.]
        [Translation: *Rassagne Italiana de Sociologia,* Vol. 9, 1986.]
1970b   "Basic and Normative Rules in the Negotiation of Status and Role." In H.P. Dreitzel, *Recent Sociology,* 2:4-45.
        [Reprinted in: A. V. Cicourel, *Cognitive Sociology.* New York: The Free Press, 1974:11-41.]
        [Translation: "Basisregeln und normative Regeln im Prozess des Aushandelns von Status und Rolle." In Arbeitsgruppe Bielefelder Soziologen (eds.), *Alltagswissen, Interaktion und gesellschaftliche Wirklichkeit.* I(1973):147-188.]
1970c   "Generative Semantics and the Structure of Social Interaction." In *International Days of Sociolinguistics.* Luigi Sturzo Institute, Rome.
        [Reprinted in: A. V. Cicourel, *Cognitive Sociology.* New York: The Free Press, 1974:74-98.]
        [Translation: "Generative Semantik und die Struktur der sozialen Interaktion." In *Sprache in der sozialen Interaktion,* München, 1975:69-112.]
1972   "Delinquency and the Attribution of Responsibility." In R.A. Scott and J.D. Douglas (eds.), *Theoretical Perspectives on Deviance.* New York: pp. 142-157.

1973a   "Cross Modal Communication. The Representational Context of Sociolinguistic Information Processing." In R.W. Shuy (ed.), *Report of the Twenty-Third Annual Round Table Meeting on Linguistics and Language Studies*, Washington (D.C.), pp. 187-222.
[Reprinted in: A. V. Cicourel, *Cognitive Sociology*. New York: The Free Press, 1974:141-171.]
[Translation: "Multisensuelle Kommunikation. Probleme der sprachlichen Darstellung sozialer Erfahrungen." In *Sprache in der sozialen Interaktion*, München, 1975:190-241.]

1973b   *Cognitive Sociology. Language and Meaning in Social Interaction.* Harmondsworth: Penguin Books Ltd.
[Translation: *Sprache in der sozialen Interaktion*, München, 1975.]

1974a   "Gestural Sign Language and the Study of Non-Verbal Communication." In *Sign Language Studies*, 4:35-76.

1974b   "Ethnomethodology." In T. A. Sebeok (ed.), *Current Trends in Linguistics.* Vol. 12:1563-1605.
[Reprinted in: A. V. Cicourel, Cognitive Sociology. New York: The Free Press, 1974:99-140.]
[Translation: *Sprache in der sozialen Interaktion*, München, 1975: 113-189.]

1974c   *Theory and Method in a Study of Argentine Fertility.* New York: Wiley Interscience.

1974d   "Some Basic Theoretical Issues in the Assessment of the Child's Performance in Testing and Classroom Settings." In *Language Use and School Performance.* New York: Academic Press.

1974e   "Interviewing and Memory." In Colin Cherry (ed.), *Theory and Decision*, Dordrecht.

1974f   *Cognitive Sociology.* New York: The Free Press

1975a   "Discourse and Text. Cognitive and Linguistic Processes." In *Versus.*

1975b   "A Response from Aaron Cicourel to the Reviews of his Argentine Fertility Study." In *Contemporary Sociology*, 5(4):397-399.

1978   "Language and Society: Cognitive, Cultural, and Linguistic Aspects of Language Use." In *Sozialwissenschaftliche Annualen*, (2): B25-B58.

1980   "Three Models of Discourse Analysis: The Role of Social Structure." In *Discourse Processes*, 3:101-132.

1981   "Notes on the Integration of Micro- and Macro-Levels of Analysis." In Karin Knorr-Cetina and A.V. Cicourel (eds.), *Advances in Social Theory and Methodology Toward an Integration of Micro and Macro Sociologies,* pp. 51-80. Boston: Routledge and Kegan Paul.

1985   "Doctor-Patient Discourse" in *Handbook of Discourse Analysis* Vol.4, pp. 193-202. T. A.Van Dijk, ed., London: Academic Press.

1987 "Cognitive and Organizational Aspects of Medical Diagnostic Reasoning," *Discourse Processes*, 10(4):347-368.

In press "Sociolinguistic Aspects of Gestural Sign Language." In I. Schlesinger and L. Namir (eds.), *Current Trends in Studies of the Sign Language of the Deaf*. Den Haag.

In press "Oral and Non-oral Representations of Communicative and Social Competence." In proceedings of a conference in *The Mentally Retarded and Society. A Social Science Perspective*. Baltimore.

Cicourel, A.V. and Robert Boèse

1972a "Sign Language Acquisition and the Teaching of Deaf Children." In C. B. Cazden, V. B. John and D. Hymes (eds.), *Functions of Language in the Classroom*, pp. 32-62. New York: Teachers College Press.

1972b "The Acquisition of Manual Sign Language and Generative Semantics," *Semiotica*, 5:225-256.

Cicourel, A. V. and S. Jennings, K. Jennings, K. Leiter, R. MacKay, H. Mehan, and D. Roth

1974 *Language Use and School Performance*. New York: Academic Press.

Cicourel, A.V. and John I. Kitsuse

1963 *The Educational Decision Makers*. New York: Bobs Merrill.

1968 "The Social Organization of the High School and Deviant Adolescent Careers." In E. Rubington and M. S. Weinberg (eds.), *Deviance. The Interactionist Perspective*, pp. 124-135. New York: Wiley.
[Translation: "Die soziale Organisation der Schule und abweichende jugendliche Karrieren." In Klaus Hurrelmann (ed.), *Soziologie der Erziehung*, Weilheim and Basel, 1974:362-378.]

Cicourel, A. V. and Analia Kornbilt

1964 "Consideraciones sociologicas sobre enfermedad mental." In *Acta Psiquiatrica y Psicologica de America Latina*, 10, Buenos Aires, Argentina.

Cicourel, A.V., et. al.

1969 "Language and Measurement in Social Research." Unpublished manuscript.

Clark, T.

1973 *Prophets and Patrons: The French University System and the Emergence of the Social Sciences*. Cambridge: Harvard University Press.

Clifford, James

1981 "On Ethnographic Surrealism." In *Contemporary Studies in Society and History*, pp. 539-564.

Clifford, James and George E. Marcus (eds.)

1986 *Writing Culture: The Poetics and Politics of Ethnography*. Berkeley: University of California Press.

Cohen, Alain J.-J.
  1974   *Marcuse: Le Scenario Freudo-Marxian.* Paris: Editions Universitaires.
  1985   "Semiotique et Ethnométhodologie en Californie." In *Societies: Revue des Sciences Humaines et Sociales*, Vol. 1, No. 5:20.
Cole, Stephen
  1975   "The Growth of Scientific Knowledge: Theories of Deviance as a Case Study." In L. A. Coser (ed.), *The Idea of Social Structure.* New York: Harcourt Brace Jovanovich.
Cole, Stephen and Jonathan R. Cole, and Lorrain Dietrich
  1978   "Measuring the Cognitive State of Scientific Disciplines." In Y. Elkoma (ed.), *Toward a Metric of Science.* New York: John Wiley and Sons, pp. 209-251.
Colfax, J. D. and J. L. Roach
  1971   *Radical Sociology.* New York: Basic Books.
Collins, H. M.
  1983   "An Empirical Relativist Program in the Sociology of Scientific Knowledge." In Knorr-Cetina and Mulkay (eds.), *Science Observed*, pp. 85-114.
Collins, Randall
  1979a   *The Credential Society.* London: Routledge and Kegan Paul.
  1979b   "The Organization of the Intellectual World." in R. Collins, *Conflict Sociology.* New York: Academic Press.
  1981   "Micro-translation as a Theory-building Strategy." In Karin Knorr-Cetina and A. V. Cicourel (eds.), *Advances in Social Theory and Methodology: Toward an Integration of Micro- and Macro-Strategies.* Boston: Routledge and Kegan Paul.
Combs, Sam Edward
  1985   *The Lessons of Devotion: Two Systems of Spiritual Semiosis in Comparative Perspective.* Unpublished Ph.D. dissertation, University of California, San Diego.
Combs, Sam. Dominique Lestel, Pierce Flynn, Susan Phaneuf
  1985   "The Local Production of Knowledge in Penguin and Ant Ethology Laboratories: Two International Settings." unpublished paper, University of California, San Diego, and The École des Hautes Études in Sciences Sociales, Paris.
Conein, Bernard
  1987   "Les Actions Politiques sont Accomplies Localement et Temporalement." *Raison Present*: 82:59-63.
Conklin, H.
  1959   "Linguistic Play in Its Cultural Context." In *Language*, 35:631-636.
Coser, Louis
  1959   "Two Methods in Search of a Substance." In *American Sociological Review*, 40:691-700.

1965　*Men of Ideas: A Sociologist's View*. New York: Free Press.
1975　"Sociology of Knowledge: In *International Encyclopedia of the Social Sciences*, Vol. 8, New York, pp. 428-435.
1984　*Refugee Scholars in America*. New Haven: Yale University Press.
Coulon, Alain
1986　"Qu'est-ce que L'ethnomethodologic?" *Quel Corps?* No. 32/33, Dec. 1986:10-36.
1987　*L'Ethnomethodogie*. Que Sais - je series, Paris: Presses Universitaires de France.
Coulter, Jeff
1971　"Decontextualized Meanings: Current Approaches to the Verstehende Investigations." In *Sociological Review*, 19 (New Series):301-333.
1973a　"Language and the Conceptualization of Meaning." In *Sociology*, 7:173-189.
1973b　*Approaches to Insanity*. New York: Wiley.
1974　"The Ethnomethodological Program in Contemporary Sociology." In *The Human Context*, 6:103-122.
1975a　"Perceptual Accounts and Interpretive Asymetrics." In *Sociology*, 9:385-396.
1975b　*The Operations of Mental Health Personnel*. Unpublished Ph.D. dissertation, University of Manchester.
1979a　*The Social Construction of Mind: Studies in Ethnomethodology and Linguistic Philosophy*. Totowa, New Jersey: Rowman and Littlefield.
1979b　"Beliefs and Practical Understanding. In George Psathas (ed.), *Everyday Language: Studies in Ethnomethodology*, pp.163-186. New York: Irvington Publishers, Inc.
Cozzens, S., et al.
1978　*Citation Analysis: An Annotated Bibliography*. Philadelphia: Institute for Scientific Information.
Crane, Diana
1972　*Invisible Colleges: Diffusion of Knowledge in Scientific Communities*. Chicago: University of Chicago Press.
Crowle, Anthony
1971　*Post Experimental Interviews. An Experiment and a Sociolinguistic Analysis*. Unpublished Ph.D. dissertation, University of California, Santa Barbara.
Cuff, E.C.
1980　"Some Issues in Studying the Problem of Versions in Everyday Life." Occasional papers in sociology, No. 3, Sociology Department, University of Manchester (January).
Culler, Jonathan
1981　*The Pursuit of Signs: Semiotics, Literature, Deconstruction*. New York: Cornell University Press.

1982   *On Deconstruction Theory and Criticism After Structuralism*. Ithaca, New York: Cornell University Press.

Danow, David K.
1986   "Temporal Strategies and Constraints in Narrative." In *Semiotica*. 58-3/4 (1986):245-268.

Davidson, J.
1978   "An Instance of Negotiation in a Call Closing." In *Sociology*. 12: 123-133.

1984   "Subsequent versions of invitations, offers, requests and proposals dealing with potential of actual rejection." In Atkinson and Heritage *Structures of Social Action: Studies in Conversation Analysis*. pp.102-128.

De Certeau, Michel
1980   "On the Oppositional Practices of Everyday Life." Translated by Frederic Jameson and Carl Lovitt. *Social Text*. Fall:3-43.

Denzin, Norman K.
1969   "Symbolic Interactionism and Ethnomethodology." A Proposed Synthesis." In *American Sociological Review* 34:922-934. Also in J. D. Douglas *Understanding Everyday Life*. Chicago 1970, pp. 259-284.

1970   "Symbolic Interactionism and Ethnomethodology." A Comment to Zimmerman and Wieder. In J. D. Douglas *Understanding Everyday Life*. Chicago, pp. 295-298.

Diner, Steven J.
1975   "Department and Discipline: The Department of Sociology at the University of Chicago, 1892-1920." *Minerva*, 13:514-543.

Dorson, Richard M.
1972   *Folklore: Selected Essays*. Bloomington: Indiana University Press.

Douglas, Jack D.
1967   *The Social Meaning of Suicide*. Princeton: Princeton University Press.

1970a   "Understanding Everyday Life." In Jack D. Douglas (ed.), *Understanding Everyday Life*. Chicago: Aldine Press, pp. 3-44.

1970b   *Understanding Everyday Life: Toward the Reconstruction of Sociological Knowledge*. Chicago: Aldine Press.

1973   Jack D. Douglas (ed.), *Introduction to Sociology*. New York: Wiley.

Douglas, Mary
1975   *Implicit Meanings*. London: Routledge and Kegan Paul.

Dreitzel, Hans Peter (ed.)
1970   *Recent Sociology No. 2: Patterns in Communications Behavior: Eight Articles that Demonstrate what Ethnomethodology is all About*. London: MacMillan Co.

Drew, P.
1974   "Domestic Political Violence: Some Problems of Measurement." *Sociological Review*. 22, pp. 5-26.
1977   *Some Moral and Inferential Aspects of Descriptions of Violent Events in Northern Ireland*. Unpublished Ph.D. dissertation, University of Lancaster.
1978   Accusations: The Occasioned Use of Members' Knowledge of 'Religious Geography' in Describing Events. In *Sociology*. 12:1-22.
1984a   Speakers' "Reportings" in Invitation Sequences. In Atkinson and Heritage *Structures of Social Action: Studies in Conversation Analysis*. pp.159-51.
1984b   Analyzing the Use of Language in Courtroom Interaction. In T. van Dijk (ed.), *A Handbook of Discourse Analysis: Vol. 3, Genres of Discourse*, New York: Academic Press.

Ducasse, C. J.
1939   "Symbols, Signs, Signals," *Journal of Symbolic Logic*, Vol. IV, No. 3.
1942   "Some Comments on C. W. Morris's Foundations of the Theory of Signs," *Philosophy and Phenomenological Research*, Vol. III, pp. 43ff.

Dundes, Alan
1964   *The Morphology of North American Folktales*. Folklore Fellows Communication No. 195. Helsinki: Academia Scientrium Fennica.
1984   *Sacred Narrative: Readings in the Theory of Myth*. Berkeley: University of California Press.

Duster, T.
1981   "Intermediate Steps Between Micro and Macro Integration: The Case of Screening for Inherited Disorders." In K. Knorr Cetina and A.V. Cicourel (eds.), *Advances in Social Theory and Methodology: Toward an Integration of Micro and Macro Sociologies*. Boston: Routledge and Kegan Paul.

Eco, Umberto
1976   *A Theory of Semiotics*. Bloomington: Indiana University Press.
1979   *The Role of the Reader: Explorations in the Semiotics of Texts*. Bloomington: Indiana University Press.
1984   *Semiotics and the Philosophy of Language*. Bloomington: Indiana University Press.

Eglin, Trent
1973   "Introduction to a Hermeneutics of the Occult: Alchemy." In Edward A. Tiryakian (ed.) *On the Margin of the Visible: Sociology, the Esoteric, and the Occult*. New York: John Wiley and Sons.

Eglin, Peter
  1976   "Leaving Out the Interpreter's Work: A Methodological Critique of Ethnosemantics Based on Ethnomethodology," *Semiotica*, 17, No. 4:339-369.
Einstein, Carl
  1929   "André Masson, étude ethnologique" in *Documents*; 1:2(1929), 95.
Eisenstadt, S.N.
  1974a   "Some Reflections on the Crisis in Sociology." *Social Inquiry*, 44: 147-58.
  1974b   *Tradition, Change, and Modernity.* New York: Wiley Press.
  1977   "The Sociological Tradition: Origins, Boundaries, Patterns of Innovation, and Crises." In J. Ben-David and T. N. Clark, (eds.), *Culture and Its Creators.* Chicago: University of Chicago Press, pp. 43-71.
Elliot, Henry C.
  1974   "Similarities and Differences between Science and Common Sense." In Roy Turner (ed.) *Ethnomethodology.* Baltimore: Penguin, pp. 21-26.
Emerson, Joan P.
  1969   "Negotiating the Serious Import of Humor." In *Sociometry.* 32: 169-181.
  1970a   "Behavior in Private Places. Sustaining Definition of Reality in Gynecological Examination." In H.P. Dreitzel *Recent Sociology* No. 2. New York, pp. 73-97.
  1970b   "Nothing Unusual Is Happening." In T. Shibutani (ed.) *Human Nature and Collective Behavior. Papers in Honor of Herbert Blumer, Englewood Cliffs.* New Jersey, pp. 208-222.
  1974   "Was Hier Geschieht ist Wirklich Nichts Besonderes." In Gruppendynamik 5:84-97.
Emerson, Robert M.
  1969   *Judging Delinquents.* Chicago: Aldine Press.
  1972   "Notes on discretion as a reflexive feature of the criminal process: Shoplifting materials." Unpublished manuscript, University of California, Los Angeles.
  1981   "On Last Resorts." In *American Journal of Sociology.* 87:1-3.
Emerson, Robert M. and Pollner, Melvin
  1976   "Dirty Work Designations: Their Features and Consequences in a Psychiatric Setting." *Social Problems*, 23:243-254.
  1981   "Studies of Psychiatric Emergency Teams." Unpublished manuscript, University of California, Los Angeles.
Ervin-Tripp, Susan
  1972   "On Sociolinguistic Rules: Alternations and Co-occurrence." In John J. Gumperz and Dell Hymes (eds.) *Directions in Sociolinguistics.* New York: Holt, Rinehart, and Winston, pp. 213-251.

Ervin-Tripp, S. and C. Mitchell-Kernan
 1977   *Child Discourse*. New York: Academic Press.
Eyerman, R., L. G. Svensson, T. Soderqvist
 1987   *Intellectuals, Universities, and the State in Western Modern Societies*. Berkeley: University of California Press.
Fabbri, Paolo
 1985   Personal Communication – Paris, France.
Fabian, Johannes
 1983   *Time and the Other: How Anthropology Makes Its Object*. New York: Columbia University Press.
Faris, R. E. L.
 1970   *Chicago Sociology, 1920-1932*. Chicago: University of Chicago Press.
Fauman, Richard
 1980   "Filmmakers' Work: On the Production and Analysis of Audio-Visual Documents for the Social Sciences." Department of Sociology, University of California, Los Angeles.
Fernandez, J. W.
 1964   "African Religious Movements-Types and Dynamics." In *Journal of Modern African Studies*. 12:531-549.
 1979   "On the Notion of Religious Movement." In *Social Research*. 46: 36-62.
Filmer, Paul
 1972   "On Harold Garfinkel's Ethnomethodology." In Paul Filmer, Michael Phillipson, David Silverman, David Walsh, *New Directions in Sociological Theory*: 203-234. Cambridge: M.I.T. Press.
Filmer, Paul, Michael Phillipson, David Silverman and David Walsh
 1972   *New directions in Sociological Theory*. Cambridge: M.I.T. Press.
Filmer, Paul, Michael Phillipson, Maurice Roche, Barry Sandywell and David Silverman
 1973   "Stratifying Practices." Unpublished manuscript, Goldsmith's College, London.
 1979   *Essays in Reflexive Sociology. Language Theorizing Difference*. London: Heineman.
Fine, Elizabeth C.
 1984   *The Folkloric Text: From Performance to Print*. Bloomington: Indiana University Press.
Fisher, Sue
 1979   *The Negotiation of Treatment Decisions in Doctor Patient Communications and Their Impact on Identity in Women Patients*. Unpublished doctoral dissertation, University of California, San Diego.
 1981   "Selling Hysterectomies." Working papers in *Sociolinguistics*, 83, SEDL.

1982   "The Decision-making Context: How Doctor and Patient Communicate." In Robert J. Di Pietro (ed.), *Linguistics and the Professions*. Norwood, N.J.: Ablex Press.

1983   "Doctor Talk/Patient Talk: How Treatment Decisions are Negotiated in Doctor/Patient Communication." In Sue Fisher and Alexandra Todd (eds.), *The Social Organization of Doctor-Patient Communication*. Center for Applied Linguistics, Washington, D.C.: Harcourt Brace Jovanovich.

1986   *In the Patient's Best Interests*. New Brunswick: Rutgers University Press.

Fisher, Sue and Alexandra Todd (eds.)

1983   *The Social Organization of Doctor-Patient Communication*. Center for Applied Linguistics, Washington, D.C.: Harcourt Brace Jovanovich.

1986   *Discourse and Institutional Authority: Medicine, Education and Law*. In series, Advances in Discourse Processes, Vol XIX. Norwood, N.J.: Ablex Press.

Fishman, Pamela

1978   "Interaction: The Work Women Do." *Social Problems*, 25:397-406.

Fleming, Donald and Bernard Bailyn (eds.)

1968   *The Intellectual Migration: Europe and America, 1930-1960*. Cambridge: Harvard University Press.

Fluer, Lewis S.

1976   "What Is an Intellectual?" In A. Gella, (ed.), *The Intelligensia and the Intellectuals*. Beverly Hills: Sage Publications, pp. 37-47.

Flynn, Pierce J.

1977   "Charismatics, Consciousness, and the Crack between Worlds." Unpublished paper, University of California, San Diego.

1985   Review. *From a Sociology of Symbols to a Sociology of Signs* by Ino Rossi; *The Hermeneutic Imagination* by Josef Bleicher; *The Perspective of Ethnomethodology* by Douglas Benson and John A. Hughes. In *Sociétés: Revue de Sciences Humaine et Sociales*, Vol. 1, No. 5, (September):24-25.

1986   "Les Générations Successives d'Ethnométhodolgues aux U.S.A." In *Practiques de Formations* (Analyses), 11-12(October):97-102.

1987a   "Waves of Semiosis: Surfing's Iconic Progression," *The American Journal of Semiotics*, 4(3-4):397-418.

1987b   Review. *Garfinkel and Ethnomethodology* by John Heritage; *The Ethnomethodologists* by Wes Sharrock and Bob Anderson. Translated by Dominique Glaub. In *Sociétés Humaine et Sociales*, Vol. 2, No. 4, (May-June):36-37.

1988   "Semiotics and Ethnomethodology." In Thomas A. Sebeok and Jean Umiker-Sebeok (eds), *The Semiotic Web 1987*. Berlin, New York: Mouton de Gruyter, pp. 355-375.

1988   *The Ethnomethodological Movement: A Sociology of Knowledge Approach*. Unpublished doctoral dissertation, Department of Sociology, University of California, San Diego.

Flynn, Pierce J. and Sam E. Combs

1985   Review. *An Ethnomethodological Investigation of the Foundations of Mathematics* by Eric Livingston; *Art and Artifact in Laboratory Science* by Michael Lynch. In *Sociétés: Revue de Sciences Humaine et Sociales*, Vol. 1, No. 5:24.

Foucault, Michel

1970   *The Order of Things, An Archeology of the Human Sciences*. New York: Vintage Books.

1972   *The Archaeology of Knowledge*. New York: Pantheon Books.

Frake, Charles O.

1961   "The Diagnosis of Disease Among the Subanun of Mindanao." In *American Anthropologist*, 63:113-132.

Frankel, Richard M.

1981   "I Wz Wondering - Uhm Could Raid Uhm Affect the Brain Permanently D'Y Know? Record Keeping on the Context of Communicative Interaction." Paper presented at the annual meetings of the American Sociological Association. Toronto: August.

1983   "The Laying on of Hands: Aspects of the Organization of Gaze, Touch, and Talk in a Medical Encounter." In Sue Fisher and Alexandra Todd (eds.), *The Social Organization of Doctor-Patient Communication*. Washington D.C.: Harcourt Brace and Jovanovich, pp. 19-54.

In press "Talking in Interviews: A Dispreference for Patient-Initiated Questions in Physician-Patient Encounters." In George Psathas (ed.), *Interactional Competence*. Norwood, N.J.: Ablex Publishers.

Friedrichs, R. W.

1970   *A Sociology of Sociology*. New York: The Free Press.

Frisby, D.

1984   *George Simmel*. Chechester, Ellis Harwood and London: Tavistock.

Gadamer, H. G.

1976   *Philosophical Hermeneutics*. Berkeley: University of California Press.

Gallant, Mary and Sherry Kleinman

1983   "Symbolic Interactionism vs. Ethnomethodology." In *Symbolic Interaction*, 6(1):1-18.

Gamson, W.

1975   *The Strategy of Social Protest*. Homewood, Ill.: Dorsey Press.

Garfield, Eugene, Norteon V. Malin, and Henry Small
    1978   "Citation Data as Science Indicators." In *Toward a Metric of Science: The Advent of Science Indicators*. Y. Elkana, J. Lederberg, R. K. Merton, et al. (eds.). New York: John Wiley and Sons, pp. 179-207.

Garfinkel, Harold
    1949   "Research Note on Inter- and Intra-Racial Homicides." In *Social Forces*, pp. 369-381.
    1952   *The Perception of the Other: A Study on Social Order*. Unpublished doctoral dissertation. Department of Sociology, Harvard University.
    1953   "A Comparison of Decisions Made on Four 'Pre-Theoretical' Problems by Talcott Parsons and Alfred Schutz." Unpublished paper.
    1956a   "Some Sociological Concepts of Methods for Psychiatrists." In *Psychiatric Research Reports*, 6:181-195. ·
    1956b   "Conditions of Successful Degradation Ceremonies." In *American Journal of Sociology*, 61:420-424.
            [Translation: "Bedingungen für den Erfolg von Degradierungszeremonien." In *Gruppendynamik* 5(1974):77-83.]
    1959a   "Aspects of the Problem of Common Sense Knowledge of Social Structures." In *Transactions of the Fourth World Congress of Sociology IV*, 4:51-65. Milan: Stressa.
            [Translation: "Das Alltagswissen über soziale und innerhalb sozialer Strukturen." In Arbeitsgruppe Bielefelder Soziologen (eds.), *Alltagswissen, Interaktion und gesellschaftliche Wirklichkeit* 1(1973):189-262.]
    1959b   *Parson's Primer*. Unpublished manuscript of Garfinkel's course "Sociology 251: Topics in the Problem of Social Order," Spring, University of California, Los Angeles.
    1960   "The Rational Properties of Scientific and Common-Sense Activities." In *Behavioral Science*, 5(Jan.):72-83.
            [Reprinted in: *Studies in Ethnomethodology*. Chapter 8:262-283. Englewood Cliffs, N.J.: Prentice Hall, 1967.]
            [Reprinted in: Anthony Giddens (ed.), *Positivism and Sociology*. London: Heineman, 1974.]
    1961   "Reflections on the Clinical Method in Psychiatry from the Point of View of Ethnomethodology." Prepared for the seminar on Ethnoscience, Stanford University, April.
    1962   "Common Sense Knowledge of Social Structures: The Documentary Method of Interpretation in Lay and Professional Fact Finding." In Jordon M. Scher (ed.), *Theories of the Mind*. New York: Free Press, pp. 689-712.
            [Reprinted in: *Studies in Ethnomethodology*. Chapter 3:76-103. Englewood Cliffs, N.J.: Prentice Hall, 1967.]

1963   "A Conception of, and Experiments with 'Trust' as a Condition of
        Stable Concerted Actions." In O. J. Harvey (ed.), *Motivation and
        Social Interaction*, 187-238. New York: Ronald Press.
1964a   "Studies of the Routine Grounds of Everyday Activities." In *Social
        Problems*, 11:225-250.
        [Reprinted in: *Studies in Ethnomethodology*. Chapter 2:35-75.
        Englewood Cliffs, N.J.: Prentice Hall, 1967.]
        [Translation: "Studien über die Routinegrundlagen vom Alltagshan-
        deln." In H. Steinert (ed.), *Symbolische Interaktion*, Stuttgart, 1973:
        280-293.]
1964b   "Comments." In William Bright, (ed.), *Sociolinguistics: Proceedings
        of the UCLA Sociolinguistics Conference*, 1964. The Hague: Mouton
        and Co., pp.102-113.
1965   "Sign Functions: Organized Activities as Methods for Making an
        Invisible World Visible." Paper delivered at the annual meeting of
        the American Sociological Association.
1967a   *Studies in Ethnomethodology*. Englewood Cliffs, N.J.: Prentice Hall.
        Paperback edition, Cambridge: Polity Press, 1984.
1967b   "'Good' Organizational Reasons for 'Bad' Clinic Records." Harold
        Garfinkel in collaboration with Egon Bittner, *in Studies in Ethno-
        methodology*. Englewood Cliffs, N.J.: Prentice Hall, pp. 186-207.
        [Reprinted in: Roy Turner (ed.), *Ethnomethodology*. Baltimore:
        Penguin, pp. 109-127.]
1967c   "Suicide, for all Practical Purposes." Excerpt from *Studies in
        Ethnomethodology*. Englewood Cliffs, N.J.: Prentice Hall, pp.11-18.
        [Reprinted in: Roy Turner (ed.), *Ethnomethodology*. Baltimore:
        Penguin, pp.96-101.]
1967d   "Practical Sociological Reasoning: Some Features in the Work of the
        Los Angeles Suicide Prevention Center." In E. S.Schneidman (ed.),
        Essays in Self Destruction. New York: International Science Press,
        pp. 171-187.
1967e   "What Is Ethnomethodology?" In *Studies in Ethnomethodology*.
        Englewood Cliffs, N.J.: Prentice Hall, pp. 1-34.
1967f   "Studies of the Routine Grounds of Everyday Activities." In *Studies
        in Ethnomethodology*. Englewood Cliffs, N.J.: Prentice Hall, pp. 35-
        75. (Reprinted with revisions from *Social Problems*, 11:225-250.)
1967g   "Some Rules of Correct Decision Making that Jurors Respect." In
        Studies in Ethnomethodology. Englewood Cliffs, N.J.: Prentice Hall,
        pp. 104-115.
1967h   "Passing and the Managed Achievement of Sexual Status in an
        Intersexed Person. Part I." In *Studies in Ethnomethodology*. Engle-
        wood Cliffs, N.J.: Prentice Hall, pp. 301-324.

1967i   "Methodological Adequacy in the Quantitative Study of Selection Criteria and Selection Practices in Psychiatric Outpatient Clinics." In *Studies in Ethnomethodology*. Englewood Cliffs, N.J.: Prentice Hall, pp.208-261.

1972   "Remarks on Ethnomethodology." In J. Gumperz and Dell Hymes (eds.), *Directions in Sociolinguistics*. New York: Holt, Rinehart, and Winston, pp. 301-324.

1973   Lecture series given as Simon Visiting Professor, Department of Sociology, Manchester University, Manchester, England.

1974   "The Origins of the Term 'Ethnomethodology'." In Roy Turner (ed.), *Ethnomethodology*. Baltimore: Penguin, pp. 15-18. Excerpt from the Purdue Symposium, 1968.

1975   "The Boston Seminar". unpublished manuscripts, UCLA., Department of Sociology

1976   "Materials for Two Bibliographies: (I) Candidates for a Corpus of Studies of Naturally Organized Ordinary Activities, and (II) Studies about Ethnomethodology." Unpublished manuscript, circulated to research seminar, University of California, Los Angeles, Winter.

1977   "University Lectures"UCLA., Department of Sociology.

1978   "Introduction to the Session on Ethnomethodology: Studies of Work," Ninth World Congress of Sociology, Uppsala, Sweden.

1979   "Lawyers' Work." Plenary session lecture presented to the British Sociological Association's National Conference on Law and Society (Easter).

1985a   Personal communication.

1985b   "Entretien avec Harold Garfinkel." by Bennetta Jules-Rosette, translated by Elizabeth Convair. In *Societes: Revue International de Sciences Humaines*. Vol. 1, No. 5, (1985):35-38.

1986a   H. Garfinkel (ed.), *Ethnomethodological Studies of Work*, London: Routledge and Kegan Paul.

1986b   "Du bon usage de la degradation." Translation of "Conditions of Successful Degradation Ceremonies," by J. M. de Quenoz. In *Sociétés*, Vol. 2, No. 6, (1986):24-27.

1987   "A Reflection." In the Discourse Analysis Research Group Newsletter, 3(2), Fall 1987:5-9.

1988   "Evidence for Locally Produced, Naturally Accountable Phenomena of Order*, Logic, Reason, Meaning, Method, etc., In and As of the Essential Quiddity of Immortal Ordinary Society: An Announcement of Studies" in The Discourse Analysis Research Group Newsletter 3(2), Fall, 1987:2-8.

1990   "Curious Absurditics in Studies of Work in the Natural Sciences: Messengers from the Domain of Lebenswelt Sciences." Paper presented at UCLA Conference on Aesthetics and Semiotics, June 1990.

In press "An Introduction for Novices to the Study of Naturally Organized Activities." A revision of a Public Lecture at Boston University Summer Session on Conversational Analysis and Ethnomethodology, June 1975, to be published in H. Garfinkel (ed.), *A Manual for the Study of Naturally Organized Ordinary Activities*. London: Routledge and Kegan Paul.

In press *A Manual for the Study of Naturally Organized Ordinary Activities*. 3 volumes including vol. I, *Introduction for Novices*, London: Routledge and Kegan Paul.

In press H. Garfinkel (ed.), *Ethnomethodological Studies of Work in the Discovering Sciences*, vol. II. London: Routledge and Kegan Paul.

In press "Recurrent Themes in Ethnomethodological Studies of Work." Introduction to *A Manual for the Study of Naturally Organized Ordinary Activities*. 3 volumes, London: Routledge and Kegan Paul.

Garfinkel, Harold and Lindsey Churchill
1964   "Some Features of Decision Making in Common-Sense Situations of Choice." Unpublished research proposal, Department of Sociology, University of California, Los Angeles.

Garfinkel, Harold and Harvey Sacks
1970   "The Formal Properties of Practical Actions." In John C. McKinney and Edward A. Tiryakian (eds.), *Theoretical Sociology*. New York: Appleton, Century, Crofts, pp. 337-366.

Garfinkel, Harold and Stacy Burns
In press "Lecturing's Work of Talking Introductary Sociology." Department of Sociology, University of California, Los Angeles. In Garfinkel (ed.), *A Manual for the Study of Naturally Organized Ordinary Activities*. London: Routledge and Kegan Paul.

Garfinkel, Harold, Eric Livingston, Michael Lynch, and Albert B. Robillard
In press "Respecifying the Natural Sciences as Discovering Sciences of Practical Action, I & II: Doing So Ethnographically by Administering a Schedule of Contingencies in Discussions with Laboratory Scientists and by Hanging Around Their Laboratories." In *Talk and Social Structure*, (ed.), Deirdre Boden and Don H. Zimmerman. Cambridge: Polity Press.

Garfinkel, Harold, Michael Lynch and Eric Livingston
1981   "The Work of a Discovering Science Construed with Materials from the Optically Discovered Pulsar." In *Philosophy of the Social Sciences*, 5:131-158.

Gella, A. (ed.)
1986   *The Intelligensia and the Intellectuals: Theory, Method, and Case Study*. Beverly Hills: Sage Publications.

Gellner, Ernst
  1975   "Ethnomethodology: The Re-Enchantment Industry ... or the Califor-
          nia Way of Subjectivity." In *Philosophy of the Social Sciences*, 5:
          431-450.
Genette, Gerard
  1980   *Narrative Discourse: An Essay in Method*. Translated by Jane E.
          Lewin. Ithaca: Cornell University Press.
Gidlow, Bob
  1972   "Ethnomethodology: A New Name for Old Practices." In *British
          Journal of Sociology*, 23:395-404.
Gieryn, Thomas
  1983   "Boundary-Work and the Demarcation of Science from Non-
          Science." *American Sociological Review*, Vol. 48, No. 6:781-95.
Gilbert, G. Nigel
  1976   "The Transformation of Research Findings into Scientific Knowl-
          edge." In *Social Studies of Studies*, 6:281-306.
Gilbert, G.N. and M. Mulkay
  1984   *Opening Pandora's Box: A Sociological Study of Scientists' Dis-
          course*. Cambridge: Cambridge University Press.
Girton, George D.
  1986   "Kung Fu: toward a praxealogical hermeneutic of the martial arts."
          in *Ethnomethodological Studies of Work*, H.Garfinkel, ed. London:
          Routledge and Kegan Paul.
Gleeson, D. and M. Erben
  1976   "Meaning in Context: Notes Towards a Critique of Ethnomethodol-
          ogy." In *British Journal of Sociology*, 27:473-483.
Glock, Charles and Robert N. Bellah (eds.)
  1976   *The New Religious Consciousness*. Berkeley: University of California
          Press.
Goffman, Erving
  1981   *Forms of Talk*. Philadelphia: University of Pennsylvania Press.
Goldberg, J.
  1975   "A System for the Transfer of Instructions in Natural Settings." In
          Semiotica, 14, 3:269-296.

  1976   *Amplitude as a Discourse Affiliation Mechanism in Sequence
          Construction*. Unpublished doctoral dissertation, School of Social
          Science, University of California, Irvine.

  1978   "Amplitude Shift: A Mechanism for the Affiliation of Utterances in
          Conversational Interaction." In Jim Schenkein (ed.), *Studies in the
          Organization of Conversational Interaction*. New York: Academic
          Press.

Goldthorpe, John H.
  1973   "A Revolution in Sociology?" Review article in *Sociology*, 7:
          449-462.
  1974   "A Rejoinder to Benson." In *Sociology*, 8:131-133.
Goodenough, Ward H.
  1956   "Componential Analysis and the Study of Meaning." In *Language*,
          32:195-216.
Goodwin, Charles
  1975   "The Social Construction of the Sentence." Paper delivered at Ameri-
          can Anthropological Association Annual Meetings, San Francisco,
          November.
  1979a   "The Interactive Construction of a Sentence in Natural Conversa-
          tion." In George Psathas (ed.), E*veryday Language: Studies in
          Ethnomethodology*, pp. 97-121.
  1979b   Review of S. Duncan Jr. and D. W. Fiske, *Face to Face Interaction:
          Research, Methods and Theory*. In Language and Society, 8:439-444.
  1981   *Conversational Organization: Interaction Between Speakers and
          Hearers*. New York: Academic Press.
  1986   "Gestures as a Resource for the Organization of Mutual Orientation,"
          Semiotica, 62-1/2:29-49.
Goodwin, Charles and M. H. Goodwin
  1982   "Concurrent Operations on Talk: Notes on the Interactive Organiza-
          tion of Assessments." Paper presented at the 77th Annual Meeting
          of the American Sociological Association, San Francisco, California.
Gottdiener, Mark and Alexandros Lagopoulas, ed.
  1986   *The City and the Sign: An Introduction to Urban Semiotics*, New
          York: Columbia University Press.
Gouldner, Alvin
  1970a   "Ethnomethodology. Sociology as a Happening." In *The Coming
          Crisis in Western Sociology*. New York: Basic Books, pp. 390-395.
  1970b   *The Coming Crisis of Western Sociology*. London: Heineman.
  1979   *The Future of Intellectuals and the Rise of the New Class*. New
          York: Seabury.
Grabinar, Gene
  1975   "The Situational Sociologies: A Theoretical Note." In *The Insurgent
          Sociologist*, 5(4):80-81.
Graham, L., W. Lepenies, P. Weingart (ed.)
  1983   *Functions and Uses of Disciplinary Histories*. Sociology of the
          Sciences Yearbook, 7. Dordrecht: Reidel.
Gramsci, A.
  1971   *Selection from the Prison Notebooks*. London: Routledge and
          Kegan Paul.

Grana, Caesar
    1964   *Bohemian versus Bourgeois.* New York: Free Press.
Grathoff, Richard (ed.)
    1978   *The Theory of Social Action: The Correspondence of Alfred Schutz and Talcott Parsons.* Bloomington: Indiana University Press.
Greatbach, D.
    1985   *The Social Organization of News Interview Interaction.* Unpublished Ph.D. disseration, Department of Sociology, University of Warwick.
Greimas, A.J.
    1976   *Semiotique et Sciences Sociales.* Paris: Seuil.
    1987   *On Meaning: Selected Writings in Semiotic Theory.* Minneapolis: University of Minnesota Press.
Greimas, A.J. and J. Courtès
    1982   *Semiotics and Language: An Analytical Dictionary.* Bloomington: Indiana University Press.
Greimas, A. J. and E. Landowski
    1979   *L'Analyse du Discours en Sciences Sociales.* Paris: Hachette.
Grice, H.P.
    1975   "Logic and Conversation." In P. Cole and J. Morgan (eds.), *Syntax and Semantics.* New York: Academic Press.
Gross, G.R.
    1970   "The Organization Set: A Study of Sociology Departments." *American Sociologist*, 5:25-29.
Gumperz, J. J.
    1982   *Discourse Strategies.* London: Cambridge University Press.
Gumperz, J. J. and Dell Hymes (eds.)
    1972   *Directions in Sociolinguistics.* New York: Holt, Rinehart, and Wilson.
Gurwitsch, Aaron
    1964   *The Field of Consciousness.* Pennsylvania: Ducuesne University Press.
    1966   *Studies in Phenomenology and Psychology.* Duduesne University Press.
Gusfield, Joseph
    1957   "The Problems of Generations in an Organizational Structure." *Social Forces*, 36(May).
    1963   *Symbolic Crusade.* Urbana: University of Illinois Press.
    1976   "The Literary Rhetoric of Science: Comedy and Pathos in Drinking Driver Research." In *American Sociological Review*, vol. 41 (Feb.), pp.16-34.
    1978   "Historical Problematics and Sociological Fields: American Liberalism and the Study of Social Movements." Research in *Sociology of Knowledge, Sciences, and Art*, vol. I:121-149.

1979   "The Modernity of Social Movements: Public Roles and Private Parts." In A. Hawley (ed.), *Societal Growth*. New York: The Free Press, pp. 290-307.

1981a   *The Culture of Public Problems: Drinking, Driving, and the Symbolic Order*. Chicago: University of Chicago Press.

1981b   "Social Movements and Social Change: Perspectives of Linearity and Fluidity." *Research in Social Movements, Conflict, and Change*. (4):317-339.

Gusfield, Joseph and J. Michalowicz

1984   "Secular Symbolism: Studies of Ritual, Ceremony, and the Symbolic Order in Modern Life." In *American Review of Sociology*, 10: 417-435.

Hackenberg, Robert A.

1974   "Genealogical Method in Social Anthropology: The Foundations of Structural Demography." In J. J. Honigmann (ed.), *Handbook of Social and Cultural Anthropology*. Chicago: Rand McNally.

Hammond, Phillip (ed.)

1985   *The Sacred in a Secular Age*. Berkeley: University of California Press.

Handel, Warren

1972   *Learning to Categorize*. Unpublished doctoral dissertation, University of California, Santa Barbara.

1979   "Using Participant Observation Research to Study Structural Phenomenon." *Humanity and Society*, 3:275-285.

1982   *Ethnomethodology: How People Make Sense*. Englewood Cliffs, N.J.: Prentice Hall.

Handel, Judith

1979   "Normative Expectations and the Emergence of Meaning as Solutions to Problems: Convergence of Structural and Interactionist Views." *American Journal of Sociology*, 84:855-881.

Hareven, Tamara K.

1978   "The Search for Generational Memory: Tribal Rites in Industrial Society." In *Daedalus*, vol. 107, no. 3:137-149.

Hayward, Peter

1978   *The Acquisition of Membership*. Unpublished Ph.D. dissertation, Department of Sociology, University of California, San Diego.

Heap, James

1978   "Toward a Phenomenology of Reading." *Journal of Phenomenological Psychology*, 8:104-115.

1980   "Description in Ethnomethodology." *Human Studies*, 3:87-106.

1986   "Sociality and cognition in collaborative computer writings," paper prepared for discussion at the University of Michigan School of

Education Conference on Literacy and Culture in Educational Settings, March, 7-9, February.

1986   "Collaborative practices during computer writing in a first grade classroom," paper prepared for presentation at the annual meetings of the American Educational Research Association, San Francisco, March.

1987   "Ethnomethodology: Disclosing Education." In *The Discourse Analysis Research Group Newsletter*, 3(2), Fall 1987:16-20.

Heap, James L. and Phillip A. Roth

1973   "On Phenomenological Sociology." In *American Sociological Review*, 38:354-367.

Heath, Christian

1982   "The Display of Recipiency: One Instance of a Sequential Relationship between Speech and Body Movement," *Semiotica*, 42, No. 214.

1984   "Talk and Recipiency: Sequential Organization in Speech and Body Movement." In J. Maxwell Atkinson and J. Heritage (eds.), *Structures of Social Action: Studies in Conversation Analysis*. Cambridge: Cambridge University Press, pp.247-265.

1986   *The Partnership: Essays in the Social Organization of Speech and Body Movement in the Medical Consultation*. Cambridge: Cambridge University Press.

Heeren, John

1970   "Alfred Schutz and the Sociology of Common Sense Knowledge." In J. Douglas (ed.), *Understanding Everyday Life*, Chicago: Aldine Press, pp. 45-56.

Heidegger, Martin

1962   *Being and Time*. New York: Harper and Row.

1967   *What Is a Thing?* Chicago: Henry Regnery.

1971   *Poetry, Language, and Thought*. Translated by A. Hofstadter. New York: Harper and Row.

Helm, David T.

1981   *Conferring Membership: Interacting with 'Incompetents.'* Unpublished doctoral dissertation, Department of Sociology, Boston University.

Henri, Adrian

1974   *Total Art: Environments, Happenings, and Performance*. New York: Praeger Publishers.

Heritage, John

1978   "Aspects of the Flexibilities of Natural Language Use: A Reply to Phillips." In *Sociology*, 12:79-103.

1983   "Accounts in Action." In Gilbert and Abell, *Accounts and Action*. Farnborough: Gower, pp. 117-131.

1984a   "A Change of State Token and Aspects of Its Sequential Placement." In Atkinson and Heritage, *Structures of Social Action: Studies in Conversation Analysis.* Cambridge: Cambridge University Press, pp. 299-345.

1984b   "Analyzing News Interviews: Aspects of the Production of Talk for an Overhearing Audience." In T. van Dijk (ed.), *Handbook of Discourse Analysis, Vol. 3: Genres of Discourse.* New York: Academic Press.

1984c   "Recent Developments in Conversation Analysis." Warwick Working Papers in Sociology, No. 1, Department of Sociology, University of Warwick.

1984d   *Garfinkel and Ethnomethodology.* Oxford: Polity Press.

1985   "Recent Developments in Conversation Analysis." *Sociolinguistics,* 15(1985), pp. 1-19.

1987a   "Ethnomethodology." In *Social Theory Today*, ed. A. Giddens and J. Turner. Cambridge: Polity Press, pp. 224-72.

1987b   "Ethnomethodology Apres La Lutte." In *The Discourse Analysis Research Group Newsletter,* 3(2), Fall, 1987:9-16.

Heritage, John and R. Watson

1979   "Formulations as Conversational Objects." In George Psathas (ed.), *Everyday Language: Studies in Ethnomethodology.* New York: Irvington Publishing Associates.

1980   "Aspects of the Properties of Formulations in Natural Conversation: Some Instances Analyzed." In *Semiotica,* 30:314, 245, 262.

Hertweck, Alma

1981   "Attributional Analysis in Context." In *Educational Decision Making in Students' Careers, end of year (1979-80) report, Part II: Prospectus for year three.* Unpublished manuscript, University of California, San Diego.

1982   *Constructing the "Truth" and Consequences: Educators' Attributions of Perceived Failure in School.* Unpublished doctoral dissertation, University of California, San Diego.

1986   "The Language of Attribution: Constructing Rationales for Educational Placement." In Fisher and Todd (eds.), *Discourse and Institutional Authority: Medicine, Education and Law.* In series, Advances in Discourse Processes, Vol. XIX. Norwood, N.J.: Ablex Publishers.

Hess, Remi

1981   *La Sociologie d'Intervention.* Paris: Presses Universitaires de France.

Hewitt, J. and R. Stokes

1975   "Disclaimers." *American Sociological Review,* 40, 1:1-11.

Heyman, Richard T.

1986   "Formulating Topic in the Classroom." *Discourse Processes,* 9(1): 37-55.

Higham, J. and P.K. Conkin
   1979   *New Directions in American Intellectual History.* Baltimore: Johns
         Hopkins University Press.
Hill, Richard J. and Kathleen S. Crittenden (eds.)
   1968   *Proceedings of the Purdue Symposium on Ethnomethodology.* Insti-
         tute for the Study of Social Change, Purdue University, Layfayette,
         Indiana, Monograph No. 1.
Hinkle, R.
   1980   *Founding Theory of American Sociology, 1881-1915.* London:
         Routledge and Kegan Paul.
Hirsh, Arthur
   1981   *The French New Left: An Intellectual History from Sartre to Gorz.*
         Boston: South End Press.
Hollier, Denis
   1979   *Le Collège de Sociologie.* Paris: Gallimard.
Holton, Gerald
   1978   *The Scientific Imagination: Case Studies.* Cambridge: Cambridge
         University Press.
Holub, Robert C.
   1984   *Reception Theory: A Critical Introduction.* New York: Methuen and
         Co. Ltd.
Hopkins, Frances L.
   1984   "New Causal Theory and Ethnomethodology: Cocitation Patterns
         Across a Decade." In *Scientometrics*, 6, 1:33-53.
Houtkoop, Hanneke
   1987   *Establishing Agreement: An Analysis of Proposal – Acceptance
         Sequences.* Dordrecht & Providence, RI: Foris.
Hughes, H. Stuart
   1958   *Consciousness and Society.* New York: Harper and Row.
   1968   *The Obstructed Path.* New York: Harper and Row.
   1975   *The Sea Change.* New York: Harper and Row.
Husserl, Edmund
   1931   *Ideas: General Introduction to Pure Phenomenology.* Translated by
         Boyce Gibson. New York: MacMillan Co.
   1964   *The Phenomenology of Internal Time-Consciousness.* Martin
         Heidegger (ed.), translated by James S. Churchill. Bloomington:
         Indiana University Press.
   1970   *The Crisis of European Sciences and Transcendental Phenomenol-
         ogy.* Translated by David Carr. Evanston: Northwestern University
         Press.
Huxley, Aldous
   1954   *The Doors of Perception.* New York: Harper.

Iser, W.
1972　"The Reading Process: A Phenomenological Approach." *New Literary History.* 3:279-299.
1974　*The Implied Reader.* Baltimore: Johns Hopkins University Press.
Ivanov, V.V.
1969　"Systemes Secondaires Modulants." In *Semiotica*, 1969.
Jacobs, Paul and Saul Landau
1966　*The New Radicals: A Report with Documents.* New York: Vintage Books.
Jamin, Jean
1980　"Un Sacré Collège ou les apprentis sorciers de la sociologie." *Cahiers Internationaux de Sociologie* no.68 (1980), 5-30.
Jaspers, Karl
1925　*Psychology of the Weltanschauung.* Berlin: J. Springer.
Jauss, Hans Robert
1970　"Literary History as a Challenge to Literary Theory." *New Literary History*, 2(1):7-37.
Jay, M.
1973　*The Dialectical Imagination: A History of the Frankfurt School and the Institute of Social Research, 1923-50.* London: Heineman.
Jefferson, Gail
1972　"Side Sequences." In D. Sudnow (ed.), *Studies in Social Interaction.* New York: Free Press, pp.294-338.
1973　"A Case of Precision Timing in Ordinary Conversation: Overlapped Tag-Positioned Address Terms in Closing Sequences." In *Semiotica*, 9:47-96.
1974　"Error Correction as an Interactional Resource." In *Language in Society*, III,2:181-199.
1978　"Sequential Aspects of Storytelling in Conversation." In Jim Schenkein (ed.), *Studies in the Organization of Conversational Interaction.* New York: Academic Press, pp. 219-248.
1979a　"A Technique for Inviting Laughter and its Subsequent Acceptance/ Declination." In George Psathas (ed.), *Everyday Language: Studies in Ethnomethodology.* New York: Irvington, pp. 79-96.
1979b　"At First I Thought ..." Unpublished lecture presented at the University of Warwick.
1980a　Final Report to the (British) SSRC on *The Analysis of Conversations in Which 'Troubles' and 'Anxieties' are Expressed.* No. HR 4805.
1980b　"On 'Trouble-Premonitory' Response to Inquiry." In *Sociological Inquiry*, 50:153-185.
1981a　"The Abominable 'Ne?': A Working Paper Exploring the Phenomenon of Post-Response Pursuit of Response." University of Manchester, Department of Sociology, Occasional Paper no. 6.

1981b　"'Caveat Speaker': A Preliminary Exploration of Shift Implicative Recipiency in the Articulation of Topic." Report to the (British) SSRC.

1983　"On exposed and Embedded Correction in Conversation." In *Stadium Linguistik*, 14:58-68.

1984a　"Caricature Versus Detail: On Capturing the Particulars of Pronunciation in Transcripts of Conversational Data." *Tilburg Papers on Language and Literature No. 31*, University of Tilburg, Netherlands.

1984b　"On Stepwise Transition from Talk About a Trouble to Inappropriately Next-positioned Matters." In Atkinson and Heritage, *Structures of Social Action: Studies in Conversation Analysis*. Cambridge: Cambridge University Press, pp. 191-222.

1984c　"On the Organization of Laughter in Talk about Troubles." In J. Maxwell Atkinson and J. Heritage (eds.), *Structures of Social Action: Studies in Conversation Analysis*. Cambridge: Cambridge University Press, pp. 346-369.

1985　"On the Interactional Unpackaging of a 'Gloss'." *Language and Society*, 14:435-466.

Jefferson, Gail and John Lee

1981　"The Rejection of Advice: Managing the Problematic Convergence of a 'Troubles-Telling' and a 'Service Encounter'." In *Journal of Pragmatics*, 5:399-422.

Jefferson, Gail and H. Sacks and E. Schegloff

1973　"Preliminary Notes on the Sequential Organization of Laughter." (Informal Seminars of the Ethology Research Groups, University of Pennsylvania.) Unpublished draft.

In press "Some Notes on Laughing Together." In M. Moerman (ed.). *International Journal of the Sociology of Language*. Berlin-New York: Mouton de Gruyter.

Jefferson, Gail and E. Schegloff

1978　"Sketch: Some Orderly Aspects of Overlap in Natural Conversation." Unpublished manuscript.

Jefferson, Gail and Jim Schenkein

1977　"Some Sequential Negotiations in Conversation: Unexpanded and Expanded Versions of Projected Action Sequences." In *Sociology*, 11:86-103.

1978　"Some Sequential Negotiations in Conversation: Unexpanded and Expanded Versions of Projected Action Sequences." In J. Schenkein (ed.). *Studies in the Organization of Conversational Interaction*. New York: Academic Press, pp. 155.

Jennings, Kenneth L.

1968　"Notes On a Theory of Experiments." Presented in partial fulfillment of M.A. program. University of California, Santa Barbara. Presented at Language, Society and the Child: Summer workshops in Sociolinguistics, University of California, Berkeley.

1971   *The Social Organization of Psycholinguistic Research.* Congress paper, American Sociological Association, Denver, Colorado.

1972   *Language Acquisition. The Development of Rational and Rationalizable Skills.* Unpublished doctoral dissertation, University of California, Santa Barbara.

Jennings, Kenneth L. and Sybillyn Jennings

1974   "Tests and Experiments." In A.V. Cicourel et al., *Language Use and School Performance.* New York: Academic Press.

Jennings, Kenneth L. and Hugh Mehan

1969   "Enjambing: A Mechanical Method to Make Interpretive Procedures Visible." Unpublished manuscript, University of California, Santa Barbara.

Johnston, Barbara

1978   "The Critical Difference." In *Diacritics*, 8(2):3.

Jules-Rosette, Bennetta

1973   *Ritual Contexts and Social Action. A Study of the Apostolic Church of John Maranke.* Unpublished doctoral dissertation, Harvard University.

1974   "Reflexive Ethnography I: Instructions as Data: The Apostolic Case." Paper presented at the University of California, Los Angeles Ethnomethodology Symposium, June.

1975a   "Song and Spirit. The Use of Song in the Management of Ritual Settings." In *Africa*, 45.

1975b   *African Apostles: Ritual and Conversion in the Church of John Maranke.* Ithaca: Cornell University Press.

1976a   "The Conversion Experience." In *Journal of Religion in Africa*, Vol. 7:132-164.

1976b   "Verbal and Visual Accounts of a Ritual Setting." Paper presented at the Sixth Annual Conference on Visual Anthropology, Philadelphia, March, 1974. In F. Sack, J. Schenkein, and E. Weingarten (eds.), *Ethnomethodologie.* Frankfort: Suhrkamp, pp. 203-243. [Translation: "Verbale und Visuelle Darstellungen einer Rituellen Situation."]

1978a   "Toward a Theory of Ethnography: The Use of Contrasting Interpretive Paradigms in Field Research." Paper presented at the Annual Meetings of the Pacific Sociological Association, April. In *Sociological Symposium*, Vol. 24:81-98.

1978b   "The Veil of Objectivity: Prophecy, Divination and Social Inquiry." In *The American Anthropologist*, Vol. 80, No. 3(Sept.):549-570.

1978c   "The Politics of Paradigms: Contrasting Theories of Consciousness and Society." In *Human Studies*, Vol. 1, No. 1:92-110.

1979a   *The New Religions of Africa.* New Jersey: Ablex Publishing.
1979b   "Art and Ideology: The Communicative Significance of Some Urban
         Art Forms in Africa." In *Semiotica: International Journal of
         Semiotic Research,* Vol. 28, No. 1(Fall):1-29.
1980a   "Ceremonial Trance Behavior in an African Church: Private Experi-
         ence and Public Expression." Paper presented in the Symposium on
         Ceremony and Ritual, Annual Meetings of the Pacific Sociological
         Association, Spokane, Washington, April 13-15, 1978. In *Journal
         for the Scientific Study of Religion,* Vol. 19, No. 1(March):1-16.
1980b   "Talcott Parsons and the Phenomenological Tradition in Sociology:
         An Unresolved Debate." In *Human Studies,* Vol. 3, No. 4(Oct.):
         311-330.
1981a   *Symbols of Change: Urban Transition in a Zambian Community.*
         Norwood, N.J. : Ablex Publishing.
1981b   "Faith Healers and Folk Healers: The Symbolism and Practice of
         Therapy in Urban Africa." Paper presented at the African Humanities
         Seminar, Indiana University, February, 23, 1979. In *Religion,* Vol.
         12, No. 2(Winter):1-21.
1981c   "Disavowal and Disengagement: A New Look at the Conversion
         Process in Religious Sects." Paper presented at the conference on
         Conversion, Coercion, and Commitment. University of California,
         Berkeley, June, 1981.
1984   *The Messages of Tourist Art: An African Semiotic System.* New York:
         Plenum Publishing.
1985a   "Conversation avec Harold Garfinkel." In *Sociétés: Revue de
         Sciences Humaines et Sociales,* Vol. 1, No. 5(Sept.):35-39.
1985b   "La Sociologie Comprehensive aux États-Unis: Paradigmes et Per-
         spectives." In *Cahiers Internationaux de Sociologie,* Vol. 78:91-101.
1986a   "The Narrative Structure of Prophecy among the Maranke Apostles:
         An Alternative System of Religious Expression." Paper presented at
         the Symposium of the Whole: Toward a Human Poetics, University
         of Southern California, Los Angeles, March 18-20, 1983. In
         Semiotica, Vol. 61, No. 1-2.
1986b   "Semiotics and Sociological Malaise." Editorial, in *Spectrum,*
         (Spring).
1986c   "You Must Be Joking?: A Sociosemiotic Analysis of Ethiopian
         Jokes." In *American Journal of Semiotics,* Vol. 4, No. 2:17-42.
1986d   "Sociosemiotics: The New Hybrid." In *Semiotic Spectrum,* (6).
1986e   "Interpretive Sociology in Comparative Perspective: Paradigms and
         Prospects." In *Canadian Journal of Sociology,* Vol. 11(4).
1987   "L'Ethnomethodologie en perspective." *Sociétés: Revue des Sciences
         Humaines et Sociales,* No. 14, (juin):5-7.

Jules-Rosette, Bennetta and Pierce Flynn
1988   "Who was Mozart? Computers and the Semiotics of Invention."
Paper presented at the Meetings of the Semiotics Circle of California,
UC Berkeley, January 30, 1988.

Jules-Rosette, Bennetta and Hugh Mehan
1986   "Schools and Social Structure: An Interactionist Perspective." In J.
Prager, D. Longshore and M. Seeman (eds.), *School Desegregation
Research: New Directions in Situational Analysis.* New York:
Plenum Publishing.

Kaiman, Ron
1969   "A Companion to Wood's Zato-Coding as a Model for Ethnomethodology." Unpublished paper presented to a seminar led by Don H.
Zimmerman. University of California, Santa Barbara, April 9.

Karady, V.
1983   "The Durkheimians in Academe: A Reconsideration." In P. Besnard,
(ed.), *The Sociological Domain.* Cambridge: Cambridge University
Press. pp. 71-89.

Keesing, Roger M.
1975   *Kin Groups and Social Structure.* New York: Holt, Rinehart and
Winston.

Kephant, William J.
1982   *Extraordinary Groups: The Sociology of Unconventional Lifestyles.*
New York: St. Martin's Press.

Kitazawa, Yutaka
1984   "Pasonu Riron to Esunomesodoroji: Shukansei Mondai ni Kansuru
HoHo Bunseki O Megutte." (Parsons's Theories and Ethnomethodology: Theoretical Perspectives for Analysis of the Problem of Subjectivity) In *Shakaigaku Hyoron/Japanese Sociological Review*, 35,
1(137), June:58-76.

Kitsuse, John and A.V. Cicourel
1970   "The High School's Role in Adolescent Status Transition." In B.J.
Chandler, J. Stiles and John Kituse (eds.), *Education in Urban
Society.* New York: Dodd, Mead, pp. 70-82.

1963   "A Note on the Use of Official Statistics." In *Social Problems*, II:
131-139.

1972   "A Note on the Use of Official Statistics." In W.J. Filstead (ed.),
An Introduction to Deviance. Chicago: Markam Publishing Co.,
pp. 244-255.

Knorr-Cetina, Karin
1981   *The Manufacture of Knowledge: An Essay on the Constructivist and
Contextual Nature of Science.* Oxford: Pergamon Press.

1983   "The Ethnographic Study of Scientific Work: Toward a Constructivist Interpretation of Science." In Knorr-Cetina and Mulkay (eds.),

Science Observed: Perspectives on the Social Study of Science. London/Beverly Hills: Sage Publications.

Knorr-Cetina and A.V. Cicourel
1981   *Advances in Social Theory and Methodology: Toward an Integration of Micro-and Macro-Sociologies.* Boston: Routledge and Kegan Paul.

Knorr-Cetina, K. and M. Mulkay (eds.)
1983   *Science Observed: Perspectives on the Social Study of Science.* London/Beverly Hills: Sage Publications.

Knox, Ronald A.
1961   *Enthusiasm: A Chapter in the History of Religion.* London: Oxford University Press.

Krauss, Rosalind
1981   "The Photographic Conditions of Surrealism." In *October*, Vol. 19: 3-34.

Kriegel, Annie
1978   "Generational Difference: The History of an Idea." In *Daedalus*, Vol. 107, No. 3:23-38.

Kristeva, Julia
1980   "The Bounded Text." In Julia Kristeva, *Desire in Language: A Semiotic Approach to Literature and Art.* New York: Columbia University Press.

Kuhn, Thomas S.
1970   *The Structure of Scientific Revolutions.* Chicago: Chicago University Press.

Kuklick, Henrika
1973   "A Scientific Revolution: Sociological Theory in the U.S., 1930-1945." *Sociological Inquiry*, 43:3-22.
1983   "The Sociology of Knowledge: Retrospect and Prospect." In *Annual Review of Sociology*, 9:287-310.

La Capra, Dominick
1983   *Rethinking Intellectual History: Texts, Contexts, Language.* New York: Cornell University Press.

Lapassade, Georges
1970   *Groupes, Organisations, Institutions.* Paris: Gauthier-Villars.
1971a   *L'Analyseur et L'Analyste.* Paris: Gauthier-Villars.
1971b   *L'Autogestion Pédagogique.* Paris: Gauthier-Villars.
1971c   *L'Arpenteur, une Intervention Sociologique.* Paris: Epi.
1975   *Socianalyse et Potentiel Humain.* Paris: Gauthier-Villars.
1976   *Joyeuse Tropiques.* Paris: Gauthier-Villars.
1986   Personal communication. University of Paris, VIII, Vincennes-St. Denis. St. Denis, France.

Latour, Bruno
  1982   "Give Me a Laboratory and I Will Raise the World." In K. Knorr-
          Cetina and Mulkay (eds.), *Science Observed: Perspectives on the
          Social Study of Science*. London/Beverly Hills: Sage Publications.
Latour, Bruno and Paolo Fabbri
  1977   "Pouvoir et Devoir dans un Article de Sciences Exactes." In *Actes de
          la Recherche*, 13:82-95.
Latour, Bruno and Steve Woolgar
  1979   *Laboratory Life: The Social Construction of Scientific Facts*. London/
          Beverly Hills: Sage Publications.
Leary, Timothy
  1968   *Politics of Ecstasy*. New York: Putnam.
Lecerf, Yves
  1985   "Éthnologie à Paris VII: Indexicalité, Journaux Recits, Quasi-
          journaux." In *Pratiques de Formation (Analyses)*, No. 9, Avril:59-77.
  1985   "Revue de Arguments Ethnométhodologiques pour 1984." In
          Pratiques de Formation (Analyses), No. 9, Avril:165-171.
  1986 ed.*Ethnométhodologies*. Special edition of *Pratiques de Formation
          (Analyses)*, No. 11-12. Paris: University of Paris VIII, Vincennes at
          St. Denis.
Leiris, Michel
  1934   *L'Afrique Phantôme*. Paris: Gallimard.
Leiter, Kenneth
  1969   *Getting It Done. An Ethnography of Coding*. Unpublished M.A.
          thesis, University of California, Santa Barbara.
  1971   *Telling It Like It Is. The Structure of Teachers' Accounts*. Unpub-
          lished doctoral dissertation, University of California, Santa Barbara.
  1974   "Ad Hocing in Schools." In A.V. Cicourel et al., *Language Use and
          School Performance*. New York: Academic Press.
  1980   *Primer on Ethnomethodology*. London: Oxford University Press.
Lemert, Charles
  1978   "Ethnomethodology and Structuralism: Linguicity and the De-Center-
          ing of Core-Values." In *Theory and Society*.
  1979   "Structuralist Semiotics and the De-Centering of Sociology." In
          Scott G. McNall (ed.), *Theoretical Perspectives in Sociology*. New
          York: St. Martin's Press, pp. 96-111.
  1981   "Reading French Sociology." In C. Lemert (ed.), *French Sociology:
          Rupture and Renewal Since 1968*. New York: Columbia University
          Press.
Lestel, Dominique
  1986   *Contribution à l'Etude du Raisonnement Expérimental dans un
          Domaine Sémantiquement Riche: Le Cas d'un Laboratoire du Biolo-*

gie. Unpublished doctoral dissertation, Ecole des Hautes Etudes en Sciences Sociales, Paris.

Levi-Strauss, Claude
1970   *The Raw and the Cooked*. Translated by J. and D. Weightman. New York: Harper and Row.

Levinson, S.C.
1983   *Pragmatics*. Cambridge: Cambridge University Press.

Levy, Carl
1987   "Socialism and the Educated Middle Classes in Western Europe, 1870-1914." In Eyerman, R., L.G. Svensson, T. Soderqvist, (eds.), *Intellectuals, Universities and the State in Western Modern Societies*, Berkeley: University of California Press, pp. 154-191.

Lewin, Kurt
1948   *Resolving Social Conflicts*. New York: Harper and Row.

Lewis, J.D. and R.L. Smith
1980   *American Sociology and Pragmatism*. Chicago: University of Chicago Press.

Liberman, Kenneth
1980   *Understanding Interaction in Central Australia: An Ethnomethodological Study of Australian Aboriginal People*. Published doctoral dissertation, University of California, San Diego.

1982   "The Economy of Central Australian Aboriginal Expression: An Inspection from the Vantage of Merleau-Ponty and Derrida." In *Semiotica*. 40, no. 3/4, pp. 267-346.

1983   Review of *The Time of the Sign: A Semiotic Interpretation of Modern Culture*. By Dean MacCannell and Juliet Flower MacCannell. In *American Anthropologist*, (85):428-429.

1985   *Understanding Interaction in Central Australia: An Ethnomethodological Study of Australian Aboriginal People*. Boston: Routledge and Kegan Paul.

Lilly, John
1972   *The Center of the Cyclone: An Autobiography of Inner Space*. New York: Julien Press.

Linton, Ralph
1943   "Nativistic Movements." In *American Anthropologist*, Vol. 65:230-240.

Livingston, Eric
1983   *An Ethnomethodological Investigation of the Foundations of Mathematics*. Published doctoral dissertation, Department of Sociology, University of California, Los Angeles.

1986   *An Ethnomethodological Investigation of the Foundations of Mathematics*. London: Routledge and Kegan Paul.

1987   *Making Sense of Ethnomethodology*. London: Routledge and Kegan Paul.

In press "An Ethnomethodological Approach to the Study of the Arts." Department of Sociology, University of California, Los Angeles, in Garfinkel (ed.), *Ethnomethodological Studies of Work*.

In press "Mathematicians' Work." Paper presented in the session on Ethnomethodology: Studies of Work, Ninth World Congress of Sociology, Uppsala, Sweden. In Garfinkel (ed.), *Ethnomethodological Studies of Work*.

Livingston, Eric and Harold Garfinkel

1983   "Notation and the Work of Mathematical Discovery." Unpublished paper, Department of Sociology, University of California, Los Angeles.

Loader, Colin

1985   *The Intellectual Development of Karl Mannheim*. Cambridge: Cambridge University Press.

Lofland, John and Norman Skonovd

1981   "Conversion Motifs." In *Journal for the Scientific Study of Religion*, 29, 4:373.

Lounsbury, Floyd G.

1956   "A Semantic Analysis of Pawnee Kinship Usage." In *Language*, 32:158-194.

Lourau, Rene

1970   *L'analyse Institutionnelle*. Paris: Minuit.

1971   *Analyse Institutionnelle et Pedagogie*. Paris: Epi.

1972   *Les Analyseurs de L'Eglise*. Paris: Anthropos.

1976   *Sociologue à Plein Temps*. Paris: Epi.

1977   *Le Gai Savoir des Sociologues*. Paris: UGE.

1978   *L'état inconscient*. Paris: Minuit.

1985   "Un Journal de Terrain: *L'Afrique Phantôme*, de Michel Leiris." In *Pratiques de Formation*, No. 9:47-57.

Lukes, S.

1973   *Emile Durkheim: His Life and Work*. London: Allen Lane.

Lynch, Michael

1974a   "Discrediting Devices in the Early History of Microscopy." Unpublished paper, School of Social Sciences, University of California, Irvine.

1974b   "Instrumental Praxis in Microscopy." Paper read at Ethnomethodology Colloquium, University of California, Los Angeles, June.

1976   "Art and Artifact in Microscopy." Unpublished manuscript, School of Social Sciences, University of California, Irvine.

1977   "Days." Unpublished Manuscript, School of Social Sciences, University of California, Irvine.

1979   *Art and Artifact in Laboratory Science: A Study of Shop Work and Shop Talk in a Research Laboratory.* Published doctoral dissertation, School of Social Sciences, University of California, Irvine.

1982a   "Technical Work and Critical Inquiry: Investigations in a Scientific Laboratory. In *Social Studies of Science*, 12(4):499-534.

1982b   "Closure and Disclosure in Pre-trial Argument." In *Human Studies*, Vol. 5:285-318.

1985a   *Art and Artifact in Laboratory Science.* London: Routledge and Kegan Paul.

1985b   "La Retine Exteriorisé: Selection et Mathematisation des Documents Visuels." In *Culture Technique*, No. 14, *Les 'Vues" de l'Esprit.* Paris: Presse Universitaire de France.

1985c   "Discipline and the Material Form of Images: An Analysis of Scientific Visibility." In *Social Studies of Science*,Vol. 15, (1):37-66.

1990   "Topical Contextures and Digital Image Processing: A Case Study of Astronomy." Paper presented at UCLA Conference on Aesthetics and Semiotics, June 1990.

Lynch, Michael with Eric Livingston and Harold Garfinkel
1983   "Temporal Order in Laboratory Work." In Karin Knorr-Cetina and Mulkay (eds.), *Science Observed.* London: Sage Publications.

MacAndrew, Craig
1969   "On the Notion that Certain Persons Who are Given to Frequent Drunkenness Suffer from a Disease Called Alcoholism." In Stanley C. Plog and Robert B. Edgerton (eds.), *Changing Perspectives in Mental Illness.* New York: pp. 483-501.

1977   "On the Notion of Drunkenness." In E. M. Pattison et al., (eds.), *Emerging Concepts of Alcohol Dependence.* New York: Springer.

MacAndrew, Craig and Robert Edgerton
1969   *Drunken Comportment.* A Social Explanation. Chicago: University of Chicago Press.

MacCannell, Dean
1986a   "Keeping Symbolic Interaction Safe From Semiotics: A Response to Harmon." In *Symbolic Interaction*, Vol. 9(1):161-168.

1986b   "Semiotics and Sociology." In *Semiotica*, 6/(3/4), 193-200.

MacCannell, Dean and Juliet Flower-MacCannell
1982   *The Time of the Sign: A Semiotic Interpretation of Modern Culture.* Bloomington: Indiana University Press.

Macbeth, Douglas
1987   *Management's Work: The Social Organization of Order and Troubles in Secondary Classrooms*, unpublished doctoral dissertation, School of Education, University of California, Berkeley.

MacKay, Robert W.
1971   *Ethnography of the Classroom and Language Learning.* Unpublished doctoral dissertation, University of California, Santa Barbara.
1973   "Conceptions of Children and Models of Socialization." H.P. Dreitzel (ed.), *Childhood and Socialization. Recent Sociology No. 5.* New York: MacMillan, pp. 27-43.
[1974 Also in R. Turner (ed.), *Ethnomethodology.* Baltimore: Penguin, pp. 180-193.]
MacKay, Robert W., Hugh Mehan and David Roth
1971   "Communicative Competence and School Performance." Congress paper, American Sociological Association, Denver, Colorado.
1974   "Standardized Tests." In A.V. Cicourel et al., *Language Use and School Performance.* New York: Academic Press.
Mannheim, Karl
1936   *Ideology and Utopia.* New York: Harcourt, Brace and World.
1952a *Essays on the Sociology of Knowledge.* P. Kecksmeti (ed.), London: Routledge and Kegan Paul.
1952b "On the Interpretation of Weltanschauung." Translated and edited by Paul Kecksemeti, in *Essays on the Sociology of Knowledge.* London: Routledge and Kegan Paul.
1982   *Structures of Thinking.* Translated by J. J. Shapiro and S. W. Nicholsen, edited by D. Kettler, V. Meja, and N. Stehr. London: Routledge and Kegan Paul.
1986   *Conservatism: A Contribution to the Sociology of Knowledge.* (translated by D. Kettler and V. Meja) London: Routledge and Kegan Paul.
Manning, Peter K.
1970   "A View of Organizational Socialization." In J. D. Douglas (ed.), *Understanding Everyday Life.* Chicago: Aldine, pp. 239-256.
1973   "Existential Sociology." In *Sociological Quarterly*, 12:200-225.
Manning, Peter K. and Horacio Fabrega, Jr.
1973   "The Experience of Self and Body: Health and Illness in the Chiapas Highlands." In G. Psathas (ed.), *Phenomenological Sociology.* New York: John Wiley and Sons, pp. 251-301.
Maroules, Nicholas
1984   "Sociolinguistics: From Hymes to Courtroom Discourse." Unpublished paper, Department of Sociology, University of California, San Diego.
1985   *The Social Organization of Sentencing.* Unpublished doctoral dissertation, Department of Sociology, University of California, San Diego.
Martindale, Don
1976   *The Romance of a Profession: A Case History in the Sociology of Sociology.* St. Paul: Windflower Publishing.

Maryl, William
  1973   "Ethnomethodology: Sociology Without Society." In *Catalyst*, 7: 15-28.
Maus, H.
  1962   *A Short History of Sociology*. London: Routledge and Kegan Paul.
Maynard, Douglas W.
  1979   *People Processing: Plea Bargaining in a Municipal Court*. Unpublished doctoral dissertation, University of California, Santa Barbara.
  1980   "Placement of Topic Changes in Conversation." In *Semiotica*, 30: 263-290.
  1982   "Person Descriptions in Plea Bargaining." In *Semiotica*.
  1983   "Language in the Court." In *American Bar Foundation Research Journal*, pp. 211-222.
  1985   "The Problem of Justice in the Courts Approached by the Analysis of Plea Bargaining Discourse." In *Handbook of Discourse Analysis* Vol 4, T. A.Van Dijk (ed.), London: Academic Press, pp. 153-179.
  1986   *Inside Plea Bargaining: The Language of Negotiation*. New York/ London: Plenum Press.
  1988   "Language, Social Interaction, and Social Problems." *Social Problems* 35:311-334.
Maynard, Douglas W. and Thomas P. Wilson
  1980   "On the Reification of Social Structure." In Scott B. McNall and Gary N. Howe (eds.), *Current Perspectives in Social Theory: A Research Annual*. Greenwich, Conn.: JAI Press.
Maynard, Douglas W. and Don H. Zimmerman
  1983   "Ritual, Topical Talk, and the Social Organization of Relationships." Revised version of a paper delivered at the annual meetings of the American Sociological Association, Boston, 1979.
  1984   "Topical Talk: Ritual and the Social Organization of Relationships." *Social Science Quarterly*, 47:301-316.
McDermott, R. P.
  1976   *Kids Make Sense: An Ethnographic Account of Success and Failure in One First Grade Classroom*. Unpublished doctoral dissertation, Anthropology, Stanford University.
  1980   "Profile: Ray L. Birdwhistell." In *The Kinesis Report*, 2(3), 1-4: 14-16.
McDermott, R.P., K. Gospodinoff and J. Aron
  1978   "Criteria for an Ethnographically Adequate Description of Concerted Activities and Their Contexts." In *Semiotica*, 24:245-275.
McGuire, Meredith
  1981   *Religion: The Social Context*. Belmont, CA: Wadsworth Publishing Co.

1983   "Words of Power: Personal Empowerment and Healing." *Culture, Medicine, and Psychiatry*, 7:221-240.

McHoul, Andrew

1978a   "Ethnomethodology and Literature: Towards a Sociology of Reading." *Poetics*, 7:113-120.

1978b   "The Organization of Turns at Formal Talk in the Classroom." In *Language and Society*, 7:183-213.

1982   *Telling How Texts Talk: Essays on Reading and Ethnomethodology.* London: Routledge and Kegan Paul.

1987   "An Initial Investigation of the Usability of Fictional Conversation for Doing Conversation Analysis," *Semiotica*, 67-3/4:83-105.

In press "Notes on the Organization of Repair in Classroom Talk." In J.N. Schenkein (ed.), *Studies in the Organization of Conversational Interaction, Volume II.* New York: Academic Press.

McHugh, Peter

1966   "Social Disintegration as a Requisite of Resocialization." In *Social Forces*, 44:355-363.

1968   *Defining the Situation: The Organization of Meaning in Social Interaction.* Indianapolis: Bobs-Merrill Co.

1970   "A Common-sense Conception of Deviance." In H. P. Dreitzel (ed.), *Recent Sociology, No. 2, Patterns of Communicative Behavior.* New York: MacMillan, pp. 152-180.

1970   "On the Failure of Positivism." In J. D. Douglas (ed.), *Understanding Everyday Life.* Chicago: Aldine, pp. 320-335.

McHugh, Peter, Stanley Raffel, Daniel C. Foss and Alan F. Blum

1974   *On the Beginning of Social Inquiry.* London: Routledge and Kegan Paul.

McLeod, Ross

1975   "Doing Snogging." *Urban Life and Culture*, 3:442-445.

McNall, Scott

1978   "On Contemporary Social Theory." In *The American Sociologist*, 13(1):2-6.

McNall, Scott and James C. M. Johnson

1975   "The New Conservatives: Ethnomethodologists, Phenomenologists, and Symbolic Interactionists." In *The Insurgent Sociologist*, 5, 4: 49-65.

Meehan, Albert Jay

1983   *For the Record: Interactional and Organizational Practices for Producing Police Records on Juveniles.* Unpublished doctoral dissertation, Department of Sociology, Boston University.

Meehan, Albert Jay and Anne Rawls (eds.)

In press *New Directions in the Study of Social Order.* Chicago: Irvington Press.

Mehan, Hugh
  1971   *Accomplishing Understanding in Educational Settings.* Unpublished
          doctoral dissertation, University of California, Santa Barbara.
  1973a   "Assessing Children's Language Using Abilities." In J. M. Armor
          and A. D. Grimshaw (eds.), *Methodological Issues in Comparative
          Sociological Research.* New York: John Wiley and Sons.
  1973b   Also in H. P. Dreitzel (ed.), *Childhood and Socialization.* New York:
          pp. 240-264.
  1974a   "Accomplishing Classroom Lessons." In A. V. Cicourel, K. H.
          Jennings, S. H. M. Jennings, K. C. W. Leiter, R. MacKay, H. Mehan
          and D. R. Roth (eds.), *Language Use and School Performance.* New
          York: Academic Press.
  1974b   "Ethnomethodology and Education." In D. O'Shea (ed.), *Sociology
          of the School and Schooling.* Washington D.C. National Institute of
          Education.
  1978a   Personal communication.
  1978b   "Structuring School Structure." In *Harvard Educational Review*,
          Vol. 45, No. 1:331-338.
  1979a   *Learning Lessons: Social Organization in the Classroom.* Cambridge,
          Mass.: Harvard University Press.
  1979b   "What Time Is It, Denise? Some Consequences of Asking Informa-
          tion Questions in Classroom Discourse." In *Theory into Practice*,
          18(4):285-294.
  1981   "Practical Decision Making in Naturally Occurring Institutional
          Settings." In Barbara Rogoff and Jean Lave (eds.), *Everyday
          Cognition: Its Development and Social Context.* Cambridge, Mass.:
          Harvard University Press.
  1982   "Social Constructivism in Psychology and Sociology." In *Sociologie
          et Sociétés*, 14(2):77-96.
  1983   "The Role of Language and the Language of Role in Institutional
          Decision Making." In *Language and Society*, 12(3):1-39.
  1985   "Oracular Reasoning in a Psychiatric Exam: The Resolution of
          Conflict in Language." In Allan Grimshaw (ed.), *Conflict Talk.*
          Cambridge: Cambridge University Press.
  1986   "The School's Work of Sorting Students." Paper presented at the
          Santa Barbara International Conference on Talk and Social Structure,
          University of California, Santa Barbara, March 25.
  1987   "Language and Power in Organizational Process," *Discourse Proc-
          esses*, 10(4):347-368.
  1988   "Educational Handicaps as a Cultural Meaning System," *Ethos*,
          Vol. 16, (1):73-91.
  1990   Review. *Making Sense of Ethnomethodology*, by Eric Livingston.
          Contemporary Sociology 19, 3(May):484-485.

Mehan, Hugh, Sue Fisher and Nicholas Maroules
In press "Students' Formulating Practices and Instructional Strategies." In
Annals, New York Academy of Science.
Mehan, Hugh, Bennetta Jules-Rosette and Gerald Platt
1984 "Perspectives on Ethnomethodology." Unpublished paper, University
of California, San Diego.
Mehan, Hugh, A. Hertweck, S. Combs and P. Flynn
1981 "Teachers' Interpretations of Students' Behavior." In L.C. Wilkinson
(ed.), *Communicating in the Classroom*. New York: Academic Press.
Mehan, Hugh, A. Hertweck and L. Meihls
1981 "Educational Decision Making in Students' Careers. Part II: Prospectus for Year Three." Unpublished manuscript. University of California, San Diego.
Mehan, Hugh, A. Hertweck and M. Crowdes
1981 "Identifying Handicapped Students." In S. B. Bacharach (ed.),
Organizational Behavior in Schools and School Districts. New York:
Praeger Press.
Mehan, Hugh, L. Meihls and A. Hertweck
1986 *Handicapping the Handicapped*. Stanford, CA: Stanford University
Press.
Mehan, Hugh and Houston Wood
1975a *The Reality of Ethnomethodology*. New York: John Wiley and Sons.
1975b "An Image of Man for Ethnomethodology." In *Philosophy of the
Social Sciences*, 5:365-376.
1976 "De-Secting Ethnomethodology." In *The American Sociologist*,
11:13-21.
Mehan, Hugh et al.
1976 *Texts of Classroom Discourse*. Report No. 67, Center for Human
Information Processing, University of California, San Diego.
Merleau-Ponty, Maurice
1962 *The Phenomenology of Perception*. London: Routledge and Kegan
Paul.
1968 *The Visible and the Invisible*. Evanston: Northwestern University
Press.
Mermell, S.
1976 "Ethnomethodology and the New Methodenstreit." In D. C. Thorn
(ed.), *New Directions in Sociology*. New York: Rowman and Littlefield, pp. 139-157.
Merton, Robert K.
1973 *The Sociology of Science: Theoretical and Empirical Investigations*.
Edited by Norman Storer: University of Chicago Press.

1977   "The Sociology of Science: An Episodic Memoir." *The Sociology of Science in Europe and America*, J. Gaston and R. K. Merton (eds.). Carbondale: Southern Illinois University Press.

Meyer, Lois.
1985   *Making a Scene: Probing the Structure of Understanding in Sibling Interaction*, unpublished manuscript, University of California, Berkeley.
1988   "It Was No Trouble: Achieving Communicative Competence in a Second Language", in Robin Scarcella, Elaine Andersen, and Stephen Krashin, (eds.) *Development of Competence in a Second Language*, Newbury House.

Mills, C.W.
1963   *Power, Politics, and People*. New York: Ballantine Books.

Moerman, Michael
1965   "Ethnic Identification in a Complex Civilization: Who are the Lue?" In *American Anthropologist*, 67:1215-1230.
1967a   "Reply to Narroll." In *American Anthropologist*, 69:512-513.
1967b   "Being Lue: Uses and Abuses of Ethnic Identification." In American Ethnological Society, *Proceedings of 1967 Spring Meetings*, pp.153-169.
1968a   "Accomplishing Ethnicity." In Roy Turner (ed.), *Ethnomethodology*. Baltimore: Penguin, pp. 54-68.
1968b   *Agricultural Change and Peasant Choice in a Thai Village*. Berkeley: University of California.
1969   "A Little Knowledge." In S.A. Tyler (ed.), *Cognitive Anthropology*. New York: Holt, Rinehart & Winston, pp. 449-469.
1970   "Analysis of Lue Conversation, Part I and Part II." Unpublished manuscript.
1972   "Analysis of Lue Conversation: Providing Accounts, Finding Breaches, and Taking Sides." In D. Sudnow (ed.), *Studies in Social Interaction*. New York: Free Press, pp. 170-228.
1973   "The Use of Precedent in Natural Conversation." In *Semiotica*, 9: 193-218.
1977   "The Preference for Self-Correction in a Thai Conversational Corpus." In *Language*, 53:872-883.
1988   *Talking Culture: Ethnography and Conversation Analysis*. Philadelphia: University of Pennsylvania Press.

Moerman M. and H. Sacks
1974   "On Understanding in Conversation." In *Festschrift for E. Voegelin*. The Hague: Mouton.

Moholy-Nagy, Lázló
1947   *Vision in Motion*. Chicago: Chicago University Press.

Molotch, Harvey L. and Deirdre Boden
1985   "Talking and Social Structure: Discourse, Domination, and the Watergate Hearings." In *American Sociological Review*, 50(3): 273-288.

Morris, Charles W.
1938   *Foundation of the Theory of Signs*. International Encyclopedia of Unified Science, 1:21. Chicago: University of Chicago Press.
1946   *Signs, Language, and Behavior*. New York: Prentice Hall.

Morrison, Kenneth
1976   *Readers Work: Devices for Achieving Pedagogic Events in Textual Materials for Readers as Novices to Sociology*. Unpublished doctoral dissertation, Department of Sociology, York University, Toronto, Canada.
1981   "Some Properties of 'Telling-Order Designs' in Didactic Inquiry." In *Philosophy of the Social Sciences*, 11(June):245-262.
In press "Some Researchable Recurrences in Science and Social Science Inquiry." In Jay Meehan and Anne Rawls (eds.), *New Directions in the Study of Social Order*. Chicago: Irvington.
         [In press Also in H. Garfinkel (ed.), *A Manual for the Study of Naturally Organized Ordinary Activities*. London: Routledge and Kegan Paul.]

Mulkay, M.
1985   *The Word and the World: Explorations in the Form of Sociological Analysis*. London: George Allen Unwin.

Mulkay, M., J. Potter, and S. Yearley
1983   "Why an Analysis of Scientific Discourse Is Needed." In Knorr-Cetina and Mulkay (eds.), *Science Observed*, 171-203.

Mullins, Nicholas C.
1973a   *Theories and Theory Groups in Contemporary American Sociology*. New York: Harper and Row.
1973b   "The Developments of Specialties in Social Science: The Case of Ethnomethodology." In *Science Studies*, 3:245-273.

Nadeau, Maurice
1965   *The History of Surrealism*. Translated by Richard Howard. New York: MacMillan.

Narens, Louis
1976   "Vorstellungssysteme der Geisteskranken." In Weingargen, Sack, Schenkein, *Ethnomethodologie: Beiträge zu einer Soziologie des Alltagshandelns*. Frankfurt: Suhrkamp.

Nash, Laura L.
1978   "Concepts of Existence: Greek Origins of Generational Thought." In *Daedalus*, Vol. 10, No. 3:1-21.

Needleman, Jacob
  1987   "When is Religion Transformative? A Conversation with Jacob Needleman." In Dick Anthony, Bruce Ecker, and Ken Wilber (eds.), *Spiritual Choices.* New York: Paragon House Publishers.

Newstadt, Richard and Ernest R. May
  1986   *Thinking in Time: The Uses of History for Decision Makers.* New York: Free Press.

Nisbet, R.
  1967   *The Sociological Tradition.* London: Heineman.

Obershall, A.
  1978   "The Decline of the 1960s Social Movements." In L. Kriesberg (ed.), *Research in Social Movements, Conflicts and Change*, Vol. 1. Greewich, Ct.: JAI Press.

Ochs, Elinor
  1982   "Talking to Children in Western Samoa." In *Language in Society*, 11:77-104.

  1984   "Clarification and Culture." In Georgetown University Rountable on Languages and Linguistics.

Ogden, D. K. and I. A. Richards
  1946   *The Meaning of Meaning.* New York: Harcourt Brace.

O'Keefe, D.
  1979   "Ethnomethodology." *Journal for the Theory of Social Behavior*, 9:187-219.

O'Neill, John
  1972   *Sociology as a Skin Trade: Essays Toward Reflexive Sociology.* New York: Harper and Row.

  1981   "The Literary Production of Natural and Social Science Inquiry: Issues and Applications in the Social Organization of Science." In *Canadian Journal of Sociology*, 6, 2:105-120.

Ong, Walter J.
  1982   *Orality and Literacy: The Technologizing of the Word.* New York: Methuen.

Orenstein, Gloria
  1973   "Women of Surrealism." In *Feminist Art Journal*.

Oromaner, Mark
  1977   "The Career of Sociological Literature: A Diachronous Study." *Social Studies of Science*, 7:126-132.

Pack, Christopher
  1982   *Interactional Synchrony Reassessed: An Attempt to Apply the Discovery of Interactional Synchrony in Neonates as an Index of Attachment in Non-organic Failure to Thrive Syndrome.* Unpublished doctoral dissertation, Department of Sociology, University of California, Los Angeles.

1986   "Features of Signs Encountered in Designing a Notational System for Transcribing Lectures." In Garfinkel (ed.), *Ethnomethodological Studies of Work*, London: Routledge and Kegan Paul.

In press "Towards a Phenomenology of Transcription." In Garfinkel (ed.), *Ethnomethodological Studies of Work*, London: Routledge and Kegan Paul.

Paget, M.A.

1983   "On the Work of Talk: Studies in Misunderstandings." In Fisher and Todd (eds.), *The Social Organization of Doctor-Patient Communication*. Washington D.C.: The Center for Applied Linguistics.

Parish, Steven M.

1981   *The Overworked Students' Practical Guide to Writing Term Papers for Anthropology (and Related Subjects)*. Regents of the University of California.

Parsons, Talcott

1937   *The Structure of Social Action*. New York: McGraw Hill.

1969   "The Intellectual: A Social Role Category." In Rieff, R. (ed.), *On Intellectuals*: pp. 3-24.

1951   *The Social System*. New York: The Free Press.

1970   "On Building Social System Theory: A Personal History." In *Daedalus: The Making of Modern Science: Biographical Studies*, 99(Fall):826-881.

Pearce, Frank

1970   "On Ethnomethodology." Congress paper, Fifth National Deviancy Symposium, April.

Pesic, Vesna

1983   "Ethnometodologija i Sociologija." In *Sociologija*, 25, 2-3, April-Sept.:261-286.

Peyrot, Mark

1982a   "Caseload Management: Choosing Suitable Clients in a Community Health Clinic Agency." In *Social Problems*, 30:157-167.

1982b   "Understanding Ethnomethodology: A Remedy for Some Common Misconceptions." In *Human Studies*, 5,4(Oct.-Dec.):261-283.

Phillips, Susan

1982   "The Social Organization of Questions and Answers in Courtroom Discourse." Paper presented at the annual meetings of the American Sociological Association, San Francisco.

Phillipson, Michael and Maurice Roche

1974   "Phenomenology, Sociology and the Study of Deviance." In Paul Rock and Mary McIntosh (eds.), *Deviance and Social Control*, London: pp. 125-162.

Piven, F.F. and R. Cloward

1979   *Poor People's Movements*. New York: Vintage Books.

Plakans, Andrejs
1984   *Kinship in the Past*. London: Basil Blackwell.
Platt, Gerald
1980   "Thoughts on a Theory of Collective Action: Language, Affect and Ideology in Revolution." In Mel Albin (ed.), *New Directions in Psychohistory*, Kentucky: Lexington, Kentucky, pp. 69-94.
1984   Personal communication, June.
Plummer, Ken
1982   *Documents of Life: An Introduction to the Problems and Literature of a Humanistic Method*. London: George Allen and Unwin.
Polanyi, Michael
1962   *Personal Knowledge: Towards a Post-Critical Philosophy*. Chicago: University of Chicago Press.
1966   *The Tacit Dimension*. New York: Anchor Books.
Pollner, Melvin
1970   *On the Foundations of Mundane Reasoning*. Unpublished doctoral dissertation, University of California, Santa Barbara.
1974   "Sociological and Common-Sense Models of the Labelling Process." In Roy Truner (ed.), *Ethnomethodology*. Baltimore: Penguin, pp. 27-40.
1987   *Mundane Reason: Reality in Everyday and Sociological Discourse*. Cambridge: Cambridge University Press.
In press "Notes on Self-Explicating Settings." In Garfinkel (ed.), *Ethnomethodological Studies of Work*, London: Routledge and Kegan Paul.
Pomerantz, Anita
1984a   "Agreeing and Disagreeing with Assessments: Some Features of Preferred/Dispreferred Turn Shapes." In J. Maxwell Atkinson and John Heritage (eds.), *Structures of Social Action: Studies in Conversation Analysis*. Cambridge: Cambridge University Press, pp. 57-101.
1984b   "Pursuing a Response." In J. Maxwell Atkinson and John Heritage (eds.), *Structures of Social Action: Studies in Conversation Analysis*. Cambridge: Cambridge University Press, pp. 152-164.
Pomerantz, Anita M. and J. M. Atkinson
1984   "Ethnomethodology, Conversation Analysis and the Study of Courtroom Behaviour." In D. J. Muller, D. E. Blackman and A. J. Chapman (eds.), *Topics in Psychology and Law*. Chichester, Wiley, pp. 283-297.
Poster, Mark
1975   *Existential Marxism in Postwar France: From Sartre to Althusser*. Princeton: Princeton University Press.

Price, D. J. de S.
   1965   "Networks of Scientific Papers: The Pattern of Bibliographic Refer-
          ences Indicates the Nature of the Scientific Research Front." In
          Science, 149(3683, July 30):510-515.
Psathas, George
   1968   "Ethnomethods and Phenomenology." In *Social Research*. 35:
          500-520.
          [Translation: "Ethnotheorie, Ethnomethodologie und Phänomenolo-
          gie." In Arbeitsgruppe Bielefelder Soziologen (eds.), *Alltagswissen,
          Interaktion und Gesellschaftliche Wirklichkeit, 2*, Reinbek: 1973:
          263-284.]
   1973   *Phenomenological Sociology. Issues and Applications.* New York:
          Wiley Interscience.
   1976a "Ethnomethodology as a Phenomenological Approach in the Social
          Sciences." In R. Zaner and D. Ihde (eds.), *Interdisciplinary Phenome-
          nology. Vol. VI, Selected Studies of the Society for Phenomenology
          and Existential Philosophy.* Den Haag.
   1976b "The Study of Everyday Structures and the Ethnomethodological
          Paradigm." In R. Grathoff and W. Sprondel (eds.), *Alfred Schutz und
          die Idee des Alltags fur die Sozialwissenschaften.* Stuttgart.
   1979   (ed.) *Everyday Language: Studies in Ethnomethodology.* New York:
          Wiley Press.
   1980   "Approaches to the Study of the World of Everyday Life." *Human
          Studies*, 3(1980), 3-17.
Psathas, George and Frances C. Waksler
   1973   "Essential Features of Face-to-Face Interaction." In G. Psathas (ed.),
          Phenomenological Sociology Issues and Applications. New York:
          Wiley Interscience, pp. 159-183.
Psathas, George and R. Frankel
   In press *Interactional Competence.* Norwood, N.J.: Ablex Publishers.
Rabinow, Paul
   1977   *Reflections on Fieldwork in Morocco.* Berkeley and Los Angeles:
          University of California Press.
   1986   "Representations are Social Facts: Modernity and Post-Modernity in
          Anthropology." In Clifford and Marcus (eds.), *Writing Culture: The
          Poetics and Politics of Ethnography.* Berkeley and Los Angeles:
          University of California Press, pp. 234-261.
Radnitzsky, Gerald
   1973   *Contemporary Schools of Metascience.* Chicago: Henry Regnery Co.
Ramos, Reyes
   1973a "The Production of Social Reality." Unpublished doctoral disserta-
          tion, University of Colorado.
   1973b "A Case in Point." In *Social Science Quarterly*, 53:905-919.

1974   "The Use of Improvisation and Modulation in Natural Talk: An Alternative Approach to Conversational Analysis." Manuscript, University of California, San Diego.

Raushenbush,W.
1979   *Robert E. Park: A Biography of a Sociologist.* Durham, N.C.: Duke University Press.

Rawls, Anne
1983   *An Interactionist Perspective on the Understanding of Social Order and Human Value.* Unpublished doctoral dissertation, Department of Sociology, Boston University.
1984a   "Interaction as a Basis for Epistemological Critique: A Comparison of Goffman and Sartre." In *Sociological Theory, II.*
1984b   "An Ethnomethodological Perspective on Social Theory." In Helm, Anderson, Meehan and Rawls (eds.), *New Directions in the Study of Social Order.*
1984c   "Micro-structures as 'Maps' of Organizational and Intra-organizational Constraints." In *Philosophy of the Social Sciences.*
1985   "Reply to Gallant and Kleinman." In *Symbolic Interaction*, 8, 1, Spring:121-140.

Reader, Keith A.
1987   *Intellectuals and the Left in France Since 1968.* London: MacMillan.

Remmling, Gunter (ed.)
1973   *Towards the Sociology of Knowledge: Origin and Development of a Sociological Thought Style.* London: Routledge and Kegan Paul.

Richards, I. A.
1955   *Speculative Instruments.* Chicago: Chicago University Press.

Ricoeur, Paul
1984   *Time and Narrative.* Volume I. Chicago: University of Chicago Press.

Rieff, Philip (ed.)
1969   *On Intellectuals.* New York: Doubleday.

Riffaterre, Michael
1978   *The Semiotics of Poetry.* Bloomington: Indiana University Press.

Robbins, T., D. Anthony and J. Richardson
1978   "Theory and Research on Today's 'New Religions'." *Sociological Analysis*, 39, 2:95-122.

Robillard, Albert R.
1980   "Applied Behavioral Analysis." Unpublished paper, Department of Human Development, Michigan State University.

Robillard, Albert R.
1983   *Pacific Island Mental Health Counselor Training Program: A Final Program Narrative and Evaluation Report*, Honolulu: Department of Psychiatry, 1983.

1984   *Pacific Islander Alternative Mental Health Services: A Project Summary Report*, Honolulu: Social Science Research Institute, March 1984.

1986   "Mental Health Services in Micronesia: A Case of Superficial Development", in Carole E. Hill (ed.). *Current Health Policy Issues and Alternatives: An Applied Social Science Perspective*, University of Georgia Press, Athens, Georgia 1986.

1986   "Community-Based Primary Health Care: Reality or Mystification?" in Trinidad S. Osteria and Jonathan Y. Okamura (eds.) *Participatory Approaches to Development: Experiences in the Phillipines*. De La Salle Universtiy, Manilla, Phillipines, 1986.

1987   *Pacific Islander Mental Health Research Center*, Grant Application, Department of Mental and Human Services, Public Health Service, September, 1987.

Robillard, Albert R. and Christopher Pack

1980   "The Clinical Encounter: The Organization of Doctor-Patient Interaction." Unpublished paper, Department of Human Development, Michigan State University.

Robillard, Albert R., G.M. White and T.W. Maretzki

1983   "Between Doctor and Patient: Informed Consent in Conversational Interaction." In Fisher and Todd (eds.), *The Social Organization of Doctor-Patient Communication*. Washington D.C.: The Center for Applied Linguistics.

Roche, Maurice

1973   "Class Analysis and the Showing of Dichotomy." In P. Filmer, *Stratifying Practices*, unpublished manuscript, Goldsmith College, London.

Rock, P.E.

1968   "Review of Aaron Cicourel, *The Social Organization of Juvenile Justice*." British Journal of Sociology, 19:474-474.

1979   *The Making of Symbolic Interactionism*. Totowa, N.J.: Rowman and Littlefield.

Rogers, Mary F.

1983   *Sociology, Ethnomethodology and Experience: A Phenomenological Critique*. Cambridge: Cambridge University Press.

Rosaldo, Michelle Z.

1980   *Knowledge and Passion: Ilongot Notions of Self and Social Life*. Cambridge: Cambridge University Press.

Roth, David

1972   *Children's Linguistic Performance as a Factor in School Performance*. Unpublished doctoral dissertation, University of California, Santa Barbara.

1974   "Intelligence Testing as a Social Activity." In A.V. Cicourel et al., *Language Use and School Performance*. New York: Academic Press, pp. 143-217.

Ryave, A.

1973   *Aspects of Story-Telling Among a Group of "Mentally Retarded."* Unpublished doctoral dissertation, Department of Sociology, University of California, Los Angeles.

1978   "On the Achievement of a Series of Stories." In J. Schenkein (ed.), *Studies in the Organization of Conversational Interaction*. New York: Academic Press, pp. 113.

Ryave, A. and J. Schenkein

1974   "Notes on the Art of Walking." In Roy Turner (ed.), *Ethnomethodology*. Baltimore: Penguin.

Ryno, Ron

1985   *The Pragmatics of Religious Belief: An Ethnography of the Cursillo Community in Palma de Mallorca*. Unpublished doctoral dissertation, Department of Sociology, University of California, San Diego.

Sacks, Harvey

1963   "On Sociological Description." In *Berkeley Journal of Sociology*, 8:1-16.

1964-
1972   Unpublished transcribed lectures, School of Social Science, University of California, Irvine. (Transcribed and indexed by Gail Jefferson.)

1966   *The Search for Help: No One to Turn to*. Unpublished doctoral dissertation, Department of Sociology, University of California, Berkeley.

1967a   "The Search for Help: No One to Turn to." In E. Schneidman (ed.), *Essays in Self-destruction*. New York: Science House, pp. 203-223.

1967b   "Das Erzählen von Geschichten innerhalb von Unterhaltungen." In Rolf Kjolseth and Fritz Sack (eds.), *Zur Soziologie der Sprache*. Opladen, 1971:307-314.

1967c   Transcripts of unpublished lectures. Department of Sociology, University of California, Los Angeles.

1972a   "On the Analysability of Stories by Children." In J. Gumperz and D. Hymes (eds.), *Directions in Sociolinguistics*. New York: Holt, Rinehart and Winston, pp. 325-345.

1972b   "On the Analysability of Stories by Children." In Roy Turner (ed.), *Ethnomethodology*. Baltimore: Penguin, pp. 216-232.

1972c   "An Initial Investigation of the Usability of Conversational Data for Doing Sociology." In D. Sudnow (ed.), *Studies in Social Interaction*. New York: Free Press, pp. 31-75.

1972d   "Notes on Police Assessment of Moral Character." In D. Sudnow (ed.), *Studies in Social Interaction*. New York: Free Press, 280-293.

1973a   "On Some Puns with Some Intimations." In R. Shuy (ed.), *Report of the Twenty-Third Annual Georgetown Roundtable in Linguistics.* Washington D.C.: Georgetown University Press, pp. 135-144.

1973b   "Tout le Monde Doit Mentir." In *Communications,* 20:182-203.

1973c   "The Sequential Organization of Conversational Interaction." Unpublished manuscript.

1974   "An Analysis of the Course of a Joke's Telling in Conversation." In R. Baumann and J. Sherzer (eds.), *Explorations in Ethnography of Speaking.* Cambridge: Cambridge University Press, pp. 337-353.

1975   "Everyone Has to Lie." In B. Blount and M. Sanchez (eds.), *Ritual, Reality, and Innovation in Language Use.* New York: Academic Press, pp. 57-79.

1976   "Agreement Notebooks, I, II and III. Compiled at the School of Social Sciences, UC Irvine. Currently held at Sociology Department University of California, Los Angeles.

1978   "Some Technical Considerations of a Dirty Joke." In J. Schenkein (ed.), *Studies in the Organization of Conversational Interaction.* New York: Academic Press, pp. 249-269.

1979   "Hotrodder: A Revolutionary Category." In G. Psathas (ed.), *Everyday Language: Studies in Ethnomethodology.* New York: Irvington Publishers, Inc., pp.7-14.

1981   "Preface: Some Programmatic Statements by Harvey Sacks." In Gail Jefferson, "The Abominable 'Ne': A Working Paper Exploring the Post Response Pursuit of Response." Occasional Paper in Sociology No. 6, Sociology Department, Manchester University, Manchester, England, (April).

1984a   "Methodological Remarks." In Atkinson and Heritage, *Structures of Social Action.* Cambridge: Cambridge University Press, pp.21-27.

1984b   "On Doing 'Being Ordinary'." In Atkinson and Heritage, *Structures of Social Action.* Cambridge: Cambridge University Press, pp. 413-429.

In press "Aspects of the Sequential Organization of Conversation." Unpublished manuscript. In *Collected Works of Harvey Sacks.* New York: Academic Press.

Sacks, Harvey, Egon Bittner and Harold Garfinkel

1963   "Reasonable Accounts." Congress Paper, Sixteenth Annual Conference on World Affairs, University of Colorado, Boulder, 11/12, April.

Sacks, Harvey, G, Jefferson and E. Schegloff

1974   "A Simplest Systematics for the Organization of Turn Taking in Conversation." In *Language,* 50,4:696-735.

Sacks, Harvey and E. Schegloff

1979   "Two Preferences in the Organization of Reference to Persons in Conversation and Their Interaction." In G. Psathas (ed.), *Everyday*

Language: Studies in Ethnomethodology. New York: Irvington
Publishers, pp. 15-21.
[Reprinted in: N.H. Avison and R.J. Wilson (eds.), *Ethnomethodology, Labelling Theory, and Deviant Behavior.* London:Routledge
and Kegan Paul.]

Sandywell, Barry
  1973a   "Introduction." In P. Filmer et al., *Stratifying Practices.*
  1973b   "Marx, Alienation, and Speech." Unpublished manuscript, Goldsmith
          College, London.

Schegloff, Emanuel
  1963   "Toward a Reading of Psychiatric Theory." In *Berkeley Journal of
          Sociology,* 8:61-91.
  1967   *The First Five Seconds: The Order of Conversational Openings.*
          Unpublished doctoral dissertation, University of California, Berkeley.
  1968   "Sequencing in Conversational Openings." In *American Anthropologist.* 70:1075-1095.
          [Reprinted in: J.J. Gumperz and D. Hymes (eds.), *Directions in
          Sociolinguistics.* New York: Holt, Rinehart Winston.]
          [Reprinted in: J. Laver and S. Hutcheson (eds.), *Communication in
          Face to Face Interaction.* Baltimore: Penguin, 1972:374-405.]
  1972   "Notes on Conversational Practice: Formulating Place." In Sudhnow,
          Studies in Social Interaction. New York: Free Press, pp. 75-119.
          [Reprinted in: Pier Paolo Gigiioli (ed.), *Language and Social
          Context.* Hardmondsworth: England, 1972:95-135.]
  1979a   "Indentification and Recognition in Telephone Conversation Openings." In G. Psathas (ed.), *Everyday Language: Studies in Ethnomethodology.* New York: Irvington Publishers, pp. 23-78.
  1979b   "The Relevance of Repair to Syntax for Conversation." In T. Givon
          (ed.), *Syntax and Semantics, 12: Discourse and Syntax.* New York:
          Academic Press, pp. 261-288.
  1979c   "Repair after Next Turn," Unpublished paper presented at the *Conference on Practical Reasoning and Discourse Processes.* St. Hugh's
          College, Oxford, England.
  1980   "Preliminaries to Preliminaries: Can I Ask You a Question?" In
          Sociological Inquiry, 50:104-152.
  1981   "Discourse as an Interactional Achievement: Some Uses of 'Uh Huh',
          etc.." Paper presented at the Georgetown University Roundtable on
          Linguistics and Language Studies. Washington D.C.
          [Reprinted in: Deborah Tannen (ed.), *Analyzing Discourse: Text and
          Talk.* Georgetown: Georgetown University Press.]
  1984a   "On Some Questions and Ambiguities in Conversation." In Atkinson
          and Heritage (eds.), *Structures of Social Action.* Cambridge: Cambridge University Press, pp. 28-52.

1984b   "On Some Gestures' Relation to Talk." In J. Maxwell Atkinson and J. Heritage (eds.), *Structures of Social Action: Studies in Conversation Analysis*. Cambridge: Cambridge University Press, pp. 266-296.

1986a   Personal communication, University of California, Los Angeles.

1986b   "The Routine as Achievement," *Human Studies*, 9, 2/3.

1987   "Entre micro et macro: Contextes et relations." *Sociétés: Revue des Humaines et Sociales*, No. 14, juin: 17-22.

1988   "Between Macro and Micro: Contexts and Other Connections." In J. Alexander, B. Giessen, R. Munch, and N. Smelser (eds.), *The Macro-Micro Link*. Berkeley/Los Angeles: University of California Press. (in press)

In press "Recycled Turn Beginnings." In G. Button, J. Lee and J. Schenkein (eds.), *Studies in the Organization of Conversational Interaction II*. New York: Academic Press.

Schegloff, E., G. Jefferson and H. Sacks

1977   "The Preference for Self-correction in the Organization of Repair in Conversation." In *Language*, 53 (June):361-382.

Schegloff, E. and Harvey Sacks

1973   "Opening Up Closings." In *Semiotica*, 8:289-327.
        [Reprinted in: Roy Turner (ed.), *Ethnomethodology*. Baltimore: Penguin, 1974:233-264.]

Schenkein, Jim

1971   *Some Substantive and Methodological Issues in the Analysis of Conversational Interaction*. Unpublished doctoral dissertation, School of Social Science, University of California, Irvine.

1972   "Towards an Analysis of Natural Conversation and the Sense of 'heheh'." In *Semiotica*, 6:344-377.

1974a   "An Introduction to the Study of 'Socialization' Through Analysis of Conversational Interaction." In Roy Turner (ed.), *Socialization Acquisition of Membership*. New York: Harper and Row.

1974b   In M. Mathiot (ed.), *Semiotica*, special edition on sociolinguistics.

1975b   "Letzte Bemerkungen zur Ethnomethodologie." In W. Weingarten, F. Sacks and J. Schenkein (eds.), Ethnomethodologie: Beiträge zu einer Soziologie des Alltagslebens. Frankfurt: Suhrkamp.

1975b   "Techniques in the Analysis of Verbal Interaction." Didactic Seminar of the American Sociological Association Seventieth Annual Meetings, ASA-43. North Hollywood, California: Convention Seminar Cassettes.

1976   Review of D.E. Allen and R.F. Guy, *Conversation Analysis: The Sociology of Talk*. In *Language in Society*, 5, 3:387-389.

1977   *A Videotape Introduction to Sociology*. Flushing, New York: Center for Instructional Development and the Queens College Portable Laboratory.

1978a   (ed.), *Studies in the Organization of Conversational Interaction.*
         New York: Academic Press.
1978b   "Sketch of an Analytic Mentality for the Study of Conversational
         Interaction." In J. Schenkein (ed.), *Studies in the Organization of
         Conversational Interaction.* New York: Academic Press, pp. 1-6.
1978c   "Identity Negotiations in Conversation." In J. Schenkein (ed.), *Studies in the Organization of Conversational Interaction.* New York:
         Academic Press, pp. 57-78.
1979   "The Radio Raiders Story." In G. Psathas (ed.), *Everyday Language:
         Studies in Ethnomethodology.* New York: Irvington Publishers,
         pp. 187-202.
In press "A Taxonomy for Repeating Action Sequences in Natural Conversa-
         tion." In J. Schenkein (ed.), *Studies in the Organization of Conversa-
         tional Interaction, Vol. II.* New York: Academic Press.
Schrecker, Frederick
In press "Doing a Chemical Experiment: The Practices of Chemistry Students
         in a Student Laboratory in Quantitative Analysis." Department of
         Sociology, University of California, Los Angeles. In H. Garfinkel
         (ed.), *Ethnomethodological Studies of Work.* London: Routledge and
         Kegan Paul.
Schutz, Alfred
1945a   "On Multiple Realities." In *Philosophy and Phenomenological
         Research,* 5, 4 (June):533-575.
1945b   "Some Leading Concepts of Phenomenology," *Social Research* 12(1).
1951   "Making Music Together: A Study in Social Relationships," *Social
         Research* 18 (1), pp. 76-97.
1955   "Symbol, Reality, and Society." In L. Bryson, L. Finkelstein, H.
         Hoagland, and R.M. MacIver (eds.), *Symbols and Society: Fourteenth
         Symposium on the Conference on Science, Philosophy, and Religion.*
         New York: Harper.
1959   "Husserl's Importance for the Social Sciences." In *Edmund Husserl
         1859-1959* (Phaenomenologica 4). The Hague: Martinus Nijhoff.
1962a   *Collected Papers I: The Problem of Social Reality.* The Hague:
         Martinus Nijhoff.
1962b   "Commonsense and Scientific Interpretations of Human Action." In
         Schutz, *Collected Papers I.* The Hague: Martinus Nijhoff, pp. 3-47.
1962c   "Symbol, Reality and Society." In Schutz, *Collected Papers I.* The
         Hague: Martinus Nijhoff, pp. 287-356.
1964   *Collected Papers II: Studies in Social Theory.* The Hague: Martinus
         Nijhoff.
1966   *Collected Papers III: Studies in Phenomenological Philosophy.* The
         Hague: Martinus Nijoff.

1967   *The Phenomenology of the Social World.* Translated by George Walsh
        and Frederick Lehnert. Evanston: Northwestern University Press.
1970   *Reflections on the Problem of Relevance.* New Haven: Yale Univer-
        sity Press.
Schutz, Alfred and T. Luckmann
1974   *The Structures of the Life World.* London: Heinemann.
Schwartz, Howard
1971   *Mental Disorders and the Study of Subjective Experience.* Unpub-
        lished doctoral dissertation, University of California, Los Angeles.
1974   *Towards a Phenomenology of Projection Errors.* Unpublished
        manuscript, Department of Sociology, Harvard University.
1974   "The Discipline of Sociology of Language: Is it One or is it Not?" In
        Contemporary Psychology, 19:728-729.
1976   "Allgemeine Merkmale." In Weingarten *et al.* (eds.), *Ethnometho-
        dologie.* Frankfurt: Suhrkamp, pp. 327-367.
1977   "Understanding Misunderstanding" *Analytical Sociology* 1, no. 3.
1980   "The Importance of Description." Unpublished manuscript, Univer-
        sity of California, San Diego.
Schwartz, Howard and Jerry Jacobs
1975   *Qualitative Sociology: A Method to the Madness.* New York: Free
        Press.
Schwartz, Theodore
1962   *The Paliau Movement in the Admiralty Islands*, 1946-1954. American
        Museum of Natural History Anthropological Papers, 49, II.
1976   "Relations Among Generations in Time-Limited Cultures." In T.
        Schwartz, (ed.), *Socialization as Cultural Communication.* Berkeley:
        University of California Press. pp. 217-230.
Schwendinger, H. and J.R. Schwendinger
1974   *Sociologists of the Chair: A Radical Analysis of the Formative Years
        of North American Sociology, 1883-1922.* New York: Basic Books.
Scott, C.
1968   "Community Reactions to Deviance." *Social Science Research
        Council* Research Report.
Searle, J.
1969   *Speech Acts.* London: Cambridge University Press.
Sebeok, Thomas A.
1953   "The Structure and Content of Cheremis Charms, Part I." In *Anthro-
        pos*, 48:369-88.
1975   "Six Species of Signs: Some Propositions and Structures." In *Semiot-
        ica*, 13:233-260.
1976   "Semiotics: A Survey of the State of the Art." In Thomas A. Sebeok
        (ed.), *Contributions to the Doctrine of Signs.* Bloomington: Indiana
        University Press, pp. 1-45.

Sebeok, Thomas A., A.S. Hayes, and M.C. Bateson (eds.)
1972   *Approaches to Semiotics: Cultural Anthropology, Education, Linguistics, Psychiatry, Psychology.* The Hague: Mouton.

Selznick, Philip
1952   *The Organizational Weapon.*

Sharratt, B.
1982   *Reading Relations: Structures of Literary Production.* Brighton: Harvestor Press.

Sharrock, W.W.
1974   "On Knowing Knowledge." In Roy Turner (ed.), *Ethnomethodology.* Baltimore: Penguin, pp. 45-53.

Sharrock, W.W. and R.J. Anderson
1978   "A Minimal Case for Ethnomethodology." Mimeo, Department of Sociology, University of Manchester.

1979   "Conceptions of Orderliness and Their Implementation." Mimeo, Department of Sociology, University of Manchester.

1980a   "Ethnomethodology and British Sociology: Some Problems of Incorporation." Paper presented at BSA Conference, Lancaster.

1980b   "On the Demise of the Native." *Occasional Paper*, No. 5, Department of Sociology, University of Manchester.

1986a   *The Ethnomethodologists.* London:Tavistock Publications.

1986b   "Methodological Tokenism, OR Are Good Intentions Enough?" *Semiotica* 58(1/2), 1-27.

Sharrock, W.W. and R. Turner
1978   "On a Conversational Environment of Equivocality." In J. Schenkein (ed.), *Studies in the Organization of Conversational Interaction.* New York: Academic Press, pp. 173-198.

Shils, Edward
1961   *The Intellectual Between Tradition and Modernity: The Indian Situation.* The Hague: Martinus.

1969   "The Intellectuals and the Powers: Some Perspectives for Comparative Analysis." In Rieff, P. (ed.), *On Intellectuals:* 25-49.

1970   "Tradition, Ecology, and Institution in the History of Sociology." *Daedalus*, 99 (Fall):760-825.

1972   "Intellectuals, Tradition, and the Traditions of Intellectuals: Some Preliminary Considerations." *Daedalus*, 101 (Spring):21-34.

Shumsky, Marshall
1971   "A Sociolinguistic Account of Encounter Groups." In *Sociological Focus*, 5 (Summer):164-174.

1972   *Encounter Groups: A Forensic Science.* Unpublished doctoral dissertation, University of California, Santa Barbara.

Shumsky, Marshall and Hugh Mehan
1974   "The Comparability Practice in Description in Two Evaluative Contexts." Congress Paper, International Sociological Association, Toronto.

Silverman, David
1972   "Methodology and Meaning." In Filmer *et al., New Directions in Sociological Theory.* Unpublished manuscript, Goldsmith College, London.

1974a   "Speaking Seriously." In *Theory and Society I*, Part I: 1-16, Part II: 341-359.

1974b   "Accounts of Organization." In J. McKinlay (ed.), *Processing People.* New York: Wiley.

1975   *Reading Castaneda: A Prologue to the Social Sciences.* London: Routledge and Kegan Paul.

1981   "The Child as a Social Object: Down's Syndrome Children in a Pediatric Cardiology Clinic." In *Sociology of Health and Illness*, 3(3):254-274.

Simmonds, A.
1978   *Karl Mannheim's Sociology of Knowledge.* Oxford: Clarendon Press.

Smith, Dorothy E.
1973   "Women, the Family and Corporate Capitalism." In M. Stephenson (ed.), *Women in Canada.* Toronto: New Press.

1974a   "Theorizing as Ideology." In Roy Turner (ed.), *Ethnomethodology.* Baltimore: Penguin Press, pp. 41-44.

1974b   "Women's Perspective as a Radical Critique of Sociology." In *Sociological Inquiry*, 4:7-13.

1974c   "The Ideological Practice of Sociology." In *Catalyst*, 8.

1974d   "The Social Construction of Documentary Reality." In *Sociological Inquiry*, 4:257-268.

1978   "K is Mentally Ill: The Anatomy of a Factual Account." In *Sociology*, 12:23-53.

Snow, David A.
1980   "The Disengagement Process": A Neglected Problem in Participant Observation Research." *Qualitative Sociology*, 3, 2:100-122.

Snow, David A. and Richard Machalek
1984   "The Sociology of Conversion." In *Annual Review of Sociology*, 10:167-190.

Speier, Mathew
1970   "The Everyday World of the Child." In J.D. Douglas (ed.), *Understanding Everyday Life.* Chicago: Aldine Press, pp. 188-217.

1972   "Some Conversational Problems for Interactional Analysis." In D. Sudnow (ed.), *Studies in Social Interaction.* New York: Free Press, pp. 397-427.

1973   "How to Observe Face to Face Communication. A Sociological Introduction." Pacific Palisades: Goodyear Publishing Co.

Spiegelberg, Herbert
1971   *The Phenomenological Movement: A Historical Introduction.* The Hague: martinus Nijhoff.

Sperber, Dan
1985   *On Anthropological Knowledge.* Paris: Maison des Sciences de l'Homme and Cambridge University Press.

Stark, Rodney and William Sims Bainbridge
1985   *The Future of Religion: Secularization, Revival, and Cult Formation.* Berkeley/Los Angeles:University of California Press.

Stehr, N. and L.E. Larson
1972   "The Rise and Decline of Areas of Specialization." *American Sociologist*, 7(3):5-6.

Stehr, Nico and Volker Meja (eds.)
1984   *Society and Knowledge: Contemporary Perspectives in the Sociology of Knowledge.* London: Transaction Books.

Stoddart, Kenneth
1974a   "The Facts of Life About Dope." *Urban Life and Culture*, 3:179-204.
1974b   "Pinched: Notes on the Ethnographer's Location of Argot." In Roy Turner (ed.), *Ethnomethodology*. Baltimore: Penguin, pp. 173-179.

Stoller, R.J., H. Garfinkel and A.C. Rosen
1960   "Passing and the Maintenance of Sexual Indentification in an Intersexed Patient." In *Archives for General Psychiatry*, 2:379-384.
1962   "Psychiatric Management of Intersexed Patients." In *California Journal of medicine*, 96:30-34.

Streeck, Jurgen
1984   "Embodied Contexts, Transcontextuals, and the Timing of Speech Acts." In *Journal of Pragmatics*, 8:113-137.

Strunk, William J. and E.B. White
1959   *The Elements of Style.* New York: Macmillan.

Sudnow, David
1965   "Normal Crimes. Sociological Features of the Penal Code in a Public Defender Office." In *Social Problems*, 12:255-276.
1967a   *Passing On. The Social Organization of Dying.* Englewood Cliffs, N.J.: Prentice Hall.
        [Translation: *Organisiertes Sterben. Eine Soziologische Untersuchung.* Frankfurt:1973.]
1967b   "Counting Deaths." In Roy Turner (ed.), *Ethnomethodology*. Baltimore: Penguin, pp. 102-108.
1972a   (ed.) *Studies in Social Interaction.* New York: Free Press.
1972b   "Temporal Parameters of Interpersonal Observation." In D. Sudnow (ed.), *Studies in Social Interaction.* New York: Free Press.

1978   *Ways of the Hand: The Organization of Improvised Conduct.* New York: Bantam Books.

1980   *Talk's Body: A Meditation Between Two Keyboards.* New York: Alfred Knopf and Co.

1983   *Pilgrim in the Micro-World: Eye, Mind, and the Essence of Video Skill.* New York: Warner Books.

Suchman, Lucy A.

1985   *Plans and Situated Actions: The Problem of Human-Machine Communication*, Xerox Palo Alto Research Center, Palo Alto, California, February.

Swanson, Guy

1968   "Review Symposium over Harold Garfinkel's *Studies in Ethnomethodology.*" In *American Sociological Review*, 33:122-124.

Tannen, Deborah, (ed.)

1984   *Coherence in Spoken and Written Discourse.* Volume XII, Advances in Discourse Processes, Roy O. Freedle, ed. Norwood, New Jersey: Ablex Publishing Co.

Tedlock, Dennis

1979   "The Analogical Tradition and the Emergence of a Dialogical Anthropology." In *Journal of Anthropological Research*, 35, 4:387-400.

TenHave, Paul

1987   *Sequenties en Formuleringen.* Dortrecht & Providence, RI: Foris.

TenHouten, Warren and Charles Kaplan

1973   *Science and Its Mirror Image.* New York: Harper and Row.

Terasaki, Arlene

1975   "A Proposal on Announcement Sequences in Conversation." Unpublished paper, School of Social Sciences, University of California, Irvine.

1976a   *A Proposal on Announcement Sequence in Conversation.* Unpublished doctoral dissertation, School of Social Science, University of California, Irvine.

1976b   "Pre-Announcement Sequences in Conversation." Social Science Working Paper, 99. University of California, Irvine.

Therborn, G.

1980   *Science, Class and Society, On the Formation of Sociology and Historical Materialism.* London: Verso.

Tilly, Charles

1978   *From Mobilization to Revolution.* Reading, MA: Addison-Wesley.

Tillyard, E.M.W. and C.S. Lewis

1939   *The Personal Heresy, A Controversy.* London/New York: Oxford University Press.

Tipton, Steven M.
  1982   *Getting Saved From the Sixties.* (Foreword by Robert N. Bellah) Berkeley/Los Angeles: University of California Press.
Tiryakian, Edward
  1971   "Introduction to the Sociology of Sociology." In E.A. Tiryakian, (ed.), *The Phenomenon of Sociology.* New York: Appelton-Century Crofts.
  1986   "Sociology's Great Leap Forward: The Challenge of Internationalisation." In *International Sociology*, 1, 2:155-171.
Todd, Alexandra
  1982   *The Medicalization of Reproduction: Scientific Medicine and the Diseasing of Healthy Women.* Unpublished doctoral dissertation, University of California, San Diego.
  1983a   "A Diagnosis of Doctor-Patient Discourse in the Prescription of Contraception." In Sue Fisher and A. Todd (eds.), *The Social Organization of Doctor-Patient Communication.* Washington D.C.: The Center for Applied Linguistics Press.
  1983b   "Women's Bodies as Diseased and Deviant: Historical Contemporary Issues." In Steven Spitzer (ed.) *Research in Law Deviance and Social Control.* Greenwich, CT: JAI Press.
  1984   "The Prescription of Contraception: Negotiations Between Doctors and Patients." In *Discourses and Processes*, 7:171-200.
Todorov, Tzvetan
  1984   *Mikhail Bakhtin: The Dialogical Principle.* Minneapolis: University of Minnesota Press.
Touhey, John
  1973   "Review of *Studies in Social Interaction*," David Sudnow (ed.), *Contempoary Sociology*, 2:504-506.
Touraine, Alain
  1977   "Crisis or Transformation." In N. Birnbaum (ed.), *Beyond the Crisis.* New York: Oxford University Press: 17-45.
  1980   *The Voice and the Eye.* Cambridge: Cambridge University Press.
Traweek, S.
  1982   "Uptime, Downtime, Spacetime and Power: An Ethnography of the Particle Physics Community in Japan and the United States." Ph.D. Dissertation, Santa Cruz: University of California.
Treichler, Paula A., R.M. Frankel, C. Kramaral, K. Zoppi and
Howard B. Beckman
  1984   "Problems and Problems: Power Relationships in a Medical Encounter." In Cheris Kamaral, Muriel Shultz, and William O'Barr (eds.), *Language and Power.* Beverly Hills, CA: Sage Pulications.

Turner, Bryan S.
  1986   "Sociology as an Academic Trade: Some Reflections on Centre and Periphery in the Sociology Market." *Australian and New Zealand Journal of Sociology*, 22, 2:272-282.
Turner, Ralph
  1969   "The Theme of Contemporary Social Movements." *British Journal of Sociology*, 20:390-405.
Turner, Roy
  1966   "The Ethnography of Experiment." In *American Behavioral Scientist*, 10:26-29.
  1970   "Words, Utterances, and Activities." In J.D. Douglas (ed.), *Understanding Everyday Life*. Chicago: Aldine Press, pp. 169-187.
          [Reprinted in: Roy Turner (ed.), *Ethnomethodology*. Baltimore: Penguin, pp. 197-215.]
  1972a   "Some Formal Properties of Therapy Talk." In D. Sudnow (ed.), *Studies in Social Interaction*. New York: Free Press, pp. 367-396.
  1972b   "Some Features of the Construction of Conversations." Congress paper, American Sociological Association, San Francisco.
  1974a   "Introduction." In Roy Turner (ed.), *Ethnomethodology*. Baltimore: Penguin, pp. 7-12.
  1974b   (ed.), *Ethnomethodology: Selected Readings*. Middlesex, England: Penguin Education.
  1974c   (ed.), *Socialization: Acquisition of Membership*. New York: Wiley.
  1976   "Utterance Positioning as an Interactional Resource," *Semiotica* 17: 233-254.
Twer, Sheldon
  1972   "Tactics for Determining Persons' Resources for Depicting, Continuing, and Describing Behavioral Episodes." In D. Sudnow (ed.), *Studies in Social Interaction*. New York: Free Press, pp. 339-366.
Tyler, Stephen A. (ed.)
  1969   *Cognitive Anthropology*. New York: Holt, Rinehart and Winston.
  1972   "Context and Alternation in Koya Kinship Terminology." In Gumperz and Hymes (eds.), *Directions in Sociolinguistics: The Ethnography of Communication*. New York: Holt, Rinehart and Winston, pp. 251-269.
  1985   "Ethnography, Intertextuality, and the End of Description." In *American Journal of Semiotics*, 3, 4:85-98.
  1986   "Post-Modern Ethnography: From Document of the Occult to Occult Document." In Clifford, J. and G. Marcus, *Writing Culture*. Berkeley/ Los Angeles: University of California Press, pp. 122-140.
Vansina, Jan
  1965   *The Oral Tradition: A Study in Historical Methodology*. Chicago: Aldine.

1970   "Cultures Through Time." In R. Naroll and R. Cohen (eds.), *A Handbook of Method in Cultural Anthropology*. Garden City, N.Y.: National History Press, pp. 165-179.

Vidich, A.J. and S.M. Lyman
1985   *American Sociology: Worldly Rejections of Religion and Their Directions*. New Haven, CT: Yale University Press.

Vygotsky, L.S.
1962   *Thought and Language*. Cambridge: MIT Press.

Wagner, H.
1983   *Alfred Schutz: An Intellectual Biography*. Chicago: University of Chicago Press.

Walker, Andrew
1975   "Sociological and Lay Accounts as Versions of Reality: Choosing Between Accounts of the 'Charismatic Renewal Movement' Among Roman Catholics." In *Theory and Society*, 2:211-233.

Wallace, Anthony F.C.
1968   "Review Symposium over Harold Garfinkel's *Studies in Ethnomethodology*." In *Amrican Sociological Review*, 33:124-126.

Watson, R.
1975   *Calls for Help: A Sociological Analysis of Telephoned Communications to a Crisis Intervention Center*. Unpublished doctoral dissertation, University of Warwick.

1978   "Categorization, Authorization and Blame Negotiation in Conversation." In *Sociology*, 12:105-113.

1986   "Doing the Organization's Work: An Examination of Aspects of the Operation of a Crisis Intervention Center." In S. Fisher and A. Todd (eds.), *Discourse and Institutional Authority*. Norwood, N.J.: Ablex, pp. 91-120.

Wedow, Susan
1973   *From the Zodiac to Everyday Life*. Unpublished doctoral dissertation, Department of Sociology, University of California, Santa Barbara.

1979   "Feeling Paranoid: The Organization of an Ideology About Drug Abuse." *Urban Life and Culture*, 8:72-93.

1980   *The Fetishism of the Self: Occult Individualism and Rites of Passage*. Unpublished manuscript, University of California, San Diego.

Weingarten, Elmer Fritz Sack and Jim Schenkein (eds.)
1976   *Ethnomethodologie: Beitrage zu einer Soziologie des Alltagshandelns*. Frankfurt: Suhrkamp Taschenbuch Wissenschaft, 71.

Weinstein, David
1975   "Drivers' Work." Unpublished manuscript, School of Social Sciences, University of California, Irvine.

West, Candace
  1978   *Communicating Gender: A Study of Dominance and Control in Conversation.* Unpublished doctoral dissertation, Department of Sociology, University of California, Santa Barbara.
  1979   "Against Our Will: Male Interruptions of Females in Cross-Sex Conversation." In *Annals of the New York Academy of Sciences,* 327:81-97.
  1982a "What Is a Medical Inteview? A Preliminary Investigation of Physician-Patient Interaction." Paper presented at American Sociological Association Annual Meetings, San Francisco.
  1982b "When the Doctor Is a Lady: Power, Status and Gender in Physician-Patient Conversations." In Ann Stromberg (ed.), *Women, Health and Medicine.* Palo Alto: Mayfield.
  1982c "Why Can't a Woman Be More Like a Man?" In *Work and Occupations,* 9, 1:5-29.
  1983   "Ask Me No Questions... An Analysis of Queries and Replies in Physician-Patient Dialogues." In Fisher and Todd (eds.), *The Social Organization of Doctor-Patient Communication.* Washington D.C.: The Center for Applied Linguistics, pp. 75-106.
  1984   *Routine Complications: Troubles in Talk Between Doctors and Patients.* Bloomington: Indiana University Press.
West, Candace and Don H. Zimmerman
  1977   "Women's Place in Everyday Talk: Reflections on Parent-Child Interaction." In *Social Problems,* 24:521-529.
  1983   "Small Insults: A Study of Interruptions in Cross-Sex Conversations Between Unacquainted Persons." In Barrie Thorne, Cheris Kramaral and Nancy Henley (eds.), *Language, Gender, and Society.* Rowley, Mass.: Newbury House.
  1985   "Gender, Language, and Discourse" in *Handbook of Discourse Analysis* Vol. 4, T.A. Van Dijk, ed. London: Academic Press, pp. 103-120.
Whalen, Jack, Don H. Zimmerman, and Marilyn L. Whalen
  1988   "When Words Fail: A Single Case Analysis." *Social Problems* 35: 335-62.
White, Hayden
  1973   *Metahistory.* Baltimore: Johns Hopkins University Press.
Whitley, Richard
  1984   *The Intellectual and Social Organization of the Sciences.* Oxford: Clarendon Press.
Widmer, Jean
  1986   *Langage et Action Sociale: Aspects Philosophiques et Semiotiques du Langage dans la Perspective de L'ethnomethodologie.* Fribourg: Editions Universitaires Fribourg Suisse.

Wieder, D. Lawrence
1970   "On Meaning by Rule." In J.D. Douglas (ed.), *Understanding Every-day Life*. Chicago: Aldine, pp. 107-135.
1974a   *Language and Social Reality: The Case of Telling the Convict Code.* The Hague: Mouton.
1974b   "Telling the Code." In Roy Turner (ed.), *Ethnomethodology.* Baltimore: Penguin, pp. 144-172.
1980   "Behavioristic Operationalism and the Life-World; Chimpanzees and the Chimpanzee Researchers in Face-to-Face Interaction." In *Sociological Inquiry*, 50, (3-4):75-103.
Wieder, D.L. and D.H. Zimmerman
1971   "The Problem of Competent Recognition of Social Action and the Phenomenon of Accounting." Congress paper, American Sociological Association, Denver, Colorado.
1974   "Generational Experience and the Development of Freak Culture." *Journal of Social Issues*, 30:137-161.
1976   "Becoming a Freak." *Youth and Society*, 7:311-344.
Wild, John
1947   "Introduction to the Phenomenology of Signs," *Philosophy and Phenomenological Research* 8(2):217ff.
Wilkins, James
1968   "Review of Harold Garfinkel's *Studies in Ethnomethodology.*" *American Journal of Sociology*, 73:642-643.
Wilkinson, J.D.
1981   *The Intellectual Resistance in Europe*. Cambridge: Harvard University Press.
Williams, Joseph M.
1981   *Style: Ten Lessons in Clarity and Grace*. Glenview: Scott, Foresman.
Wilson, Bryan
1970   *Religious Sects*. World University Library: McGraw-Hill.
Wilson, Thomas P.
1970a   "Conceptions of Interaction and Forms of Sociological Explanation." In *American Sociological Review*, 35:697-710.
        [Translation: "Theorien der Interaktion und Modelle Soziologischer Erklärung." In Arbeitsgruppe bielefelder Soziologen (eds.), *Alltagswissen, Interaktion und Gesellschaftliche Wirklichkeit I*, Reinbek: pp. 54-79.]
1970b   "Normative and Interpretive Paradigms in Sociology." In J.D. Douglas (ed.), *Understanding Everyday Life*. Chicago: Aldine, pp. 57-79.
1971   "The Infinite Regress and the Problem of Evidence in Ethnomethodology." Paper presented to the Annual Meetings of American Sociological Association, Denver, Colorado.

1982   "Qualitative 'Versus' Quantitative Methods in Social Research." Published in German as "Qualitative 'Oder' Quantitative Methoden in der Sozialforschung." In *Külner Zeitschrift Für Soziologie und Sozial Psychologie.* 34:487-508.

Wilson, Thomas P. and Don H. Zimmerman
    1980   "Ethnomethodology, Sociology, and Theory." In *Humbolt Journal of Social Relations,* 7:52-88.
    1986   "The Structure of Silence." *Discourse Processes,* 9(4):375-390.

Wiser, William
    1983   *The Crazy Years: Paris in the Twenties.* New York: Atheneum.

Wood, Houston L.
    1968   *The Labelling Process on a Mental Hospital Ward.* Unpublished Master's thesis. University of California, San Diego.
    1969a   "Zatocoding as a Model for Ethnomethodology." Paper presented to a seminar led by Harold Garfinkel, University of California, Los Angeles, February 14.
    1969b   "Notes on Some Criteria for Doing Science." Unpublished manuscript, Department of Sociology, University of California, Santa Barbara.

Woolgar, Steve W.
    1976   "Writing an Intellectual History of Scientific Development: The Use of Discovery Accounts." In *Social Studies of Science,* 6:395-422.

Wooten, A.
    1981   "The Management of Grantings and Rejections by Parents in Request Sequences." In *Semiotica,* 37:59-89.

Yates, Frances
    1964a   *The Art of Memory.* Chicago: Chicago University Press.
    1964b   *Giordano Bruno and the Hermetic Tradition.* Chicago: University of Chicago Press.
    1978   *The Rosicrucian Enlightenment.* Boulder: Shamballa Publications.

Yearley, S.
    1981   "Textual Persuasion: The Role of Social Accounting in the Construction of Scientific Arguments." *Philosophy of the Social Sciences,* 11:409-435.

Zablocki, Benjamin
    1971   *The Joyful Community.* Baltimore: Penguin.

Zald, M. and R. Ash
    1966   "Social Movement Organizations: Growth, Decay and Change." *Social Forces,* 327-341.

Zald, M. and J. McCarthy (eds.)
    1979   *The Dynamics of Social Movements.* Cambridge, MA: Winthrop Publishers.

378   *Bibliography*

Zimmerman, Don H.
1966   *Paper Work and People Work: A Study of a Public Assistance
Agency.* Unpublished doctoral dissertation, University of California,
Los Angeles.
1969   "Tasks and Troubles: The Practical Basis of Work Activities in a
Public Assistance Agency." In D.H. Hansen (ed.), *Explorations in
Sociology and Counselling.* New York: Houghton Mifflin.
1970a   "The Practicalities of Rule Use." In J.D. Douglas (ed.), *Understanding Everyday Life.* Chicago: Aldine, pp. 221-238.
1970b   "Record Keeping and the Intake Process in a Public Welfare
Agency." In Stanton Wheeler (ed.), *On Record: Files and Dossiers
in American Life.* Russell Sage Foundation, 1969:319-354.
[Abridged in Roy Turner (ed.), *Ethnomethodology.* Baltimore:
Penguin, pp. 128-143.]
1974   *Preface* to D.L. Wieder's *Language and Social Reality: The Case of
Telling the Convict Code.* The Hague: Mouton, pp. 9-26.
1976   "A Reply to Professor Coser." In *American Sociologist,* 11:4-13.
1978   "Ethnomethodology." In *American Sociologist,* 13(1):6-15.
1984   "Talk and Its Occasions: The Case of Calling the Police." In D.
Schriffrin (ed.), *Meaning, Form, and Use in Context.* Washington
D.C.: Georgetown University Press, pp. 210-228.
1987   "Studies in Ethnomethodology: Twenty Years Later." In The Dis-
course Analysis Research Group Newsletter 3(2), Fall 1987:20-25.
Zimmerman, Don H. and Melvin Pollner
1970   "The Everyday World as a Phenomenon." In Harold Pepinsky (ed.),
People and Information. Pergamon Press.
[Reprinted in: J.D. Douglas (ed.), *Understanding Everyday Life.*
Chicago: Aldine, pp. 80-102.]
Zimmerman, Don H. and D. Lawrence Wieder
1970   "Ethnomethodology and the Problem of Order: Comment on
Denzin." In J.D. Douglas (ed.), *Understanding Everyday Life.*
Chicago: Aldine, pp. 285-298.
1970   "The Social Basis for Illegal Behavior in the Student Community.
First Year Report." Scientific Analysis Corporation, San Francisco
and Santa Barbara.
1977   "You Can't Help But Get Stoned: Notes on the Social Organization
of Marijuana Smoking." In *Social Problems,* 24:198-207.
Zimmerman, Don H. and Thomas P. Wilson
1973   "Prospects for Experimental Studies of Meaning Structures." Congress paper, American Sociological Association, New York City.

Zimmerman, Don H. and Candace West
  1975   "Sex Roles, Interruptions and Silences in Conversation." In B. Thorne
         and N. Henley (eds.), *Language and Sex: Difference and Dominance.*
         Rowley. Mass.: Newbury House, pp. 105-129.
  1980a Special Issue on Verbal Behavior. *Sociological Inquiry*, 50 (3-4).
  1980b *Language and Social Interaction.* United Chapters of Alpha Kappa
         Delta: Urbana, Illinois.
Zimmerman, Don, and Jack Whalen,
  1987   "Multi-party management of single telephone calls: The verbal and
         gestural organization of work in an emergency dispatch center."
         presented at The Surrey Conference on Video, University of Surrey,
         Guildfor, England, July 7-9.
Zito, George V.
  1984   *Systems of Discourse: Structures and Semiotics in the Social
         Sciences.* London: Greenwood Press.

Index of names

Note. This index includes entries from the bibliography, some of which are collaborative.

Subject Index

Bennetta Jules-Rosette

Terminal Signs
Computers and Social Change in Africa

1990. XVI, 424 pages. Cloth. DM 178,–
ISBN 3 11 012221 9
(Approaches to Semiotics 90)

This research monograph presents cross-cultural comparisons of interpretations surrounding computerization in Africa.

Plans for the introduction of computers have influenced daily practices in the workplace and the technological advances are altering the aspirations and career patterns of an emerging group of computer professionals.

Parts 1 and 2 introduce a narrative program for computer adoption based on a semiotics of narrative developed by A. J. Greimas as well as ethnographic studies of computer adoption in Kenya and the Ivory Coast.

In Part 3, implications of these case studies are explored and compared with data from other African nations, Western Europe and the United States through a detailed examination of human-machine interaction and a sociosemiotic analysis of the contractual exchanges essential to technological diffusion. The book concludes with a consideration of terminal signs, or the interpretive strategies and processes of signification that accompany Africa's entry into the postmodern era, which provide the basis for projecting the future of new technologies.

mouton de gruyter
Berlin · New York

Stephen Harold Riggins (Editor)

Beyond Goffman

Studies on Communication, Institution, and Social Interaction

1990. 15.5 x 23 cm. VIII, 456 pages. Cloth. DM 178.00
ISBN 3 11 012208 1
(Approaches to Semiotics 96)

This collection of 18 original articles analyzes cross-cultural examples of face-to-face interaction and other forms of social situations, using approaches inspired by the sociologist Erving Goffman (1922–1982).

The point of departure for this volume was the general opinion that a systematic multi-disciplinary examination of Goffman's theory was needed. Thus, the authors of the contributions include sociologists, semioticians, anthropologists, philosophers, linguists, specialists of the mass media, and political scientists.

The resulting collection addresses the question of how Goffman's theory can be improved by applying it to a greater diversity of subjects than he himself investigated, including religion, mass media, politics, the law, and popular entertainment, and by expanding it cross-culturally.

mouton de gruyter

Berlin · New York